Outlines of English Law

THIRD EDITION

S. B. Marsh
B Com LL B, Ph D, Barrister-at-Law
Head of the Department of Law, Manchester Polytechnic

and

J. Soulsby
LL B, Solicitor
Principal Lecturer in Law, Manchester Polytechnic

McGRAW-HILL Book Company (UK) Limited
London · New York · St Louis · San Francisco · Auckland · Bogotá ·
Guatemala · Hamburg · Johannesburg · Lisbon · Madrid · Mexico ·
Montreal · New Delhi · Panama · Paris · San Juan · São Paulo ·
Singapore · Sydney · Tokyo · Toronto

Published by
McGRAW-HILL Book Company (UK) Limited
MAIDENHEAD · BERKSHIRE · ENGLAND

British Library Cataloguing in Publication Data
Marsh, S. B.
  Outlines of English law.—3rd ed.
  1. Law—England
  I. Title   II. Soulsby, J.
  344.2 KD661

ISBN 0-07-084655-3

Library of Congress Cataloging in Publication Data
Marsh, Stanley Brian, 1926–
  Outlines of English law.

  Includes index.
  1. Law—Great Britain—Outlines, syllabi, etc.
I. Soulsby, J. II. Title.
KD661.M37 1982   349.42   82-4661
ISBN 0-07-084655-3   344.2

Copyright © 1982 McGraw-Hill Book Company (UK) Limited. All rights reserved. No part of this publication may be reproduced, stored in a retrieval system, or transmitted, in any form or by any means, electronic, mechanical, photocopying, recording, or otherwise, without the prior permission of McGraw-Hill Book Company (UK) Limited, or of the original copyright holder.

345 WC 865

Filmset by Eta Services (Typesetters) Ltd, Beccles, Suffolk
Printed and bound in Great Britain by William Clowes Limited, Beccles and London

Contents

Preface vi

Table of Cases vii

Table of Statutes xii

Unit 1   **The Nature and History of English Law 1**
- A The Nature of Law 1
- B Civil and Criminal Law 1
- C The Common Law 3
- D Other Historical Sources of Law 5

Unit 2   **Legislation as a Source of Law 10**
- A The Nature and Effect of Legislation 10
- B The Legislative Process 11
- C Delegated Legislation 15

Unit 3   **Precedent and Other Sources of English Law 19**
- A Judicial Precedent 19
- B Law Reporting 22
- C The Judges and Statutes 23
- D Other Sources of Law 25

Unit 4   **The Criminal Courts 26**
- A Magistrates and their Courts 26
- B The Crown Court 30
- C Appeals in Criminal Cases 32
- D The Prerogative of Mercy 33

Unit 5   **The Civil Courts 35**
- A Inferior Courts 35
- B The High Court 38
- C Appeals in Civil Cases 39

Unit 6   **Other Courts and Tribunals 43**
- A Modern Special Courts and Tribunals 43
- B Administrative Tribunals 46
- C Historical Survivals 49
- D Domestic Tribunals 49
- E Arbitration 50

Unit 7   **The Legal Profession 53**
- A The Division of the Legal Profession 53
- B Legal Education 54
- C Legal Practice 55
- D Judges 57
- E Judicial Offices 59
- F Administration and Reform of the Law 60

Unit 8   **Court Proceedings 62**
- A Preliminary Considerations 62
- B Civil Procedure Before Trial 65

CONTENTS

         C   The Civil Trial   67
         D   Enforcement of Civil Judgments   67
         E   Criminal Proceedings   69

Unit 9   English Law and the European Communities   71
         A   The European Communities   71
         B   Community Institutions   72
         C   Sources of Community Law   75
         D   The Acceptance of Community Law by the United Kingdom   77

Unit 10   Legal Personality and Capacity   80
         A   Natural and Legal Persons   80
         B   Corporations   81
         C   Unincorporated Associations   82
         D   Partnerships   83
         E   The Crown   90

Unit 11   Companies   92
         A   Formation of Companies   93
         B   Capital   94
         C   Membership and Management   96
         D   The Company and Outsiders   101
         E   Public Controls over Companies   103
         F   Winding Up   103

Unit 12   Liability for Wrongful Acts   106
         A   Crimes and Torts   106
         B   Liability in Tort   107
         C   Defences   110
         D   Parties   113
         E   Remedies   115

Unit 13   Negligence and Breach of Statutory Duty   119
         A   The Tort of Negligence   119
         B   Dangerous Goods   123
         C   Employers' Liability   123
         D   Dangerous Premises   124
         E   Breach of Statutory Duty   126

Unit 14   Torts against Land and Goods   130
         A   Trespass to Land   130
         B   Nuisance   132
         C   The Rule in Rylands v. Fletcher   136
         D   Wrongful Interference with Goods   137

Unit 15   Other Specific Torts   140
         A   Trespass to the Person   140
         B   Intentional Physical Harm   142
         C   Malicious Prosecution   142
         D   Defamation   142
         E   Deceit   147
         F   Liability for Animals   147

Unit 16   The Nature of a Contract in English Law   150
         A   Essential Requirements   150
         B   Intention to Create Legal Relations   152
         C   Consideration   153
         D   Form   155

Unit 17 Agreement 158
  A   Offer 158
  B   Acceptance 161
  C   Certainty of Terms 164

Unit 18 Matters which Affect the Validity of Contracts 166
  A   Mistake 166
  B   Misrepresentation 169
  C   Duty to Disclose 171
  D   Duress and Undue Influence 172
  E   Lack of Capacity to Contract 172

Unit 19 The Terms of the Bargain 176
  A   Express Terms 176
  B   Implied Terms 177
  C   Problems of Unequal Bargaining Power 179
  D   Exclusion Clauses 180

Unit 20 Performance, Breach, and Remedies 185
  A   Performance 185
  B   Breach of Contract 186
  C   Damages for Breach of Contract 188
  D   Other Remedies for Breach 190

Unit 21 Discharge, Limitation, and Privity 194
  A   Discharge by Agreement 194
  B   Discharge by Frustration 195
  C   Limitation of Actions 197
  D   Privity of Contract 198

Unit 22 Contracts and Public Policy 202
  A   Contracts which are Illegal at Common Law 202
  B   Contracts which are Illegal by Statute 204
  C   Contracts in Restraint of Trade 205
  D   Other Contracts which are Void 208

Unit 23 Sale of Goods 211
  A   Obligations of the Seller and the Buyer's Remedies 211
  B   Obligations of the Buyer and the Seller's Remedies 216
  C   Transfer of Property between Seller and Buyer 218
  D   Transfer of Title by a Non-Owner 221

Unit 24 Credit and Security 225
  A   Consumer Credit 226
  B   Goods as Security 228
  C   Land as Security 231
  D   Borrowing by Companies 232

Unit 25 Negotiable Instruments 235
  A   The Concept of Negotiability 235
  B   Bills of Exchange 236
  C   Cheques 242

Unit 26 Agency, Banking, and Insurance 247
  A   Agency 247
  B   The Relationship between Banker and Customer 251
  C   Insurance 254

Unit 27 Property and Legal Estates in Land 261
  A   The Nature and Classification of Property 261
  B   Land 263

CONTENTS

   C Freehold 264
   D Leasehold 266

Unit 28 **Further Aspects of Property Law** **269**
   A Interests in Land 269
   B Sale of Land 271
   C Trusts 274

Unit 29 **Succession on Death** **279**
   A Testate Succession 279
   B Intestate Succession 282
   C Administration of Estates 284

Unit 30 **The Law in Practice** **288**
   A Accidents—The Problems 288
   B Prevention and Criminal Sanctions 289
   C Compensation 292
   D Social Security 294
   E Defective Goods—The Problems 296
   F Prevention and Criminal Sanctions 296
   G Compensation 299

Index **301**

Preface

  Law is an important part of business and professional courses in further and higher education. The content of these courses varies, but in most cases the student begins with an introductory study of legal institutions and the most important principles and rules of the main branches of law.
  This book covers the subject-matter normally included in these introductory law courses which appear under different names. It is hoped that it will be useful for students preparing for professional examinations, particularly in accountancy, banking, and insurance or taking business education courses. This third edition therefore includes additional material of a business nature covering business associations, commercial contracts, credit and security, and negotiable instruments.
  As in earlier editions, the text is not divided into chapters according to subject. A division is made instead into teaching units, each unit representing the subject-matter that might be covered in one week in a course extending over a normal college session. Thus, the Contents list provides a suggested scheme of work which will normally leave some time to spare for revision purposes. Any unit not required by a particular syllabus may be omitted or used for background reading and the time saved devoted to other units upon which that syllabus places emphasis. The final unit—which may be omitted if there is no time available—attempts to show how the various branches of law are interrelated and may come together to affect common situations.
  At the end of each unit there are a number of questions which may be used for discussion or for written work. These questions attempt to test both knowledge of the subject-matter of that unit and its application.

S. B. Marsh
J. Soulsby

Table of Cases

Adler *v.* Dickson [1955] 1 QB 158 **198**
Alexander *v.* North-Eastern Rail Co. (1865) 6 B & S 340 **145**
Allcard *v.* Skinner (1887) 36 Ch D 145 **172**
Allen *v.* Rescous (1676) 1 Freem. (KB) 433 **202**
Aluminium Industrie Vaassen BV *v.* Romalpa Aluminium Ltd [1976] 2 All ER 552 **217–9, 231**
Anderson Ltd *v.* Daniel [1924] 1 KB 138 **205**
Anns *v.* Merton London Borough Council [1977] 2 All ER 492 **120**
Appleson *v.* Littlewood Ltd [1939] 1 All ER 464 **152**
Archbolds (Freightage) Ltd *v.* Spanglett Ltd [1961] 1 QB 374 **205**
Armory *v.* Delamirie (1722) 1 Stra 505 **138**
Armstrong *v.* Jackson [1917] 2 KB 722 **250**
Ashbury Carriage Co. *v.* Riche (1875) LR 7 HL 653 **82, 92, 100**
Avery *v.* Bowden (1855) 5 E & B 714 **188, 196**
Ayrey *v.* British Legal Assurance [1918] 1 KB 136 **257**

Balfour *v.* Balfour [1919] 2 KB 571 **152**
Ballett *v.* Mingay [1943] KB 281 **113**
Bankers Trust Company *v.* Shapira [1980] 3 All ER 353 **253**
Beale *v.* Taylor [1967] 3 All ER 253 **212**
Bebee *v.* Sales (1916) 32 TLR 413 **113**
Belvoir Finance Ltd *v.* Stapleton [1971] 1 QB 210 **204**
Benham *v.* Gambling [1941] AC 157 **116**
Beswick *v.* Beswick [1968] AC 58 **199**
Bettini *v.* Gye [1874–80] All ER Rep 242 **177**
Bird *v.* Jones (1845) 7 QB 742 **141**
Bolton *v.* Stone [1951] AC 850 **23, 121, 133, 135**
Bolton Partners *v.* Lambert (1889) 41 Ch D 295 **249**
Boston Deep Sea Fishing & Ice Co. *v.* Ansell (1888) 39 Ch D 339 **98**
Bourhill *v.* Young [1942] AC 92 **120**
Bowater *v.* Rowley Regis Corporation [1944] KB 476 **112**
Bradford Corporation *v.* Pickles [1895] AC 587 **108**
Bradley and Essex and Suffolk Accident Society, *Re* [1912] 1 KB 415 **259**
Bridge *v.* Campbell Discount Co. Ltd [1962] AC 600 **190, 229**
Bridges *v.* Hawksworth (1851) 21 LJ QB 75 **139**
Bridlington Relay Ltd *v.* Yorkshire Electricity Board [1965] Ch 436 **133**
British Railways Board *v.* Herrington [1972] AC 877 **125**
Brown *v.* Gould [1972] Ch 53 **164**
Brown *v.* Zurich Insurance Co. [1954] 2 Lloyd's Rep 243 **258**
Bull *v.* Pitney-Bowes Ltd [1966] 3 All ER 384 **207**
Bushell *v.* Faith [1970] 1 All ER 53 **98**
Byrne *v.* Van Tienhoven (1880) 5 CPD 344 **163**

Capital Finance Ltd *v.* Bray [1964] 1 All ER 603 **230**
Car and Universal Finance Co. Ltd *v.* Caldwell [1965] 1 QB 535 **171**
Carlill *v.* Carbolic Smoke Ball Co. [1893] 1 QB 256 **159, 163**
Cassell *v.* Lancashire and Yorkshire Accident Insurance Co. (1885) 1 TLR 495 **259**
Cassidy *v.* Daily Mirror Newspapers [1929] 2 KB 331 **143**
Castle *v.* St Augustine's Links (1922) 38 TLR 615 **133, 135**

TABLE OF CASES

Central London Property Trust *v.* High Trees House [1947] KB 130   **155**
Chandler *v.* Webster [1904] 1 KB 493   **196**
Chapleton *v.* Barry UDC [1940] 1 KB 532   **180**
Charles Rickards Ltd *v.* Oppenheim [1950] 1 KB 616   **187**
Christie *v.* Davey [1893] 1 Ch 316   **133**
City Equitable Fire Insurance Co., *Re* [1925] Ch 407   **99**
City of London *v.* Wood (1702) 12 Mod 669   **11**
Cleaver *v.* Mutual Reserve Fund Life Assurance [1892] 1 QB 147   **258**
Clemens *v.* Clemens Bros Ltd [1976] 2 All ER 268   **101**
Close *v.* Steel Company of Wales Ltd [1962] AC 367   **127**
Cohen *v.* Roche [1927] 1 KB 169   **191–2, 216**
Colling, *Re* [1972] 3 All ER 729   **280**
Cook *v.* Deeks [1916] 1 AC 554   **99, 100**
Cooper *v.* Phibbs (1867) LR 2 HL 149   **168**
Cooper *v.* Wandsworth Board of Works (1863) 14 CB (NS) 180   **132**
Cope *v.* Rowlands (1836) 2 M & W 149   **205**
Couturier *v.* Hastie [1843–60] All ER Rep 280   **167, 220**
Cowern *v.* Nield [1912] 2 KB 419   **173**
Cramer *v.* Giles (1883) 1 Cab & El 151   **230**
Craven-Ellis *v.* Canons Ltd [1936] 2 KB 403   **191**
Cundy *v.* Lindsay (1878) 3 App Cas 459   **168**
Curtice *v.* London, City and Midland Bank [1908] 1 KB 293   **252**
Curtis *v.* Chemical Cleaning Co. [1951] 1 KB 805   **180**
Cutler *v.* Wandsworth Stadium [1949] AC 398   **127**

D & C Builders Ltd *v.* Rees [1966] 2 QB 617   **154, 195**
Daniels *v.* Daniels [1978] Ch 406   **100**
Dawsons Ltd *v.* Bonnin [1922] 2 AC 413   **256**
Department of Trade and Industry *v.* St Christopher's Motorists Association Ltd [1974] 1 All ER 395   **254**
Derry *v.* Peek (1889) 14 AC 337   **147**
Dick Bentley Productions Ltd *v.* Harold Smith (Motors) Ltd [1965] 2 All ER 65   **170, 229**
Dickinson *v.* Dodds (1876) 2 Ch D 463   **160**
Donoghue *v.* Stevenson [1932] AC 562   **41, 119, 123, 199**
Doughty *v.* Turner Manufacturing Co. Ltd [1964] 1 All ER 98   **123**
Doyle *v.* White City Stadium [1935] 1 KB 110   **173**
Dunlop Ltd *v.* New Garage Ltd [1915] AC 79   **190**

Eastern Distributors Ltd *v.* Goldring [1957] 2 QB 600   **221, 248**
Eastham *v.* Newcastle United Football Club [1964] Ch 413   **207**
Eastwood *v.* Kenyon [1835–42] All ER Rep 133   **153**
Ebrahimi *v.* Westbourne Galleries Ltd [1972] 2 All ER 492   **88, 104**
Entores *v.* Miles Far East Corporation [1955] 2 QB 327   **163**
Esso Petroleum Co. Ltd *v.* Harper's Garage Ltd [1968] AC 269   **208, 232**

Fairclough *v.* Swan Brewery Co. Ltd [1912] AC 565   **232**
Farr *v.* Motor Traders Mutual Insurance Society [1920] 3 KB 669   **256**
Felthouse *v.* Bindley (1863) 7 LT 835   **162**
Fibrosa Case [1943] AC 32   **197, 203**
Financings Ltd *v.* Stimson [1962] 3 All ER 386   **161, 227**
Fisher *v.* Bell [1961] 1 QB 394   **159**
Fisher *v.* Ruislip-Northwood UDC [1945] KB 584   **111**
Foley *v.* Classique Coaches Ltd [1934] 2 KB 1   **164**
Folkes *v.* King [1923] 1 KB 282   **221, 248**
Ford Motor Co. Ltd *v.* Armstrong (1915) 31 TLR 267   **190**
Forster & Sons Ltd *v.* Suggett (1918) 35 TLR 87   **207**
Foss *v.* Harbottle (1843) 2 Hare 461   **100**
Foster *v.* Driscoll [1929] 1 KB 470   **84, 202–3**
Foster *v.* Mackinnon (1869) LR 4 CP 704   **167, 240**

Fouldes v. Willoughby (1841) 8 M & W 540 **138**
Freeman and Lockyer v. Buckhurst Park Properties Ltd [1964] 2 QB 480 **102, 248**
Frost v. Aylesbury Dairy Co. Ltd [1905] 1 KB 608 **186, 214, 299**
Fullwood v. Hurley [1928] 1 KB 498 **250**

Galloway v. Galloway (1914) 30 TLR 531 **167**
Glasbrook Bros v. Glamorgan County Council [1925] AC 270 **154**
Glasgow Corporation v. Taylor [1922] 1 AC 44 **125**
Godley v. Perry [1960] 1 All ER 36 **214**
Grant v. Australian Knitting Mills [1936] AC 85 **213**
Great Northern Railway Co. v. Swaffield (1874) LR 9 Exch 132 **248**
Greenwood v. Martins Bank Ltd [1932] 1 KB 371 **240, 252, 254**
Griffiths v. Peter Conway [1939] 1 All ER 685 **213**
Grist v. Bailey [1967] Ch 532 **168**
Groves v. Lord Wimbourne [1898] 2 QB 402 **126-7**

Hadley v. Baxendale [1843-60] All ER Rep 461 **189, 215**
Hall v. Brooklands Racing Club [1933] 1 KB 205 **112**
Halsey v. Esso Petroleum Co. Ltd [1961] 2 All ER 145 **63, 135**
Hamlyn v. Houston & Co. [1903] 1 KB 81 **85**
Hampstead Guardians v. Barclays Bank Ltd (1923) 39 TLR 229 **243**
Harris v. Nickerson (1873) LR 8 QB 286 **159**
Harse v. Pearl Life Assurance Co. [1904] 1 KB 558 **204, 254**
Harvey v. Facey [1893] AC 552 **160**
Haynes v. Harwood [1935] 1 KB 146 **112**
Hedley Byrne v. Heller & Partners [1964] AC 465 **120, 122, 253**
Herd v. Weardale Steel, Coal & Coke Co. Ltd [1915] AC 67 **141**
Heron II, The [1969] 1 AC 350 **189**
Hickman v. Maisey [1900] 1 QB 752 **131**
Hill v. C. A. Parsons & Co. Ltd [1972] Ch 305 **192**
Hillas & Co. Ltd v. Arcos Ltd [1932] All ER Rep 494 **164**
Hippisley v. Knee Bros [1905] 1 KB 1 **250**
Hochster v. De La Tour [1843-60] All ER Rep 12 **188**
Hollins v. Fowler (1875) LR 7 HL 757 **137**
Home Counties Dairies Ltd v. Skilton [1970] 1 All ER 1227 **206**
Hong Kong Fir Shipping Co. Ltd v. Kawasaki Kisen Kaisha Ltd [1962] 2 QB 26 **177, 187**
Horne v. Midland Railway Co. (1873) LR 8 CP 131 **189**
Houghton v. Trafalgar Insurance Co. Ltd [1953] 2 All ER 1409 **258**
Howard Smith Ltd v. Ampol Petroleum Ltd [1974] 1 All ER 1126 **99**
Hulton & Co. v. Jones [1910] AC 20 **143**
Hyde v. Wrench (1840) 3 Beav 334 **161**

Inglis v. Stock (1855) 10 App Cas 263 **220**
Introductions Ltd v. National Provincial Bank Ltd [1969] 1 All ER 887 **82, 92**

Jarvis v. Swans Tours Ltd [1973] QB 233 **189**

Keppel v. Wheeler [1927] 1 KB 577 **250**
King's Motors (Oxford) Ltd v. Lax [1969] 2 All ER 665 **164**
King's Norton Metal Co. Ltd v. Edridge Ltd (1897) 14 TLR 98 **168**
Kirk v. Gregory (1876) 1 Ex D 55 **137**
Kores Ltd v. Kolok Ltd [1959] Ch 108 **207**

Leaf v. International Galleries [1950] 2 KB 86 **166, 170**
Leslie Ltd v. Shiell [1914] 3 KB 607 **113**
L'Estrange v. Graucob Ltd [1934] 2 KB 394 **180**
Letang v. Cooper [1965] 1 QB 232 **140**
Lewis v. Averay [1972] 1 QB 198 **168**

TABLE OF CASES

Liggett Ltd v. Barclays Bank Ltd [1928] 1 KB 48 **252**
Limpus v. London General Omnibus Co. (1862) 1 H & C 526 **109**
Lister v. Romford Ice & Cold Storage Co. Ltd [1957] AC 555 **110**
Lloyd v. Grace, Smith & Co. [1912] AC 716 **108**
Lloyds Bank Ltd v. Bundy [1975] QB 326 **253**
Lloyds Bank Ltd v. Savory [1933] AC 201 **244**
London Assurance v. Mansel (1879) 11 Ch D 363 **169, 256**
London Borough of Bromley v. Greater London Council [1982] 1 All ER 129 **82**
London Joint Stock Bank v. Macmillan and Arthur [1918] AC 777 **253**
London Street Tramways Ltd v. LCC [1898] AC 375 **20**
Lowery v. Walker [1911] AC 10 **126**
Lynn v. Bamber [1930] 2 KB 72 **198**

Macaura v. Northern Assurance Co. Ltd [1925] AC 619 **255**
McLoughlin v. O'Brian [1982] 2 All ER 298 **121**
McWilliams v. Sir William Arrol & Co. Ltd [1962] 1 All ER 623 **110**
Malins v. Freeman (1837) 2 Keen 25 **191**
Malone v. Laskey [1907] 2 KB 141 **134**
Maple Flock Co. Ltd v. Universal Furniture Ltd [1934] 1 KB 148 **188, 216**
Marfani Ltd v. Midland Bank Ltd [1968] 2 All ER 573 **244**
Marquess of Bute v. Barclays Bank Ltd [1954] 3 All ER 365 **244**
Marsh v. Joseph [1897] 1 Ch 213 **249**
Mason v. Provident Clothing Co. Ltd [1913] AC 724 **207**
Mercantile Credit Ltd v. Garrod [1962] 3 All ER 1103 **85**
Mercantile Union Guarantee Corporation Ltd v. Ball [1937] 2 KB 498 **173**
Merchants and Manufacturers Insurance v. Hunt & Thorne [1941] 1 KB 295 **256**
Metropolitan Asylum District v. Hill (1881) 6 App Cas 193 **111, 135**
Metropolitan Water Board v. Dick, Kerr & Co. [1918] AC 119 **196**
Miller v. Karlinski (1945) 62 TLR 85 **203**
Moorcock, The [1886–90] All ER Rep 530 **177**
Moore & Co. and Landauer & Co Re [1921] 2 KB 519 **185. 212**
Morison v. Kemp (1912) 69 TLR 70 **240**
Munro Ltd v. Meyer [1930] 2 KB 312 **188, 216**
Mutual Life Assurance v. Evatt [1971] AC 793 **120**

Nash v. Inman [1908] 2 KB 1 **173**
National Coal Board v. J. E. Evans Ltd [1951] 2 KB 861 **111**
Neale v. Merrett [1930] WN 189 **161**
Newtons of Wembley Ltd v. Williams [1965] 1 QB 560 **223**
Nichols v. Marsland (1876) 2 Ex D 1 **111**
Nicolene Ltd v. Simmonds [1953] 1 QB 543 **164**
Nordenfeldt Case [1894] AC 535 **208**

Olley v. Marlborough Court Ltd [1949] 1 KB 532 **180**
Orbit Mining and Trading Co. Ltd v. Westminster Bank Ltd [1963] 1 QB 794 **244**
Oscar Chess Ltd v. Williams [1957] 1 All ER 325 **170, 299**

Panorama Developments Ltd v. Fidelis Furnishing Fabrics Ltd [1971] 2 QB 711 **102, 248**
Paradine v. Jane (1647) Aleyn 26 **195**
Paris v. Stepney Borough Council [1951] AC 367 **121**
Parkinson v. College of Ambulance Ltd [1925] 2 KB 1 **203**
Pathirana v. Pathirana [1967] AC 233 **87, 89**
Pearce v. Brooks (1866) LR 1 Exch 213 **203**
Pender v. Lushington (1877) 6 Ch D 70 **100**
Peter Darlington Partners Ltd v. Gosho Ltd [1964] 1 Lloyd's Rep 149 **185, 212**
Pharmaceutical Society of Great Britain v. Boots Cash Chemists [1953] 1 QB 401 **159**
Philip Head & Sons Ltd v. Showfronts Ltd (1970) 113 Sol J 978 **219**
Phillips v. Brooks [1919] 2 KB 243 **168**

Piercy v. Mills Ltd [1920] 1 Ch 77 **99**
Planché v. Colburn [1824–34] All ER Rep 94 **191**
Poussard v. Spiers & Pond [1876] 1 QBD 410 **177**
Powell v. Lee (1908) 99 LT 284 **163**
Pride of Derby Angling Association v. British Celanese Ltd [1953] Ch 149 **134**

Raffles v. Wichelhaus (1864) 2 H & C 906 **167**
Ramsgate Hotel Co. v. Montefiore (1866) LR 1 Exch 109 **161**
Rawlinson v. Ames [1925] Ch 96 **157, 191**
Read v. J. Lyons & Co. Ltd [1946] AC 156 **136**
Reed v. Dean [1949] 1 KB 188 **178**
Reffell v. Surrey County Council [1964] 1 All ER 743 **127**
Regal (Hastings) Ltd v. Gulliver [1942] 1 All ER 378 **99**
Reid v. Commissioner of Metropolitan Police [1973] QB 551 **222**
Richley v. Faull [1965] 3 All ER 109 **122**
Robinson v. Davison [1861–73] All ER Rep 699 **196**
Roe v. R. A. Naylor Ltd (1918) 87 LJKB 958 **180**
Roles v. Nathan [1963] 2 All ER 908 **125**
Rondel v. Worsley [1969] 1 AC 191 **120**
Roscorla v. Thomas (1842) 3 QB 234 **153**
Rose and Frank v. Crompton Bros Ltd [1925] AC 445 **152**
Routledge v. Grant (1828) 4 Bing 653 **160**
Rowland v. Divall [1923] 2 KB 500 **212**
Royal British Bank v. Turquand (1856) 6 E & B 327 **102**
Rylands v. Fletcher (1868) LR 3 HL 330 **107, 109, 132, 136, 265**

Salomon v. Salomon & Co. Ltd [1897] AC 22 **82, 92**
Saunders v. Anglia Building Society [1971] AC 1004 **167**
Sayers v. Harlow UDC [1958] 2 All ER 342 **112, 116**
Scammell v. Ouston [1941] AC 251 **164**
Sedleigh-Denfield v. O'Callaghan [1940] AC 880 **134**
Shaw v. Groom [1970] 2 QB 504 **205**
Shipton, Anderson & Co. v. Weil Bros & Co. [1912] 1 KB 574 **185**
Simpkins v. Pays [1955] 3 All ER 10 **152**
Sky Petroleum Ltd v. VIP Petroleum Ltd [1974] 1 WLR 576 **192**
Slingsby v. District Bank Ltd [1932] 1 KB 544 **253**
Smith v. Charles Baker & Sons [1891] AC 325 **112**
Smith v. Leech Brain & Co. Ltd [1962] 2 QB 405 **116**
South Staffordshire Water Co. v. Sharman [1896] 2 QB 44 **138**
Spartan Steel & Alloys Ltd v. Martin & Co. (Contractors) Ltd [1972] 3 All ER 557 **122**
Square v. Model Farm Dairies Ltd [1939] 2 KB 365 **127**
Stapley v. Gypsum Mines Ltd [1953] AC 663 **113**
Steer v. Durable Rubber Co. Ltd, *The Times*, 20 November 1958 **123, 299**
Stennett v. Hancock [1939] 2 All ER 578 **123**
Stevenson Ltd v. Cartonnagen-Industrie [1918] AC 239 **88**
Stewart v. Casey [1892] 1 Ch 104 **154**
Stone v. Reliance Mutual Insurance Co. [1972] 1 Lloyds Rep 469 **255**
Sturges v. Bridgman (1879) 11 Ch D 852 **133, 135**

Tarling v. Baxter (1827) 6 B & C 360 **220**
Taylor v. Caldwell (1863) 3 B & S 826 **195, 196**
Taylor v. Laird (1856) 1 H & N 266 **160**
Thompson v. LMS Railway Co. [1930] 1 KB 41 **180**
Thornton v. Shoe Lane Parking Ltd [1971] 2 QB 163 **180**
Tiedmann & Ledermann Frères, *Re* [1899] 2 QB 66 **248**
Tower Cabinet Co. Ltd v. Ingram [1949] 2 KB 397 **86**
Tsakiroglou Ltd v. Noblee & Thorl G.m.b.H. [1962] AC 93 **196**
Tulk v. Moxhay (1848) 2 Ph 774 **200, 270**
Tweddle v. Atkinson [1861–73] All ER Rep 369 **198**

TABLE OF CASES

Underwood *v.* Bank of Liverpool [1924] 1 KB 775 **244**
Universe Tankships *v.* ITF [1982] 2 All ER 67 **172**

Valentini *v.* Canali [1886–90] All ER Rep 883 **174**
Victoria Laundry (Windsor) Ltd *v.* Newman Industries Ltd [1949] 2 KB 528 **189**

Wagon Mound Case [1961] AC 388 **20, 116, 123**
Wakelin *v.* London & South Western Railway Co. (1886) 12 App Cas 41 **122**
Wallis, Son & Wells *v.* Pratt & Haynes [1911] AC 394 **181**
Ward (R.V.) Ltd *v.* Bignall [1967] 1 QB 534 **218**
Warner Brothers Pictures Incorporated *v.* Nelson [1937] 1 KB 209 **192**
Warren *v.* Henlys Ltd [1948] 2 All ER 935 **109**
Watt *v.* Hertfordshire County Council [1954] 2 All ER 368 **121**
Watt *v.* Longsdon [1930] 1 KB 130 **146**
Watteau *v.* Fenwick [1893] 1 KB 346 **248**
Westminster Fire Office *v.* Glasgow Provident Investment Society (1888) 13 App Cas 699 **255**
White *v.* John Warrick & Co. Ltd [1953] 2 All ER 1021 **181**
Wickham Holdings Ltd *v.* Brook House Motors Ltd [1967] 1 All ER 117 **138**
Wilkinson *v.* Downton [1897] 2 QB 57 **142**
Williams *v.* Bayley [1861–73] All ER Rep 227 **172**
With *v.* O'Flanagan [1936] Ch 575 **171**
Wood *v.* General Accident, Fire and Life Assurance (1948) 65 TLR 53 **258**
Woods *v.* Martins Bank Ltd [1959] 1 QB 55 **253**
Woolcott *v.* Sun Alliance Insurance [1978] 1 All ER 1253 **257**

Yenidje Tobacco Co. Ltd, *Re* [1916] 2 Ch 426 **89, 104**
Yonge *v.* Toynbee [1910] 1 KB 215 **250, 251**
Youssoupoff *v.* Metro-Goldwyn-Mayer Pictures (1934) 50 TLR 581 **142**

Table of Statutes

Act of Settlement 1701 **58**
Administration of Estates Act 1925 **282, 286**
Administration of Justice Act 1969 **41**
Administration of Justice Act 1970 **39**
Animals Act 1971 **12, 132, 147–9**
Arbitration Acts 1950–79 **50**
Attachment of Earnings Act 1971 **68**

Bankers' Books Evidence Act 1879 **253**
Banking Act 1979 **245**
Bills of Exchange Act 1882 **14, 236–43**

Carriage of Goods by Sea Act 1971 **179**
Charities Act 1960 **276**
Cheques Act 1957 **243–5**
Civil Aviation Act 1949 **131, 265**
Companies Act 1844 **81**
Companies Act 1948–81 **81, 84, 92–104, 172, 225, 253**
Congenital Disabilities (Civil Liability) Act 1976 **113**
Consumer Credit Act 1974 **156, 195, 209, 211, 225–9, 231–2**
Consumer Protection Act 1961 **297**

TABLE OF STATUTES

Consumer Safety Act 1978 **126, 297**
Control of Pollution Act 1974 **24, 126, 130**
County Courts Act 1959 **35**
Courts Act 1971 **4, 30, 37, 38, 39, 43**
Criminal Appeal Act 1966 **32**
Criminal Damage Act 1971 **130, 137**
Criminal Justice Act 1967 **30**
Criminal Justice Act 1972 **70**
Criminal Law Act 1977 **29**
Crown Proceedings Act 1947 **90**

Defamation Act 1952 **143, 145**
Defective Premises Act 1972 **179**
Distress Act 1276 **13**
Domestic Proceedings and Magistrates' Courts Act 1979 **37**

Employers' Liability (Compulsory Insurance) Act 1969 **294**
Employers' Liability (Defective Equipment) Act 1969 **209**
Employment Protection Act 1975 **45**
Employment Protection (Consolidation) Act 1978 **90, 194, 209**
European Communities Act 1972 **8, 13, 25, 77–8, 82, 101, 241**

Factories Act 1961 **15, 109, 127, 191, 294**
Factors Act 1889 **221**
Fair Trading Act 1973 **183, 297**
Fatal Accidents Acts 1846–1976 **114–5**
Food and Drugs Act 1955 **296–9**

Gaming Act 1845 **255**

Health and Safety at Work etc. Act 1974 **24, 291**
Hire Purchase Act 1964 **223**
Hire Purchase Act 1965 **229**
Housing Act 1980 **47, 268**

Income and Corporation Taxes Act 1974 **253**
Industrial Relations Act 1971 **24, 46, 114**
Infants' Relief Act 1874 **173**
Inheritance (Provision for Family and Dependants) Act 1975 **281**
Insurance Companies Act 1974 **254–5**
Interpretation Act 1889 **11**
Interpretation Act 1978 **11, 23**

Judicature Acts 1873–75 **6, 38**
Judicial Committee Act 1833 **41**

Land Charges Act 1925 **273**
Land Registration Act 1925 **273**
Law Commissions Act 1965 **60**
Law of Property Act 1925 **156, 231, 235–6, 264, 269**
Law Reform (Contributory Negligence) Act 1945
Law Reform (Frustrated Contracts) Act 1943 **197, 220**
Law Reform (Husband and Wife) Act 1962 **113**
Law Reform (Married Women and Tortfeasors) Act 1935 **110**
Law Reform (Miscellaneous Provisions) Act 1934 **115**
Law Reform (Personal Injuries) Act 1948 **124, 295**
Leasehold Reform Act 1967 **268**
Legal Aid Act 1974 **64**

xiii

TABLE OF STATUTES

Legal Aid Act 1979 **64**
Life Assurance Act 1774 **204, 209, 255**
Limitation Act 1980 **60, 117, 197**
Limited Partnerships Act 1907 **89**
Local Government Act 1972 **13, 81**

Marine Insurance Act 1906 **179**
Misrepresentation Act 1967 **147, 170–1, 182, 299**

National Insurance Act 1965 **46**

Occupiers' Liability Act 1957 **124–5, 132**

Parliament Acts 1911–49 **12**
Partnership Act 1890 **83–9**
Payment of Wages Act 1960 **205**
Powers of Criminal Courts Act 1973 **70, 291–2, 294, 298–9**
Prescription Act 1832 **270**

Race Relations Act 1976 **24, 267**
Registration of Business Names Act 1916 **84**
Rent Act 1977 **47, 268**
Resale Prices Act 1976 **200, 204–5, 208**
Restriction of Offensive Weapons Act 1961 **159**
Restrictive Trade Practices Act 1976 **44, 205, 207**
Road Traffic Act 1930 **24**
Road Traffic Act 1972 **24, 112, 126, 199, 209, 289, 297–8**

Sale of Goods Act 1893 **12, 14, 23**
Sale of Goods Act 1979 **14, 178–9, 182, 187, 197, 211–23, 230, 261, 263, 299**
Slander of Women Act 1891 **145**
Statute of Frauds 1677 **156**
Social Security Acts 1975–80 **46, 295**
Stock Transfer Act 1963 **95**
Supply of Goods (Implied Terms) Act 1973 **179, 182, 230**
Supreme Court Act 1981 **38**

Theatres Act 1968 **145**
Theft Act 1968 **130**
Third Parties (Rights Against Insurers) Act 1930 **199**
Torts (Interference with Goods) Act 1977 **138**
Trade Descriptions Acts 1968–72 **70, 296–8**
Trade Disputes Act 1906 **114**
Trade Disputes Act 1965 **60**
Trade Union and Labour Relations Act 1974 **83, 114**
Trading Stamps Act 1964 **179**
Tribunals and Inquiries Act 1958 **48**
Truck Acts 1831–1940 **205**
Trustee Act 1925 **276–7, 286**

Unfair Contract Terms Act 1977 **125, 182–3, 215, 258**
Unsolicited Goods and Services Act 1971 **162**

Water Act 1973 **266**
Water Resources Acts 1963–68 **266**
Weights and Measures Acts 1963–79 **297**
Wills Act 1837 **280**
Wills Act 1968 **279**

Unit 1. The Nature and History of English Law

A. The nature of law

The word 'law' suggests the idea of rules; rules affecting the lives and activities of people. Some of these rules, such as the laws of science, enable us to predict what will happen in a given situation, but we have no control over them. We must accept, for example, the law of gravity; we regulate our conduct by it, but we cannot alter it.

In any community or group of people, man-made rules will develop to control the relationships between members. These rules are essential if the community is to work and will be found in all forms of activity which depend upon some form of cooperation—in games, in schools, in clubs. The rules come into existence in varying ways, although in most cases there must have been agreement between at least some of the members of the community that the rule was desirable. When a person or persons having power in the community enforces the rule, then that rule will acquire the status of a 'law' in the generally accepted meaning of the word.

Even in primitive societies, traditions and customs will affect conduct. Such customary rules tend to be too vague and imprecise at this stage to merit the use of the term 'law', although they may provide the basis of later law. As the society develops and becomes more complex, rules of a more definite nature emerge and a body of law comes into existence. At the same time some machinery for its enforcement must be established.

B. Civil and criminal law

As legal systems develop, the different rules tend to fall into two main categories, criminal law and civil law, and the objectives of each, although closely connected, are different. Criminal law is concerned with conduct of which the state disapproves so strongly that it will punish the wrongdoer. It is felt that society cannot work if people are allowed to take the property of others at will; therefore, theft is forbidden and thieves are punished to deter them, and others of a like mind, from repeating this conduct. There are other aims of punishment but it is not the objective of criminal law to compensate the victim, except perhaps incidentally.

Civil law has a complementary function. If a dispute arises between two individuals, each believing himself to be in the right, a quarrel may ensue and violence or other criminal conduct may result. To prevent this, rules of civil law were developed in order to determine which of the two parties was in the right. The party in the wrong was then obliged to make redress by compensating the other for any loss he may have caused. The object of the civil law therefore is to resolve disputes and give a remedy to the persons wronged, not to punish wrongdoers.

Most countries, including England, find it convenient to set up separate systems of criminal courts and civil courts. In England, a criminal prosecution is usually begun in the name of the Crown (i.e. the state) through the machinery of the police, and the decision as to whether or not to press the prosecution is not the concern of the victim. In a civil case, the law is set in motion by a private individual, or a firm, who has the right to determine how far the action shall continue.

Thus the parties and the terminology differ. In the criminal case of *R.* v. *Smith*, the Crown (*R.* signifying *Regina* or the Queen) prosecutes the accused, who may also be referred to as the prisoner or defendant. In the civil case of *Jones* v. *Smith*, the plaintiff sues the defendant.

Differences also exist in the rules of evidence and procedure, reflecting the fact that a criminal conviction is likely to be far more damaging to a person's character than failure in a civil action. The rules of evidence are much stricter in criminal cases, for example, a confession will be carefully examined to see if any pressure was brought to bear upon the accused, but an admission in a civil case will be fully accepted. The standard of proof required in criminal cases is greater, for the accused must be proved guilty beyond all reasonable doubt. A plaintiff in a civil action will succeed if he can convince the court that he has only a marginally stronger case than the defendant.

Finally, it is important to note that the same series of events may sometimes give rise both to criminal and civil proceedings. For instance, if A is alleged to have driven carelessly and injured B, two types of issue arise. Careless driving is conduct which has been made a criminal offence and A may be prosecuted by the Crown in a criminal court and, if found guilty of the offence, punished. The issue of whether A has caused loss to B through negligence and should therefore pay B compensation will be determined in a separate civil action brought by B in a civil court, although in this type of situation the loss will normally be met by A's insurance company. There are many other instances, such as the failure to guard dangerous factory machinery and the sale of misdescribed goods, where the same incident may give rise to both criminal and civil actions.

C. The common law

Origins of English law

Most legal systems in Europe, including that of Scotland, and indirectly those in many other parts of the world are based upon Roman law. In England and Wales, on the other hand, Roman law has had very little influence except in a few specialized fields such as marriage and the succession to property upon death, matters in which the Church was particularly interested.

The body of law which at present applies in England and Wales developed very gradually over a long period. Like so many of our institutions, it was not systematically created. Drawing upon many different sources, the English common law system finally emerged and has become the basis of law not only in this country but also in the United States and in many Commonwealth contries.

The period of local justice

Until and for some time after the Norman Conquest, it could scarcely be said that there was such a thing as English law. The population was small, settlements were often widely separated and travel was difficult. Justice and other aspects of administration tended to be local. Each local community would have its own court in which, for the most part, *local customs* would be applied. These customs, the beginnings of legal rules, varied considerably from one area to another.

There was a court in each shire and one in each hundred, a sub-division of a shire, but frequently these courts would be under the control of a local baron or other powerful person. Issues connected with the holding of land came to be dealt with in the court of the lord of the manor and revenues from these courts, an important source of wealth, went largely to the local lord himself. The methods of trial, for example, trial by ordeal, may appear a little peculiar to us today, but it was felt that, if the appropriate situation were created, Divine intervention would occur and be preferable to the judgment of men. Those in charge of the ordeal may sometimes have varied what was demanded of the accused according to whether they themselves felt him to be guilty.

The Middle Ages

The Norman Conquest made little immediate impact upon English law. William I promised that the English should keep their rights and their law, which meant the customary law. At the same time, the Normans developed a strong central government and over the following 200 years greatly increased central control over the administration of the law. This was a gradual process bringing with it the decline of the local and manorial courts.

One innovation was the concept of the King's Peace by which a crime was made a wrong against the peace of the King rather than against the peace of an individual. Crimes were, therefore, punishable only by the Crown and the royal courts acquired sole jurisdiction in criminal matters.

Central courts gradually developed when special committees of the King's Council were entrusted with jurisdiction over legal disputes. Three courts came into existence, and one by one they ceased to follow the King and his Council around the country, and sat permanently in Westminister. The Court of Exchequer was probably the first and while it originally heard disputes arising out of taxation, it later acquired a wider civil jurisdiction. The Court of Common Pleas was next established to deal with various types of civil disputes between private individuals. The Court of King's Bench was concerned at first with criminal matters but later acquired a certain amount of civil jurisdiction by means of the writ of trespass. The King occasionally sat in the Court of King's Bench and because of this, and the fact that it followed the King around the country until a later date than the other two courts, it became the most important court and acquired some supervisory powers over the other two.

At the same time, the practice grew up of sending royal judges to visit most parts of the country so as to establish closer royal control over the administration of justice. William I had used travelling commissioners to compile his national inventory known as the Domesday Book and this system had also been used to enquire into matters of local administration. The next step was to send out travelling commissioners with judicial powers.

These powers were given in the form of commissions to be exercised at the sittings, or Assizes, of the itinerant justices. Criminal jurisdiction eventually came to be based upon the Commission of Oyer and Terminer by which they were able to 'hear and determine' all criminal offences arising since their last visit. Civil jurisdiction came to depend upon the Commission of Assize, sometimes called *nisi prius* because the litigants were summoned to appear before the courts in London on an appointed day 'unless before' (*nisi prius*) that date an itinerant judge had heard the case locally. These commissions formed the basis of Assize jurisdiction until the latter was abolished by the Courts Act 1971.

The supremacy of the royal courts, both centrally and at Assize, was ensured by these methods and by the offer of a better method of trial. Trial by jury gradually superseded other forms of trial. The 12 jurors were originally local men who informed the judge of any local matter applicable to the case. Later, they acquired their present function of deciding questions of fact.

The emergence of common law

The new institutions, particularly the travelling judges, brought with them a most important change in the law itself, the unification of the varying local customs. As they went around the country on circuit the judges tended to select and apply certain customary rules in all cases rather than rely in every case upon enquiring into local customs. This process was assisted by the King who sometimes created new legal rules which were to apply nationally, and by the permanent courts which had nation-wide jurisdiction. In particular, Henry II created important new remedies in relation to land law. The different local customs were, therefore, replaced gradually by a body of rules common to the whole country and known eventually as the common law. This process was substantially completed by the end of the thirteenth century.

The formulation of the common law took place when there were few statutes or other forms of written law. The judges accordingly looked to previous decisions for guidance in order to maintain consistency. In other words the doctrine of precedent, to be discussed in Unit 3, began to merge. If previous decisions were to be followed, it was essential that the judges' decisions be recorded, and we see the beginning of law reporting, at first by anonymous lawyers in the Year Books. The main stream of English law, therefore, began with the unification of local customs to form the common law and has been developed down to the present day by the judges as precedent has been built upon precedent.

D. Other historical sources of law

Deficiencies of the early common law

A legal rule aims at making provision for a large number of cases of a particular kind. It is impossible to provide for every eventuality, however, and some special situations will arise where the application of the rule will cause hardship. Since 'hard cases make bad law', most legal systems have some machinery to deal with these special cases which would otherwise bring the law into disrepute.

An established legal system may overcome this difficulty by a liberal interpretation of its legal rules. A new system tends to place greater emphasis upon the letter of the law rather than upon its spirit or intention, and to disapprove of liberal interpretation. This was so with the early common law which, by the end of the thirteenth century, was well established but which had already acquired a degree of rigidity. As the common law courts became separated from the King's Council, they became increasingly reluctant or unable to grant remedies for new and unfamiliar types of wrong. As conditions changed and new forms of property and interests in property developed, there came to be many types of wrong for which the courts could grant no remedy.

In particular, in order to begin an action it was necessary to obtain a writ from the Chancellor's office, this being the King's command to the defendant to submit to the court's jurisdiction. The types of writ were limited and if it was not possible to frame your action within the scope of an existing writ there was no remedy. Even if a writ was obtained, the judges were so concerned with procedural matters that they might spend more time examining the validity of the writ than upon the case itself, and might decide against plaintiff on this ground alone.

If the action went forward and succeeded, the only remedy was monetary compensation. This was often inadequate in cases such as trespass where it was undesirable to have to wait and suffer the injury before being able to do anything about it. Furthermore, wrongs such as a breach of trust were not recognized by the common law courts, partly because the trust was looked upon as a device to escape feudal obligations. It was also possible for a powerful person to overawe a local jury and obtain a perverse verdict.

Equity

Subjects unable to obtain a remedy from the common law courts would petition the King asking for justice, and these petitions were usually passed to the Chancellor. The latter was empowered to order the parties to appear before him under penalty (subpoena) for refusal and, after hearing the petition, he could make such order as appeared to him to be fair, just or 'equitable'. These sittings of the Chancellor became more regular and by the end of the fourteenth century had developed into a new Court of Chancery, administering its own form of justice known as equity.

During the sixteenth century, rivalry developed between the three common law courts and the Court of Chancery. The latter proved popular with litigants because of its greater powers and flexibility, its superior procedure and, in some cases, its more appropriate remedies. The Chancellor, while not expressly overruling common law decisions, would sometimes, for instance, refuse to allow a *legal* owner of property to enforce his *legal* rights. After the period of rigidity which had led to the birth of equity, the common law again began to develop new rules and a struggle ensued between the courts over the extent of their respective jurisdictions. In the reign of James I, the principle was established that, in the event of a conflict between common law and equity, equity should prevail.

The early Chancellors were clergymen, and at first, and for a long time, each petition was simply dealt with on the basis of what the individual Chancellor felt to be just. It gradually came to be recognized, however, that there were some situations in which the Chancellor would almost always grant relief and a doctrine of precedent began to appear. This process quickened from the seventeenth century onwards when the office of Chancellor was held by lawyers trained in the common law. By the early nineteenth century, equity was as much tied by precedent as was common law and we had the unique system of two bodies of legal rules administered in two sets of courts, each with its own particular procedure and remedies. Many litigants were not only disappointed if they eventually found that they had chosen the wrong court but were utterly bewildered.

A number of reforms were introduced culminating in the Judicature Acts 1873–75. These statutes swept away the common law courts and the Court of Chancery and replaced them by one Supreme Court of Judicature in which each branch had the power to administer both common law and equity according to the same rules of procedure. The rule that equity should prevail in the event of a conflict was also restated.

The administration of the two systems was therefore combined, although it is still necessary to distinguish between them for some purposes. Thus, the common law remedy of damages may be claimed as of right but the action will be barred after a fixed period, normally six years. On the other hand, the award of equitable remedies remains at the discretion of the court and will be refused if it is felt that the plaintiff has delayed unnecessarily even for a short time in seeking them.

Equity was never a comprehensive system of law as was common law, but was for the most part a collection of individual rules or principles. If common law was the book, equity was a page of errata. Nevertheless, equity played an important part in developing certain aspects of law. It recognized and protected the trust by compelling the trustees, the legal owners, to deal with the property on behalf of the beneficiaries, the equitable owners. It treated the mortgage as the parties intended it to be treated, as a device for borrowing money, and would not allow the lender to exercise his legal rights over the property if repayment was not made on the exact contractual date. It protected the separate property of a married woman even though the husband was the legal owner. It granted relief where a contract was entered into as a result of misrepresentation or undue influence by allowing the innocent party to abandon the contract and be returned to his original position—the remedy of rescission. It also provided the remedies of specific performance and injunction which are court orders compelling the performance or non-performance respectively of certain acts under pain of fine or imprisonment for contempt if not obeyed.

It should be noted that the phrase 'common law' is sometimes used today to describe the whole body of judge-made rules of law, whether the rules originated in equity in the Court of Chancery or were common law rules in the strict sense, emanating from the old common law courts. In this wider sense, common law is contrasted with statute law which is discussed later.

Law merchant

The early common law courts were concerned largely with problems of land tenure and gave little attention to the growing number of mercantile transactions and the disputes arising therefrom. Procedure in the common law courts was slow and in order to obtain the quick decisions they needed, the merchants set up their own tribunals. These were of two types. The Courts of Staple was found mainly in the ports and dealt with external trade. The Courts of Pie Powder, as they came to be called, were found more widely and dealt with trade generally. The name of the latter is probably derived from *pieds poudrés* or the dusty feet of the traders who required speedy settlements before they moved on the next fair.

The rules administered in these courts were based upon mercantile customs and became known as the law merchant. Some of these customs became internationally recognized, while others were applied only in a particular locality or trade.

The common law courts realized the growing importance of this work and gradually took it over. Various types of commercial documents and procedures were recognized in legal decisions, thereby forming precedents and becoming part of the common law itself. At the same time, the modern law of contract was developed. The law merchant had been incorporated into the common law by about the end of the eighteenth century and the mercantile courts had disappeared. Even today, however, the ordinary courts will often take account of business practice in reaching a decision and this still plays a part in the evolution of English law.

Canon law

The medieval Church had an extremely wide jurisdiction, over the clergy in all matters and over other people in matters affecting their faith and morality; these terms were interpreted quite liberally. The law applied was canon or ecclesiastical law, which had been developed from Roman law.

After the Reformation, the power of the church courts declined as their functions were taken over by the royal courts. Two important matters, their jurisdiction over marriage and over succession to personal property, remained until the nineteenth century when they too were finally taken away. Today, their jurisdiction is confined to church property and the discipline of clergy.

Statute law

Statute law, or legislation, consists of rules which are formally enacted by a body which has constitutional power to do so. Parliament is now the only body with inherent power to legislate under English law, and statutes today take the form of Acts of Parliament. Sometimes legislative powers are delegated to subordinate bodies.

From earliest days, legislation, often in the form of royal decrees, played some part in the growth of English law. The early statutes would supplement or amend the rules of common law, and later equity, but the main framework of law grew through the decisions of the courts.

Over the last 150 years, the Government has concerned itself to an unprecedented degree with such matters as public health, education, transport, the use and conservation of natural resources, the management of the economy, and the concept of the welfare state. Industrialization, the population explosion, and the growth of large conurbations created social, economic, and human problems to which the common law and equity could not adapt. New institutions and new legal rules and concepts had to be created quickly, and this was done through Parliament. Vast numbers of statutes have been enacted creating new areas of law and, as will become apparent in later units, legislation has become a major source of new legal rules.

The courts have recognized the legislative sovereignty of Parliament and will always obey and apply an Act of Parliament even where it conflicts with or abolishes the rules of common law or equity. Legislation as a source of law today will be examined in some detail in the next unit.

Entry into Europe

One of the most potentially important legal developments in the history of this country took place in January 1972 when the United Kingdom signed the Treaty of Accession in Brussels. By this Treaty and the subsequent European Communities Act 1972, Community law was accepted as part of the law of the United Kingdom, in some respects without the necessity for further action by Parliament (Unit 9).

For further consideration

1. Give an example of a rule (or law) from as many different activities as possible in which you participate. In each instance, state the sanction for breach.
2. Explain, with examples, the difference between criminal law and civil law. Why is it necessary to draw this distinction? What problems might arise if both types of case were heard in the same courts?
3. Smith drives at a dangerously fast speed through the centre of a town. His car overturns, hits another vehicle, injures a pedestrian, and finishes up in the front garden of a house.
    What possible court proceedings might arise?
4. Describe and explain the contribution made by equity to the development of English law, both historically and today. (Do not confine your answer to the subject-matter contained in this unit; use the Index to draw upon material included later in this book.)
5. Explain briefly the following
    (a) Writ
    (b) King's Peace
    (c) Specific performance
    (d) Year Books
    (e) Courts of Staple
    (f) Plaintiff

Unit 2. Legislation as a Source of Law

The expression 'sources of law' can mean at least two different things. It can refer to the historical origins from which the law has come, such as common law and equity, which were discussed in the last unit. Second, it can refer to the body of rules which a judge will draw upon in deciding a case, and where these rules are to be found. In this second sense there are two main sources of English law today: precedent and legislation. This unit will deal with the latter.

A. The nature and effect of legislation

Legislation is the body of rules which have been formally enacted or made. Many bodies in England have power to lay down rules for *limited* purposes, for example, social clubs, but fundamentally the only way in which rules can be enacted so as to apply *generally* is by Act of Parliament. For various reasons, some of Parliament's legislative functions are delegated to subordinate bodies which, within a limited field, are allowed to enact rules. Local authorities, for instance, are allowed to enact by-laws. But local authorities can only do this because an Act of Parliament has given them the power to do so.

In constitutional theory, Parliament is said to have legislative sovereignty and, provided that the proper procedure is followed, the statute passed must be obeyed and applied by the courts. The judges have no power to hold an Act invalid or to ignore it, however unreasonable or 'unconstitutional' they may consider it to be.

In this respect England differs from many countries which have written constitutions. In the United States, for instance, the Supreme Court has power to declare legislation passed by Congress to be invalid if it is, in the opinion of the Court, inconsistent with the written constitution. The attitude of the courts in this country, on the other hand, is perhaps best expressed in words attributed to Holt C.J. in a report of *City of London* v. *Wood* in 1702: 'An Act of Parliament can do no wrong, though it may do several things that look pretty odd.'

On the other hand, although they cannot question the validity of an Act, the courts do have the task of applying it to specific problems. The Government, by Act of Parliament, states what the law is to be, but having done so, it must then abide by the words which it has used. What those words *mean* is a matter for the courts to decide. If the Government disapproves of the interpretation, it must pass another Act in an attempt to state its intentions more clearly. The courts have, in fact, evolved rules of interpretation which they will use to discover the 'true' meaning of the words of a statute and Parliament helped the courts to some extent by passing the Interpretation Act 1889, which is now replaced by the Interpretation Act 1978 (Unit 3).

B. The legislative process

Government bills

The process by which an Act is passed is a long one. The first and most important step in most cases is for the Government to decide that it wishes the legislation to be passed. Once this decision has been taken, and so long as public opinion does not cause the Government to change its mind, the legislation will pass through Parliament and become law.

The Government is the key to the legislative process because, to a great extent, it can control the way in which the House of Commons will vote. By convention, the Prime Minister, his Cabinet and other Ministers are chosen by and from the political party which holds a majority in the House of Commons. Having been chosen, members of the Government can then demand the loyalty of their supporters and, therefore, within limits, ensure that Parliament does what the Government wishes. In particular, they can decide how Parliament is to spend its time and which bills can be debated. In most Governments the decision as to which bills have priority will be taken by a committee of Ministers—usually part of the 'Legislation Committee'— and, subject to Cabinet approval, this determines broadly what legislation will be enacted. Much of the work on Government legislation will, in fact, already have been done before it reaches Parliament; there will often have been consultation with interested bodies, and a draft bill will have been prepared by Parliamentary draftsmen.

This is not to say, however, that the time spent in Parliament is wasted. Parliament is not merely a rubber stamp. It does have at least two very important functions in relation to legislation: it gives the chance for public debate and criticism, and it enables changes to be made when defects are pointed out in debate or in committee. While the essential decision is that of the Government, this is subject to the power of Parliament to criticize, explain, and amend.

Legislative procedure

Before legislative proposals, at this stage known as bills, can become Acts of Parliament or statutes, they must be approved by both Houses of Parliament and receive the Royal Assent. In the absence of any special provision, the Act will operate from the day of assent. Sometimes an Act contains a section delaying commencement in order to give time for people affected to comply with the new rules. Thus, powers may be given to a Government Department to bring the Act into operation in parts.

When a bill is introduced in the Commons there are five steps.

1. It is given a purely formal first reading. The title of the bill is read to the House and copies are printed so that Members and others can inspect the draft.
2. On the second reading, a debate takes place on the merits of the bill, upon which a vote is taken.
3. If the bill passes its second reading, it will then be referred to a standing committee which will consider it in detail, clause by clause. Bills of great importance may be considered by a Committee of the Whole House.
4. The Committee will then 'report' the bill back to the House, and any amendments proposed in Committee will be voted on.
5. Finally, the bill is given a third reading which, if the bill is controversial, can provide an opportunity for another debate and vote.

When it has passed all of these stages, the bill is sent to the House of Lords, where it goes through a similar procedure, with similar opportunities for debate and voting. Finally, when it has passed through the Lords, it is sent for the Royal Assent, which is today never refused. Two official copies of the Act are kept, but for all practical purposes the copies published by the Queen's printers through HM Stationery Office are accepted as evidence of what Parliament has decided.

Difficulties would arise if the Lords refused to pass a bill sent to them by the elected Commons. The powers of the Lords are accordingly restricted by the Parliament Acts 1911 and 1949. Briefly, a 'money bill' containing only financial provisions may be passed without the approval of the Lords. Other public bills may be submitted directly for the Royal Assent by the Commons if passed by the Commons in two successive sessions and rejected by the Lords each time, provided that at least one year has elapsed between the second reading in the Commons in the first session and the third reading in the second session. The Lords may thus delay, but cannot veto, bills which the Commons wish to pass. The only exception to this rule is that the Lords may delay indefinitely a bill to extend the life of a Parliament beyond five years.

Not all Government bills are introduced initially in the Commons. Sometimes non-controversial bills are first introduced in the House of Lords for discussion and amendment before being sent to the Commons, in order to save the time of the latter House. The Animals Act 1971 and the Sale of Goods Act 1979 are examples of Acts which became law in this way. It must also be mentioned that any bill which has not passed through all its stages at the end of a Parliamentary session will automatically lapse and must be re-introduced as a new bill during the following session.

There are still some instances where a bill introduced by a private Member of Parliament, without Government backing, can become law. About 12 Fridays each year are set aside in the Commons for private Members' bills. Unless the Government opposes the bill, it is just possible for it to pass through all of its stages in this time. The time allocated, however, is not enough for all bills which private Members may wish to introduce, and Members therefore draw lots for priority. Sometimes, if the Government is in sympathy with the provisions, it may help a private Member's bill by giving extra time for it.

Private bills

The procedure discussed so far applies to *public* bills, which alter the general law of the land on a nation-wide basis. A bill can be a public one whether introduced initially by the Government or by a private Member. *Private* bills, on the other hand, do not affect the public at large, but give additional powers to some specified person or body. The Manchester Corporation Acts, for instance, operate to confer extra powers on Manchester Corporation or on other people or bodies within the area of Manchester. It was by private Acts such as these that Manchester acquired many of its powers to take water from the Lake District. A private bill will be sponsored and introduced by the person or body which is desiring the extra powers and, although nominally it passes through the same stages as a public bill, it will not be debated in either House. Most of the discussion takes place in a small Private Bill Committee which will hear arguments on the merits of the proposals. The importance of such Acts, however, can be considerable. Manchester Corporation has had no fewer than 148 private Acts passed since 1844, and many of its powers have derived from these. The position is similar in most other local authorities, although few will have so many Acts as Manchester does. Under the Local Government Act 1972, some local authorities have taken the opportunity to tidy up the mass of private legislation which affects their area.

Amendment and repeal

A statute, once enacted, remains in force permanently. However old it may be, it remains law unless and until it is *repealed*, and it can only be repealed by another statute. The Distress Act of 1276 still appears in the current edition of Halsbury's Statutes of England, for instance. Similarly, a statute can only be *amended* by another Act of Parliament unless, as rarely happens, an Act delegates to a Minister or some other body the power to make minor changes. Most Acts today, in fact, do have to repeal or amend some earlier statutory provisions, and they will usually contain a schedule specifying what earlier provisions have been affected.

Conversely, Parliament can never take away its own power to amend or repeal earlier legislation. Nor can it otherwise restrict its own freedom to legislate in future as it thinks fit. The European Communities Act 1972 could, for instance, be construed as purporting to restrict the power of Parliament to legislate in a manner inconsistent with the European Treaties. Nevertheless, this Act could always be repealed by a future Parliament, although this would mean the withdrawal of the United Kingdom from the European Communities.

Consolidating and codifying Acts

Governments have always tended to introduce legislation as and when some specific need arises, and several closely connected Acts on a particular topic may well exist side by side. In such circumstances, the Government will often do some tidying up. A *consolidating* Act will be passed which will repeal all of the piecemeal provisions, and re-enact them in one logically arranged Act. This is periodically done, for instance, with tax legislation. Other examples include Acts dealing with road traffic, social security, safety at work, and companies.

Sometimes a Government may decide not only to consolidate all of the legislation, but also to replace some of the *case law* on the subject by a new Act. Such an Act is called a *codifying* one. It reduces most of the law on the subject into a single code. There are good examples in commercial law, particularly the Bills of Exchange Act 1882 and the Sales of Goods Act 1893. (The Sale of Goods Act 1893 was subsequently amended by several other Acts, and this legislation is now consolidated in the Sale of Goods Act 1979.)

The drafting of bills

When an Act becomes law the courts must, when called upon to do so, give effect to the words which Parliament has used. The drafting of bills, therefore, has to be done with the greatest possible skill, to avoid any unnecessary misunderstanding. This is done by a very small body of draftsmen known as Parliamentary Counsel to the Treasury who have an enormous volume of work to tackle. The normal procedure is for the Ministry responsible for the bill to prepare a draft in everyday language of what the legislation is to contain, and from this draft Counsel will draw up a bill expressed in the precise language required. Counsel will also work closely with Members of Parliament and with the Government as the bill goes through Parliament, helping to draft any amendments which may be incorporated into the Act.

The complaint is often made that the wording of Acts is too complicated, and therefore difficult to follow. One of the problems facing the draftsmen, however, is that if the rules are complex, then complex language is needed to express them accurately. The draftsman of the Sale of Goods Act 1893 expressed some quite complicated ideas in simple language, but as a result the Act was seriously ambiguous in places. On the other hand, even the judges have been irritated by the complexity of some more recent statutory drafting.

C. Delegated legislation

Forms of delegated legislation

The vast extension of the functions of Government during the last 150 years was mentioned in Unit 1. The task of making the detailed rules needed to translate this new development into practice was beyond the capacity of any one legislative body. What the Government has often done, therefore, is to pass an 'enabling' Act setting up the main framework of the reform on which it has decided, and then empowering some subordinate body—often a Minister—to enact the detailed rules necessary to complete the scheme. Thus, the Factories Act 1961 provides for sufficient and suitable lighting in factories, but leaves to the responsible Minister the work of laying down specific standards of lighting that shall be deemed sufficient and suitable for different types of work. Rules enacted under such powers are called 'delegated legislation'. The following are the principal forms that this may take:

1. *Orders in Council.* An Act may sometimes give the Privy Council power to make legislative orders. The Privy Council itself is largely an honorary body and, since all senior members of the Government will be members, the order will be made by a committee of Ministers. It must receive the assent of the Queen, but this is purely formal. An Order in Council enacted in this way is simply Government legislation which does not have to go through the full Parliamentary procedure.
2. *Ministerial regulations.* Like the Privy Council, individual Ministers have no power in their own right to make rules which must be obeyed by the courts. Parliament does, however, often delegate such powers to a Minister in some limited sphere, for instance, the power of the Minister of Transport to make traffic regulations. Once again, this is Government legislation which does not have to pass through the full procedure in Parliament.

    Most orders and rules of each of these kinds are published through HM Stationery Office under the description of *statutory instruments.*
3. *Local authorities* are given powers by many Acts of Parliament to make *by-laws* which will have the force of law within the geographical area of the authority.
4. *Other statutory authorities*, such as nationalized industry boards, harbour commissions, and bodies such as the Peak Park Planning Board, are often given power to make *by-laws* within the scope of their functions.
5. *Certain professional bodies* are given power by Parliament to make rules governing the conduct of their members. The Law Society, for example, has this power under the Solicitors Acts.

Advantages of delegation of powers

1. Parliamentary time is saved on relatively trivial matters.
2. Greater flexibility can be assured. Just as the rules can be enacted more quickly, so they can be changed more quickly. This can be particularly useful where the rules

are of an experimental nature, as is often the case with traffic regulations, or where changes can make the old rules obsolete.
3. In national emergencies it may sometimes be necessary for the Government to act at short notice. Powers of this type must normally be exercised by Orders in Council rather than merely by Ministerial regulations, because emergency powers are obviously more serious matters than, say, traffic regulations.
4. Many regulations have to cover very technical subjects which no ordinary Member of Parliament would feel able to discuss adequately. In subjects such as the construction and use of motor vehicles, therefore, it is felt better that Parliament should only lay down the general requirement that motor vehicles should be safe, and leave it to experts in the Ministry of Transport to provide for the technical details.
5. Local knowledge is usually desirable in deciding what local by-laws should be passed. This task, therefore, is given to the local authorities. Similarly, the specialist knowledge of the Law Society, and of nationalized industry boards is relied upon by Parliament.

Criticisms of the growth of delegated legislation

In the first half of this century, there were widespread criticisms of the growth of delegated legislative powers. It was felt to be an erosion of the constitutional role of Parliament to allow such wide powers to be given to other bodies, particularly to individual Ministries. Moreover, it was pointed out, delegated legislation need not ever be debated or even mentioned in Parliament, and might, therefore, become law without people really being aware of the fact. There are usually over two thousand different statutory instruments alone coming into force each year, and some of these can make substantial changes in the law.

It is generally felt today that these criticisms were exaggerated, and to some extent simply an expression of resentment at the sheer volume of legislation needed in a modern industrialized country. Certainly some safeguards do exist against abuse of delegated powers; how adequate these safeguards are is a matter which is still sometimes discussed.

Control of delegated legislation

1. *Parliamentary control*
(a) Parliament, having given the power to legislate, can obviously take the power away at a future date. This is the ultimate control.
(b) Ministers are usually answerable to Parliament for the content of regulations made by their departments, and can be questioned on this by individual Members.
(c) The enabling Act will sometimes require that an instrument be 'laid' before Parliament. In some cases the procedure is that the instrument will not become law unless it is positively approved by a resolution either of one or of both

Houses. In other cases, the instrument does not need positive approval, but it is left open to any member to take the initiative and move a negative resolution against anything in the regulations to which he objects. Provision can, therefore, be made for limited Parliamentary debate, but this depends on the enabling Act. Where approval by a resolution of the Lords is required, the Lords can effectively veto *delegated* legislation.

(d) Committees of Members of Parliament examine certain types of secondary legislation. For example, a 'sifting' committee examines European Community legislation, and reports important Community proposals. A Joint Select Committee of Lords and Commons examines most Ministerial orders to report on the drafting, whether the Minister has followed the correct procedure, and whether the instrument contains certain constitutionally questionable provisions. Another committee even examines the merits of certain instruments.

(c) Local authority by-laws have usually to be approved by the Department of the Environment, and a certain amount of Governmental (although not necessarily Parliamentary) control does exist.

2. *Judicial control*

(a) *Ultra vires*. There is a vitally important distinction between the attitude of the courts to an Act of Parliament and their attitude to delegated legislation. The courts can never challenge the validity or reasonableness of a statute. They can, and do, sometimes challenge the validity of delegated legislation. The delegate body only has power to legislate in so far as Parliament has given it this power, and the courts keep it firmly within this limit. If it exceeds its powers in any way, the rules are *ultra vires* (outside of its powers) and therefore *void*. The Minister of Transport cannot, for instance, make rules for food and drugs.

(b) *Unreasonableness*. The courts will sometimes take the view that Parliament has only given the power on the understanding that it be exercised *reasonably*. They have, therefore, held some local authority by-laws to be void, because the court felt that they were unreasonable. The courts are much less ready to hold that Ministerial regulations are unreasonable, however, because the Minister is responsible more directly to Parliament and the courts are much more wary of intervention.

For further consideration

1. Explain and criticize the present procedure by which legislative proposals become Acts of Parliament.
2. Examine the role of the House of Lords. Should it be abolished?
3. What is delegated legislation? Give as many examples as possible, particularly those which are likely to affect you.
4. The courts may influence the effect of legislation through their powers of interpretation (see Unit 3). Would it be desirable or practicable to give the courts

wider powers in this respect, even to the extent of deciding whether an Act of Parliament is invalid in specified circumstances?
5. Explain briefly the following
   (a) Consolidating Act
   (b) Private Member's bill
   (c) By-law
   (d) *Ultra vires*
   (e) Codify
   (f) Statutory instrument

Unit 3. Precedent and Other Sources of English Law

A. Judicial precedent

The development of precedent

The idea of binding judicial precedent is a special feature of common law jurisdictions, that is to say, systems of law based on that of England. The doctrine is based on the general principle that once a court has stated the legal position in a given situation, then the same decision will be reached in any future case where the material facts are the same.

We have already seen how the common law and equity both owe their existence to the way in which judges, faced with a familiar set of facts, would apply the same principles this time as they had last time. Suppose that, two years ago, the judge had held that what Mr A did amounted to trespass. If Mr B now did more or less the same thing, the new judge would hold that Mr B had also committed a trespass. The new judge would follow the earlier decision. From past decisions it became possible to forecast how a judge would decide in future, and judges came to rely on the legal (or equitable) rules which developed in this way rather than on their own unfettered discretion.

This was not yet the same as the modern doctrine of *binding* precedent. In the early common law courts the position was complicated by the writ system. Moreover, although normally a judge *would* follow a previous decision, it was not yet established that he *must* do so. Indeed, the absence of reliable reports of previous decisions probably made binding precedent impracticable until the nineteenth century, when the present system of law reporting came into being. The final steps were probably the creation of the Council of Law Reporting in 1865, and the rationalization of the court system in 1873–75.

In 1898, the House of Lords, in *London Street Tramways* v. *LCC*, said expressly that it regarded itself as bound by its own previous decisions, and in doing so it was probably just stating the position as it had existed for some time previously. Clearly, if the House of Lords must follow its own decisions, then those decisions must also bind all inferior courts.

Precedent today

Whether a court today is bound depends to a very large extent on which court gave the previous decision. Generally, if the decision was of a superior court then the lower court must follow it, but a superior court is not bound by the previous decisions of an inferior one. The following table outlines the main rules.

1. Decisions of the House of Lords bind all other courts for the future, and until recently were even binding on the House of Lords itself in subsequent cases. In 1966, however, the Lord Chancellor issued a statement on behalf of the House that it would no longer regard itself as rigidly bound if this would cause injustice by reason of changing social circumstances.
2. The Court of Appeal is bound by previous decisions of the Lords and, in the opinion of most of the judges, by its own previous decisions. Its decisions are binding on all lower courts but not upon the House of Lords.
3. A High Court judge is bound by decisions of the House of Lords and the Court of Appeal but not by other High Court decisions.
4. A County Court judge is bound by decisions of all higher courts. The decisions of the County Courts themselves are not binding in any future case, and they are not normally reported at all.

This does not mean that decisions of lower courts will be disregarded by higher courts. These decisions may not be *binding* precedents, but they will have *persuasive* value. They may be long standing, recognized by people as the law, and acted upon accordingly. Similarly, decisions of the House of Lords in appeals from Scotland or Northern Ireland, and decisions of the Judicial Committee of the Privy Council in appeals from some Commonwealth countries, while not binding on English courts, have very strong persuasive influence. Note, for instance, the *Wagon Mound* case in 1961 (Unit 12). An English court may even turn for guidance to a decision in the United States or the Commonwealth, where the legal systems have the same basis as our own.

Where seen in operation, the doctrine of precedent works in quite a complex manner. When he gives his decision in a case the judge does, in effect, three things:

1. He gives his actual decision between the parties: 'I find for the plaintiff', or 'the appeal must fail'. This is obviously the part which is of most interest to the parties themselves.
2. He will also give his reasons for reaching that decision: what facts he regards as 'material', the legal principles which he is applying to those facts and why. This is

called the *ratio decidendi* (the reasoning vital to the decision), and it is this part of the judgment which may bind future courts.
3. He may also, at the same time, discuss the law relating to this type of case generally, or perhaps discuss one or two hypothetical situations. These will be *obiter dicta* (other comments), and while they may have persuasive force in future cases, they are not binding.

Having become a precedent, a decision need not continue to be one indefinitely. It can cease to be binding in various ways. A decision can be *reversed* when the party who lost the case appeals to a higher court, which allows the appeal. Where similar facts come before the courts in a later case, then a higher court can *overrule* the previous decision of a lower one. This does not affect the parties to the earlier case; so far as they are concerned their decision still stands, but the earlier case is no longer binding in future. If a later court is not in a position to overrule a previous decision, for instance, because the legal principles involved are not the same, it may nevertheless *disapprove* it, usually by way of an *obiter dictum*. Disapproval by a higher court obviously casts doubt on the correctness of an earlier decision. Similarly, a later court which is not bound can simply *not follow* a previous decision, which will itself cast doubt on the earlier case. Finally, a previous decision can often be *distinguished* where the material facts of the earlier case differ from the present ones. There will always be some difference between the facts of two separate cases, and if the later judge feels that the differences is sufficient to justify a different decision, he will distinguish the earlier case, In this way, even a lower court can avoid holding itself bound by a previous higher decision.

Precedent or code?

Many other countries, particularly in Continental Europe, have no doctrine of binding precedent. Instead, the main source of law in these countries will be a code. Almost all of the rules of civil and of criminal law have been written out fairly simply, and then formally enacted by the legislature.

It is largely for historical reasons that the English legal system is based mainly on precedent rather than on a code, and each alternative has its advantages.

1. In favour of the English system of judge-made or case law, it is argued that it gives more flexibility. The law steadily grows as new cases come before the courts, and new rules develop to meet new situations. A code, once enacted, can only be changed by a complex legislative process, and can sometimes work injustice as the rules become out-dated. Many European codes, for instance, date from the early years of the nineteenth century, and social, political, and economic circumstances have changed greatly since then. On the other hand, this argument may be less than fair to codified systems. In the first place, continental codes are drafted much more loosely than English statutes, and the courts in codified systems can often change the interpretation put on the words used, so as to adapt the rules to meet

changing circumstances. Second, even a case law system can become rigid where the later courts are bound by an old House of Lords decision.
2. Systems based on precedent are claimed to be more realistic and practical in character, being based on actual problems that have come before the courts. They are based on practical problems, not on mere theory. On the other hand, since the courts do not give decisions on academic points, it is sometimes necessary to wait until an actual dispute arises before the law can be known. This can lead to uncertainty, and bringing a case to find out the law can be a costly business. A code can, within limits, legislate in advance, so that the parties know what their legal position is without having to go to court to find out.
3. Finally, although case law provides us with many detailed rules, this can itself be a drawback. In English law there are at least 1000 volumes of law reports in which precedents are to be found, and in the White Paper which preceded the setting up of the Law Commission in 1965 it was estimated that there were about 300 000 decided cases which could be cited as authority.

B. Law reporting

The development of a doctrine of precedent has been very closely tied to the growth of good law reporting in this country. Without a clear and reliable record of earlier decisions, a doctrine of precedent simply could not work.

Law reporting in England began in the thirteenth century with the Year Books, which were very brief notes written by anonymous lawyers, often in a curious mixture of English and Norman French. The invention and development of printing in the fifteenth and sixteenth centuries made the dissemination of information much easier. From about 1530 the Year Books were replaced by private reports published under the names of those compiling them. These continued until the nineteenth century, but they vary considerably in value according to the accuracy of the reporter. In 1865 the Council of Law Reporting was established by the legal profession to provide for systematic publication of professionally prepared and officially revised volumes of reports.

Today the main reports are still produced by what is now the Incorporated Council of Law Reporting. It publishes about two volumes each year of reports of decisions in the Queen's Bench Division of the High Court, one or two volumes of Chancery Division cases, and about one volume per year of Family Division decisions. Court of Appeal cases are included in the volumes for the High Court Division from which the appeal came, but House of Lords decisions are found in a separate volume of Appeal Cases. Since 1953 the Council has also issued the Weekly Law Reports, to enable reports of certain cases to be available more quickly.

Some private reports did survive after the nineteenth century, but the only general ones now issued are the All England Law Reports, published in about three volumes each year, and also periodically, about weekly. Some very specialized private reports also continue in fields such as commercial law, taxation, and industrial law.

None of these sets of reports covers all of the cases decided. Unpublished reports of some other decisions are kept in the library of the Bar Council in London. Any report certified by a barrister may be produced in court, but if there is any conflict the Law Reports will be preferred. The Law Reports are submitted in draft form to the judge before being published, so that accuracy can be checked, and the judge may even alter slightly the words which he used when giving judgment in court. Judges now also revise and correct some of the private reports.

The report of a civil case is referred to by the names of the parties as, for example, *Bolton* v. *Stone*, but in speech the 'v.' is said as 'and' (*not* 'versus'). The plaintiff's name is placed first and the defendant's second. If the case goes to appeal the parties are known as the appellant and the respondent, but the order is not changed unless it is a House of Lords case, when the appellant's name is placed first. After the name of the case will be found details for easy reference: the year, the series of reports with the volume number if necessary, and the page. Thus, in the Law Reports, the House of Lords decision in *Bolton* v. *Stone* [1951] AC 850 is to be found on page 850 of the Appeal Cases reports for 1951. The Court of Appeal decision in the same case was reported under the name *Stone* v. *Bolton* [1950] 1 KB 201 (Miss Stone being the original plaintiff), and is found on page 201 of the first volume of King's Bench Division Reports for 1950. In the All England Law Reports, the Court of Appeal decision in this case is reported under the reference *Stone* v. *Bolton* [1949] 2 All ER 851, and the House of Lords decision as *Bolton* v. *Stone* [1951] 1 All ER 1078.

C. The judges and statutes

Construction and interpretation of statutes

The other major way in which the judges contribute to the development of English law is in interpreting and construing the words used in statutes and other legislation. Once a higher court has decided that the words of an Act apply in a particular way to a set of facts, this decision will form a precedent to be followed should a similar problem arise in a future case. Sometimes a complex body of case law may arise out of the interpretation of a single statute, as happened with parts of the Sale of Goods Act 1893, for example.

The Interpretation Act 1978 gives certain statutory rules of interpretation, for example, that the masculine gender shall include the feminine, and the singular shall include the plural, and vice versa, unless a contrary intention is obvious. Moreover, almost all Acts contain a series of definitions of technical and other terms which the enactment contains.

Subject to this, it is for the judges to say what the words of an Act mean should any doubt arise. Words will be given their literal or everyday meaning unless this would lead to absurdity. If particular words are followed by general words, the general words are restricted to things similar to those specified particularly. Thus 'wheat, barley, and other crops' would include oats but not potatoes. On the other hand, if there is particular mention only, nothing else is included. Thus 'wheat and barley' would not include oats.

If the words used are ambiguous, or if their application is uncertain, then more difficult questions of construction can arise. The courts will look at the Act as a whole; often the way in which a word is used in other parts of the Act will make it plain what it is intended to mean here. If the meaning is still not clear, the courts will try to discover from the wording of the Act what 'mischief' the Act was designed to deal with, and will try to interpret the words so as to give effect to what the Act was intended to achieve. The court will *not*, however, ask the Government what the Act was intended to achieve, partly because the Government might be tempted to give a meaning which best suited its own immediate purposes; nor will account be taken of Parliamentary debates or statements published by Ministers when the bill was first proposed. It is the words of the Act alone which constitute the law.

Finally, there are certain presumptions which a court will make. Thus, it is presumed that a statute is not intended to bind the Crown unless the statute expressly so provides. Since 'the Crown' includes all crown servants (e.g. civil service departments) this presumption can be very important. Similarly, it is presumed that an Act is not intended to create a strict criminal offence; the courts will assume that the defendant is guilty only if he intended to commit the offence, or acted carelessly. This presumption will, of course, be rebutted if the words of the Act make it plain that the legislature wishes to impose strict liability.

Codes of Practice

Section 45 of the Road Traffic Act 1930 provided that 'The Minister shall . . . prepare a code (in this section referred to as the "Highway Code") comprising such directions as appear to him to be proper for the guidance of persons using roads . . .'. In exercise of this duty (now imposed by the Road Traffic Act 1972) the Minister of Transport produced the Highway Code. This Code is *not* a piece of legislation; it does not have binding force, it is not a criminal offence to break it, nor will breach of it give rise to civil liability. It can always, however, be cited in evidence, and a person who breaks it is much more likely to be held negligent, or guilty of careless driving, than a person who observes the provisions. The Code must be treated as a source of law to the extent that a court *must* accept its provisions in evidence.

The use of this type of code seems likely to increase in future. Under the Industrial Relations Act 1971, a Code of Industrial Relations Practice was produced, having the same practical effect as the Highway Code. Subsequent legislation preserved this Code of Practice, which is now governed by the Employment Protection Act 1975, and further codes have since been added. Codes with similar effect have been produced under the Health and Safety at Work etc. Act 1974, the Control of Pollution Act 1974, and the Race Relations Act 1976.

In addition, there are many non-statutory codes of practice, produced by professional bodies, making recommendations as to safety in such matters as handling chemicals or other materials. Unlike statutory codes of practice, these are not sources of law, in that the courts have no *duty* to accept them in evidence. Nevertheless they may in practice influence a court in deciding whether or not particular conduct is reasonable.

D. Other sources of law

Law of the European Communities

By section 2 of the European Communities Act 1972, the law of the Communities is incorporated into English law, and therefore becomes a very important source of rules which will have effect in this country. This was an extremely important change, and will be examined in detail in Unit 9.

Custom

Custom formed the basis of common law. General customs, almost without exception, have now fallen into disuse or been recognized by the courts and incorporated into precedent. Occasionally, a local custom may be put forward in support of an argument, but the court will only accept this on very stringent conditions. The most important of these are that the custom shall be certain, reasonable, and have existed since time immemorial. By historical accident, legal memory is deemed to go back until 1189; but it will be presumed that this is the case if the custom has existed longer than anyone living can remember. More frequently, the courts will take into consideration what amount to special customs, such as commercial and business practice, in cases where they have to decide how existing legal rules should be applied in business situations.

Books by legal authors

These are not cited very frequently in the English courts, contrary to the practice in many continental countries. At one time this practice was seldom allowed here, and was restricted to a few notable authorities. More recently the rule has been relaxed and the number of acceptable authors increased. It is now, for instance, no longer necessary for the author to be dead before his work can be cited.

For further consideration

1. Explain the expression 'sources of law'.
2. To what extent, if at all, do the judges in England *make* the law?
3. When may a court avoid following a previous decision?
4. Should the whole of English law be codified?
5. Explain briefly the following
   (a) Code of Practice
   (b) *Ratio decidendi*
   (c) Time immemorial
   (d) Overruling
   (e) Book of authority
   (f) *Obiter dictum*

Unit 4. The Criminal Courts

A. Magistrates and their courts

Justices of the peace

The office of justice of the peace or magistrate (the two expressions mean the same thing) can be traced back to the thirteenth century when 'conservators of the peace' were appointed in each county to assist in the maintenance of order. Shortly afterwards they were given the power to try minor offences to save the time of the Assize judges. For this purpose the justices met quarterly for the more serious offences and informally when required for the less serious ones. From these meetings developed the Courts of Quarter Sessions and Petty Sessions.

From the fifteenth century, in the absence of a system of local government, the justices were given various administrative duties to carry out. Responsibility was acquired for such matters as poor relief, highways, and even the fixing of wages. As local government developed, most of these functions were taken over by new local authorities; liquor licensing is perhaps the most important remaining administrative function performed by the justices today.

The judicial functions of justices, regulated from time to time by statute, have now existed for over 600 years. In the present century these functions have increased considerably; greater powers to hear more serious cases have been given to justices and our increasingly complex society has required more regulation, for example, road traffic legislation. The ready solution to most problems, whether these be concerned with untrained dogs, false trade descriptions or litter, is apparently to make it an offence triable summarily, that is before the justices. Over 98 per cent of all crimes are dealt with in this way.

Appointment of justices

Justices are appointed by the Lord Chancellor on the recommendation of local advisory committees. (In Lancashire, Merseyside, and Greater Manchester, appointments are made by the Chancellor of the Duchy of Lancaster.) Any person may be recommended for appointment, good character and achievements in other walks of life being primary considerations. No legal qualifications or knowledge of law are necessary and the only requirement is residence within 15 miles of the area for which the appointment is made.

It is not surprising that controversy surrounds the office. It is argued that too many appointments are rewards for political services; on the other hand such people would probably be appointed anyway by reason of the fact that they tend to be leaders of the community. The Lord Chancellor attempts to maintain a balance of interests, politically and in other ways, on each Bench. Since 1966, all newly appointed justices have been required to undergo an initial course of training and 'refresher' courses are held from time to time on a voluntary basis.

The Lord Chancellor may remove a justice from the Commission of the Peace for misconduct or for failure to take a fair share in the work of the Bench; a justice may also resign for reasons such as illness. At the age of 70 a justice is placed on the Supplemental List which enables him to act in such matters as signing documents but not to sit in court.

Magistrates' Courts

These courts, sometimes known as courts of summary jurisdiction or petty sessions or, incorrectly, as police courts, are held in most places; the number of courts and the frequency of their sitting depends upon the amount of work to be done. The court must be composed of at least two and not more than seven justices. The usual number is three, so that in the event of a conflict a majority decision will be given. While it is possible for a justice to sit alone, his powers are then so limited that this rarely occurs today.

In a few towns the place of the lay justices may be taken by one full-time *stipendiary magistrate*, who must be a barrister or solicitor of at least seven years' standing. Stipendiary magistrates are appointed by the Crown on the recommendation of the Lord Chancellor but are paid by the local authority. There are 50 stipendiaries, most of whom sit in central London, and yet some 1000 Magistrates' Courts are held each day.

The jurisdiction of Magistrates' Courts, which is normally confined to offences arising in the locality, is regulated closely by statute. There is power to try all summary or non-indictable offences; these are offences where there is no right to trial by jury on charges set out in a document known as the indictment. Most minor offences fall into this category, for example, common assult, drunkenness, and the less serious motoring offences. Many of these cases are now disposed of in the absence

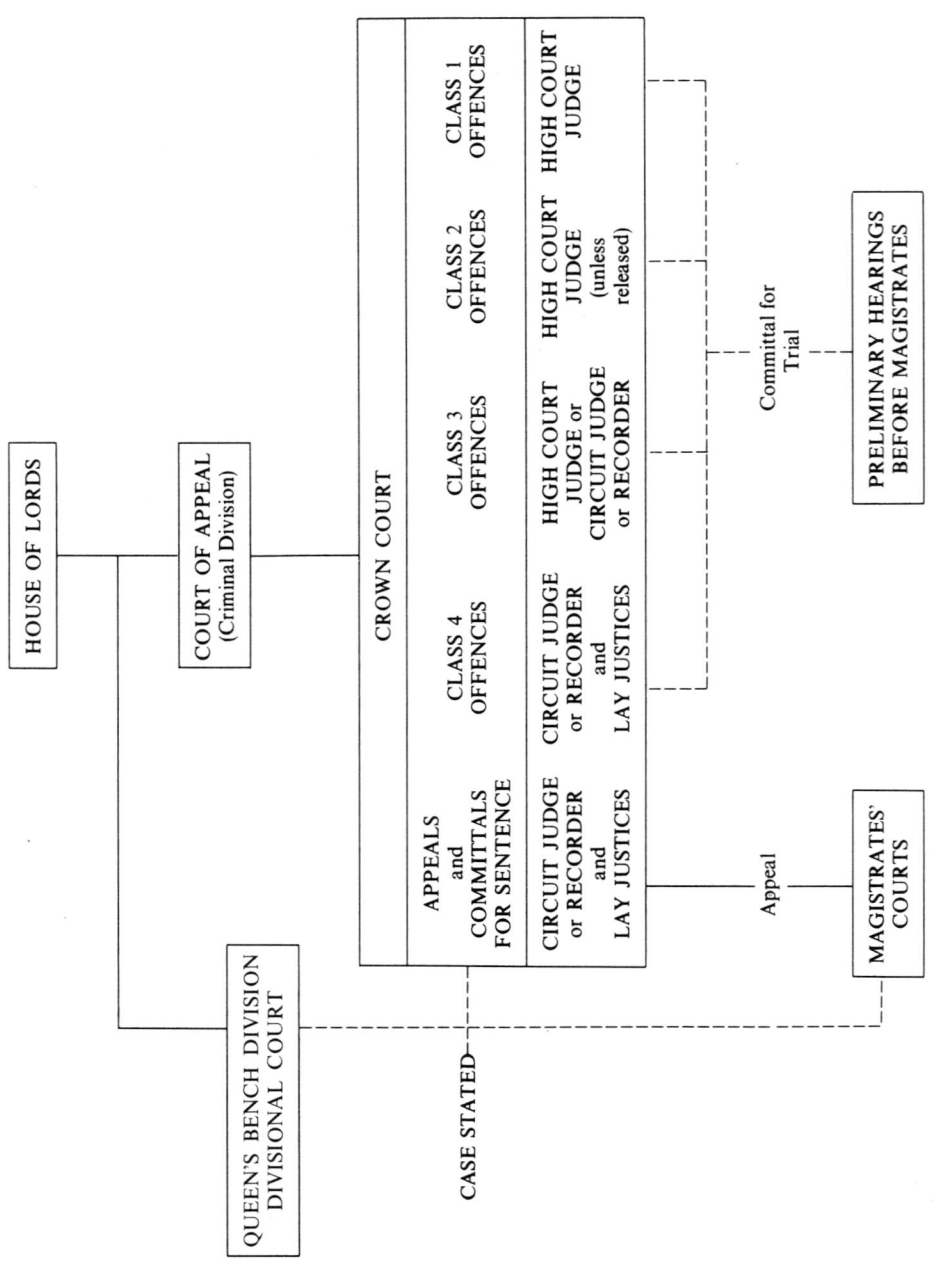

of the defendant who may plead guilty by letter, but an absent defendant may not be sentenced to imprisonment or disqualified from driving.

Certain indictable offences of a more serious nature, for example, theft and certain crimes of violence, may be, and in fact usually are, tried in Magistrates' Courts. If the defendant elects for this form of trial instead of trial by jury in the Crown Court, he must be warned that there is power to send him to the Crown Court for sentence; this may be done where he is found guilty and the justices, having heard of his previous record, feel that their powers of punishment are inadquate. An offender has a right to trial by jury in all cases except those which may only be tried summarily under the provisions of the Criminal Law Act 1977.

The punishment that may be imposed by justices depends upon the offence, but in general they may not fine more than £1000 or imprison for more than six months. If there are two or more offences, a sentence of up to 12 months may be given. Magistrates' Courts cannot sentence a young offender to Borstal training; if it is felt that this is appropriate, the offender must be committed to the Crown Court for sentence with a recommendation to this effect.

Young persons under the age of 17 must normally be dealt with in the *juvenile court*. Three justices must sit, not all of the same sex, and the justices must be drawn from a panel appointed to deal with juvenile offenders and who have had training in this field. The juvenile court must sit separately from the normal adult court, the public are not admitted, and press reporting is restricted.

The supervision of the court and matters arising before and after trial rests with the *Clerk to the Justices*. He must normally be a solicitor or barrister of at least five years' standing, although it is possible to qualify for appointment in exceptional cases by length of service. The Clerk, or his deputy, is also available in court to give advice to the justices on a point of law, but he must not influence their decision. The justices decide questions of fact without the assistance of a jury and also decide upon the appropriate sentence. The accused person may be represented in court by either a barrister or a solicitor.

In each local government area which has a Commission of the Peace, the justices will elect a *Magistrates' Courts Committee*. This body is responsible for the administration of the Magistrates' Courts in that area including the appointment of staff and the provision of accommodation. To preserve local connections, the necessary finance is provided by the local authority, though 80 per cent is normally reimbursed by the Home Office. In the larger county areas the courts and the justices are divided into petty sessional divisions.

Committal proceedings

Justices have another important function to perform in the case of more serious crimes which they cannot try. Their duty is to hear the evidence presented by the prosecution against the accused and decide whether there is a prima facie or reasonable case to go forward for trial. This preliminary examination of the evidence, known as committal proceedings, avoids wasting the time of higher courts on frivolous charges. One justice may sit alone for this purpose and, by the Criminal Justice Act 1967, it is now possible to submit all or part of the evidence against the accused by handing to the court previously prepared written statements, provided that the accused is legally represented and does not object. In consequence these proceedings have tended to become little more than a formality in most cases.

If it is decided that the evidence is not sufficient, the accused will be released but, since this is not a trial and therefore not an acquittal, a fresh prosecution may be brought later if new evidence comes to light. If it is decided that an arguable case has been made out, the accused will be committed, either on bail or in custody, for trial in the Crown Court.

B. The Crown Court

The Beeching Commission

Until 1971, the structure of criminal courts was the result of a development which dated back to the Middle Ages. Serious cases were tried at Assizes by High Court judges under powers derived from special commissions. Less serious cases were tried at about 150 county and borough Quarter Sessions. London had its Central Criminal Court (Old Bailey) and there were Crown Courts with a similar jurisdiction in Liverpool and Manchester.

These courts were also hampered by territorial limits upon their jurisdiction which prevented the transfer of business from busy courts to courts which had less business. Court administration, staffing, and buildings were the responsibility of a number of different bodies. In general, the criminal courts presented an extremely fragmented and inefficient pattern which required reform.

In 1966, the Royal Commission on Assizes and Quarter Sessions was set up under the chairmanship of Lord Beeching 'to inquire into the present arrangements for the administration of justice', and 'to report what reforms should be made for the more convenient, economic and efficient disposal of the civil and criminal business'. The Commission reported in 1969 and the recommendations were largely embodied in the Courts Act 1971 which came into effect on 1 January 1972. The object of this statute was a simplified, more rational, and more flexible court structure in which resources could be used to the best advantage.

The changes made by the Courts Act 1971

All criminal cases triable on indictment above the level of Magistrates' Courts are heard in one court, the Crown Court. This court is part of the Supreme Court and replaces Assizes and Quarter Sessions. There are no territorial limitations and the Crown Court may sit at any convenient centre, taking into account the volume of work and the convenience of the public. Cases may be transferred from one centre to another if necessary.

Centres are divided into three tiers. There are 26 first-tier centres at which High Court Judges will deal with civil business, and High Court judges and Circuit judges will deal with criminal business. There are 17 second-tier centres for criminal cases only, at which both High Court judges and Circuit judges will sit. There are 52 third-tier centres for less serious cases at which only Circuit judges will sit. Part-time judges or Recorders may sit instead of Circuit judges (Unit 7).

Criminal offences have been divided into four classes for the purpose of trial. The first class, which comprises the most serious offences, must be tried by a High Court judge. The second class must be similarly tried unless a particular case is released as being suitable for trial by a Circuit judge. The third class may be tried by a High Court judge or a Circuit judge and the fourth class, the least serious offences, are normally tried by Circuit judges only. While the division of work between High Court and Circuit judges approximates to the previous division between Assizes and Quarter Sessions the new system is far more flexible in the use of 'judge power'.

Magistrates formerly sat with a legally qualified chairman at county Quarter Sessions but not in the boroughs where the Recorder was the sole judge. It is now provided that not less than two and not more than four magistrates may sit with a Circuit judge; this will normally be when he is dealing with class four offences. Magistrates also form part of the Bench when appeals are heard from Magistrates' Courts or in proceedings on committal for sentence.

Administration of the Crown Court

There is now one authority, the Lord Chancellor, responsible for the administration of all courts, except Magistrates' Courts, and there is a unified court service. The Lord Chancellor has divided the country into six circuits for administrative purposes—Northern (based upon Manchester), North Eastern (Leeds), Midland (Birmingham), Wales and Chester (Cardiff), Western (Bristol), and South Eastern (London). Organization of each circuit is controlled by a circuit administrator, assisted by court administrators and other staff, and by an advisory committee. Judicial matters such as the disposition of judges and the supervision of the disposal of business are controlled by two High Court judges, known as presiding judges. Two appointments are made so that one of the judges would be present on the circuit whenever the courts are sitting. All court and other accommodation is the sole responsibility of the Secretary of State for the Environment.

Procedural improvements have been made by the Courts Act regarding such matters as juries and costs. The Act also confers wide powers upon the Lord Chancellor and Lord Chief Justice to make rules and directions for the more efficient working of the courts. Of particular interest is the power given to the Lord Chancellor to grant a right of audience in the Crown Court to solicitors where the public interest demands this. An example would be in an area where there is a shortage of barristers.

C. Appeals in criminal cases

Appeals from Magistrates' Courts

Appeals against a conviction or the severity of a sentence may be made to the Crown Court. Only the defence, and not the prosecution, may appeal. The appeal takes the form of a complete re-hearing of the case by a Circuit judge, normally sitting with two magistrates but without a jury. When juvenile court appeals are heard, the Circuit judge sits with two magistrates from juvenile court panels.

Appeals may be made on a point of law by either the prosecution or defence to the Divisional Court of the Queen's Bench Division. This is known as *case stated*, since the magistrates are required to make a statement of their findings on the facts of the case. The Divisional Court will then gives its decision on the law applicable to these facts. If this decision is contrary to that given by the magistrates, the case will be remitted to the magistrates with instructions that the Divisional Court's ruling on the law shall be applied.

An appeal by way of case stated may also be made from the Crown Court. A further appeal from a decision of the Divisional Court on a case stated may be taken to the House of Lords.

Court of Appeal (Criminal Division)

Before 1907 there was no formal system of criminal appeals, only an informal arrangement whereby the trial judge, in effect, consulted his brother judges. Following a miscarriage of justice, which came to light in 1907, the Court of Criminal Appeal was established. This existed until 1966 when the Criminal Appeal Act transferred its powers, with some additions, to the Court of Appeal, which was reconstituted with a Civil Division and a Criminal Division.

This court is composed of the Lord Chief Justice, the Master of the Rolls (nominally), the Lord Justices of Appeal and any judges of the Queen's Bench Division who are requested to sit. No judge may sit if an appeal is being considered from a trial which took place before him. An uneven number of judges, normally three, sits to hear appeals from the Crown Court.

An appeal may be made by the defence against a conviction but not by the prosecution against an acquittal. Appeals on points of law do not require permission but appeals on questions of fact or of mixed law and fact can only be made with the permission of either the trial judge or of the Court of Appeal itself. The court may confirm or quash the conviction or, in very limited circumstances when fresh evidence has become available, order a new trial. An appeal must be allowed if it is felt in all the circumstances the verdict is unsafe or unsatisfactory, if there was a wrong decision given on a question of law, or if there was a material irregularity in the course of the trial. If the appeal would succeed on a technicality, the court may refuse to quash the conviction if it considers that no miscarriage of justice has occurred.

If an appeal is made against the sentence, the court may confirm or reduce it or substitute one form of punishment or treatment for another; the sentence cannot be increased as in the past. The time during which a person is in custody pending an appeal is counted as part of his sentence unless the court gives a direction to the contrary. Such directions may only be given in the case of appeals without permission and which are considered to be frivolous. One interesting clause in the 1966 Act enables the rules of court to provide for the recording of proceedings at a trial by means of tape recordings.

The Home Secretary may ask for the advice of this court when considering the exercise of the royal prerogative of mercy and, following an acquittal on a criminal charge, the Attorney-General may refer to the court for an opinion on a point of law which has arisen in the case.

House of Lords

A further appeal may be made by either the prosecution or the defence from a decision of the Criminal Division of the Court of Appeal to the House of Lords. The Court of Appeal must first certify that a point of law of general public importance is involved. Permission to appeal must then be obtained from either the Court of Appeal or the House of Lords. These requirements prevent frivolous appeals and the number of criminal appeals heard by the House is very small compared with the number of appeals on civil matters. Appeals may also be made on the same conditions from a Divisional Court of the Queen's Bench Division. The powers of the House of Lords when considering criminal appeals are similar to those of the Court of Appeal.

The constitution of the House of Lords is outlined in Unit 5.

D. The prerogative of mercy

Although this is not part of the structure of criminal courts, it may be exercised following a conviction and normally after all possibilities of appeal have been exercised.

From earliest times the Crown has had the prerogative or power to administer justice and therefore to pardon offenders. As with other royal powers this is now exercised by a Minister, the Home Secretary, on behalf of the Crown.

The first step may be to grant a *reprieve* or a suspension for a period of the execution of the sentence. It is the grant of a *pardon* which affects the sentence. A free pardon quashes both the conviction and the sentence and may be accompanied by the payment of compensation if some or all of the sentence has been carried out. It is also possible to substitute one form of sentence for another, for example, a fine instead of imprisonment, or to reduce the amount of the sentence without altering its character.

There are a few limited occasions when a pardon cannot be granted, for example, for a public nuisance so long as this remains unabated.

For further consideration

1. Consider the advantages and disadvantages of entrusting the trial of so many offences to magistrates who are not professional lawyers. Should all magistrates be stipendiaries?
2. Swifty has been charged with theft. Which court or courts may deal with the case? What provisions exist for appeal?
3. With reference to Question 2, state whether each hearing or appeal would take place locally where the incident took place, and indicate the composition of the court or courts concerned.
4. Explain briefly the meaning of
   (a) Committal proceedings
   (b) First-tier centre
   (c) Clerk to the Justices
   (d) Pardon
   (e) Case stated
   (f) Juvenile court

Unit 5. The Civil Courts

A. Inferior courts

County Courts

After the medieval local courts had largely disappeared, there was little provision for the hearing of minor civil claims until the County Courts were created in 1846. They were originally designed for the settlement of small claims and the collection of debts where the amount at stake did not exceed £20, but their jurisdiction was subsequently extended by various statutes. The County Courts Act 1959 consolidated the rules governing their operation, but it has since proved necessary to make further statutory amendments.

There are some 400 of these courts in England and Wales. They have no connection either with the earlier courts which carried the same name or with the geographical counties. County Courts are grouped in circuits varying from as many as 15 courts in country areas to one court in almost continuous session in parts of London. They are presided over by Circuit judges (Unit 7), of whom there are just over 100 and, while it is usual for there to be one judge to each circuit, the busier courts may have more than one judge.

The majority of civil cases in this country are disposed of in the County Courts by the judge sitting without a jury. Procedure tends to be quicker and less formal than in the High Court and, particularly since the cases are heard locally, less costly. Solicitors, wearing gowns but not wigs, have a right of audience as well as barristers.

There are limits to the jurisdiction of the County Courts, normally based upon the amount of the claim. Actions in contract and tort, such as the collection of contractual debts and accident claims, can be brought where the amount claimed does not exceed £5000; this sum, and those following, may be raised further when necessary by Order in Council. Since even a small claim can raise difficult issues of

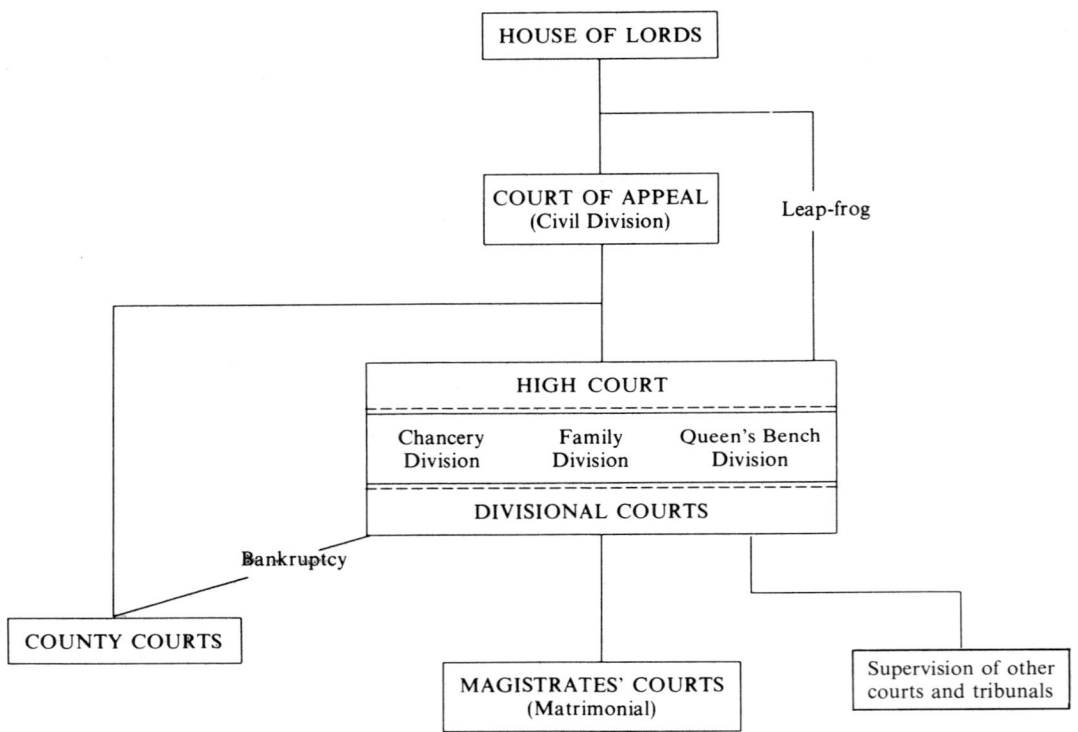

law, the amount at stake does not necessarily measure the difficulty or complexity of the case. Actions for defamation, which invariably require trial by jury, must always be brought in the High Court.

In equity matters and related proceedings, which include actions on trusts and mortgages, the administration of estates and the dissolution of partnerships, the amount at issue must not exceed £30 000. In actions concerning land, such as the recovery of possession and the determination of title, the annual rateable value must not exceed £1000. Certain County Courts can deal with bankruptcies and the winding up of companies whose paid-up share capital does not exceed £120 000.

The County Courts also have jurisdiction in certain family matters such as undefended divorces, adoption, guardianship, and legitimacy. Some courts near the coast can hear admiralty cases, particularly small salvage claims. Many statutes confer jurisdiction in other matters, important examples being hire purchase, rent restriction and complaints of racial discrimination. Actions begun in the High Court may be remitted to the County Court if the amount at issue is small and other actions may be so transferred with the consent of the parties.

In addition to the restrictions regarding the nature and amount of the claim as outlined above, there are also territorial limitations. In general, actions must be brought in the court for the district where either the defendant resides or carries on business or where the reason for the action arose. If possession of land is sought, the venue of the trial depends upon where the land is situated.

The administration of County Courts is carried out by *Registrars*, who must be solicitors of at least seven years' standing. Registrars also perform limited judicial functions and now have the power to act as judge if the action is not defended, if the amount at issue does not exceed £500, and in other cases if the parties agree.

The Courts Act 1971 did not greatly affect the County Courts. This Act did, however, abolish a number of civil courts of long standing—the Mayor's and City of London Court, the Salford Hundred Court, the Liverpool Court of Passage, and the Bristol Tolzey Court—and the work formerly carried out by these courts has now passed to the County Courts.

In relation to very small claims, it is sometimes felt that the County Courts are no longer fulfilling the purpose for which they were originally created. Although procedure is much quicker and cheaper than that in the High Court, it is still expensive. A defended County Court action could now cost hundreds of pounds in fees and disbursements and many solicitors would advise against suing if only a small sum was at stake. The County Court arbitration scheme (Unit 6) has reduced costs considerably but, in consequence, costs of legal representation in court are not awarded to a successful party where the amount involved does not exceed the arbitration limit of £500.

Magistrates' Courts

The work of these courts is largely criminal (Unit 4), but they do have a limited civil jurisdiction. This covers such miscellaneous matters as the recovery of rates, income tax and social security contributions. Magistrates also have important powers to grant or refuse the statutory licences required for businesses such as the sale of alcoholic liquor to the public, and for betting and gaming. They may also hear appeals against the refusal to grant or the withdrawal of certain licences by local authorities, for example, to operate a taxi service or open a nursing home.

The most important civil matters are dealt with separately from criminal cases in what are known as domestic proceedings, now largely governed by the Domestic Proceedings and Magistrates' Courts Act 1979. A court must be constituted by at least one male and one female magistrate drawn from a domestic panel of magistrates who have received additional training in this field. There is no divorce jurisdiction but orders may be made for the payment of maintenance and for the custody of children, and some relief against violence may be obtained by protection and exclusion orders. In addition, affiliation orders may be made for the support of illegitimate children, permission to marry may be granted where one of the parties is under 18 and parental consent has been refused, and adoption orders may be made. This jurisdiction is the nearest approach in this country to a family court.

B. The High Court

Supreme Court of Judicature

The Judicature Acts 1873–75 reorganized the system of civil courts by sweeping away the many separate courts which then existed and replacing them by the Supreme Court of Judicature (divided into the Court of Appeal and the High Court of Justice). The system then established has remained in operation with only minor alterations to the present day. It is now governed by the Supreme Court Act 1981.

High Court

Any civil action may be begun in the High Court, apart from a few matters such as rent restriction and hire purchase where the County Courts are given exclusive jurisdiction by statute. There is, therefore, an overlap in the jurisdiction of the County Court and the High Court where small claims are concerned. In these cases litigants are encouraged to use the County Courts by the power of the High Court Registrars and Masters to transfer High Court actions to the County Courts, in some instances without the consent of the parties. If there is an insistence upon the use of the High Court, the successful plaintiff may be penalized by a smaller award of costs on the County Court and not the High Court scale, or even by a refusal to award any costs at all.

The High Court is divided into three divisions, the Queen's Bench Division, the Chancery Division, and the Family Division. Any division is legally competent to deal with any matter arising, but in practice cases must be assigned to the division specializing in that particular type of action.

Before 1972, High Court cases outside London were tried at Civil Assizes. The cases were heard by High Court judges, mainly from the Queen's Bench Division, drawing their power from a special commission. The Courts Act 1971 abolished Civil Assizes and provided that the High Court might sit throughout the country wherever convenient. In practice this will be the 26 first-tier centres outside London (Unit 4) where almost any type of High Court case may be heard. The exception concerns Chancery matters which will be confined to certain centres in the north of England; in effect, this is a continuation of the former jurisdiction of the old Palatine Courts of Lancaster and Durham which were abolished by the 1971 Act.

Queen's Bench Division
This division, presided over by the Lord Chief Justice, has succeeded to the jurisdiction formerly exercised by the old common law courts of Queen's (or King's) Bench, Common Pleas, and Exchequer. It deals with the greatest number of cases, notably those arising out of breaches of contract, the commission of torts and claims for the recovery of land. Typical cases would include an action for non-performance of a contract, an allegation that the defendant has published a defamatory statement, and a claim for damages arising out of a road accident or an injury suffered at work.

Any action not specifically assigned to one of the other two divisions will be heard in the Queen's Bench Division.

In this division are to be found the few remaining civil juries. While most actions are now tried by a judge sitting alone, a jury will normally be empanelled whenever a person's character is likely to be in issue, as in actions based upon fraud and defamation. The Courts Act 1971 extended majority verdicts to civil proceedings.

Two specialized courts sit within the Queen's Bench Division, the Admiralty Court and the Commercial Court. Judges may be assigned to these courts and thereby specialize in these types of case.

Chancery Division

This division inherited the jurisdiction formerly exercised by the old Court of Chancery and other matters have since been allocated to it by statute. It is concerned with the administration of the estates of deceased persons, trusts, mortgages, partnerships, companies, bankruptcies, and revenue and planning matters. The nominal president is the Lord Chancellor but his many other duties prevent him from taking any direct part in the work of the division; the organization of the day-to-day business is carried out by a senior judge, the Vice-Chancellor.

When a judge of this division sits for the purpose of dealing with the estate of a mentally disordered person, the court is known as the Court of Protection. A specialized court within this division is the Patents' Court, established in 1978.

Family Division

This division was created by the Administration of Justice Act 1970 to deal with matters arising out of marriage, divorce, matrimonial property, and children. The senior judge in the division is known as the President.

This was formerly the Probate, Divorce, and Admiralty Division, a collection of apparently unrelated matters which the 1970 Act attempted to reform. Admiralty cases, such as salvage claims and prize jurisdiction, were then transferred to a special court within the Queen's Bench Division. Probate cases were transferred to the Chancery Division, except for non-contentious matters which remained within the Family Division for administrative reasons. Jurisdiction over minors, for example, wardship, was transferred from the Chancery Division to the Family Division.

C. Appeals in civil cases

Divisional Courts

In addition to its original jurisdiction whereby cases are first tried by one judge, the High Court also exercises certain appellate jurisdiction. For this purpose two or three judges sit together and constitute a Divisional Court.

Divisional Courts of the Queen's Bench Division may exercise criminal and civil jurisdiction. Criminal appeals are heard by way of 'case stated' from Magistrates' Courts and the Crown Court (Unit 4). Civil appeals are heard from the decisions of certain tribunals. Divisional Courts in the Chancery Division hear appeals from the County Courts on bankruptcy questions, while in the Family Division appeals are heard from Magistrates' Courts on domestic matters.

The Divisional Court in the Queen's Bench also hears applications for various prerogative orders, through which various special courts and tribunals are kept under review (Unit 6). Thus, if an administrative tribunal exceeds its jurisdiction or otherwise acts wrongfully, its decision can be quashed by the Divisional Court. This is not strictly an appellate jurisdiction, but in many cases it is so similar as to be almost indistinguishable.

Court of Appeal (Civil Division)

Appeals from the County Court (except on bankruptcy matters), the High Court, and certain tribunals, for example, the Lands Tribunal, are normally heard by three judges of this court. The court, for all practical purposes, is constituted by the Master of the Rolls and 18 Lord Justices of Appeal, though other judges from the High Court may be asked to sit if necessary. An appeal may generally be made as of right but leave is required in some cases. In County Court cases the permission of the trial judge or of the Court of Appeal is necessary except where the appeal is on a question of law, or where the amount of the claim exceeds £20, or where the remedy sought is an injunction.

The appeal takes the form of a rehearing of the case through the media of the judge's notes and the transcript of the official shorthand writer's notes, and by listening to argument from counsel. Witnesses are not heard again nor is fresh evidence usually admitted. The court has all the powers of the court below and may uphold or reverse the decision in whole or in part, it may alter the sum of damages awarded, and it may make a different order as to costs. In certain prescribed circumstances, for example, the discovery of fresh evidence, a new trial may be ordered.

House of Lords

A further right of appeal exists from the Court of Appeal to the House of Lords; leave is required from the Court of Appeal or from the Appeals Committee of the House itself.

The House of Lords when it sits as a judicial tribunal differs in constitution from the legislative body which forms one of the Houses of Parliament. All the lay peers are now excluded, by convention if not by law, and the judges are drawn from the Lord Chancellor, peers who have held or are holding high judicial office such as ex-Lord Chancellors, and the 10 life peers who are known as Lords of Appeal in Ordinary or Law Lords. Some of the Law Lords are appointed from Scotland and Northern Ireland since the House is also the highest civil court of appeal for these countries and the highest criminal court of appeal for Northern Ireland.

Appeals heard by the House of Lords require a minimum of three judges but in practice five will normally sit. Since the court is technically part of the House, the judgments are given in the form of 'speeches', not usually read out aloud today. If their lordships disagree, the view of the majority will prevail, and an appellant or respondent may succeed by only three votes to two. This was so in the case of *Donoghue* v. *Stevenson* (Unit 13).

It had long been felt in some quarters that two appeals from the High Court to the Court of Appeal and then to the House of Lords were unnecessary. Accordingly, the Administration of Justice Act 1969 introduced a 'leap-frog' procedure whereby the Court of Appeal could be avoided and the appeal could go direct from the trial judge to the House of Lords.

The trial judge must grant a certificate that the case is suitable for an appeal direct to the House of Lords on the grounds that it involves a point of law of general importance, which either relates to a matter of statutory interpretation or is a case in which the judge was bound by a previous decision of the Court of Appeal or the House of Lords. The parties must also consent to the 'leap-frog'. Finally, the House of Lords must grant leave for the direct appeal. It is worth noting that since this change was introduced there have been very few instances where it has been used.

Judicial Committee of the Privy Council

This body does not form part of the court structure of this country but, since it corresponds in structure with the House of Lords and its decisions have a strong persuasive influence, it is more conveniently dealt with here.

The Privy Council developed from the small body of advisers to the Crown which met frequently, in contrast to the Great Council, a much larger body, which met at irregular intervals. The functions of the Privy Council today are largely of a formal nature and appointments to it are made as an honour.

In the seventeenth century, when the Council lost its remaining judicial powers in so far as this country was concerned, it still retained the right to hear appeals made to the Crown from overseas territories. These were heard by its Judicial Committee, the importance of which increased with the increase in the size of these territories. It was reorganized by the Judicial Committee Act 1833 which, as amended, still forms the basis of its jurisdiction.

The Judicial Committee is the final court of appeal from the Commonwealth in both civil and criminal matters, except where self-governing countries have exercised their right to abolish such appeals; most countries have now done this. The Committee also hears appeals from the Channel Islands, the Isle of Man, the ecclesiastical courts, the prize courts in wartime, and from certain other tribunals such as the Disciplinary Committee of the General Medical Council.

In practice, membership is restricted to those persons holding high legal qualifications and it is very similar in composition to the House of Lords when that body sits as a court of appeal, with the addition of certain judges from Commonwealth countries. Although its judgments are not binding upon English courts, they are treated with considerable respect in view of the Committee's composition. The judgment takes the form of advice to the Crown which is then formally implemented by Order in Council. A recent change now provides for the delivery of dissenting opinions.

For further consideration

1. State with reasons the courts in which the following cases could be heard.
    (a) A claim for £10 000 for breach of contract.
    (b) A claim for £400 for the tort of negligence.
    (c) An action for the recovery of land of a rateable value of £2000.
    (d) An action for a breach of trust in which a loss of £30 000 is claimed.
    (e) An undefended divorce.
    (f) An action for defamation.
    (g) A salvage claim.
    (h) A dispute concerning a hire purchase agreement.
    (i) An application to make a child a ward of court.
    (j) A complaint of racial discrimination.
    (k) A defended divorce.
    (l) A winding up of a company with a paid-up share capital of £100 000.
    (m) A dispute over the estate of a mentally disordered person.
    (n) An application by a wife for maintenance from her husband.
    (o) An adjudication on a contested will.
    (p) An application for an affiliation order.
2. In each instance in Question 1, state whether the case would be heard locally where the facts arose and indicate the composition of the court or tribunal which would hear it.
3. To what extent is an appeal possible from decisions of the following courts and tribunals?
    (a) The County Court in an action for breach of contract.
    (b) The Magistrates' Court on a domestic matter.
    (c) The Queen's Bench Division of the High Court.
    (d) An administrative tribunal.
    (e) The Court of Appeal.
    (f) The County Court on a bankruptcy matter.
    (g) An ecclesiastical court.
    (h) The High Court, involving a point of law of general importance.
4. Explain briefly the meaning of
    (a) Lord of Appeal in Ordinary
    (b) 'Leap-frog' procedure
    (c) Judicial Committee of the Privy Council
    (d) Divisional Court
    (e) Registrar

Unit 6. Other Courts and Tribunals

The existence of special courts outside the ordinary system has always been a feature of the English legal system throughout its history. The mercantile courts, the ecclesiastical courts, and the Court of Chancery itself in its early days are all examples which were mentioned in Unit 1. Most of these older special courts have been incorporated into the ordinary system, although there are still a few which, for various reasons, did not perish in the nineteenth-century reforms or in the Courts Act 1971.

More recently, in the last 100 years, governments have created a large number of new special courts and tribunals. This has been another result of the great expansion of Government into social and economic fields. The special nature of some of the disputes arising from these new activities makes the composition and procedure of the ordinary courts inappropriate for this purpose.

A. Modern special courts and tribunals

Reasons for their creation

1. The ordinary courts are courts of *law*, and are not equipped to deal with the economic, social, business, industrial relations, and other considerations which lie behind certain types of dispute. As an illustration, in the last century the private railway companies had to get the permission of a government body before they were allowed to raise fares. If permission was refused, the railway company could appeal to the ordinary courts. The judges did not welcome this task, feeling that this was an economic decision, not a legal one; the Lord Chief Justice complained that the judges were being turned into railway directors. A special tribunal was

therefore established to hear such appeals, and the matter was taken away from the ordinary courts.
2. The procedure of the ordinary courts is slow, for reasons which will be discussed later. Administrative decisions often have to be acted upon fairly quickly, otherwise the job will never be done. Special tribunals may, therefore, be set up to hear and decide on appeals very quickly. A very early illustration can be given. After 1666 a special body was set up to settle disputes arising out of property destroyed in the Great Fire of London. People dissatisfied with the decisions given tried to appeal to the Lord Chancellor. He refused to hear them, saying that Parliament had made the special tribunal's decision final, 'otherwise London could never have been rebuilt'.

In other circumstances, delay can cause great financial hardship to the claimant. A person claiming to have been wrongly refused social security benefits can hardly be expected to starve while an appeal awaits a hearing in the ordinary courts. Such appeals, therefore, now go to special social security and other tribunals which operate relatively quickly.
3. Procedure in the ordinary courts is also very expensive, again for reasons which will be discussed later. The quicker and less formal procedure of special tribunals can be much cheaper, and this can outweigh the fact that evidence may sometimes be presented and examined less thoroughly.
4. The formal atmosphere of the ordinary civil courts can be very forbidding, and can often deter claimants from pursuing certain types of claim. Most special tribunals operate in a much more relaxed and informal manner.
5. Finally, the rules of common law and equity concentrate on protecting and enforcing *individual* rights, and on giving the individual the right to help himself. The social legislation which has played such an important part in the development of English law in the last century has a rather different basic objective, and concentrates more on those who are not very good at helping themselves. This difference in approach has sometimes influenced governments in deciding that disputes over social legislation should normally go to special tribunals.

A description of some of the special courts and tribunals which have been created may help to illustrate some of these points.

Special courts with High Court status

In some instances it has been possible to create a new court very similar to a Division of the High Court, but in fact quite separate and specifically adapted to some special type of dispute. There are two main examples:

1. The Restrictive Practices Court
The Restrictive Trade Practices Act 1976, which consolidated earlier statutes, is aimed at suppressing restrictive trade agreements on matters such as price fixing and restraining the production or supply of goods. Such agreements will normally only be

valid if the agreement can be shown to be in the public interest, to be determined by reference to certain criteria set out in the Act. Decisions on such issues demand business and economic knowledge not normally available in the ordinary courts, and a special court, the Restrictive Practices Court is, therefore, constituted under the Act.

The Act provides that the court will have 15 members, 5 of whom are lawyers, the other 10 normally not. The 5 lawyers will be 3 judges of the High Court, and 1 judge each from Scotland and Northern Ireland. The 10 other members will be appointed on the recommendation of the Lord Chancellor, each being 'a person appearing to the Lord Chancellor to be qualified by virtue of his knowledge of or experience in industry, commerce or public affairs'. Cases are heard normally by one judge and two lay members sitting together. Points of law are decided by the judge, but the more important issues are usually questions of fact, which must be decided by a simple majority. Members with necessary business experience to judge properly whether a restrictive agreement is really justifiable are, therefore, involved in the decision, and can if they so wish outvote the judge on questions of fact.

The court does not operate particularly speedily, but this is not an area where delay is likely to cause great hardship. An appeal is possible on a point of law, and in England and Wales will be heard by the Court of Appeal.

2. *The Employment Appeal Tribunal*
This court was set up by the Employment Protection Act 1975 to hear appeals from industrial tribunals (see later). Its main work, therefore, concerns appeals with regard to redundancy payments and compensation for unfair dismissal, complaints of discrimination in employment on grounds of race or sex, and other complaints under employment protection legislation.

The Employment Appeal Tribunal may sit at any time and in any place in Great Britain, and can sit in two or more divisions concurrently. Like the Restrictive Practices Court, its members fall into two main categories. First, a hearing will be presided over by a judge. Judges from the High Court or Court of Appeal in England are nominated by the Lord Chancellor to be available for this purpose, and there is at least one further judicial member from Scotland. Second, the judge will be assisted by lay members, nominated by the Lord Chancellor and the Secretary of State for Employment from persons who 'have special knowledge or experience of industrial relations, either as representatives of employers or as representatives of workers'. Cases are heard by one judge, sitting normally with between two and four of the lay members although, with the consent of both parties, the judge can hear the case assisted by only one lay member.

The rules of the Appeal Tribunal provide that it must avoid being too formal wherever possible. The ordinary rules of evidence may be relaxed, and the Tribunal operates relatively speedily. The parties can be represented either by a lawyer or, if they so wish, by some other person such as a trade union colleague or simply a friend. An appeal is possible on a point of law and, in England and Wales, this will go to the Court of Appeal.

This court replaced the National Industrial Relations Court which had been set up under the Industrial Relations Act 1971 and which was abolished when that Act was repealed in 1974.

B. Administrative tribunals

Types of tribunals

In most cases where special courts were established, it was not felt necessary to set up a powerful body like the courts just described. The nature of the disputes likely to arise made smaller 'administrative' tribunals more appropriate, and very many of these have been created. The Franks Committee on Tribunals and Inquiries in 1957 estimated that there were then over 2000 different tribunals in existence. These differ from each other in many respects, but they do have some common features: the judges are usually not lawyers, although some do have legally qualified chairmen; they operate informally, cheaply, and fairly quickly; most of them sit locally; there is usually no appeal to the courts on a point of fact, and only sometimes on a point of law. It is not possible here to describe all of these tribunals, but a few of the main categories will serve as an example.

1. *Tribunals dealing with social security and personal welfare*
The Social Security Acts 1975–80, which totally replace the National Insurance Act 1965, provide that benefits shall be payable to people out of state funds, subject to certain conditions, in the event of sickness, death, unemployment, maternity or similar situations giving rise to financial problems. Under the industrial injuries provisions of the 1975 Act, benefits may be paid to persons suffering injury or disease arising out of and in the course of employment. Disputes can often arise as to whether a claimant is entitled to benefit, and as to the amount due.

If the local insurance officer rejects a claim, the claimant can appeal to a local tribunal, of which there are some 200 in England and Wales. The tribunal will have three members: a chairman who will usually be a local barrister or solicitor, and two lay members, one from a panel representing employees, the other from a panel representing employers and self-employed persons.

A further right of appeal lies from the local tribunals to one of the Social Security Commissioners, who are barristers or solicitors of at least 10 years' standing, and are appointed full-time. Some decisions of the Commissioners are published in a series of reports but, unlike in the ordinary courts, there is no system of binding precedent.

Where an appeal under the industrial injuries provisions is on medical grounds, for example, a dispute as to the extent of the injury, there is a slightly different procedure to allow the appeal to be heard by people who are medically qualified.

Other groups of tribunals in this broad category include supplementary benefits tribunals, national health service tribunals, and mental health review tribunals.

2. Tribunals concerned with the valuation and use of land

Many permanent and *ad hoc* tribunals operate in connection with public control over land use and value. Appeals from rating valuations, for instance, go to local valuation courts composed of laymen. A further appeal from the local valuation court lies to the Lands Tribunal, which is a much more powerful body whose chairman and some other members will be legally qualified. The Lands Tribunal also hears appeals concerning compensation for compulsory purchase.

Another group of tribunals in this field are the Rent Assessment Committees which have power to fix rents of residential tenancies, furnished and unfurnished, which fall within the terms of the Rent Act 1977. They may also decide upon security of tenure for some furnished tenancies, but these powers were largely removed by the Housing Act 1980 and transferred to the County Court. However, where a tenant feels that he is paying too much rent to a private landlord he may appeal to one of these committees which sit normally with legally qualified chairmen. The other members will be people who know the locality or who have practised as surveyors or valuers, and who can, therefore, make an informed assessment of what rent is reasonable. These are not strictly 'administrative' tribunals, in that they deal with private disputes between landlord and tenant, but they are special tribunals and are mentioned here for convenience.

Where a person wishes to appeal against a compulsory purchase order on his land, or against refusal of planning permission, there is no special tribunal to which he can go. He can, however, appeal to the Minister, who will send an 'inspector' to hold a public inquiry. This will be conducted almost like a court, with all interested parties having the right to give evidence, but unlike a court or tribunal this inquiry will not give a decision. It will merely make recommendations to the Minister, and the Minister need not follow these recommendations when he eventually makes the final decision.

3. Transport

A number of special tribunals exist in this field. One example is the Transport Tribunal, which deals with appeals over road haulage licences, among other matters. The President must be an experienced lawyer and the four other members must include two who have experience in transport business, one with experience in commercial affairs and one with experience in financial matters or economics.

4. Tribunals dealing with employment

The Industrial Tribunals which have already been mentioned are some of the most important of all local tribunals. Their main work arises from disputed claims for redundancy payments and complaints of unfair dismissal, and they are extremely busy. They sit locally, and will have a legally qualified chairman with two other members, one from a panel representing employers, the other from a panel representing employees. They work informally and fairly quickly. An appeal lies to the Employment Appeal Tribunal.

Control over tribunals

Administrative tribunals have sometimes come in for criticism: it is suggested that the legal and lay members appointed by a Minister might be more likely to give a decision favourable to the Government and civil service than would the independent judges in the ordinary courts, and the looser procedure may sometimes make a wrong decision seem more likely. There is little evidence that these criticisms are justified, but in any event tribunals are subject to two main controls.

1. *Judicial control by the courts*

In the first place there is usually a provision for an appeal on a point of law to the ordinary courts. This can cause delay, however, and occasionally no right of appeal is allowed.

Second, the courts exercise some other controls, often by an extended use of very old 'prerogative' orders. *Mandamus*, which means 'we command', is used to compel the performance of some duty, such as the duty of a tribunal to allow an appeal when it ought to do so. *Prohibition*, as the name suggests, is used to prevent a tribunal exceeding its jurisdiction or otherwise acting wrongfully. *Certiorari*, the most important of these orders, is used to compel a tribunal to inform the High Court of the facts of the case under discussion so that the High Court may certify whether the tribunal has acted wrongfully, in which event the decision will be quashed. It is no longer necessary to ask the High Court for a specific order; instead, a request is now made for a *judicial review* of the decision in question and the High Court is able to make such order as it deems appropriate.

These controls can be exercised if a tribunal has acted *ultra vires*, i.e., exceeded its powers. The tribunals only have the powers conferred on them by statute, and can only exercise them in the ways and for the purposes intended by Parliament. The courts can, therefore, intervene if these powers are, in the opinion of the court, exceeded or seriously abused. Thus the courts can insist that tribunals observe the principles of 'natural justice', for instance that no man shall be judge in his own cause, that is, that no member of the tribunal shall have any personal interest in the subject-matter under discussion, and that both parties shall have a right to be heard.

This supervisory jurisdiction of the courts is exercised largely by the Queen's Bench Division, usually by a Divisional Court.

2. *The Council on Tribunals*

Criticism of tribunals and inquiries led to the setting-up of the Franks Committee, which reported in 1957. Following its recommendations, the Tribunals and Inquiries Act 1958 established a Council on Tribunals to keep under review the constitution and working of administrative tribunals. The members of the Council are appointed by the Lord Chancellor, and report to him on matters referred to it. The Council also has an important power to examine any rules of procedure that a tribunal may introduce. Thus in most cases tribunals must now give reasons for their decision upon request from one of the parties and give a right of appeal on a point of law to the ordinary courts.

C. Historical survivals

1. *Military courts*

Members of the armed forces are subject both to the ordinary law of the land and to additional statutory rules imposed for the enforcement of discipline. Offences against these rules are tried by special courts known as Courts Martial consisting of at least three officers or, in the case of more serious offences or offences committed by officers, of at least five officers. Assistance is given on points of law by a civilian barrister from the department of the Judge-Advocate General.

Court Martial sentences are subject to confirmation by the commanding officer and, since 1951, there is a right of appeal to the Court Martial Appeals Court. This is similar in constitution to the Criminal Division of the Court of Appeal and, as from that Court, an appeal may be made to the House of Lords in certain circumstances.

2. *Ecclesiastical courts*

These courts lost their important jurisdiction over matters such as divorce and probate work in the last century. Jurisdiction today is confined to disputes on doctrine, the discipline of clergy for moral offences, and matters affecting churches and consecrated ground. In each diocese there is a Consistory Court presided over by its Chancellor, a barrister appointed by the bishop. Appeals lie to the appropriate Provincial Court of Canterbury or York and from there to the Judicial Committee of the Privy Council.

3. *Coroners' courts*

The office of coroner has existed since the twelfth century at least. The coroner was then a royal official, a deputy to the sheriff, with a particular interest in violent deaths since the Crown revenues often benefited from the resulting fines and forfeitures.

Coroners today must be barristers, solicitors or doctors, and they are usually appointed by the local authority either on a full-time or a part-time basis according to the amount of work to be done. Their main function is to inquire into cases where death is sudden or violent, or where the cause of death is unknown, or where it occurred in prison or in a mental hospital. Minor functions also include holding inquiries where gold, silver or money is found hidden and the owner cannot be traced. If it has been deliberately hidden, the coroner can declare it 'treasure trove', and it then belongs to the Crown, although the finder will usually be rewarded.

Procedure is by way of inquest or inquiry and is not a trial. The coroner's court is primarily concerned with finding facts and not with deciding issues. Proceedings are usually in public and are informal. Anyone with an interest in the proceedings may give evidence and examine witnesses with the consent of the coroner. In most cases the coroner must also summon a jury of from 7 to 11 persons.

D. Domestic tribunals

When people form an association, they usually prescribe rules which members must obey, and provide a committee or other machinery for enforcement where necessary.

All persons joining the association agree to be bound and to submit to the judgment of the committee in the event of a dispute.

In the case of solicitors, allegations of unprofessional conduct are heard by the Disciplinary Committee set up under the Solicitors Acts. This Committee has the power to impose fines, to suspend from practice, or to strike off the Roll. A right of appeal lies to the Divisional Court of the Queen's Bench Division.

Charges against a barrister are heard by the Benchers of the Inn to which he belongs. There are similar disciplinary committees for medical practitioners, dentists, and architects. Trade associations often set up tribunals to enforce uniform trading practices on their members, and trade unions ensure discipline by powers given to their committees.

Many such disciplinary bodies exercise wide powers, particularly where membership of the association may be a condition for carrying on the particular trade, profession or business, so that expulsion can take away a person's ability to earn a living in that field. The ordinary courts do exercise some controls where domestic tribunals exceed or abuse the powers given them by the rules of the association, in much the same way as the courts can review the actions of administrative tribunals.

E. Arbitration

Arbitration is a means of settling disputes other than by court action and it arises when one or more persons are appointed to hear the arguments submitted by the parties and to give a decision on them. The type of arbitrator depends upon the nature of the case. In some instances a legal practitioner may be chosen, while in others of a highly technical nature it may be more appropriate to appoint a person with knowledge or experience of the subject-matter.

The most common way in which arbitration arises is by the voluntary agreement of the parties either before or after a dispute has arisen. Many commercial contracts, for example insurance policies, contain a clause providing for this method of settling disputes. It is often preferred to court action, for it is usually cheaper, quicker, more informal, and does not involve publicity.

Provided that the submission is in writing, which is usually the case, the machinery of arbitration is governed by the Arbitration Acts 1950–79. Once arbitration has been agreed upon and is being carried out in a proper manner, the court will not interfere or hear the dispute itself. An arbitration award properly arrived at will be enforced by the court. Points of law which arise may be submitted separately to the court for decision, by means of *case stated*. In these ways the court allows the parties to settle their own disputes, but at the same time maintains a supervisory role.

Various statutes provide for reference of certain types of issue to arbitration, and the courts themselves can refer a matter to arbitration where, for instance, the case requires prolonged examination of documents, scientific investigation or involved accounting.

In 1973, the County Court Rules provided for the setting-up of an arbitration service within the County Court structure. The Registrar now has the power to refer any proceedings to arbitration, even against the wishes of one of the parties, where the claim is not in excess of £500. If both parties agree to arbitration, it can be ordered where the sum involved exceeds this amount. Thus, small claims, particularly consumer claims, may be settled privately and informally without rigid adherence to the rules of evidence and procedure.

Legal representation is permitted but discouraged since the fees of a lawyer cannot be recovered as costs and must be paid by the litigants themselves, even if they win the case. Arbitration awards are enforceable in the same way as a County Court judgment.

This new development was influenced by earlier voluntary experiments such as the Manchester Arbitration Scheme for Small Claims. It is largely replacing them since, unlike in the voluntary schemes, the Registrar can compel a party to submit to the arbitration. On the other hand, the paper-work which the plaintiff faces in the local voluntary schemes is usually much simpler than that demanded by the County Court. Moreover, local schemes do not usually allow any legal representation at all, so that a wealthy business litigant is unable to buy himself an advantage. Unfortunately, local schemes now seem to be disappearing because of shortage of funds.

A specialized use of arbitration, which has become very important in recent years and which is outside the scope of this work, is for the purpose of settling industrial disputes.

For further consideration

1. In what ways does the operation of an administrative tribunal differ from that of a court? Give examples of cases for which a tribunal is more suitable.
2. Many tribunals are composed of a legally qualified chairman and two other members who are normally chosen for their special experience and knowledge. Would there be advantages if judges in the ordinary courts were similarly assisted by experts? In what types of case would this be particularly useful?
3. Why do businessmen often prefer to settle a dispute by arbitration rather than by an action in the courts? Should the use of arbitration as a means of settling disputes be extended?
4. To what extent is an appeal possible from the following.
    (a) A decision by an industrial tribunal that a dismissal was fair.
    (b) A decision by the Restrictive Practices Court that a price fixing agreement was invalid as being against the public interest.
    (c) A decision by the Employment Appeal Tribunal on a claim for redundancy payment.
    (d) A refusal by an insurance officer to accept a claim for industrial injury benefit.
    (e) A compulsory purchase order made by a local authority.

(f) A court martial sentence.
   (g) A decision by a local tribunal on a claim for social security benefit.
   (h) A decision by the Disciplinary Committee to suspend a solicitor from practice.
5. Explain briefly the meaning of
   (a) Council on Tribunals
   (b) *Ultra vires*
   (c) Court Martial
   (d) Treasure trove
   (e) Mandamus
   (f) Social Security Commissioner

Unit 7. The Legal Profession

A. The division of the legal profession

Unlike most other countries the legal profession in England and Wales is divided into two branches and the expression 'lawyer' may be used to refer to either a solicitor or a barrister. This distinction may be explained by drawing an analogy from the medical profession.

A person suffering from a pain in the head, the back or the foot will consult his local general practitioner; similarly a person who wishes to sell his house, make a will or divorce his wife will consult a solicitor. In the more difficult or serious cases the medical practitioner will seek the opinion of a specialist; likewise the solicitor may ask for the written advice of a barrister who specializes in the field of law under consideration. This advice is known as *counsel's opinion*.

Let us carry the analogy a stage further and liken surgery to litigation. Many complaints about which a doctor is consulted do not require an operation and every consultation with a solicitor does not result in a court appearance. Minor surgery such as lancing a boil may be done by the local practitioner but more serious matters such as the removal of an appendix will be done by a surgeon. A solicitor may appear for his client in the County Court or in the Magistrates' Court but, except in a very limited number of instances, he must brief a barrister if the case goes to a higher court. *Advocacy* is the second and more important aspect of a barrister's work.

A solicitor tends, therefore, to be the general practitioner of the law while the barrister is the specialist and surgeon.

B. Legal education

The Ormrod Report

The Report of the *Committee on Legal Education* under the Chairmanship of Mr Justice Ormrod (1971) recommended certain changes in the training of solicitors and barristers. The first or *academic* stage would normally be satisfied by a law degree; as with the medical profession the degree course would thereby be integrated into the system of training. As an alternative, non-law graduates and mature students (over 25) would take a common professional examination. The second or *professional* stage would consist of a full-time one-year vocational course based upon the work and problems likely to be encountered in practice. These proposals, with some modifications, have now been brought into effect, but a further proposal to abolish articles was not accepted by the profession. Thus entrants are required to take the Bar or Law Society vocational course, pass the Final examination and then undergo articles or pupillage.

Another recommendation of the Ormrod Committee, the establishment of a standing *Advisory Committee on Legal Education* to act as a link between the universities and polytechnics on the one hand and the practising profession on the other has also been put into effect.

Training of solicitors

Most intending solicitors will now either be law graduates or will have passed the common professional examination; there still remains a very limited provision for the entry of school-leavers with GCE Advanced Level qualifications by way of the Solicitors' First Examination. All are required to take the one-year full-time Law Society Finals Course, which is offered at the four branches of the College of Law and seven recognized Polytechnics, and to pass the Final Examination. After completion of the prescribed period of articles the entrant will be *admitted* as a solicitor.

The system of *articles* or apprenticeship is the means by which the practical experience is acquired. For a period of two years (five years for school-leavers) the articled clerk attends at his principal's office and sees the various matters which arise and how they are dealt with. The payment of a premium for the privilege of receiving instruction is rarely required today but the remuneration received by articled clerks is not high. The value of this method of training depends upon the ability and willingness of the principal to instruct and the nature of the practice in which articles are served. A busy solicitor may not be able to spend much time in instruction and a highly specialized practice will not give a wide experience.

Training of barristers

It is first necessary to be admitted to one of the four *Inns of Court*—Gray's Inn, Lincoln's Inn, Inner Temple, and Middle Temple. These are very old institutions dating from the fourteenth century. Each Inn is a combination of club, college, and professional organization and is governed by its senior members or *Benchers*, who are often judges. Twelve terms must be kept by dining in hall on three occasions during each term, although it is now possible to enter into practice after eight terms and keep the remaining four terms afterwards. This tradition of dining is supported on the grounds that it helps to promote the corporate spirit of the Inn; opponents doubt this and stress the cost of the journeys to London.

All intending barristers must be law graduates or have passed the common professional examination, so that there is now no provision for entry under the age of 25 without a degree in law or in another discipline. A student intending to practise must attend a full-time one-year course in London in preparation for Bar Finals and it may be possible for him to satisfy the dining requirements during this period. Educational matters, in particular the provision of courses and the conduct of examinations, are controlled by the *Council of Legal Education.*

After keeping the required number of terms and passing the examinations, the student will be *called to the Bar* by his Inn. Before practising on his own account, it is compulsory for him to undergo a period of *pupillage* by *reading in chambers*. For 12 months he will be the pupil of a senior barrister, inspecting and drafting documents under supervision and accompanying his pupil master when the latter appears in court. The value of this practical training will vary considerably, depending upon the commitments and conscientiousness of the pupil master.

C. Legal practice

The practising solicitor

After admission, the solicitor may take a salaried position in private practice or may seek an appointment with a local authority, the civil service, the Magistrates' Court Service, a nationalized undertaking or in the legal department of a business concern. Solicitors may form partnerships but not limited companies, though entry into an existing partnership usually requires capital. There is nothing to prevent a new practice being established but, since solicitors are only allowed to advertise to a very limited extent, success may depend upon available capital, local connections and good fortune, in addition to ability.

The work of a solicitor may cover a very wide field. He is the person to whom an individual first turns for advice and, in addition to dealing with a variety of legal problems, he may be asked to advise on business and family matters. Much of his time may be devoted to dealings with property, in particular the conveyancing of land and houses and the execution of mortgages, but he may also be concerned with drawing up wills, the administration of estates and trusts, matrimonial disputes, the formation of partnerships and companies, taxation problems, and representation of clients involved in criminal prosecutions and civil actions. Some solicitors may specialize in one or more of these matters or there may be specialization by the different partners in a firm.

Where the solicitor does not appear as advocate himself, he will be responsible for matters preparatory to the trial such as the preparation of documents and the collection of evidence. In many cases he will try to negotiate a settlement with the other side, for instance, with the insurance company in accident claims. In civil disputes, he may be primarily concerned with getting redress for his client *without* recourse to the courts.

Much of the work of a solicitor's office is carried out under the supervision of a solicitor by unadmitted staff known as legal executives. The more senior of these, who are still referred to as managing clerks, are very skilled and experienced in practical work such as litigation and conveyancing. In 1963, the Institute of Legal Executives was formed and introduced a system of qualifying examinations for its various grades of membership.

There are some 37 000 practising solicitors in England and Wales. Most matters appertaining to the profession are subject to statutory powers administered by the *Law Society*. While a solicitor need not necessarily be a member of the Law Society, he must take out an annual practising certificate and produce an annual accountant's certificate relating to clients' money. Compulsory insurance is required for the purpose of compensating members of the public who suffer loss through the negligence or fraud of a solicitor. Allegations of misconduct against solicitors are heard by the Disciplinary Committee, which has the power in serious cases to disqualify them by 'striking off the Roll'. The Law Society is also responsible for the training of solicitors and for the administration of the Legal Aid and Advice Scheme (Unit 8).

The practising barrister

Barristers are not allowed to form partnerships but a number will normally combine to share rooms or *Chambers* and share the cost of a clerk and other expenses. The newly called barrister will take a room or a seat in existing chambers and wait for work to be given to him by a solicitor. He is not allowed to advertise and may not deal with clients directly, but only through a solicitor. Early years at the Bar may be hazardous since solicitors are reluctant to entrust their work to an untried barrister and without work he is likely to remain untried. Some barristers do not practise but take salaried appointments of a legal nature with public authorities and private concerns.

As stated above, the barrister is the consultant and the advocate with the right to appear in every court. The work in the early years will tend to consist of many small cases of a varied nature; later will come specialization. A solicitor will select the barrister whom he considers to be the most appropriate for the type and importance of the case and deliver the brief to that barrister's chambers. The *brief* is the document which outlines the case and to which are attached any other relevant papers. The fee is marked upon the brief, which may not be refused, provided that the fee is a proper one, that the case is of the type normally taken and that the barrister is not otherwise engaged. The brief fee is not a contractual payment and cannot be sued upon if it is not paid.

It is the duty of every barrister in presenting a case to the court to put forward all the relevant facts and authorities and not to suppress anything, even though it might prejudice his client's case. As a specialist in advocacy he is submitting arguments on behalf of his client and his own opinions do not matter. This explains the popular misconception of a barrister defending a person whom 'he knows to be guilty'. In any event, the guilt or otherwise of the accused is for the court to decide. Unlike a solicitor, a barrister may not be sued for his negligence in conducting a case, for this would amount to a retrial of the original case.

After at least 10 years of practice, a barrister may apply to the Lord Chancellor for recommendation to the Crown to be made a QC or *Queen's Counsel*. If successful, he is said 'to take silk' since he exchanges his stuff gown for a silk one. In court he will still normally be accompanied by junior counsel. He tends to be restricted then to fewer and more important cases and this may not always be as remunerative as the more numerous smaller cases in which he previously appeared.

The duties of barristers are governed by rules of professional etiquette which depend upon custom and tradition rather than upon statute. Responsibility for the conduct of their own members rests with the individual Inns. They investigate complaints and may dis-bar a barrister for serious misbehaviour. In 1967, the Inns set up a joint body known as the *Senate* to deal with matters affecting the profession as a whole and the Council of Legal Education became a committee of the Senate. In addition there was the *Bar Council*, an association of practising barristers (of whom there are some 4600), which was concerned with the more day-to-day matters arising from practice. The position was simplified in 1974 when all the functions then exercised by the Senate and the Bar Council were taken over by a new governing body, the *Senate of the Inns of Court and the Bar*.

D. Judges

Contrary to the practice in some continental countries, there is no separate judicial profession in England and all judgeships, subject to one exception mentioned below, are filled by the appointment of practising barristers. The impartial approach to cases required of a judge means that not all barristers would be suitable for apointment. Successful barristers may suffer a substantial fall in income, though this is counterbalanced by the prestige attaching to the office, the certain salary to a comparatively advanced age, and a pension upon retirement.

Another feature of the judiciary in this country is that there is no established system of promotion. Judgeships at any level, including the offices of Lord Chancellor and Lord Chief Justice, may be filled by practising barristers with no previous experience as judges. It is still comparatively uncommon for a Circuit judge to be appointed to the High Court. Appointments to the Court of Appeal are invariably made from the High Court but this involves little change of status, function or salary.

Independence of judges

Although judicial appointments are political, in the sense that they are made by the Government of the day, every attempt is made to maintain the independence of judges after appointment. Their salaries are charged upon the Consolidated Fund, which means that the statute authorizing payment does not require annual Parliamentary discussion and approval, as does the statute providing for the payment of the salaries of civil servants and members of the armed forces.

Judges appointed after 1959 must now retire at 75. Apart from this, a judge of the Supreme Court can only be removed from office in very exceptional circumstances. Removal requires misconduct on the part of the judge and a petition to the Crown from both Houses of Parliament. Since this provision was made in the Act of Settlement 1701, no judge of a superior court in England has been removed from office and the exact procedure for dismissal is a little uncertain. Unless such a petition is being considered, it is a convention that the conduct of a judge may not be criticized in Parliament.

Further protection is given by the fact that superior court judges are immune from any proceedings arising out of acts done within their jurisdiction; since their jurisdiction is virtually without restriction, they have in effect complete immunity. No action may thus be brought for defamation, for any statement they may make, or for false imprisonment, for any sentence they may award. Judges of inferior courts such as Circuit judges are similarly protected but their limited jurisdiction means that the protection is not so wide.

Circuit judges and Recorders

Circuit judges are appointed by the Crown on the advice of the Lord Chancellor from barristers of at least 10 years' standing or Recorders who have held office for at least five years; they may be removed from office by the Lord Chancellor on the grounds of incapacity or misbehaviour. There are at present some 340 Circuit judges who serve in the Crown Court (Unit 4) and the County Courts (Unit 5). They must retire at 72 with a possible extension for a further three years. The salary changes frequently in a period of rising prices, but in 1981 it was £22 000. Circuit judges are referred to as Judge, for example, Judge Wisdom, and are addressed in court as 'Your Honour'.

The Courts Act 1971 provides for additional judicial assistance in the Crown Court by the appointment of part-time judges known as *Recorders* who must be practising barristers or solicitors of at least 10 years' standing. Solicitors are therefore for the first time able to enter the ranks of the judiciary and there are about 30 solicitors out of some 440 Recorders who have been appointed. The office of Recorder enables use to be made of the talents of practitioners who would not wish to give up private practice to become a full-time judge and it makes possible an assessment of likely candidates for the High Court Bench. Recorders are appointed for a limited period of time and may sit in any Crown Court. They are not restricted to a particular borough Quarter Sessions as in the past.

Supreme Court judges

High Court judges are also appointed by the Crown on the advice of the Lord Chancellor and must be barristers of at least 10 years' standing. They are assigned to one of the three Divisions of the Court, 47 out of a total of 74 being assigned to the Queen's Bench Division, since from this Division are largely drawn the judges for the Crown Court. Upon appointment they receive a knighthood and a salary which was £32 000 per year in 1981. They are referred to, for example, as Mr Justice Wisdom, in writing as Wisdom, J, and are addressed in court as 'My Lord' or 'Your Lordship'.

Higher judicial appointments are made by the Crown on the advice of the Prime Minister. The 18 *Judges of the Court of Appeal* are referred to, for example, as Lord Justice Wisdom or in writing as Wisdom, LJ. The 10 *Lords of Appeal in Ordinary* or Law Lords who are given life peerages to enable them to sit in the House of Lords are referred to, for example, as Lord Wisdom, or by any other title that has been taken on the creation of the peerage.

E. Judicial offices

The *Lord Chancellor* (abbreviated as LC) holds an office which is partly political and partly judicial. As a Minister of State and member of the Cabinet, he holds office only for the duration of the Government. He presides over proceedings of the House of Lords but may take part in debates as the Government spokesman.

As head of the judicial system of the country he presides over the House of Lords when it is sitting as a Court of Law, over the Judicial Committee of the Privy Council and, nominally, over the Chancery Division. He is responsible for court administration, except Magistrates' Courts, and for appointment of most judges and magistrates.

The *Lord Chief Justice* (LCJ) holds the senior judicial office in the country. He presides over the Queen's Bench Division of the High Court and the criminal division of the Court of Appeal. He has supervisory and procedural duties relating to the administration of justice generally.

The *Master of the Rolls* (MR) presides over the civil division of the Court of Appeal and may sit in its criminal division. He has certain supervisory duties relating to solicitors, in particular their formal admission, the appointment of the Disciplinary Committee, and the approval of regulations made by the Law Society.

The *Attorney-General* is a barrister with almost invariably a seat in the House of Commons. As a member of the Government his principal function is to give advice on points of law and to represent the Crown in important cases, both criminal and civil. He can initiate civil proceedings on behalf of the public, for example, to prevent a public nuisance, and certain other proceedings, for example, prosecutions under the Official Secrets Act, can only begin with his consent. He is regarded as the leader of the English Bar, though he may not engage in private practice while in office. His deputy is the *Solicitor-General* who, contrary to his title, is also a barrister. The two are known as the *Law Officers*.

The *Director of Public Prosecutions* (DPP) is a barrister or solicitor appointed by the Home Secretary, who acts under the supervision of the Attorney-General. His duties include the initiation and conduct of certain criminal cases, in particular those of importance and complexity. Certain other prosecutions can only begin with his consent and he may give advice to police forces on possible prosecutions. He acts for the Crown in criminal appeals to the Court of Appeal and to the House of Lords.

F. Administration and reform of the law

The administration of justice

There is no single person or body in this country responsible for the administration of the law in general or for particular matters such as the maintenance of the courts, judicial appointments, the legal profession, and law reform. While it would be true today to say that the major role is played by the Lord Chancellor, many functions rest with the Home Secretary, the Lord Chief Justice, the Attorney-General, the Director of Public Prosecutions, the Senate, and the Law Society. Suggestions have been made from time to time that these functions should be concentrated in a Ministry of Justice, but this has not been accepted by any Government. Perhaps some inefficiency is the price to pay to avoid the danger of vesting so much power in the hands of a single department.

Law reform

Largely in consequence of the above division of functions, systematic reform of the law tends to have been neglected until recently. Even when generally acceptable recommendations for reform come forward, it is difficult to find Parliamentary time to implement the proposals. Reforming legislation is often non-controversial, but it tends to lack popular appeal and support. Sometimes legislation is forced upon Parliament in order to reverse an unpopular decision of the House of Lords, for example, the Trade Disputes Act 1965 and the Limitation Act 1963. Occasionally time is found to tidy up the law by codifying or consolidating legislation (Unit 2).

There are a number of *Standing Committees* of lawyers which advise the Lord Chancellor on matters of law reform. The most fruitful of these has perhaps been the Criminal Law Revision Committee, whose work has led to changes in the law relating to felonies and misdemeanours and to theft; its most controversial report in 1972 suggested fundamental changes in the law of evidence. A particular question may be referred to a *Departmental Committee* set up for that particular purpose, for example, the Ormrod Committee on Legal Education. Where the question is of wider public importance, for example, marriage and divorce, it is more usual to set up a *Royal Commission* which includes non-lawyer members. All of these bodies suffer from the fact that their work is done on a part-time basis.

The *Law Commissions Act 1965* set up two Law Commissions for England and Wales and for Scotland, with the functions of keeping the law under constant review and of making proposals where necessary for reform. Five full-time Law Commissioners, who are judges, legal practitioners or academic lawyers, are appointed by the Lord Chancellor for each commission and they are assisted by a permanent staff. The practice is to publish a working paper first, to provoke discussion and representations, and then a final report embodying a draft bill which could put the recommendations into effect. Reforms have already come from the work of the Law Commissions; a long-term project of considerable magnitude is the embodiment of the law of contract in statutory form. This latest means of law reform is important in that a permanent body has been established for the first time. There still remains the problem of finding Parliamentary time to put the changes into effect.

Royal Commission on Legal Services

This Royal Commission reported in 1979 after three years' study of the structure, organization, training, and entry to the legal profession, and their effect upon the provision of legal services to the public. No fundamental changes were proposed with respect to the two-branch structure of the profession, the solicitors' conveyancing monopoly, the barristers' exclusive right of audience or the system of education and training. At the same time, a number of important recommendations were made relating to law centres, tribunal proceedings, criminal legal aid, and other matters.

Some of the proposals require action by the legal profession itself, for example, improvements to the system of articles, and the presumed intention is that the Government will act if the Bar and the Law Society do not. Other proposals require action by the Government itself, and one recommendation was adopted in 1980 when the Lord Chancellor's Department, formerly responsible for civil legal aid only, took over responsibility also for criminal legal aid. Legislation will be necessary for some of the proposals, however, and it is, again, always a problem to find the necessary Parliamentary time. More important in these days of financial restraint is the need to find public money to effect changes such as the setting up of law centres. In consequence, it is likely to be many years before the Report of the Royal Commission has any noticeable effect on the provision of legal services.

For further consideration

1. There is evidence that women obtain better results than men in the Bar and Law Society Final Examinations. Why, therefore, is the proportion of women in the legal profession still relatively small?
2. Explain the relationship between barrister, solicitor, and client. To what extent does the division of the legal profession into barristers and solicitors serve a useful purpose?
3. It has been suggested that there should be a national legal service, just as there is a national health service. What would be the advantages and disadvantages of such a service?
4. Explain the machinery that exists for keeping the law up to date.
5. Explain briefly the meaning of
   (a) Recorder
   (b) Legal executive
   (c) Q.C.
   (d) Brief
   (e) Articles

Unit 8. Court Proceedings

This unit will be concerned primarily with the course taken by typical civil proceedings, including matters likely to arise before trial, the trial itself, and the ways in which any judgment given by the court may be enforced. It will conclude with a brief outline of criminal proceedings.

Civil proceedings vary according to the type of action. It is not possible here to deal with petitions for divorce, for the bankruptcy of a private individual or for the winding up of a company. Cases in the Chancery Division and the Family Division are also governed by special rules. The emphasis here will be on common law actions in the Queen's Bench Division such as are likely to arise following a breach of contract or an accident at work or on the road. It should be remembered that many such actions are brought in the County Courts, but the more important are heard in the High Court, and in any event the problems facing the litigant in the County Court are very similar.

A. Preliminary considerations

To sue or not to sue

Any person may begin and conduct proceedings himself without legal assistance, but because of the difficulties involved it is highly desirable to obtain legal advice by consulting a solicitor. The solicitor may advise that further legal action is not worth while at all. It has been said that only lawyers benefit from the law, and the litigant might be best advised simply to drop the matter. The following factors may be relevant.

1. Is the other party worth suing? There is always the possibility that, because of lack of means, he will not be able to pay any damages that may be awarded against him. Even if he has the means it might be difficult to enforce the judgment against him; the methods of enforcing judgments will be discussed later in this unit. If there are two possible defendants, for example, a bus driver whose negligence caused the accident and his employers who are responsible for his actions, it is desirable to bring the action against the one most likely to be able to pay the damages, in this example the bus company.
2. Another consideration is the likely cost of the proceedings. The plaintiff's costs in a defended High Court action will run to hundreds, often thousands, of pounds. The costs of a defended County Court action may be hundreds of pounds. Moreover, unless there are good reasons for deciding otherwise, the unsuccessful party will be required to pay not only his own costs, but also those of his opponent, at the discretion of the court. The cost of losing an action can therefore be very substantial indeed.

    The winner does not, in fact, get all of his costs from the unsuccessful party. The actual legal costs incurred by the winner will be scrutinized by a court offical known as a taxing-master, and anything not strictly essential to winning the case, such as a very high fee paid to counsel, will be struck out. Even winning the action, therefore, can still be expensive, and the action might not be worth while if the damages recovered are small. There may, of course, be good reasons for bringing an action at a loss, for example, a business firm does not wish to acquire a reputation among its debtors that it does not bother to collect small debts.
3. The length of time which proceedings will take must also be borne in mind, particularly in cases where an appeal is likely. The plaintiff might have to wait several years for his remedy, which would make it hardly worth the effort involved.

    > In *Halsey* v. *Esso Petroleum Co. Ltd* (1961), Halsey sought damages for harm done to his property by chemical discharges from an Esso plant. He also sought an injunction ordering Esso to stop the discharges and reduce noise. The damage occurred in 1958, but he did not get compensation or an injunction until 1961. Many plaintiffs would not wish to engage in proceedings of this length, particularly since the damages ultimately awarded were only £235.

    Readers will be aware of the length of time taken to settle the action on behalf of the thalidomide children.
4. A final consideration may be the publicity which a court action will bring. Even a successful action by a business may have a bad effect upon its public reputation or on its industrial relations, for example, where the firm brings or defends an action against an employee.

Legal aid

If, in spite of the above considerations, a decision has been made to proceed with the action, the next step is to consider the finance of the proceedings. For the private client, there may be the possibility of obtaining legal aid if the client cannot himself afford the cost.

The statutory provisions for legal aid and advice are contained in the Legal Aid Acts 1974 and 1979. Aid is available for most civil proceedings before the ordinary courts, but not in most instances for proceedings before administrative tribunals. The legal aid scheme is administered by the Law Society through a series of area and local committees which are made up of solicitors and barristers who practise locally.

The applicant must satisfy two requirements if he is to qualify for aid: (a) he must satisfy the local certifying committee that he has a good arguable case which, if he could pay his own costs, a solicitor would advise him to proceed with; and (b) he must show that he genuinely cannot afford to proceed.

The rules for determining what an applicant can afford are very detailed. In 1982, he will only get legal aid if his 'disposable income' does not exceed £4440 a year, and aid *may* be refused if his 'disposable capital' exceeds £2725 and he appears able to proceed without legal aid. Disposable income is arrived at by making deductions for such matters as tax, rent, and maintenance of dependants; disposable capital similarly takes account of deductions for things like furniture, and most of the value of the applicant's own house. If income and capital are below these figures, he will get some legal aid, but be required to pay a contribution to his costs, on a sliding scale as income and capital figures decrease. Only if disposable income is less than £1850 and disposable capital less than £1310 will legal aid be free.

Apart from legal assistance with proceedings, there are also provisions for legal advice, either free or on a payment of a small fee depending upon income and capital. Assistance may also be given towards the costs of negotiating a settlement without court proceedings. In particular, under the Legal Aid Act 1974 and its regulations, preliminary advice, and assistance towards negotiating a settlement can be given free of charge to persons whose income falls below certain limits, provided that solicitors' fees and other charges do not normally exceed £40 (£75 in matrimonial cases). The Act empowers the Law Society to employ its own solicitors specially for various purposes, principally giving free advice and assistance to those within the income limit, acting in proceedings for those receiving legal aid, and furnishing legal assistance to bodies such as citizens' advice bureaux.

The present legal aid scheme, although almost universally regarded as valuable, is not without its critics, largely those who feel that it does not go far enough. It is sometimes suggested, for instance, that the scheme should be extended to proceedings before more administrative tribunals. A second criticism is that the financial limits are too low, but when the 'disposable income' figures are translated into gross income, a married man with a young child will now get free help if he earns less than about £6000 per year; if he earns more than that figure he will have to pay a contribution until, at about £10 000 per year, he will get no legal aid at all. Finally, there are sometimes variations between different local committees as to the merits of certain types of claim. Some local committees, for example, are less willing than others to grant legal aid for small consumer claims. All of the above figures will periodically be revised, if only to take account of inflation.

B. Civil procedure before trial

Negotiating a settlement

As a first step it is customary for the solicitor to try to settle the dispute without litigation by writing to the opposing party or his solicitor. If no opportunity at all is given to the other party to settle, a successful plaintiff might be penalized by not getting some of his costs from the other side. In most cases this initial letter will be followed by other correspondence, and possibly meetings between representatives of the two sides with a view to reaching a settlement. In an accident claim the negotiations will usually be between the injured person's solicitor and the other party's insurance company.

Simultaneously with this, each side will be concerned with collecting evidence. In accident claims this will normally include medical reports, statements from witnesses, and possibly technical reports about, for example, the condition of the motor vehicle or the defective premises. Medical reports, in particular, can be extremely important, because the amount of any settlement will depend upon how bad, and how permanent, the injuries prove to be. Where the injuries take some time to heal, doctors cannot always answer these questions immediately, and this is often a major reason for delay in reaching a legal settlement. During this period, the solicitor will usually also obtain 'counsel's opinion' on any difficult points of law or of evidence which might arise.

The vast majority of claims in tort or for breach of contract are in fact settled without actual resort to the courts. As a rule, it is only where a settlement proves impossible that proceedings have to be started.

Commencing proceedings

The first formal steps in civil proceedings are designed to do two things: (a) to bring the parties together before the court; and (b) to ensure that everyone concerned clearly understands what issues are in dispute. The plaintiff, normally through his solicitor, takes the first step. In Queen's Bench Division cases, he prepares a draft *writ of summons*, notifying the defendant in general terms of the nature of the claim against him, and ordering him to submit to the jurisdiction of the court. The plaintiff (or more usually his solicitor) must attend at the court office to file the writ, which will be formally sealed by the court officers and returned to him. Either on the writ itself, or with it, there will normally appear a brief, clear *statement of claim*, indicating what facts the plaintiff alleges, and what remedy he seeks against the defendant. A copy will be retained by the court.

The next step is to notify the defendant that a claim has been made against him. The writ, together with the statement of claim, must therefore be 'served' on him, normally by being handed to him personally. If the statement of claim is not filed and served with the writ, it must be served within a limited time afterwards. In High Court proceedings it is the responsibility of the plaintiff or his solicitor to arrange for service, whereas service of the equivalent documents in County Court proceedings will be done by the court officers.

In High Court proceedings, the defendant must then, within 14 days, *acknowledge service* of the writ. The acknowledgement must be filed at the court office, and state whether the defendant intends to contest the action. If he does not acknowledge, judgment can sometimes be entered against him in default. After acknowledgement he has a further 14 days in which to submit a written *defence* if he so wishes. Indeed, if he so wishes, he can also make a *counterclaim*, alleging that it is he who is the injured party, and that it is the plaintiff who has broken the contract or committed a tort. The plaintiff has the right to deliver a *reply* to the defence within a specified period. All of this can sometimes be accompanied by further exchanges of documents; either party can ask for *further and better particulars* to clarify vague allegations made by the other side in any of these *pleadings*.

After the close of the pleadings, *discovery of documents* may take place. Each side will give the other the opportunity to inspect documents relevant to the case, and if either side refuses, disclosure can usually be compelled. If it is thought that the other party has further information which should be disclosed, it is possible to apply for permission to deliver *interrogatories*, written questions on issues of fact which must be answered on oath.

Within a month of the close of pleadings, the plaintiff must also take out a *summons for directions* to settle any outstanding matters preliminary to the trial itself. This summons will be heard before court officials known as Masters in London, or before Registrars in the local District Registries of the High Court. In the Queen's Bench Division these officials are barristers, and in the Chancery Division the Masters are solicitors. At the hearing of the summons for directions, the Master will fix a date and venue for the trial, for example, whether it is to be a case for the Commercial Court. He can also examine the evidence which the parties propose to call at the trial. Some allegations may be ones which the other side is willing to admit, and therefore formal proof is unnecessary; other matters can be proved by sworn written statements or *affidavits*, and attendance of witnesses in person is unnecessary. He can also restrict the number of expert witnesses, such as doctors, who can be called by either side. He will decide whether the case is one of the rare instances where there should be a jury. If the claim is a small one, he may order that it be transferred to a County Court.

These *interlocutory* steps can fulfil a useful function in saving the time of the judge and witnesses at the trial itself. On the other hand, they are sometimes felt to be unnecessarily complicated, with the result that a litigant finds it difficult to conduct the case himself and is obliged to seek expensive legal assistance. Procedure is governed in the High Court by the Rules of the Supreme Court, which are kept in continual review by a special Rules Committee which amends the rules as and when required. The Rules are published each year in the Annual Practice, a weighty volume known as the White Book from the colour of its cover. A corresponding volume is the annual County Court Practice, with a green cover.

It must be added that procedure in the County Courts is usually a good deal simpler than the High Court procedure just described. In particular, the interlocutory proceedings are usually less complex.

C. The civil trial

At the trial both parties are usually represented by counsel and, since the burden of proving the case generally rests upon the plaintiff, counsel for the plaintiff begins. He outlines the facts of the case and the evidence he proposes to call in support of these facts. This evidence is then produced, and any witnesses who are examined may be cross-examined by the defence. The defence will then put its case to the court in the same manner. After the defence case has been completed, each counsel will address the court in turn, first the counsel for the defendant and then the counsel for the plaintiff. During these closing speeches any points of law may be argued with the judge.

In the rare cases where a jury is present in civil proceedings, the judge will sum up the case, outlining the evidence, giving any directions on questions of law, and telling them what questions of fact are for their decision and the various conclusions open to them. If there is no jury, the judge will deliver his judgment, either immediately or, if the case is particularly complicated, at a later date. The latter is known as a *reserved judgment*.

A defended action in the County Court follows a similar pattern, except that in many areas the parties will usually be represented in court by solicitors rather than barristers. Reserved judgments, and indeed detailed arguments on points of law, are not very common.

If the plaintiff is successful in proving his case, there are several remedies which the judge may grant. The most common will be an order for the defendant to pay damages to the plaintiff, a fixed sum of money by way of compensation. If he has been asked to do so by the plaintiff, the judge has power to grant an injunction or to make various other orders, such as an order for the possession of land or goods.

Immediately after judgment has been given, it is usual for counsel for the successful party to ask for costs and, as mentioned earlier, this is a matter for the judge's discretion. If an appeal is to be made against the judgment it must be made within a limited period of time.

D. Enforcement of civil judgments

It is one thing to obtain judgment, it can be another thing to force the defendant to comply with it. If the judgment orders the defendant to pay damages to the plaintiff, for instance, what happens if the defendant still refuses to pay? Equally important, what happens if the defendant fails to comply with an injunction, or an order to return the land or goods to the plaintiff?

Money judgments

In the High Court there are various ways (enumerated below) by which money can be obtained from a judgment debtor who will not pay.

1. The plaintiff can obtain a writ of *fieri facias* (*fi. fa.*), ordering the sheriff to seize the defendant's goods and, if necessary, sell them to pay the plaintiff out of the proceeds.
2. The plaintiff can apply to the court for a *charging order* on the defendant's land or on shares held by him in a company. If the money is still not paid, the plaintiff can ultimately have the house or shares sold, and recover his damages from the proceeds.
3. The court may grant a *garnishee* order, under which money owed to the defendant by someone else must be paid directly to the plaintiff. In this way, the plaintiff can obtain payment directly from the defendant's bank account, if it is in credit.
4. The court has power to appoint a *receiver* who, if the defendant owns property, can intercept income such as rent, and apply it in payment of the plaintiff.
5. If the plaintiff applies by *writ of sequestration*, the court can, in effect, take control of all of the defendant's property, and deprive him of the right to manage it until the plaintiff has been paid. This can sometimes be useful where the defendant is a small company.
6. In addition to methods of enforcement such as these, High Court judgments can also be enforced through the County Courts. This can have several advantages, not least that the County Court can order payment by instalments, which is often the most practicable way of collecting the money from an individual.

The following are the main powers available in the County Courts.

1. The plaintiff can obtain a *warrant of execution* which, like the writ of *fi. fa.* in the High Court, directs a court officer—in this case the County Court bailiff—to seize the defendant's goods and, if necessary, sell them to pay the plaintiff.
2. Under the Attachment of Earnings Act 1971, the creditor will be able to obtain an *attachment of earnings* order through the County Court. Where the defendant is in employment, his employer can be ordered to deduct a specified sum each week or month from the defendant's wages or salary, and to pay this money into court to pay the plaintiff.

In addition to these methods of enforcement, the judgment creditor can also threaten to make the defendant bankrupt where the defendant's total debts amount to over £200.

Non-money judgments

If the defendant fails to obey an injunction, which is an order of the court to refrain from doing something, then he is in contempt of court, and the court can, on application by the plaintiff, punish him. The main methods of punishment are: (a) by an order for committal under which, if he still refuses to comply, the defendant can ultimately be imprisoned; and/or (b) by a writ of sequestration.

An order to deliver land to the plaintiff can be enforced by a *writ of possession*, and an order to deliver goods by a *writ of delivery* or of *specific delivery*. In each of these instances, the sheriff is ordered to seize the property and deliver it to the plaintiff. Delivery can sometimes be obtained by the threat of committal or sequestration, as described above.

E. Criminal proceedings

Procedure before trial

In the case of less serious offences, a summons is served upon the accused directing him to appear before the court at a specified time, date, and place. Proceedings against companies for such offences as false trade descriptions, unguarded factory machinery and incorrect weights and measures are invariably begun in this way. If the offence is more serious and the accused is unlikely to appear voluntarily, a warrant for his arrest will be signed by a magistrate and executed by the police. For some offences, usually the most serious ones, the offender may be arrested without a warrant.

As already mentioned, Magistrates' Courts deal with 98 per cent of all criminal prosecutions and, therefore, once the attendance of the offender has been secured, the court may proceed to trial. If the offender has only recently been arrested, an adjournment may first be necessary to allow time for both parties to prepare their cases. The prosecution is normally conducted by a legal practitioner or police officer but various statutes give the power to prosecute to such officials as factory inspectors, inspectors of trading standards and public health inspectors, in respect of offences against statutes which it is their duty to enforce. If the offence is one that must be tried in the Crown Court, committal proceedings will be held to determine whether or not there is a sufficiently strong case against the accused to justify a trial.

The trial

In both the Magistrates' Court and the Crown Court the accused will be asked to plead guilty or not guilty. If the plea is guilty, the prosecution will summarize the evidence and give details of the background of the accused, the defence may plead for mitigation, and sentence is passed.

If the plea is not guilty, the prosecution will outline the case against the accused and call witnesses to give evidence on oath to support this; these witnesses may be cross-examined by the defence. The defence case will then be put in a like manner. After closing speeches by both sides, the verdict of the court will be given, either by the magistrates or by the jury following a summing-up by the judge. A verdict of guilty will place a duty upon the court of imposing the most appropriate form of sentence, for example a custodial sentence of imprisonment or the payment of a monetary sum by way of a fine.

Compensation

The punishment of the offender will not of itself compensate the victim of a crime. It is always possible for the latter to bring a civil action, normally in tort, but this may not be worth while (see above). To avoid hearing the same evidence twice in different courts it would seem desirable to settle small amounts of compensation in the same (criminal) proceedings.

The power to award compensation was considerably extended by the Criminal Justice Act 1972. A criminal court may now, at its discretion, award compensation for personal injury, loss or damage, excluding loss arising from fatal and road traffic accidents; in Magistrates' Courts there is a restriction of £1000 for each offence for which there is a conviction. Any compensation ordered is deducted from any damages subsequently awarded in a civil action arising from the same facts.

This power is now contained in the Powers of Criminal Courts Act 1973. It has been used to compensate some victims of offences under the Trade Descriptions Acts 1968–72 (Unit 30) who might not have brought a separate civil action because of the time and cost involved.

Wider powers are also given to order the restitution of stolen goods or money which represents the proceeds of their sale. Another new provision empowers the Crown Court to make a criminal bankruptcy order in the interests of the victims where the loss amounts to £15 000.

For further consideration

1. A debtor has persistently refused to pay £500 which he owes to your company on the grounds that trade is bad and that he will pay later. What considerations are relevant in deciding whether or not to begin legal proceedings to recover the money?
2. It is said that to litigate, it is necessary to be either very rich or very poor. Explain whether this is true.
3. You have obtained judgment against a defendant for £500. Discuss critically the various methods of enforcing this judgment.
4. Outline the main stages in a civil action in the Queen's Bench Division, explaining why there is normally a long period of time between the first consultation with a solicitor and the trial of the case.
5. Explain briefly the meaning of
   (a) Discovery of documents
   (b) Writ of summons
   (c) Taxing master
   (d) Disposable income
   (e) Garnishee order

Unit 9. English Law and the European Communities

A. The European Communities

Although it is convenient to speak of the European Community, there are in fact three distinct communities, each with its own constitution in the form of the treaty which established it. These are:

1. *European Coal and Steel Community* (*ESSC*). This was established by the Treaty of Paris 1951 for the purpose of managing a common market in coal and steel.
2. *European Atomic Energy Community* (*Euratom*). This was set up by the second Treaty of Rome 1957 for the purpose of developing a common market in nuclear energy and distributing the power produced.
3. *European Economic Community* (*EEC*). This was set up by the first Treaty of Rome 1957. Unlike the other two specialist communities, the EEC has wider and more general objectives. Its immediate aim is the integration of the economies of the participating states; the long-term aim is political integration.

The six original signatories to the Treaties of Paris and Rome were France, Germany, Italy, Belgium, the Netherlands, and Luxembourg. The United Kingdom, Ireland, and Denmark joined in 1973 and Greece in 1981. By accession, these countries surrendered sovereign powers to the new Communities and accepted the supremacy of Community law over their national systems of law if a conflict should arise. While it is theoretically possible for a country to regain this loss of sovereignty by withdrawing from the Communities, this will become more unlikely with the passage of time when their economies will become more and more enmeshed and difficult to separate.

The Communities are legal persons with the normal characteristics and powers attaching to legal persons, for example, holding property, entering into contracts, and employing servants. Since they are sovereign legal persons they also have the powers under international law of entering into treaties and exchanging envoys with other countries.

B. Community institutions

There are four main institutions responsible for discharging the functions of the Communities—the Commission, the Council of Ministers, the Assembly, and the Court of Justice. There was originally a separate Commission and Council for each Community but it was soon realized that this was unsatisfactory. The need to coordinate policy in fields which overlapped led to the Merger Treaty 1965. In consequence there has been a single Commission and a single Council since 1969.

The Commission

This is the executive body of the Communities and consists of 14 Commissioners appointed by mutual agreement of the member Governments. There must be not more than two from any country and the present practice is for the four larger countries—France, Germany, Italy, and Britain—to appoint two each and the six smaller countries one each. One of the Commissioners is appointed President and there are five Vice-Presidents.

The Commissioners are chosen on the grounds of general competence. They must act with complete independence in the interests of the Communities and not take instructions from their own national Governments. Their term of office is a renewable period of four years but they may resign or be retired compulsorily for misconduct by the Court of Justice before the expiration of this period. A vote of censure carried by a two-thirds majority in the Assembly will bring about the compulsory retirement of the whole Commission.

While the Commission acts collectively, individual Commissioners specialize in the functions allotted to them—agriculture, transport, social affairs, regional policy, etc. Each Commissioner has a private staff (*cabinet*) under a *chef de cabinet* of the same nationality. There are departments responsible for exercising the various functions of the Commission, each headed by a Director-General of a nationality different from the Commissioner who has overriding responsibility. In the appointment of staff generally, an attempt is made to secure equitable representation from the member states.

The Commission is responsible for the formulation of Community policy after consultation with interested parties, having regard to the overriding objectives of the three Communities and the need to coordinate their policies. It has wide legislative functions. It initiates and drafts most Community legislation, and puts its proposals before the Council for enactment. In some instances the Commission has the power to enact the legislation itself, either under the Treaties or by delegation from the Council, in particular with regard to agriculture.

UNIT 9. ENGLISH LAW AND THE EUROPEAN COMMUNITIES

The Commission also has executive functions to ensure the enforcement of Council decisions. Allegations that a member state or a commercial undertaking is not fulfilling its Community obligations are investigated and, if necessary, brought before the Court of Justice. The Commission represents the Communities in negotiations with non-member states and administers certain budgets and funds. In general, it acts as the day-to-day executive of the Communities.

The Commission even has functions which are semi-judicial in nature. Thus it has the task of investigating alleged breaches of the anti-monopoly and restrictive practices provisions of the EEC Treaty. It is then the Commission which decides whether there has been any infringement and proposes appropriate measures to remedy the breach.

The Council of Ministers

The Council, which represents the sovereignty of the member states, is composed of one representative from each of the states. This is normally the Foreign Minister, but another minister, for example the Minister of Agriculture, may attend if the matter under discussion justifies this. Assistance, particularly with preliminary discussions, is given by a Committee of Permanent Representatives made up of the ambassadors to the Communities, and this Committee has come to exercise considerable power.

The Council is formally the legislative body for the Communities but in most cases it may only act on proposals put forward by the Commission. A system of weighted voting is provided for under which the larger countries have more votes, and most decisions require more than a simple majority to take effect. Since the 1966 Luxembourg Agreement, however, unanimity in voting has become common practice, although only strictly required in a limited number of cases such as the admission of new member states.

The Assembly

The Assembly, which represents the peoples of the member states, is now frequently referred to as the European Parliament. Until June 1979 the members were nominated by their national parliaments but they are now directly elected by voting in the member states. There are at present 434 members, who sit in political rather than national groups.

The Assembly is not a parliament in the normal meaning of that term. It has no legislative powers and is largely an advisory or consultative body. It is a forum where Community problems can be discussed and there is a power to put questions to the Council and the Commission. Consultative functions are largely exercised through 12 standing committees dealing with specialist topics.

There is, however, the power to remove the Commission by a vote of censure passed by a two-thirds majority. There are also limited powers over the Communities' budget. It is possible that the Assembly's powers will be increased in future.

The Court of Justice

The European Court of Justice, which sits in Luxemburg, holds the judicial power of the Communities with the function of ensuring that the law is observed in the interpretation and implementation of the Treaties. It is a court of first instance whose decisions must be accepted by the national courts and against which there is no right of appeal. While the business of the court is normally disposed of in plenary session before all the judges, it is possible for certain preliminary and other matters to be dealt with by a division or chamber of three judges.

There are at present 11 judges, at least one being appointed by each member state, and the judges in turn elect the President of the Court. Judges must be persons whose independence is beyond doubt and who are either qualified to hold high judicial office in their own country or are legal experts of recognized competence. In practice, the Bench is made up of a mixture of professional judges, academic lawyers, and public servants, unlike the English courts where the judges must all have been practising barristers. Privileges and immunities are granted to help ensure independence and impartiality, and a judge may only be removed from office by a unanimous decision of the other judges.

Compared with English procedure, much greater emphasis is placed upon written submissions or pleadings than upon oral argument. The Bench also plays a more active or inquisitorial part in the hearing; preliminary proceedings are conducted by a judge—the reporting judge—and the Court itself may summon and examine witnesses. The Court will be assisted by one of five advocates-general who must be qualified in the same way as the judges and whose function is to give an independent view of each case, particularly by way of a reasoned submission at the close of the proceedings. Following continental practice again, the Court will give a single judgment and dissenting opinions are not expressed. The language in which proceedings are conducted will vary from one case to another. This will normally be chosen by the plaintiff, except where the defendant is a member state when it will be the language of that state. There is no machinery for enforcing judgments. Where this is necessary it must be done by the member states through their national courts.

The jurisdiction of the Court, derived from the Treaties, includes the following:

1. Actions may be brought against member states either by other member states or by the Commission on the grounds that Treaty obligations are not being fulfilled. The Court's judgment will then be of a declaratory nature and compliance with the judgment depends upon the good faith of the member state.
2. Actions may also be brought against Community institutions by other institutions (for example, the Commission against the Council), by member states or by private individuals or corporate bodies who are directly concerned. In this way the act of an institution may be challenged on the grounds of lack of competence, infringement of a procedural requirement, infringement of the Treaties or for misuse of power, when a power has been used for a purpose other than that for which it was conferred. The Court may pronounce on the legality or otherwise of the act in question and, if necessary, either annul it by declaring it to be void or, in

certain instances, substitute its own decision for that of the institution. If appropriate, compensation may be awarded.

3. The Court has jurisdiction to settle disputes between the Communities and their employees arising from the latter's contracts of employment. It may also deal with the non-contractual liability of Community institutions for damage caused by their servants in the performance of their duties. It is provided that this shall be done in accordance with the general principles common to the laws of the member states. The Court may also hear appeals against penalties imposed by the Commission.

4. Finally, the Court has a consultative function to give preliminary rulings on the intepretation of the Treaties or of any acts of Community institutions. Any court or tribunal in a member state may ask for such a ruling. If the court is one from whose decision there is no appeal, such a ruling must be sought. It is arguable whether, in the case of this country, this court is the Court of Appeal or the House of Lords since there is no appeal as of right to the House of Lords (Units 4 and 5).

C. Sources of Community law

Membership of the Communities means the incorporation of Community law into a state's internal legal system. This law must be accepted without question and applied in the national courts. Moreover, in the event of a conflict between Community law and national law, Community law shall take precedence.

It is necessary to consider the sources from which Community law is derived.

The Treaties

The primary sources of Community law are the three foundation Treaties of Paris and Rome with their supplementary schedules and appendices. To these have been added subsequent treaties such as the Treaty of Merger 1965 and the Brussels Treaty of Accession 1972. It is likely that further treaties or conventions will be ratified by the member states in the future, either of a general nature dealing with the Communities as a whole or on specific topics such as patents and companies. Also included are treaties, such as trade agreements, concluded between the Communities and states in the outside world.

These treaties are 'self-executing' in the sense that ratification by a member state means that the provisions automatically become the law of that state. The state does not have the right to decide whether or not to implement the treaty by its own legislation. Thus the courts in the United Kingdom must accept and apply Article 85 of the EEC Treaty which prohibits specified restrictive practices agreements between commercial undertakings.

Community legislation

The Treaties set out in broad terms the objects to be achieved and leave many of the detailed means of achieving them to the Council and the Commission. To this end, the Council and Commission have law-making powers which they may exercise from time to time in accordance with the procedure laid down by the Treaties. The rules of law emanating from these administrative acts constitute secondary sources of law. They may take one of the following forms.

1. *Regulations* are of general application, binding in their entirety and directly applicable in all member states without the need for further legislation. The object is to obtain uniformity of law throughout the Communities.
2. *Directives* also have a general scope but are simply addressed to member states. The directive will require some or all of the states to make such changes in their own law as are necessary to bring it into line with the Community requirements set out in the directive. It is for each state to decide the manner and the form of the changes necessary in its own law, so long as the end result is achieved. The principal use of directives is to bring the laws of member states on certain topics into line with those of the other states in the Communities.

Other law-making powers of the Council and Commission

Decisions of the Council or Commission are binding in their entirety *upon those to whom they are addressed*. The decision may sometimes be addressed only to a single firm or group of companies. Unlike regulations, they do not have general legislative effect. They do, however, take effect directly; it is not left to member states to implement them.

Recommendations and opinions merely express the views of the Council and the Commission on Community policies. They are persuasive only and not binding and, therefore, cannot strictly be regarded as sources of Community law.

Case law

The powers and jurisdiction of the Court of Justice to ensure the observance of Community law have already been outlined. In so doing it is necessary for the Court to interpret 'statutory' provisions and from this rules of 'law' may emerge.

In accordance with the normal continental approach the Court has no law-making powers and there is no doctrine of binding precedent. Nevertheless, through interpretation—and there is considerable scope for this since the Treaties are widely drafted—a body of rules is emerging in the Court's judgments which has a strongly persuasive influence. Previous decisions of the Court are cited in argument and even in judgments and, while decisions are not based on these precedents, the desire for consistency does lead to their being given some weight.

In the interpretation of legislation the Court has wider powers than those possessed by a court in this country which is carrying out a similar task. The Court is not tied to the words of the Treaty or regulation only but may consider the reason for its enactment in the light of the general objectives of the Communities. It may consider, for example, statements and publications arising during the negotiations prior to enactment (*travaux préparatoires*) and the views of learned writers on what the law should be (*doctrine*).

D. The acceptance of Community law by the United Kingdom

Treaty of Accession

After two earlier and unsuccessful attempts to join the Communities, the United Kingdom signed the Treaty of Accession in Brussels in January 1972. (The Treaty was also signed by Denmark, Norway, and Ireland, although Norway later withdrew.) It was provided that the Treaty should be ratified in time for the new member states to enter the Communities on 1 January 1973 but there were transitional provisions applying to the following four years designed to ease the entry and soften the impact upon certain aspects of their economies.

It is part of the Crown's prerogative power to enter into agreements with other states and the approval of Parliament is not legally required. The Brussels Treaty was accordingly signed on behalf of the Crown by her Ministers. The United Kingdom thereby accepted an international obligation but without this affecting the internal law of the country. Membership of the Communities, however, requires that Community law shall become part of the internal law and shall be accepted and applied by the national courts. It was therefore necessary to change our internal law by Act of Parliament and this was done by the European Communities Act 1972.

European Communities Act

The Act provides that the Treaties and all secondary legislation, such as regulations which are intended to take direct effect within the member states, shall become part of the law of the United Kingdom. This includes secondary legislation already made and that which may be made in the future. No further enactment by Parliament is necessary. Thus, while Parliament may in future devise a procedure whereby draft regulations are considered and representations made to the Commission or Council, there is no direct Parliamentary control over whether or not such regulations become law.

Some secondary legislation such as directives must be implemented by the member state, but a choice of the way of doing this is left to the state. The Act provides that so far as this country is concerned much of this can be done by Orders in Council or by Ministerial regulations (Unit 2). There are, however, some measures which must still be implemented by Act of Parliament, such as provisions imposing or increasing taxation or creating new criminal offences which carry more than certain specified maximum penalties.

Some secondary legislation enacted by the Communities before the Treaty of

Accession has been given effect in English law already, by the Act itself. For instance, Section 9 of the European Communities Act is intended to implement the requirements of the First Directive on Company Law, enacted by the Council of the EEC in 1968. It amends the *ultra vires* doctrine (Unit 10).

Further provisions of the Act include the obligation to take account of the principles laid down by the European Court where these are relevant to legal proceedings before our courts. It is also provided that future Acts of Parliament are to be interpreted and have effect subject to the European Communities Act, that is on the assumption that Community law is part of our internal law and is supreme.

As a condition of the United Kingdom becoming a member state, Parliament has therefore been obliged to give up its sovereignty so far as Community matters are concerned. In theory, there is no reason why the 1972 Act should not be repealed by a later Act but this would mean the renunciation of membership.

Effect of Community law

The immediate impact of Community law on English law is not likely to be very great. The Communities are concerned primarily with economic and commercial matters and the effect is being felt initially in those branches of law which govern relationships in these fields.

As already mentioned, some changes in the law relating to companies were made by the European Communities Act itself and further changes are likely in a gradual movement towards a uniform set of legal rules applicable to business organizations throughout the Communities. Commercial law, particularly in the fields of agency and distribution agreements and of monopolies and restrictive trade practices, the law relating to taxation and, to some extent, industrial law will also be affected. Article 100 of the EEC Treaty provides for the issue of directives for the harmonization or approximation of the laws of the member states where these directly affect the establishment or functioning of the Common Market.

For the time being there will be little effect upon our system of courts and our rules of procedure. Contract, tort, criminal law, property, and family law will remain essentially the same as before. On the other hand the movement towards greater integration between the member states in general and the greater contact between the legal professions and the work of the European Court in particular must inevitably lead, albeit slowly, to more uniformity in the laws of the member states. This process will be quickened if the Communities should develop a policy of greater political integration. Nevertheless, complete integration of the laws and legal systems is many, many years in the future.

For further consideration

1. In what ways does the Commission discharge the functions of the European Communities? What controls exist to prevent it exceeding its powers?
2. Outline the composition and jurisdiction of the European Court of Justice.

3. Explain the purpose, principal provisions, and effect of the European Communities Act 1972. To what extent does this Act affect the principle of Parliamentary sovereignty?
4. The Commission has produced several draft directives on company law. What steps must be taken (a) in the European Communities, and (b) in this country before these can affect English law?
5. Explain briefly the meaning of
   (a) Assembly
   (b) Directive
   (c) Treaty of Rome
   (d) Regulation
   (e) Council of Ministers

Unit 10. Legal Personality and Capacity

A. Natural and legal persons

Legal personality

A legal person is anything recognized by law as having legal rights and duties. With one main exception, a legal person in this country is simply a person in the ordinary sense: a human being. In general, his or her rights begin at birth and end at death and, subject to rules such as those of capacity (below), the same rules apply to everyone.

In one important instance, English law also grants legal personality to an artificial person. This arises where a group of persons together form a *corporate* body of some sort. The corporate body can acquire a personality separate from that of its members, with some of the legal powers of a natural person. It can, for example, own property and make contracts, even with its own members, in its own name. The ways in which such *incorporation* can occur are described later.

Capacity

English law limits the legal capacity of certain categories of natural person. For example, special rules protect minors, i.e., those under 18 years of age. A minor is not generally liable on his contracts (Unit 18) and may escape liability in tort (Unit 12). He may own personal property, such as books or even a car, but he cannot own land except indirectly as beneficiary under a trust. He cannot make a will to dispose of his property on death unless he is on active military service. Other special rules apply at different ages: a person under 16 cannot marry, and there are special provisions for young criminal offenders. A young person is not allowed a full driving licence until 17.

The legal capacity of *mentally disordered* persons is similarly restricted. In general, they cannot enter into valid contracts, transfer property or make wills, or validly marry.

Many of the restrictions formerly placed on *aliens* have been removed, but generally they still do not have a right of free entry to the country. They remain liable to deportation in some circumstances, and they cannot vote or become MPs. There are now also restrictions on entry and powers to deport some Commonwealth citizens, but new rights of entry for citizens within the European Communities. *Foreign sovereigns* and ambassadors are normally granted the privilege of immunity from legal actions.

The main limits on the capacity of *corporate bodies* arise from their very nature. First, there are things which they cannot physically do, such as marry. Second, they are the creation of law and therefore only have such powers as the law gives them; anything outside of those powers (*ultra vires*) is void.

B. Corporations

Corporations may come into being in one of three ways.

1. The earliest form of incorporation was by Royal Charter, issued under the Royal prerogative upon the advice of the Privy Council. This form of incorporation was used to create the Bank of England and the great trading companies such as the East India Company and the Hudson's Bay Company. The issue of a charter today is confined to non-commercial undertakings, for example, new universities.
2. A corporation may be created by Act of Parliament. This method was used for the early railway and gas companies and more recently for the nationalized industries such as the National Coal Board. Most undertakings of a public nature, for example, the Independent Broadcasting Authority, are statutory corporations. So far as local authorities are concerned, while some towns first received their status by Royal Charter, the new authorities administering our system of local government from 1974 onwards owe their existence to the Local Government Act 1972. Some have also received new Royal Charters since then.
3. It was found in the nineteenth century that the cumbersome and expensive method of forming chartered and statutory corporations was not ideal for private business concerns. Hence the Companies Act 1844 provided a third and easier method of incorporation, by registration following a few relatively simple formalities. In 1855, limited liability was introduced, whereby shareholders who invested in companies could only be called upon for the amount they had agreed to contribute and were not liable to creditors to the extent of all their wealth. Formation by registration and limited liability together helped provide the capital which the increasing scale of business then needed. The law governing companies is now largely contained in the Companies Act 1948, as amended in 1967, 1976, 1980, and 1981. Several other statutes allow incorporation by registration today. Building societies are created by registration under the Building Societies Acts, and many

organizations such as working men's clubs and cooperative societies are incorporated under the Industrial and Provident Societies Acts.

As we have seen a corporation, once formed, acquires *separate legal personality*. It can sue its own members and be sued by them. It can employ its own members. Its property belongs to the corporation, not to the members. *Limited liability* developed naturally from this: the corporation's debts and liabilities are its own and, in general, members are not responsible for them.

> In *Salomon* v. *Salomon & Co. Ltd* (1897), Salomon, who manufactured boots, formed his business into a company. Six members of his family held one share each, and he held the remaining 20 000. He lent money to the company on the security of its assets and, when the company ran into financial difficulties, it was held that he took preference over the ordinary creditors. Although he *was*, in effect, the company, he was treated in law as an entirely separate person.

If a corporation exceeds its powers, the act in question will be *ultra vires* and void. While a natural person can do whatever the law does not prohibit, an artificial person can only do what the law and the documents creating it will permit. A statutory corporation only has the powers bestowed by legislation, and a company only has the powers given by the 'objects clause' in its memorandum of association.

> In *Ashbury Carriage Co.* v. *Riche* (1875), a company formed to make railway carriages contracted to finance the building of a railway in Belgium. Although the shareholders ratified the agreement, it was held *ultra vires* and the company was not bound.
>
> In *Introductions Ltd* v. *National Provincial Bank Ltd* (1969), a company formed in 1951 with the objects of promoting tourism was not bound by contracts made when it went into pig farming many years later.
>
> In *London Borough of Bromley* v. *Greater London Council* (1982), it was held *ultra vires* and unlawful for the GLC to subsidize public transport out of rates in the way in which it had done so.

The reason for the objects clause of a company was largely to protect shareholders who invested their money on the understanding that the company would only do the things specified therein. In practice, objects clauses are today drawn widely and may later be extended, so that little protection is actually given. The European Communities Act 1972, section 9, makes further inroads. Outsiders dealing with a company in good faith may assume that a transaction entered into by the directors is within the company's capacity, so that the company is bound whether or not it is within its objects.

C. Unincorporated associations

People may combine to further a common interest without creating an independent legal personality. Such interests may be sporting, social, political or business. In the absence of incorporation, the law does not normally recognize the association as a separate entity but regards it instead as a number of individual persons. Any property belongs to the members jointly, not to the association.

In some instances, however, limited recognition is given to the association.

1. If its property is held by trustees on behalf of the members, the trustees are then the legal owners, and they may bring and defend actions and do other things necessary to safeguard it.
2. If the management of affairs is entrusted to a committee, all the members of that committee may be liable for an act done with their authority.
3. Under the rules of court it is possible for some members to sue or be sued on behalf of all the others in a representative action. In *Bolton and Others* v. *Stone* (Unit 13), Miss Stone sued Bolton, the secretary, and three other committee members of the cricket club, which was an unincorporated association.

Special rules exist for particular types of unincorporated association. For example, most *trade unions* are unincorporated. In the early nineteenth century, they were unlawful, and members could be prosecuted for the crime of conspiracy. Gradually their status was recognized by law and, since 1871, their status (if not always their activities) has been regarded as lawful. Today they can acquire some features similar to those of corporations, particularly if they register with the Certification Officer under the Trade Union and Labour Relations Act 1974.

Most unincorporated associations for *business* purposes are governed by the Partnership Act 1890 (below).

D. Partnerships

The Partnership Act 1890, section 1, defines a partnership as 'the relation which subsists between persons carrying on business in common with a view to profit'.

Formation

When a partnership is created, the parties often draw up a deed or 'articles' of partnership. This usually covers such matters as the provision of capital, management, and the sharing of profits. The Partnership Act provides for these matters, but only in the absence of agreement to the contrary by the partners. This contrasts sharply with the provisions of the Companies Acts, with which companies must comply.

In some instances, partnerships are not formal or long term. They may be created informally, or even inadvertently. If X and Y cooperate in a once-only business venture, being paid to remove rubbish from Lord Z's back garden, then X and Y are partners under the Act, although the thought may never have occurred to them. It is similar with many very small or part-time businesses.

Difficulties do sometimes arise as to whether there is a partnership, and the Act contains rules to help determine this. First, the persons involved must be in *business*. Therefore, by section 2, the mere fact that two or more people are co-owners of property does not *of itself* render them partners, even if the property brings in income such as rent or dividends. Similarly, the sharing of *gross* returns (not profits) does not of itself create a partnership. Second, they must be carrying on the business 'in common'. If both carry on the business, then they are partners under section 1. If someone shares in the profits *without* taking part in the business, then section 2 applies. As a general rule anyone sharing profits is *presumed* a partner, but this can be rebutted. For example, repayment of a loan or debt out of profits, or at a rate varying with profits, does not necessarily make the creditor a partner; nor is the seller of a business who is being paid off out of the buyer's profits necessarily still a partner. The section also provides that paying an employee or agent at a rate varying with the profits does not necessarily make him a partner.

In forming a partnership, the ordinary rules of contract apply. It is voidable if induced by misrepresentation. It is void if formed for an illegal purpose; see *Foster* v. *Driscoll* (Unit 22). By the rules of capacity, a company, being a person, can be a partner. A minor can be a partner, but can repudiate before or within a reasonable time after majority. He is not liable for partnership debts, but cannot be credited with profits without also being debited with losses.

By the Companies Acts 1948 and 1967, a partnership cannot validly have more than 20 members, although exceptions exist for professions such as solicitors and accountants, who cannot practise as companies. A partnership is, therefore, at a disadvantage when raising large amounts of capital. It is a suitable form of business organization where close cooperation between members is required, and where they do not wish to have to publish their accounts (see later).

The partners are known collectively as a 'firm', and the name under which they carry on business is the 'firm name'. They can, within limits, choose whatever name they think fit, subject only to the Companies Act 1981. This repeals and replaces the Registration of Business Names Act 1916, and provides that wherever a firm carries on business in a name which does not consist of the surnames of all partners, with or without 'permitted additions' such as first names, initials, phrases such as 'and Sons' or, where two or more partners have the same surname, the addition of an 's' at the end of that surname ('Smiths'), then it is subject to limits. It must not, for example, use a firm name which suggests Government or local authority connections, is offensive, or falsely suggests connection with another business. Other important checks are that a partnership must not use 'limited' or 'public limited company' as the last words of its name, although it can use 'company' or an abbreviation thereof. In any event, the true surnames of all partners must appear on letter headings (although there are exceptions for firms with more than 20 partners), and must be displayed in a prominent place to which customers have access at the firm's business premises. Non-compliance with any of the above provisions is a criminal offence.

Relations between the partners and outsiders

Four main issues arise under this head.

When can the acts of one partner render the whole firm liable?
By the Partnership Act, section 5, the rules are those of agency. The firm is bound by

anything which an individual partner was *expressly* authorized to do. The firm may also be bound if the partner does something for '*carrying on in the usual way business of the kind carried on by the firm*', so that there is nothing to make the outsider suspicious. The partner has *implied* authority, and the firm is bound even if he has exceeded his actual authority. It follows, however, that the firm will not be bound if the outsider either knows that the partner has no authority, or does not know or believe him to be a partner.

The key question as regards the unauthorized acts of a partner is what sort of thing *is* it 'usual' for an individual partner to do. This depends largely upon what sort of business it is, but the following can normally be assumed to be within a partner's powers, so long as his actions are not so unusual as to raise suspicions: selling the firm's goods; buying goods normally bought by the firm; giving receipts for debts; engaging and dismissing employees; signing ordinary cheques. In trading partnerships, as opposed to professional ones, it may also be usual for one partner to borrow money on the firm's behalf.

> In *Mercantile Credit Ltd* v. *Garrod* (1962), G and P were partners in a garage business concerned with *repairing* cars and letting lock-up garages. They had expressly agreed *not* to *sell* cars. Nevertheless P, without G's knowledge, sold a car to M Ltd for £700. It then transpired that P had had no title to the car, so M Ltd demanded back the £700. When P did not pay, G was held liable as his partner. There was nothing to make M Ltd suspect that P and G had restricted their authority to repairing contracts. Therefore the firm, all partners, were liable.

An outsider can always protect himself by contacting the other partners to see whether they do in fact agree with what the one partner proposes.

When is the firm liable for wrongs, such as torts, committed by one partner?
By section 10, where one partner commits an act which is wrong in itself, as opposed to merely being outside his authority, the firm will be civilly liable for any harm caused, and criminally for any penalty incurred if either:

(a) the act was done with the actual authority of his fellow partners; or
(b) the act was within his 'usual' authority, in the ordinary course of the firm's business.

> In *Hamlyn* v. *Houston & Co.* (1903), it was held to be quite 'usual' for a partner to obtain information about a rival business. His firm was therefore held liable when, without actual authority, he used bribery for this purpose.

Section 11 applies where a partner misapplies money or property received for, or in the custody of, the firm. The problem can arise in two ways. First, a *partner* may receive money or property *for* the firm, and misapply it before it reaches the firm. Here, the firm is liable if it was within the actual or 'usual' authority of that partner to receive the property. Second, the *firm* may already have custody of someone else's money or property, and a partner then takes it from the firm. In this case, so long as the money or property was in the firm's custody in the ordinary course of its business, the firm and all of its partners are liable.

When is an individual partner personally liable for the firm's debts and liabilities?
Partners do not have limited liability. By section 9, they are jointly liable on the firm's contracts. Each partner is liable for the full amount due, but can apply to the court to have the others joined as co-defendants. In practice, plaintiffs usually sue the firm in the firm's name, but can then enforce the full judgment against any partner. By section 12, partners are liable jointly and severally for torts committed by or on behalf of the firm. Again, each can be made liable for the full amount.

New partners are not liable for things done or debts incurred before they became partners. A *retiring partner* remains liable for debts incurred *before* his retirement, but can be discharged if a contract of 'novation' is made between himself, the other partners, and the creditor. He may also be liable for debts incurred *after* he leaves. Someone dealing with a firm after a change in its constitution is entitled to treat all apparent members of the old firm as still being members until he has notice of the change. The retiring partner should therefore protect himself by notifying all existing customers and suppliers of his retirement, so that he no longer appears to them to be a partner. He should also advertise his retirement in the *London Gazette*, which serves as notice to those who have not previously dealt with the firm. In any event, he is not liable to those who have not previously dealt with the firm, and who did not even know that he had been a partner.

In *Tower Cabinet Co. Ltd* v. *Ingram* (1949), I and C traded as partners under the name 'Merry's' until 1947. I then left, but C carried on under the old name. In 1948, C ordered furniture from T Ltd, and failed to pay. T Ltd obtained judgment against 'Merry's', and tried to enforce this against I. It was held that I was not liable: T Ltd had never dealt with Merry's while I was a partner, and only knew of him because C had confirmed the order on some old headed notepaper which still showed I's name. Until then, T Ltd did not know that I had been a partner, and discovery at this late stage did not make I an 'apparent member'. (Nevertheless, I would have saved himself much trouble had he destroyed *all* of the old headed notepaper before leaving.)

The estate of a partner who dies or becomes bankrupt is not liable for partnership debts incurred after the death or bankruptcy.

When is a person who is not *a partner liable for the debts of the firm?*
We have seen that a retiring partner can sometimes be liable for debts incurred after he left. By section 14, others may also be liable. A non-partner can be liable for the debt if he has by his words, spoken or written, or by his conduct, represented himself to be a partner and, as a result, an outsider has given credit to the firm. Similarly, a non-partner can be liable if he has *allowed* himself to be 'held out' as being a partner, and the creditor has relied on this misapprehension. The 'apparent' partner can be liable whether or not he knows that the representations which he has made or allowed have been used to persuade a potential creditor in this way.

In *Tower Cabinet* v. *Ingram*, I was not liable under section 14 because he had not *allowed* the use of the old headed paper.

Relations of partners to each other

This is basically a matter for agreement between the partners. Section 24, however, sets out rules which apply in the absence of express or implied agreement to the contrary.

1. All partners are entitled to share equally in capital and profits, and must contribute equally to losses.
2. The firm must indemnify partners in respect of expenses and personal liabilities incurred in the ordinary and proper conduct of the business, or in anything necessarily done to preserve the firm's business or property.
3. A partner is entitled to interest on payments or loans which he makes to the firm beyond his agreed capital.
4. He is not, however, entitled to interest on his capital before ascertainment of profits.
5. Every partner may take part in managing the firm's business.
6. No partner is entitled to remuneration (such as salary) for acting in the partnership business.
7. No new partner may be introduced without the consent of all the existing partners. (This is sometimes expressly varied in practice, so as to give a partner the right to introduce a son or daughter.)
8. Ordinary management decisions can be by a majority, but any change in the *nature* of the business must be unanimous.
9. The records and accounts must be kept at the main place of business, and be open to all partners, or their proper agents such as accountants, to inspect and copy.
10. By section 25, no majority can expel a partner unless a power to do so has been conferred by express agreement between the partners.

Partners also owe statutory duties of good faith to each other.

1. Section 28 imposes a statutory duty to account: 'Partners are bound to render true accounts and full information of all things affecting the partnership to any partner or his legal representative.'
2. Section 29 deals with secret or unauthorized profits: 'Every partner must account to the firm for any benefit derived by him without the consent of the other partners from any transaction concerning the partnership property, name or businesss connection.'

   In *Pathirana* v. *Pathirana* (1967), R and A were partners in a petrol service station. A gave R three months' notice that he intended to leave. Without waiting, R almost immediately took full control, and pocketed the entire profits. A was held entitled to his own share of profits for the rest of the notice period.

3. Section 30 imposes a duty not to compete with the firm: 'If a partner, without the consent of the other partners, carries on any business of the same nature as and competing with that of the firm, he must account for and pay over to the firm all profits made by him in that business.'

Dissolution of a partnership

Partnerships may be dissolved in various ways. For example, a partnership for a fixed term, or for a single venture or undertaking, *expires* automatically when the term or undertaking ends. If the partners continue working together after this, it is a new partnership.

If the partnership was for an indefinite period, as is more usual, it can be ended by any partner giving *notice* to *all* of the others. Notice can be oral unless the original partnership was created by deed, in which case notice must be written.

Death or *bankruptcy* of any partner automatically dissolves the entire partnership, unless otherwise provided. This can be inconvenient, so partnership agreements often exclude this rule and provide, for example, that the partnership shall continue, and that the others shall buy the deceased or bankrupt's share at a valuation.

If a court makes a *charging order* over any partner's share as a result of his private debts, the other partners may dissolve the firm.

A partnership is automatically dissolved by any event which makes it *illegal* to carry on the business, or for the members to carry it on in partnership.

> In *Stevenson Ltd* v. *Cartonnagen-Industrie* (1918), the outbreak of war in 1914 automatically ended the partnership between a British company and a German firm.

Any partner may apply for a *court order* to dissolve the partnership if any of the following conditions apply.

1. If any partner becomes a patient under the Mental Health Acts, or is shown to be permanently of unsound mind; application can be either on behalf of the mentally ill partner, or by the others.
2. If a partner other than the one applying becomes in any other way incapable of performing his partnership contract.
3. If a partner, other than the one suing, is guilty of such conduct as, in view of the nature of the business, is calculated to affect it prejudicially; an order might be made under this head if, for example, a solicitor, accountant or other professional partner was convicted of dishonesty, either within or outside of the business.
4. If a partner, other than the one suing, wilfully or persistently breaks the partnership agreement, or otherwise so conducts himself that it is not reasonably practicable for the others to carry on business with him; examples might include persistent absence or laziness, or simply unpleasantness.
5. If the partnership business can *only* be carried on at a loss; merely making a loss *at present* is not necessarily enough.
6. If circumstances have arisen which, in the court's opinion, render it just and equitable that the partnership be dissolved.

> In *Ebrahimi* v. *Westbourne Galleries Ltd* (1973), E and N had been equal members for many years in a successful partnership. They then formed a company to run the business, with themselves as the sole shareholders and directors. Later, as a favour, E allowed N to introduce N's son into the business, and E voluntarily transferred some of his shares to the son. N and his son then combined deliberately to force E out. The court granted E's

application to wind up (dissolve) the company, under provisions of the Companies Act 1948 very similar to those of the Partnership Act.

In *Re Yenidje Tobacco Co. Ltd* (1916), similarly, the court ordered winding up when a company's directors and sole shareholders quarrelled and could no longer work together, even though the company was profitable.

Finally, like any other contract, a partnership can be *rescinded* within a reasonable time of formation if it was induced by fraud or misrepresentation.

If a partnership is dissolved for any of the above reasons, the authority, rights, and duties of the partners continue, but only for the purpose of winding up. Any partner may publicize the dissolution, and the others must concur.

By section 39, partnership property must be applied in payment of the firm's debts and liabilities. Any surplus must then be paid to the individual partners as, in effect, repayment of capital. Any partner can insist on this and, if necessary, ask the court to supervise it.

In settling accounts between the partners, the rules in section 44 apply unless otherwise agreed. Losses, including deficiencies in capital, must be paid (a) out of profits, (b) then out of capital, and (c) lastly, if necessary, by the partners themselves in the proportions in which they were entitled to share profits. If there are no outstanding losses, assets are to be applied (a) in paying trade and other creditors, (b) then in repaying to partners any loans which they have made to the firm, (c) then in repaying to each partner what he has contributed in capital, and finally (d) anything left goes to the partners in the proportions to which they were entitled to profits.

When there ought to be a final settlement and it does not take place, for example, if a partner dies or retires and the remaining partners carry on without settling with him or his estate, then the outgoing partner may claim either such share of the profits after he left as are attributable to use of his share of the assets, or interest on the amount of his share; see *Pathirana* v. *Pathirana* again.

In practice, partnership agreements often expressly exclude this part of the Act. For example, the agreement may provide that the partnership shall not end on the death or retirement of one partner, but that the surviving partners shall buy the interest of outgoing partner at a valuation.

Limited partnerships

The Limited Partnerships Act 1907 allows the creation of firms where, unlike in ordinary partnerships, some members can have limited liability. Limited partners contribute a stated amount of capital, and then have no further liability for the firm's debts. At least one member, however, must have unlimited liability. A limited partner takes no part in management, his death, bankruptcy or mental illness do not dissolve the firm, and he cannot end the firm by notice. Unlike ordinary firms, limited partnerships must register details of the firm, the business, and the partners with the Companies' Registrar, who issues a certificate of registration. In practice, limited partnerships are rare.

E. The Crown

At common law, the Crown was above the law, and no action could be brought against the King in the King's courts. This was summarized in the maxim, 'The King (or Queen) can do no wrong'. This legal immunity applied also to public acts carried out in the King's name by Ministers and Government departments.

As the activities of state vastly increased, the extent of this immunity brought many cases of injustice. Thus, the Crown was not liable for the negligent driving of an army lorry or for a dangerous post office floor, as an ordinary employer would have been; nor were Government departments liable if they broke their contracts. At common law there was, in practice, some mitigation of this severe position, but the important changes were made by the Crown Proceedings Act 1947, which now largely governs the matter.

In tort, the Crown can now be liable for the wrongful acts of its servants, for injuries arising out of the ownership and control of premises and, where the statute expressly states that the Crown is to be bound, for breach of statutory duty. There are still some immunities, however: for example, no action lies for death or personal injury suffered during service in the armed forces if the Minister responsible certifies that this injury ranks for entitlement to pension. Although the Post Office changed in 1969 from a Government department to a public corporation, there is still no liability for loss or delay of unregistered letters, parcels, telegrams or for telephonic communications.

In contract, similarly, the Crown can be liable, particularly for commercial agreements. It is doubtful if it is bound by the service contracts of its employees (civil servants) but, in any event, they are now protected by the unfair dismissal provisions of the Employment Protection (Consolidation) Act 1978.

Civil actions may now be brought against the appropriate departments or against the Attorney-General, who is empowered to defend such actions on the Crown's behalf. There is still no legal way of enforcing judgments against the Crown, although this is normally not necessary. The Crown (i.e., the Government) can still stop disclosure of certain evidence for which Crown privilege is claimed. The Queen in her private capacity still enjoys complete immunity.

For further consideration

1. Discuss whether the following are partners within the Partnership Act 1890.
   (a) The committee of a tennis club.
   (b) Mr A and his son B who take turns in driving Mr A's van to deliver flowers and vegetables from a market garden to retail grocers' shops.
   (c) C and D who organize a jumble sale for charity.
   (d) E, who runs a business, and F who has loaned him money to help him expand it.
2. To what extent is a partnership firm liable in respect of contracts made in its name by one of the partners?

3. In what ways can a retiring partner protect himself against liability for the firm's debts?
4. 'The Queen can do no wrong.' Explain the legal meaning of this phrase, and discuss whether it is true today.
5. Explain briefly the meaning of the following
    (a) Separate legal personality
    (b) *Ultra vires*
    (c) A minor
    (d) An unincorporated association
    (e) The Crown

Unit 11. Companies

Since 1844, companies have been created by registration under various Acts. The position today is governed by the Companies Act 1948, as amended in 1967, 1976, 1980, and 1981. There are three main types of company. In an *unlimited* company, each member is fully liable for the company's debts in the same way as members of a partnership. In a company *limited by guarantee* a member, on joining, guarantees the company's debts, but only up to a stated figure. Again these are uncommon, but are sometimes used for non-business bodies such as cricket clubs. The vast majority of companies are *limited by shares*: each member holds one or more 'shares' issued by the company in return for payment. A shareholder's liability to the company's creditors is normally limited to that part of the nominal value of his shares which he has not yet paid to the company. Most shares today are fully paid up, and such shareholders therefore have no liability for the company's debts; see *Salomon* v. *Salomon & Co. Ltd* (page 82).

Most of this unit deals with companies limited by shares, of which there are two types. Some become *public limited companies*. To qualify for this status they must have issued at least £50 000 worth of shares, with at least one-quarter of the nominal capital (see later) paid up. The memorandum of association must specifically state that the company is public, and the name must end with the words 'public limited company' ('p.l.c.'). Any company not satisfying these requirements is a *private company* and therefore, by the Companies Act 1980, section 15, must not offer its shares for sale to the public. A private company can turn itself into a public one and vice versa. In practice, most companies are formed as, and remain, private.

There are other classifications for special purposes which have little to do with the Companies Acts. For example, if a public company wishes its shares (or debentures, see later) to be dealt with on a stock exchange, it must apply to the exchange, which will only grant permission if the requirements *of the exchange* (as to total value of the shares, and as to disclosure, etc.) are met. A stock exchange 'quotation' or 'listing' is often desirable in order to increase the saleability and value of a company's shares. By no means all public companies are 'listed'.

For tax purposes, it can be an advantage for a company to remain a 'close' company, that is, one 'controlled' by directors who are also shareholders or creditors, or 'controlled' by five or fewer shareholders or creditors.

One company can hold shares in another, and most large companies do control many subsidiary companies, for instance by holding most of the shares in the subsidiary. Although in law each of these companies is a separate person, in reality they are controlled by the 'parent' company. Often the arrangements are much more complex, and may involve companies or their equivalents in many different countries. Some such 'multinational' enterprises include hundreds of companies throughout the world.

A. Formation of companies

Those forming a company are called its 'promoters'. The term includes people doing any of the work necessary, those who acquire property or a business for the company, and those who set out to provide finance. The main tasks of the promoters are to prepare various documents, and to lodge these, with the necessary fees, with the Registrar of Companies (an official of the Department of Trade). Several documents must be lodged.

1. *The memorandum of association.* This, in effect, defines the company and what it can do. It must contain the following details.
   (a) It must state the *company's name*. The choice rests with the promoters but, under the Companies Act 1981, the Registrar can refuse a name on the same basis as he can reject the name of a partnership (Unit 10). For example, he will reject a name too like that of an existing business, or which falsely suggests Government or local authority connections. The last words must normally be 'public limited company' or simply 'limited', depending on the type of company. Members can later change the name by special resolution, but again the Registrar's consent is required.
   (b) If the company is to be a public one, the memorandum must expressly say so.
   (c) A clause must state whether the *registered office* is to be in England and Wales, or in Scotland. Every company must have a registered office, which is its *legal* home. It need not be anywhere near the main, or any, place of business. The actual address of the registered office must be given in the statement concerning directors, delivered with the memorandum.
   (d) The '*objects clause*' states the objects for which the company is formed, and the powers which it is to have. Anything which the company later does outside of these objects and powers is *ultra vires*, and may be void; see *Ashbury Carriage Co. Ltd* v. *Riche* and *Introductions Ltd* v. *National Provincial Bank* (Unit 10).

   A company can later extend its objects, within limits, by special resolution of shareholders, under the 1948 Act, section 5. In practice, objects clauses today are usually drafted very widely in the first place.

(e) A clause must state that the members have *limited liability*.

(f) There must be a statement of the *nominal capital*, and how it is to be divided into shares. This clause may be changed subsequently, for example, so as to increase the capital if the company expands.

The memorandum ends with a request by the 'subscribers', whose names and addresses appear at the end, to be formed into a company. There must be at least two subscribers. Each must take at least one share, and the memorandum must state how many he does take. Each must sign, and the signatures must be witnessed.

2. *Articles of association* are usually submitted too. These regulate the internal management, and the rights and duties of shareholders *vis-à-vis* the company and each other. They deal with matters such as transfer of shares, meetings, voting and other rights of shareholders, dividends, and the directors' powers of management.

A company need not, in fact submit any articles. If it does not do so, it will be taken to have adopted Table A, a model set of articles in Schedule 1 of the 1948 Act, as amended. In any event, Table A always applies except in so far as it is expressly or impliedly overruled by actual articles.

The articles of association may later be altered under the 1948 Act, section 10, but the alteration must not (a) clash with the memorandum, (b) discriminate between members, or take away the rights of any class of shareholders, and (c) the alteration must be for the benefit of all shareholders.

3. There must be a separate *statement of the nominal capital.*

4. A statement containing *particulars of directors and company secretary* must be filed with the memorandum. It must be signed by the subscribers, and contain a signed consent by each director to act as such. It must also contain the address of the registered office.

5. A *statutory declaration* by a solicitor engaged in forming the company, or by a person named in the articles as a director or the company secretary, must also be filed. This must declare that the requirements of the Act have been complied with, and may be accepted by the Registrar as evidence of this.

If all the requirements in respect of registration and matters incidental to it have been satisfied, the Registrar issues a *certificate of incorporation*, which is the company's 'birth certificate'. A company registered as private can start business immediately. A public company, however, must not do business or borrow money until it has gone on to satisfy the Registrar that the necessary share capital has actually been raised. It must also show details of the expenses of formation, and of any payments to promoters. If he is satisfied, the Registrar issues a further certificate, whereupon the public company too can start to do businesss.

B. Capital

It takes money to set up and run a business. In companies with a share capital, the money is raised partly by issuing shares in the company. A shareholder must pay the company for each share allotted to him, and the money thus produced provides, in theory, the basic finance. In its memorandum, a company must state its *nominal capital*. This is the face value of the total number of shares which the company has, at present, *authorized* itself to issue. The nominal (or 'authorized') capital may, for example, be £60 000, divided into 60 000 shares of £1 each. This does not necessarily mean that all of these shares have been issued yet, only that the company *can* issue them.

The *issued capital* is so much of the £60 000 nominal capital as has actually been issued. The company need not even demand that the full nominal price be paid immediately by the new shareholder. It can issue £1 shares for 50p now, with the right to call for the other 50p later. The second 50p is known as 'uncalled' capital. This is rare today, because most shares are issued fully paid.

The real value of shares may be more than the nominal value. Thus if a company's assets are worth much more than its nominal capital, its shares may reflect this. If would-be shareholders pay £5 for each of the £1 shares issued, the shares are said to be issued at a premium of £4.

In theory, an amount equal to the money actually paid to a company in return for its shares has to be kept available in order, in the last resort, to pay off creditors and repay the shareholders if the company is wound up. The Companies Acts, therefore, still contain detailed rules to prevent or control reduction of this capital, although the rules have been relaxed slightly by the 1981 Act.

When a company invites the public to buy its shares, it must issue a *prospectus*, which must contain detailed information about the company so that investors can make an informed choice. False statements in prospectuses can be a criminal offence, and can also render the share issue voidable.

When a company has allotted a share it must, within two months, issue a share certificate to the holder. This is evidence of ownership, and one certificate can cover a number of shares. The company must also keep a register of shareholders, normally at its registered office.

Once issued, shares can be transferred by the shareholder. For example, if the business prospers, the shares may increase in real value, and a shareholder may wish to sell his shares to someone else (at a profit to *himself*, not to the company). The company's capital is maintained; the shares are simply held by someone new. The procedure for transferring shares is set out in the Stock Transfer Act 1963, as amended: broadly, the share certificate and a stock transfer form are sent to the company's secretary, who alters the register and issues a new certificate to the new holder.

Shareholders may periodically be rewarded by the company by the payment of a *dividend* out of profits. This must come either from current profits, or from money set aside from the profits of previous years. If it were paid otherwise than from profits, it could be regarded as a payment out of capital, which generally is not permitted.

Another way in which a company can raise finance is by borrowing it. A document issued by a company evidencing a loan to it is called a *debenture*. Debenture holders are not members of the company, although they can acquire rights to influence management. Money borrowed is not strictly 'capital', although in practice it is often called 'loan capital'. It will be discussed in Unit 24.

C. Membership and management

Shareholders

We have seen that there are three ways in which someone can become a shareholder: the subscribers of the memorandum must each take at least one share; new shares may later be issued by the company; or the shareholder may have acquired existing shares from another holder.

The general position of shareholders is set out in the 1948 Act, section 20: '... the memorandum and articles shall, when registered, bind the company and the members thereof to the same extent as if they respectively had been signed and sealed by each member, and contained covenants on the part of each member to observe all the provisions of the memorandum and articles'. Shareholders, therefore, have rights, based on the memorandum and articles, as between themselves and the company, and as between themselves. Their rights also depend upon the terms of issue of the shares: some shares, for instance, carry voting rights while others do not. The following are some common types of share.

Ordinary shares usually carry rights to vote at company meetings, and therefore to take part in electing directors and in other management issues. Holders of ordinary shares are not, however, *entitled* to any dividend. The directors *may* (and usually will if they can) recommend at the annual general meeting that a stated dividend be paid that year. Shareholders then have a right to vote themselves a dividend up to, but not more than, that amount.

Holders of *preference shares*, on the other hand, *are* entitled to a fixed rate of dividend before anything becomes available for ordinary shareholders. Note, however, that even preference dividends can only be paid out of profits; no profits, no dividends. Moreover, the preference only extends to dividends. Unless the articles provide otherwise, preference shareholders receive no preferential repayment of capital on a winding up if, for example, the company is insolvent. Normally the articles give no voting rights to preference shareholders.

Different varieties of preference share exist. For example, preference shares are 'participating' if, in addition to the preferential dividend, the holders are also entitled to participate in the ordinary dividend, if one is declared. Unless otherwise provided, preference shares are presumed to be 'non-participating'. Preference shares are 'cumulative' if, should the preference dividend not be paid in one year, it is carried forward, so that in the next year all arrears of preference dividend must be paid before anyone else gets anything. Unless otherwise provided, preference shares *are* presumed cumulative.

If authorized by its articles, a company limited by shares can issue *redeemable* shares. Either the shareholder or the company can be empowered to insist that the shares be bought back by the company and, under the Companies Act 1981, both preference and ordinary shares can be made redeemable. Normally, redemption must be made either out of profits, or out of the proceeds of a new share issue made for the purpose. Exceptionally, a private company may also redeem or buy its own shares out of capital.

Company meetings

Shareholders can exercise their voting rights by voting on resolutions at company meetings.

There are two types of meeting. An *annual general meeting* ('a.g.m.') must be held initially within 18 months of incorporation, and thereafter at least once in every calendar year, with not more than 15 months between any two meetings. At least 21 days' notice of the a.g.m. must be given to members. Any other general meeting is an *extraordinary general meeting* ('e.g.m.'). Under Table A, directors can call an e.g.m. whenever they think fit. Furthermore, they *must* call one if holders of at least one-tenth of paid-up shares so demand. Those requiring the meeting must say why they want it, and at least 14 days' notice must be given to members.

The notice calling a general meeting must, under Table A, include details of any *special business* to be discussed there. All business at an e.g.m. is 'special'. At an a.g.m., standard items such as declaring a dividend, considering the accounts, balance sheets, directors' and auditors' reports, and electing directors to replace those retiring, are *ordinary business*, and need not be mentioned in the notice. Even at an a.g.m., however, anything else will be 'special' business.

Irrespective of the type of business, there are three different types of *resolution* at company meetings. *Ordinary resolutions* can be passed by a simple majority of those voting. It should be emphasized, however, that the normal rule is one vote *per share*, not one per person. Therefore, if one person holds most of the voting shares, he can determine what is passed and what is not. Sometimes the articles and terms of issue can give weighted voting rights, so that some shares carry several votes. Second, by the Companies Acts and/or the articles, some powers of shareholders can only be exercised by *extraordinary resolution*. This can only be passed by a three-quarters majority of votes cast. Notice of intention to move an extraordinary resolution must have been given when the meeting was called. Third, some things can only be done by *special resolution*—for example, altering the objects clause or the articles. Again a three-quarters majority is needed. Furthermore, in this case at least 21 days' notice of the resolution must be given to members, even if it is moved at an e.g.m. for which only 14 days' notice is required.

Finally, as we have seen, *notice* must be given of meetings and/or resolutions, and the periods of notice required vary. In some situations, for instance on a resolution to dismiss a director, *special notice* of 28 days must be given to the company, which must then give notice of the resolution to members when it calls the necessary general meeting.

Directors and other officers

Every company must have directors, who are the persons responsible for managing the company. The actual numbers depend upon the articles, but a public company must have at least two, and a private company at least one. No qualifications are needed, except that a director of a public company must retire at 70 unless either the articles, or a resolution of which special notice has been given specifying his age, provide otherwise. The court can disqualify a person from being or acting as a director for up to five years if he has been convicted of an offence under the Acts, and an undischarged bankrupt may not act as a director.

A director need not be a shareholder, although 'qualification' shares are often required by the articles in practice.

The first directors are those named in the statement filed with the memorandum. Subsequent elections normally take place at the a.g.m. Articles commonly provide that directors must retire or offer themselves for re-election every three years, with one-third doing so each year. Changes of directors must be notified to the Registrar of Companies.

Even if elected for a three-year term, directors can be removed at any time, under the 1948 Act, section 184, by an ordinary resolution of shareholders, with special notice. However, if a director holds voting shares, he can vote for himself.

> In *Bushell* v. *Faith* (1969), a director's shares validly gave him two votes per share on such a resolution, and this was enough to defeat the attempt to sack him.

Directors are not as such employees of the company, and they are not automatically entitled to payment. In practice, the articles often provide for directors to receive fees and expenses, and executive directors such as a 'managing director' often, in addition to being directors, have employment contracts under which they receive a salary.

Every company must also have a *company secretary*, who is the administrative officer responsible for meetings, notices, resolutions, records, registers, and accounts. A director, but not a sole director, may serve as secretary.

A company must keep a register of directors and secretaries at its registered office, and notify the Companies' Registrar of its contents. The register is open to public inspection. Detailed statutory provisions also require directors to disclose to the company and members matters such as their financial interests in this and connected companies.

Duties of directors

In addition to their duties to manage, the directors owe duties of good faith to the company. These duties are similar to those of partners (Unit 10), agents (Unit 26), or trustees (Unit 28). The following are some examples.

1. A director must not make a secret profit from his position.

> In *Boston Deep Sea Fishing and Ice Co.* v. *Ansell* (1888), a director received an undisclosed commission from the builders of a new boat for his company, and

undisclosed bonuses from a company supplying ice. After he had been dismissed as director, and his employment contract ended, he had to account to the company for the money.

2. A director must not allow an undisclosed conflict of interest to occur. For example, he must not take for himself contracts negotiated for the company.

In *Cook* v. *Deeks* (1916), the directors of a construction company negotiated a contract in the usual way, as if they were making it for the company. Then, however, they made the contract in their own names, and took the profit. They ultimately had to account to the company for the profit.

In *Regal* (*Hastings*) *Ltd* v. *Gulliver* (1967), the company bought and sold some cinemas at a profit. Some directors, who had also invested their own money in the project, shared in the profit without the knowledge or consent of the other shareholders. They had to account for their profits, which were only made because of knowledge and opportunities arising from their position as directors. (They could have protected themselves by making full disclosure and seeking the consent of the other shareholders in advance.)

Under the Companies Acts, a director who is in any way, directly or indirectly, 'interested' in a contract which the company is making must disclose his 'interest' to the board of directors and, if it is a substantial property transaction, to a general meeting. Failure to do so is an offence. Subject to this and the above common law and equitable rules, however, there is no reason why a director should not contract with his own company. It is *undisclosed* conflicts of interest which are unlawful.

3. Directors must exercise their powers for the *company's* benefit, not for their own or for any other ulterior motive. This has often arisen when shares are issued:

In *Piercy* v. *Mills Ltd* (1920), the directors issued extra voting shares to themselves and their supporters, not because the company needed the extra capital, but solely to prevent the election of rival directors. The share issue was held void.

In *Howard Smith Ltd* v. *Ampol Petroleum Ltd* (1974), the directors of M Ltd issued 4.5 million new shares to Smith Ltd, so as to change the balance of power in M Ltd. After the issue, the previous majority shareholder, Ampol, would no longer have a majority. The issue was set aside, because destroying Ampol's majority was not a proper motive for issuing shares.

4. Directors must show reasonable care and skill.

In *Re City Equitable Fire Insurance Co.* (1925), the managing director was able to defraud his own company partly because the ordinary directors were careless in not checking suspicious entries in the annual accounts. It was accepted that the negligence of the ordinary directors was a breach of their duties to the company.

Relations between members and management

Directors and officers owe their duties *to the company*, not to individual shareholders. Therefore, it is the company which must sue them if they break their duties, and if the company decides not to sue, then no further action can be taken. The company will not sue if the majority of votes in a general meeting resolve not to do so. Therefore, if the directors have the support of the majority of votes (or if they *have* the majority of votes), the wrong can be condoned.

> In *Foss* v. *Harbottle* (1843), two directors sold their own land to the company, allegedly for much more than its true value. Some shareholders tried to sue the directors, but the court would not hear the action. It was up to the company to decide whether or not to sue.

The rule in *Foss* v. *Harbottle* does not, however, allow the majority to get away with everything. In some situations, the court will hear an action by minority shareholders, even against the majority's wishes.

1. The majority cannot ratify something which is *ultra vires* the company; see *Ashbury Railway Carriage Co.* v. *Riche* (Unit 10). Even one shareholder can restrain an *ultra vires* act.
2. If the directors try to do something which requires a special or extraordinary resolution (with a three-quarters majority and appropriate notice) without first obtaining such a resolution, a *simple* majority cannot ratify it. To allow this would be to destroy the whole protection given to minorities by special or extraordinary resolutions, namely that a 26 per cent minority can defeat them.
3. Sometimes the directors may commit a wrong to the member personally, not to the company. If this occurs, the individual member can sue to protect his own rights.

> In *Pender* v. *Lushington* (1877), the chairman wrongfully refused to accept the votes of certain shareholders and, as a result, a resolution which they wished to oppose was passed. It was held that the chairman had infringed the shareholders' personal rights to vote, and the court granted them an injunction restraining the company from acting on the resolution.

4. The court will not permit a 'fraud on the minority'. 'Fraud' is used loosely here as meaning grossly inequitable conduct, not necessarily criminal.

> In *Cook* v. *Deeks* (page 99), the directors were made to account notwithstanding that, as majority shareholders, they had passed a resolution declaring that the company had no interest in the contract.

5. The court can also allow minority shareholders to sue to prevent directors from benefiting personally, at the company's expense, from their own negligence or misconduct.

> In *Daniels* v. *Daniels* (1978), it was alleged that the directors and majority shareholders had sold land belonging to the company to one member of the board for less than its value. It was sold by the company in 1970 for £4250, and re-sold by the director in 1974 for £120 000. It was held that, even though no fraud was alleged, a minority shareholder could sue the directors for breach of their duties.

Duties of majority shareholders

Unlike directors, shareholders as such owe no detailed duties of good faith to the company. Generally, they can exercise their powers for whatever motive they think fit. There are now, however, limits on this freedom. For example, as we have seen, the activities of directors cannot always be ratified by majority shareholders. Second, in altering the articles, it is established that shareholders must act in good faith for the benefit of the company. Third, oppression by the majority of the minority may be a ground for winding up the company. Fourth, a shareholder's powers are subject to equitable principles which may make it unjust to exercise them in a particular way.

> In *Clemens* v. *Clemens Bros Ltd* (1976), the defendant used her majority holding to pass resolutions issuing new shares, with the effect (and apparent motive) of increasing her own control, and reducing the plaintiff's holding to below 25 per cent. The court therefore set aside the resolutions.

D. The company and outsiders

Agency of directors and officers

Since a company is an artificial person and cannot do anything by itself, it must act through human beings. Most companies are larger than partnerships and, therefore, unlike in partnerships, not every member is presumed to have authority to act on a company's behalf. A shareholder as such, even a majority shareholder, has no implied authority to make contracts for the company. Even an individual director has no implied authority to bind the company. Most of a company's activities are carried on by the directors, acting as a board.

A company will normally be bound by the activities of its board of directors. This can be the case even if the board is acting outside of its actual powers under the articles, or even *ultra vires* the company. By the European Communities Act 1972, section 9(1):

> 'In favour of a person dealing with a company in good faith, any transaction decided on by the directors shall be deemed to be one which it is within the capacity of the company to enter into, and the power of the directors to bind the company shall be deemed to be free of any limitation under the memorandum or articles of association; and a party to a transaction so decided on shall not be bound to enquire as to the capacity of the company to enter into it or as to any such limitation on the powers of the directors . . .'

The company only escapes liability for the acts of the *board*, therefore, if it proves that the outsider knew or suspected that the board was exceeding its or the company's powers, so that the outsider was not in good faith.

Almost invariably, boards of directors delegate some of their powers. Some directors will be given executive responsibilities, either specific (sales director), or more general (managing director). Similarly, powers are often delegated to officers such as the company secretary. Such *executive* directors or officers *are* agents of the company, and do have authority to bind it. If a delegate such as a managing director is acting within the actual authority given him by the board, then section 9(1) can protect outsiders. The main legal difficulties have arisen where a director or officer has exceeded the actual authority given him by the board, or has no such authority. Is the company still bound? Several other rules can protect outsiders.

1. By the 1948 Act, section 180, the acts of a director or manager shall be valid notwithstanding any defect which may later be discovered in his *appointment* or

qualification. This is a limited provision, and does not cover either persons who purport to be executive directors without ever having been appointed at all, or who, having been properly appointed, exceed their actual authority.

2. If an outsider has no means of checking, he is entitled to assume that the internal procedures of the company have been properly carried out.

> In *Royal British Bank Ltd* v. *Turquand* (1855), two directors borrowed money on behalf of the company. They only had authority to borrow on such terms if they had first been authorized to do so by an ordinary resolution of members, and no such resolution had been passed. Nevertheless the company was bound to repay the loan, because the lender—who had no means of checking—was entitled to assume that the proper resolution had been passed.

3. In any event, an executive such as a managing director has, from his position, certain *implied* powers. An outsider is entitled to assume that such a director or officer, acting within his 'usual' authority, can in fact bind the company. The company will only escape liability if (a) the director or officer has no actual authority, and (b) there were suspicious circumstances which should have made the outsider enquire further.

> In *Panorama Developments Ltd* v. *Fidelis Furnishing Fabrics Ltd* (1971), the company secretary of Fidelis Ltd hired cars in the company's name, but used them for his own purposes. Although he had no authority from the board to do this, the company had to pay the bill. It was quite usual for a senior officer such as the secretary to hire cars for the firm, to meet important visitors, for example, and there was nothing to make the car company suspect that the secretary was acting outside his actual authority.

4. Furthermore, if a company has previously honoured contracts made by someone on its behalf, or has otherwise 'held him out' as having authority to bind the company, it may be estopped from denying his authority. The company may be bound by future unauthorized contracts which he makes.

> In *Freeman and Lockyer* v. *Buckhurst Park Properties Ltd* (1964), the board of B Ltd had allowed one of its number, K, to act as if he were managing director, although he had never been appointed to that position. The board had previously honoured contracts made by K, but now claimed not to be bound by a contract which he made with the plaintiffs. It was held that (a) B Ltd was estopped from denying that K was managing director, and (b) it was within the usual powers of a managing director to make such contracts. Therefore, B Ltd was bound.

Personal liability of members

We have seen in Unit 10 that fully paid-up shareholders in a company have no liability for the company's debts. There are only a few exceptions to this, two of which are the following.

1. Under the 1948 Act, section 31, if a company carries on business without at least two members for six months, then the remaining member is personally liable for the company's debts incurred thereafter, if he knows that he is the only member.

Creditors can sue the company and/or the member personally. (This section can affect a 'parent' company which owns *all* of the shares in a subsidiary.)
2. Under the 1948 Act, section 332(1), if in the course of winding up a company, it appears that any business has been carried on with intent to defraud creditors, or for any fraudulent purpose, the court may declare that persons knowingly party to such 'fraudulent trading' shall be personally responsible for all or any of the company's debts or liabilities.

E. Public controls over companies

Companies have the privileges of separate legal personality and, usually, limited liability. In return, public controls are imposed, largely requiring disclosure and publication of material regarding membership, management, debts, and financial position generally. The purpose is mainly to protect members, creditors, and those dealing with the company. The following are some examples.

1. *Annual returns.* The Acts require a company to submit a detailed 'annual return' within 42 days after each a.g.m. (except in the year of incorporation). The returns must contain, for example, current particulars of members and officers, shares issued, and charges on the company's property. There must also be certified copies of balance sheets, profit and loss accounts, and auditors' and directors' reports.
2. *Registers* of various kinds must be kept at the company's registered office and/or at the Companies Registry. Examples are mentioned at several places in this unit. Most registers can be inspected by members and, in some instances, by outsiders. Accounts must also be kept, usually at the registered office, but these are normally only open to inspection by directors.
3. *Inspection and investigation.* The Department of Trade has wide powers under the Acts to inspect a company's books, and to conduct far-reaching investigations of its affairs if need be.

F. Winding up

Voluntary winding up

The shareholders can resolve at any time to end ('wind up') the company. The resolution must usually be a special one, needing a three-quarters majority. Alternatively an extraordinary resolution may be passed that the company is insolvent and should be wound up.

The job of winding up is carried out by a *liquidator* (unlike a partnership, which is dissolved by the members themselves). The liquidator's tasks are (a) to settle lists of contributories, (b) to collect the company's assets, (c) to pay off its creditors, and (d) to distribute any surplus to the contributories. The 'contributories' are present and past shareholders who, if the shares were not fully paid up, would have to contribute towards payments of debts. For practical purposes today, the relevant contributories are the current shareholders, and they will not in fact have to contribute if the shares are fully paid.

If the directors have made a statutory declaration that the company can within 12 months pay its debts in full, and filed this with the Registrar, matters will proceed as a *members' voluntary winding up*. The members appoint the liquidator, who is responsible to them. If the directors are unable to make a 'declaration of solvency', then it will be a *creditors' voluntary winding up*. The liquidator may be appointed by the creditors, and will largely be responsible to them.

Compulsory winding up

A petition may be presented to the court by the company itself, the Department of Trade or, most commonly, by a creditor, asking that the company be wound up by the court. There are various grounds on which such a petition may be granted, the most important being that the company cannot pay its debts, or that 'it is just and equitable that the company should be wound up'; see *Ebrahimi* v. *Westbourne Galleries*, and *Re Yenidje Tobacco* (Unit 10).

If a winding up order is made, a court officer, the Official Receiver, acts as liquidator unless and until the creditors or shareholders apply for the appointment of another. Having realized the assets, the receiver or liquidator pays debts in the following order:

1. Costs of winding up.
2. Preferential debts, such as rates and tax arrears for the last year, up to three months' arrears of employees' wages, to an £800 maximum, and arrears of national insurance contributions.
3. If all preferred creditors have been paid in full, the remaining money goes to pay off ordinary creditors.

If there is not enough to pay off any category, each gets a dividend of so much in the pound. If anything remains after ordinary creditors are fully paid, it goes in repayment of capital, and then division among shareholders.

Secured creditors are in a fortunate position in that they are entitled to payment in full from the proceeds of sale of the asset charged, before anyone else gets any part of that money.

The court can order that a winding up which started voluntarily shall be conducted thenceforth under the court's supervision. Such an order is rare today.

For further consideration

1. (a) If you and a friend were starting a small company and needed extra money, discuss the factors which would influence you in deciding whether to issue further shares, or debentures.
   (b) Distinguish between nominal capital and issued capital.

2. What controls can shareholders exercise over the directors of a company limited by shares? In particular, discuss the position of the holders of
   (a) one share
   (b) 30 per cent of the shares
   (c) 51 per cent of the shares
3. To what extent do the following have power to make contracts on behalf of the company?
   (a) The holder of one share
   (b) The holder of 60 per cent of the shares
   (c) A single director
   (d) The board of directors
   In each instance, discuss whether the company would be bound by what was purportedly done on its behalf.
4. Distinguish between
   (a) a voluntary winding up and a compulsory winding up, and
   (b) a members' voluntary winding up and a creditors' voluntary winding up.
5. Explain briefly the meaning of
   (a) p.l.c.
   (b) Objects clause
   (c) Prospectus
   (d) Dividend
   (e) Preference share
   (f) Special resolution
   (g) Extraordinary general meeting
   (h) Annual return

Unit 12. Liability for Wrongful Acts

A. Crimes and torts

The many activities carried on in society by individuals and groups inevitably lead to conflicts. As society has become more complex, so have the potential areas of conflict become more numerous. Conflicts may arise, for example, between competing businesses, out of the ownership and use of property, or out of the relationships between individuals.

As has been noted in Unit 1, the law meets this problem in two main ways. First, certain conduct is deemed to be so undesirable that the law prohibits it and makes it a criminal offence. Second, certain conduct harms other members of society, and the rules of civil law provide for the victim to receive compensation or some other appropriate civil remedy. Breach of contract and its remedies will be discussed in Units 16–22. The law of tort is concerned with other types of conduct which give the victim a right to a civil remedy.

There is often a large overlap between crime and tort. If a criminal act harms the victim, it will usually be a tort as well, thus making the offender liable to be prosecuted, and also to be sued for damages by the victim. Thus the factory occupier who fails to fence dangerous machinery both commits a criminal offence and, if an employee is injured, commits a tort against the employee. He may also be liable to the employee for breach of contract, because he owes a duty, under the contract of employment, to provide a reasonably safe system of work.

A second preliminary point must be made. Not all undesirable conduct, however much we disapprove of it, is necessarily either a crime or a tort. Thus if a builder erects a block of flats on the field behind your house, he may not only ruin your view, but also cause your house to fall in value. Nevertheless, the builder has probably committed neither a crime nor a tort. A similar situation arises where a new supermarket deliberately cuts prices with the sole intention of driving the old corner shop out of business, thereby depriving the shop-owner of his livelihood. No one is a criminal unless he has committed one or more of the crimes recognized by law; similarly, no one can be liable in tort unless he has committed one or more of the recognized torts.

The remainder of this unit will be devoted to an outline of the principles of liability in tort, and the following three units will deal with details of specific torts.

B. Liability in tort

Infringement of rights

The law recognizes certain rights, both personal and in respect of property, and will protect them against infringement, not by punishing the wrongdoer in a criminal court, but by compelling him to pay damages to the victim. In appropriate cases the court will issue an injunction, restraining the wrongdoer from repeating his act.

The infringement of one of these rights is known as a tort. Thus interference with the person of another causing physical harm could give rise to an action for the torts of battery or negligence. Damaging the reputation of another could lead to an action for defamation. Interests in land are protected by the torts of trespass and nuisance, and interests in goods by trespass to goods and conversion.

Liability in tort normally requires an element of fault or blame on the part of the wrongdoer or 'tortfeasor'. The plaintiff must show that the act or, in a few cases the omission, was committed either intentionally or negligently. On the other hand there are a few torts which may arise without fault. These are known as torts of strict liability, where a person acts at his peril and will be obliged to compensate for any injury he causes, irrespective of whether or not the plaintiff can prove that he is to blame. Examples arise in the case of dangerous things escaping from land (*Rylands* v. *Fletcher*), dangerous animals, and breach of some statutory duties (see later).

Loss suffered by the plaintiff

An essential element of most torts is that the plaintiff must have suffered some physical or financial harm as a result of the defendant's conduct. Thus if someone drives negligently, he does not necessarily commit the tort of negligence against anyone. It is only if the negligent driver harms or injures someone that the tort has been committed.

There are still some torts, however, where the defendant's wrongful act itself is sufficient to constitute the tort, without the plaintiff having to show loss. Notable examples are the torts of trespass and libel. These are said to be actionable *per se*, i.e., for themselves, without proof of loss. The man who stands on your lawn without your permission commits the tort of trespass even if he does not damage the lawn in any way. Although an action may lie in theory in such a case, it might not be worth while to sue for, with no loss, damages are likely to be nominal.

However, it must again be emphasized that merely causing harm to someone does not necessarily amount to a tort if there is no infringement of a legal right. In many situations it is impossible to act without causing loss to someone. Every sale by a shopkeeper means one less for his competitors.

> In *Bradford Corporation* v. *Pickles* (1895), the defendant, in order to induce the corporation to buy his land at a high price, dug wells and extracted water that would otherwise have found its way into the town's water supply. Although the corporation had suffered loss, there had been no infringement of a legal right, for Pickles had only done what he was fully entitled to do on his own land.

This case illustrates a further principle that, in general, the motive or reason why an act is done is not relevant in the law of torts. With few exceptions, good motive will not excuse an otherwise wrongful act nor, as in this case, will an improper motive change a lawful act into a tort.

Vicarious liability

In some situations a person may be held responsible for torts committed by others, even though the wrongful act was no fault of his. This is known as vicarious liability. Thus, a principal may be liable for the torts of his agent, and a partner may be liable for the torts of another partner in connection with the partnership business. The owner of a car may be liable for another who is driving with the owner's permission and for the owner's benefit or purposes. The most important example is the liability of an employer for the torts of his servant committed by the latter in the course of employment.

> In *Lloyd* v. *Grace, Smith & Co.* (1912), a firm of solicitors were held liable when their managing clerk, while dealing with some property in the course of his duties, fraudulently induced a client to make over the property to him. The partners had employed the clerk to convey property, and were therefore liable to their client when the clerk did so dishonestly.

The fact that an employer is vicariously liable does not affect the liability of the original wrongdoer. Thus, in *Lloyd* v. *Grace, Smith & Co.*, the client could have sued the clerk instead of the partners. Since employers are more likely to be able to pay the damages, the action is usually brought against the employer.

The vicarious liability of an employer depends upon two conditions.
1. The employer is only liable for torts committed by his *employees*. The wrongdoer must, therefore, have been acting under a contract of employment, and not have been, for instance, an independent contractor. Usually this distinction is fairly simple; a chauffeur is an employee, a taxi-driver is an independent contractor. Not all cases are so simple however, for example, whether a consultant surgeon is an employee of the hospital authority or an independent contractor. The old test of whether a person was an employee or an independent contractor was based upon the right of an employer to tell an employee not only what to do but also how to do

it. In the case of an independent contractor there was no such control over the manner of performance and hence if anything went wrong, the employer was not liable. Today, the courts will also take into account other factors such as the power to appoint and dismiss, whether payment is on a time or job basis, whether the times of working are specified, and the payment of national insurance contributions and income tax.

2. Assuming that the wrongdoer is an employee, the employer is only vicariously liable for torts committed by the wrongdoer *in the course of his employment*. The tort must be an authorized act, or a wrongful way of doing what is authorized, or something necessarily incidental to what is authorized. The test is whether the servant has done what he is employed to do, even though he was employed to do the act carefully and honestly and he has done it negligently or dishonestly.

Liability cannot be avoided merely by prohibiting a particular way of working, for this will be ineffective so far as an injured third party is concerned.

> In *Limpus* v. *London General Omnibus Co.* (1862), the bus driver had printed instructions not to race with or obstruct the buses of a rival company. In breach of these instructions, the driver did obstruct a rival bus, and caused a collision which damaged it. His employer was held vicariously liable. At the time of the collision, the driver was doing what he was employed to do, namely driving the bus. He was simply doing so disobediently.

There will be no vicarious liability, however, if the servant departs from the course of employment by engaging on 'a frolic of his own', or if the wrongful act is completely unconnected with the employment.

> In *Warren* v. *Henlys Ltd* (1948), a garage attendant thought wrongly that a customer was driving away without paying. A quarrel ensued, which ended when the attendant punched the driver. It was held that the garage company was not vicariously liable for the attendant's assault. He was not employed to punch customers, and the blow arose from his personal feelings during the quarrel rather than the exercise of his duties.

The torts of an independent contractor do not as a general rule give rise to vicarious liability, but there are a number of qualifications and exceptions.

1. Where strict liability is imposed by law on some person, he cannot escape this by delegating work to another. Thus, if I build a dam on my land, I am strictly liable to anyone harmed should a rush of water escape on to someone else's land (see *Rylands* v. *Fletcher*, later). It will be no defence that the water escaped only due to the fault of the independent contractor who built the dam. Strict liability also arises for breach of various statutory duties, for instance some of the duties under the Factories Act 1961.
2. Where a contractor is engaged to do work on or adjoining a highway, then the person who engages the contractor is strictly liable for torts causing danger on the highway committed by the contractor.
3. Where a contractor is engaged to do something ultra-hazardous there is a similar exception.

4. The person who engages the contractor will be vicariously liable if he previously authorizes or subsequently ratifies what the contractor has done
5. A person can also be liable for his own negligence in selecting an incompetent contractor, or in not giving adequate instructions.

Indemnity

Where an employer has to pay damages because of the tort of his employee, the employer has a right to *contribution* or *indemnity* from the employee under the Law Reform (Married Women and Tortfeasors) Act 1935. This right also arises in other instances of vicarious liability.

> In *Lister* v. *Romford Ice and Cold Storage Co. Ltd* (1957), Lister was employed as a lorry driver. He reversed the lorry carelessly, and injured his father, who recovered damages from the employer. The employer (at the insistence of the insurance company) sued Lister for indemnity, which he obtained.

C. Defences

It is always possible for a defendant to argue simply that the alleged tort has not been committed. In the case of torts requiring proof that loss was caused to the plaintiff, he may also argue, for example, that his negligence or misconduct did not cause such loss. The plaintiff may be the sole author of his own misfortune.

> In *McWilliams* v. *Sir William Arrol & Co. Ltd* (1962), a steel erector fell to his death. His employer had not provided a safety belt, but evidence was given that he would not have worn one even had it been provided. The employers were held not liable because, on this evidence, their failure was not the cause of death.

Certain torts have special defences, particularly the tort of defamation, and these will be dealt with in later units. The following are the 'general' defences that may be raised in actions to almost all torts.

Statutory authority

Nothing authorized by statute is unlawful. Much, therefore, depends upon the interpretation of the statute, which may sanction an act even though it involves what would otherwise be a tort. Thus British Rail, which has statutory authority to run the railways, could not be sued for making such noise as is an inevitable result of running a railway, even though, but for the statutory authority, this might constitute the tort of nuisance.

On the other hand, the courts are reluctant to hold that Parliament authorized a harmful act unless the statute is quite unambiguous. So, if the statute gives someone power to do something, the courts will assume that the power was given only on the understanding that it be exercised carefully.

In *Fisher* v. *Ruislip-Northwood UDC* (1945), the local authority had, by statute, been given power to erect air-raid shelters on the highway. In the black-out, Fisher drove his motor cycle into such a shelter, and was injured. When sued for the tort of public nuisance, the Council pleaded that they had statutory authority to put up the shelter. The defence failed, because the Council could, even in the black-out, have put up small, shaded warning lights for motorists. They only had statutory authority on condition that they exercised it with care for the safety of others.

Similarly, in *Metropolitan Asylum District* v. *Hill* (1881), the authority had statutory power to erect a smallpox hospital. They chose to put it in a residential part of Hampstead, and it was held that statutory authority was no defence. They could have exercised their powers so as to cause much less danger.

It is presumed that an act authorized by statute will be carried out with reasonable care and statutory authority is therefore no defence if there is negligence. It should also be noted that when a statute takes away a right of action, it may at the same time make provision for some compensation to be paid.

Inevitable accident

The defendant pleads here that he did not intend that act in question and that it was caused by something over which he had no control, and which he could not reasonably have foreseen.

In *National Coal Board* v. *J. E. Evans Ltd* (1951), the defendants damaged an electric cable during excavations, but were held not liable since they did not know of the existence of the cable and had no reason or opportunity to know of it.

This defence does not apply to torts of strict liability which do not depend upon establishing fault. Accident, where there is no intention, must be distinguished from mistake, where there is an intended act but it is based upon a mistaken belief. Mistake is generally no defence.

Act of God

This is similar to inevitable accident except that the cause of the act under consideration is some natural phenomenon and no human element is involved. This defence has only been accepted in one reported case.

In *Nichols* v. *Marsland* (1876), exceptionally heavy rainfall caused three artificial lakes to burst, and the flood water destroyed four bridges on the plaintiff's land. It was held that there was no liability.

Consent

If a person consents to suffer damage or run the risk of it, he cannot later bring an action. This is expressed in the maxim *volenti non fit injuria*, or willing assumption of risk. The risk may be assumed by express agreement, for example, by giving consent to an operation, or may be implied from the circumstances, as by participating in a vigorous game.

> In *Hall* v. *Brooklands Racing Club* (1933), a spectator who was injured while watching a motor race was held to have agreed to take the risk of such injury.

It is not sufficient to prove that the plaintiff knew of the risk; there must be evidence of a willing consent to undergo it. For this reason the defence has failed when pleaded by employers in actions brought by employees for injuries suffered at work. The courts have demanded evidence of positive consent as opposed to mere acquiescence, and the nature of the employer–worker relationship has made this impossible.

> In *Bowater* v. *Rowley Regis Corporation* (1944), a carter was injured by a dangerous horse which he took out under orders after protesting. It was held that he had not genuinely consented to run the risk.

> In *Smith* v. *Charles Baker & Sons* (1891), a workman was injured by falling stone when he worked under an overhead crane. He had not objected, even though he must have known it was dangerous. He recovered damages nevertheless. His silence was evidence of acquiescence, not necessarily of consent.

This defence will also fail in 'rescue' cases where the plaintiff acted under a strong moral compulsion, if not a legal one.

> In *Haynes* v. *Harwood* (1935), a policeman succeeded in his claim for damages when he was injured while stopping a runaway horse and cart which was endangering the safety of people, including children, in a crowded street. He would not have been injured if he had stayed out of the way, but he intervened under a moral duty and could hardly be said to have freely consented. The legal position would have been different if he had acted in a similar voluntary manner in a country lane with no people about.

Finally, the defence of consent may be excluded by statute on grounds of public policy. The Road Traffic Act 1972 prevents a car driver from raising this defence against a passenger who has suffered injury by reason of his negligent driving.

Contributory negligence

Although this defence is normally raised to actions for negligence, it is also applicable to other torts. It arises when damage is suffered partly by the fault of the defendant and partly by the fault of the plaintiff. The defendant, therefore, attempts to reduce the damages by proving the plaintiff partly responsible for the injury. The Law Reform (Contributory Negligence) Act 1945 provides that in such cases the court shall reduce the damages by an amount proportionate to the plaintiff's share of responsibility. Thus if damages are assessed at £100 and the plaintiff is 30 per cent to blame, he will receive only £70.

> In *Sayers* v. *Harlow UDC* (1958), Mrs Sayers found herself locked in a public lavatory. Unable to summon help, she tried to climb out over the top of the door. She found this impossible and, when climbing back down, allowed her weight to rest on the toilet roll which 'true to its mechanical requirement, rotated'. Mrs Sayers fell and was injured. It was

held that 75 per cent of her injury was the fault of the Council for providing a defective lock which jammed, and 25 per cent was her own fault.

In *Stapley* v. *Gypsum Mines Ltd* (1953), two miners who worked, in breach of instructions, under a dangerous roof were held 80 per cent contributorily negligent.

D. Parties

Subject to only a few exceptions, everyone may sue or be sued in tort and may also be liable to criminal prosecution. The legal rules applicable to some of these exceptional cases have already been mentioned in Unit 10. Thus, the Crown may now be sued as defendant in an action in tort but foreign sovereigns, ambassadors and their staffs may avoid liability for a civil action by claiming 'diplomatic immunity'. Formerly, it was not normally possible for husbands and wives to sue each other in tort but the Law Reform (Husband and Wife) Act 1962 made this possible.

Consideration will now be given to the more important of the remaining exceptions.

1. *Minors*, as a general rule, are fully liable for torts which they commit, but there are some instances where they may avoid liability. In the first place, the courts will not allow the minor's liability in tort to be used as an indirect way of obtaining a remedy for a contract which would be unenforceable against the minor (Unit 18).

    In *Leslie Ltd* v. *Shiell* (1914), a minor fraudulently pretended to be of age in order to obtain a loan of money. The lender could not sue on the contract of loan, so he sued the minor for the tort of deceit. It was held that this was merely an indirect attempt to recover for breach of contract, and the action therefore failed.

On the other hand, if the infant does something quite outside the contract, then the general rule applies and he can be liable in tort.

   In *Ballet* v. *Mingay* (1943), a minor had an amplifier under a contract of loan. He could not have been sued for the torts of detinue or conversion for simply refusing to return the goods. He was held liable in tort, however, for parting with the goods to someone else, because this was quite outside the original contract of loan.

Second, a minor may escape liability if the tort requires a mental element, as with fraud and negligence, and the minor is too young for this to be present. A minor who is alleged to have been negligent will be judged by what might reasonably have been expected of a person of that age and not by what might have been expected of an adult. Thus a minor may escape liability where an adult would not.

A parent or guardian is not in general liable for the torts of a minor. If the minor is employed by his parent and commits a tort in the course of his employment, the parent will be liable as would any employer. A parent will also be liable if the parent's *own* negligence contributed to the tort, as in the case of *Bebee* v. *Sales* (1916) when a 15-year-old boy was allowed to use an airgun without proper control.

A minor may sue if injured by a tortious act. In addition, the Congenital Disabilities (Civil Liability) Act 1976 now clarifies the law and gives a right of

action for pre-natal injuries where the child is subsequently born disabled. The child's mother is exempted from liability except where she is negligent in driving a motor vehicle.
2. *Trade unions* enjoyed almost complete immunity from actions in tort as a result of the Trade Disputes Act 1906, and their members were protected against certain torts committed in contemplation or furtherance of a trade dispute. The Industrial Relations Act 1971 took away this protection from unregistered unions but the Trade Union and Labour Relations Act 1974 largely restored the pre-1971 position.
3. In order to protect the administration of justice, judges, advocates, jurors, and witnesses have substantial immunity for otherwise defamatory statements made in the course of proceedings. Judges, police officers, gaolers, and bailiffs also have protection when making or executing court orders.

Joint wrongdoers

A joint tort arises when a tort is committed by two or more persons acting together, for example, if A and B assault or defraud C. Liability is said to be joint and several, in that the plaintiff may sue both of the tortfeasors, or each separately, or only one of them. If A is sued and cannot pay, another action can be brought against B, provided that the total damages recovered do not exceed the amount awarded in the first action.

If A has to pay the whole of the damages to C, A can claim a *contribution* from B. The court will, if called upon to do so, apportion liability as between A and B, either in the course of the original claim by C, or at a separate action by A against B. In some cases, B might be ordered to *indemnify* A completely. None of this, however, affects C's right to claim the whole amount from either of the defendants.

Effect of death

It has been assumed so far that both parties are alive at the time the action is brought. Problems may arise if one is dead, either as a result of the wrongful act or otherwise.

At one time, death effectively put an end to actions in tort by reason of two common law rules. One provided that the causing of death should not give rise to an action on the grounds that no one should profit out of another's death, and the second provided that a personal action died with the person. The effect of the first rule was the anomalous situation that a tort causing injury was actionable but not one causing death, so that it could be cheaper to kill than to maim. The resulting hardship to dependants and the increase in the number of deaths from railway accidents led to the Fatal Accidents Act 1846.

The Fatal Accidents Acts 1846–1976 now provide that, if the deceased could have sued had he lived, his dependants will have a right of action arising from his death.

The right to sue is limited to certain classes of dependants, similar to those who can claim on intestacy (see Unit 29), who can claim for monetary loss that they have suffered as a result of the death. Thus a wife may claim for the maintenance and support she could have expected from her husband, and a husband may claim if the death of his wife obliges him to incur expense by employing someone to look after his children.

There still remained the second rule, which prevented a claim for things such as pain and suffering and loss of expectation of life which could have been claimed by the deceased had he lived. Furthermore, the death of the tortfeasor put an end to a plaintiff's claim. The increase in the number of road deaths led to the Law Reform (Miscellaneous Provisions) Act 1934 which provides that, on the death of any person, any causes of action existing in favour of or against him shall survive and exist in favour of or against his estate. Thus if A injures B and B dies, the estate of B may, in general, sue A for all that B could have claimed had he lived. On the other hand, if A were the one to die, his estate would be liable to B to the same extent as if he had lived. A few personal actions, in particular defamation, are excluded and are still brought to an end by the death of either party.

If the victim of a tort dies, therefore, two possible claims arise, one by the dependants under the 1846 Act, as amended, and one by the estate under the 1934 Act. The two claims are quite distinct even though in practice they may be settled in the same action. If the same people are to benefit under both claims, an adjustment will be made to prevent duplication of damages. It can be to the advantage of the dependents to claim as much as possible under the Fatal Accidents Acts, since these damages go directly to the dependants and not into the estate of the deceased, and are therefore not liable to capital transfer tax payable on death.

E. Remedies

Damages

The principal remedy in tort is an award of *damages* to compensate the injured party for the loss he has suffered. The aim is to put the plaintiff back in his original position so far as money is able to do this. This can frequently be done satisfactorily where property has been damaged by assessing the value of the things destroyed or the cost of repairs.

Injuries to the person present more difficulties, for much depends upon the individual in question. Fixed tariffs for compensation cannot be laid down and many things must be considered in attempting to arrive at an assessment of loss. These include pain and suffering, loss of ability to pursue previous activities or interests, loss of actual and prospective earnings, medical expenses and, in cases of severe injury, shortening of expectation of life. Payments received from other sources such as national insurance benefits must be taken into account, and compensation for loss of earnings adjusted for taxation. Although damages are occasionally assessed by a jury, it is usual for this to be done today by a judge sitting alone. Appeals may be made against the amount of damages awarded, but the Court of Appeal is reluctant to interfere unless there has been an obvious error in the assessment.

Damages for loss of expectation of life presented particular difficulty until the House of Lords laid down certain rules in the case of *Benham* v. *Gambling* (1941), when the damages awarded in respect of the death of a child of two in a road accident were reduced from £1200 to £200. The House held that in such cases the basis of the award was not the length of time that the deceased might have been expected to live, but the probable prospects of happiness of which that person had been deprived. Damages for a young child should therefore be smaller since no confident estimate can then be made of prospects of happiness.

Other remedies

In some situations, as with threatened or repeated trespass or nuisance, damages will not provide an adequate remedy. The court may then, at its discretion, grant an *injunction* ordering the defendant to refrain from committing or repeating the wrongful act. If the length of time before the case can come to trial might lead to irreparable damage being caused, it is possible to apply for an interlocutory or temporary injunction which will either be confirmed or discharged at the later trial.

Remoteness of damage

It is possible for a wrongful act to give rise to a succession of events ultimately terminating in injury to another, but the tortfeasor will only be liable if that injury is not too remote. The general rule is that only damage which was reasonably foreseeable may be recovered.

> In the *Wagon Mound Case* (1961), a ship negligently discharged oil while bunkering, and the oil was carried under a wharf. A piece of cotton waste floating on the oil was set alight by sparks from welding operations. The oil caught fire and the wharf was severely damaged. The action failed because the fire was not reasonably foreseeable, particularly since expert opinion was that oil would not ignite under these conditions.

If, however, the type of damage is foreseeable, there will be liability for its full extent, even though the consequences are much more serious than could have been anticipated.

> In *Smith* v. *Leech Brain & Co. Ltd* (1962), a labourer was splashed and burned by a piece of molten metal and, because of an existing pre-malignant condition, died later of cancer. It was held that the damage was not too remote since the burn was foreseeable, even though the ultimate consequences were not.

It is sometimes said that the defendant must take his victims as he finds them, in the sense that if a (slight) injury was foreseeable and the victim has, for example, a thin skull, there will be liability for all the (serious) consequences.

The damage will be too remote if the chain of events is broken by some independent or new act intervening between the wrongful act and the resulting injury (*novus actus interveniens*) over which the defendant has no control. A defendant whose negligence caused a road accident will not normally be liable for further injury suffered by the victim which is caused by negligent hospital treatment. The intervening act must be a conscious and independent act. It must not be an instinctive, or even a reasonable, attempt to deal with the danger which the defendant has created.

> In *Sayers* v. *Harlow UDC*, mentioned earlier, the defendants pleaded that Mrs Sayers's attempt to climb over the door was a *novus actus interveniens*, so that it was this, and not the defective lock, which caused her injury. This defence failed.

Limitation of actions

The Limitation Act 1980 provides that in general no action in tort may be brought after six years have elapsed. There are exceptions to this period, in particular, 12 years are allowed for the recovery of land, whereas an action which includes a claim for damages for personal injuries or which arises from a fatal accident must be brought within three years.

The time is calculated from the date when the cause of action accrued, that is from the date when the action could first have been brought. In some cases of personal injuries, however, the harmful effects of the wrongful act may not become apparent until after the three-year period has expired. The Acts accordingly permit an action on an otherwise statute-barred claim for three years after the discovery of material facts of which the plaintiff had not previously been aware. There are also similar rules to those in contract for extending the period on account of a disability such as minority or insanity, or of fraud.

For further consideration

1. Charles is injured when unroping a load of timber which has been delivered to his employer's factory. Discuss the validity of the following defences which may be raised by the employer if Charles sues for damages.
   (a) The accident was caused by a defect in the rope which could not have been discovered by a reasonable inspection.
   (b) Charles willingly accepted what he knew to be a dangerous job.
   (c) Charles was at fault for not waiting for the load to be inspected to see that it was safe.
2. Rich engages two labourers, A and B, to demolish a house and enters into a contract with E under which E is to remove certain electrical fittings. A, B, and E are to receive a higher payment if the work is speedily completed and they set to work without taking proper safety precautions. In consequence, V, who is passing by, is injured. Discuss the liability of the parties involved for V's injuries.

3. The law of tort provides compensation for loss suffered in consequence of other people's actions. This may put a heavy burden of proof on the victim who may or may not recover damages. Consider the advantages and disadvantages of introducing a state insurance scheme under which accidents are automatically compensated. What problems would arise and how might these be solved?
4. (a) A tort is committed and the victim dies. Can an award of damages be made to his estate? If so, for what loss?
   (b) Can an award of damages to his estate be justified when the deceased is not alive to receive the benefit of compensation for an injury which he alone has suffered?

Unit 13. Negligence and Breach of Statutory Duty

A. The tort of negligence

Negligence is perhaps the most important of all torts, affecting many aspects of life. It arises when damage is caused to the person or property of another by failure to take such care as the law requires in the circumstances of the case. To succeed in an action for negligence, the plaintiff must prove three things.

1. The defendant owed him a legal duty of care.
2. The duty was broken.
3. Damage was suffered in consequence.

Each of these requirements will be discussed further.

1. The duty of care

There are many situations where a legal duty of care has been recognized as existing, for example, the duty of one road user towards another and of an employer towards his employees. These situations have been extended and added to by judicial decisions. In the case of *Donoghue* v. *Stevenson* (1932) (see later), Lord Atkin tried to replace this piecemeal approach to the law of negligence by suggesting a general duty of care which could be applied to all situations. His view was that reasonable care should always be taken to avoid injury to your 'neighbour', that is, to any person closely affected by your conduct, and whom you should *reasonably foresee* might be injured by it.

This 'neighbour' principle has been increasingly accepted and applied by the courts during the past 50 years, particularly in novel situations. It has now become the general test for determining whether or not a duty of care exists and perhaps the outstanding example of its application came in 1964.

> In *Hedley Byrne* v. *Heller and Partners* (1964), a firm of advertising agents gave credit to a client in reliance upon a banker's reference, and suffered loss when the client became insolvent. The reference had been given carelessly but, since the bank had expressly disclaimed liability when giving it, the action failed. Nevertheless, the House of Lords stated that, contrary to what had previously been believed, liability for negligence may extend to careless words as well as to careless deeds and that damages may be awarded for financial loss as well as for physical injury to persons and property.

It remains to be seen how these rules will develop. Since the *Hedley Byrne* case it is clear that a professional man, such as a banker, solicitor or accountant, owes a duty of care not only to his own client who employs or pays him, but also to another whom he knows is relying on his skill. On the other hand, there are still situations where no duty is owed for statements, for example, where the statement was made casually in circumstances where it is unlikely to be relied on, or if it is made by someone who could claim no special professional knowledge of what he is talking about.

> In *Mutual Life Assurance* v. *Evatt* (1971), the insurance company made negligent statements to Mr Evatt about the financial state of an associated company. In reliance on this, Mr Evatt invested money in the other company, and as a result suffered loss. It was held that he could not recover damages. The insurance company and its employees were not professional advisers on investment, and therefore owed no duty of care to Mr Evatt.

However, there are still exceptions to the 'neighbour' principle where, although harm is foreseeable, no duty exists. Thus a limited duty only is owed to trespassers, and a barrister owes no duty to those for whom he acts as advocate. It would seem that considerations of public policy may also influence decisions on the existence or otherwise of a duty.

> In *Rondel* v. *Worsley* (1969), the plaintiff, who had been convicted of causing grievous bodily harm, brought an action against his barrister on the grounds that he would have been acquitted if his case had been conducted properly. The House of Lords held that, despite the decision in the *Hedley Byrne* case, no action lay against a barrister for professional negligence in the conduct of a case. It was said to be in the public interest that this immunity should be preserved and that a case should not be retried by hearing an action against a barrister who appeared in it.

The present attitude of the courts to this matter was summarized in *Anns* v. *Merton London Borough Council* (1978) by Lord Wilberforce who said that it was no longer necessary to bring the facts of the situation within those of previous situations where a duty had been held to exist. Instead, there were two stages: to establish first whether the 'neighbour' principle applied and, if so, then to determine whether there are any considerations (of public policy) which ought to negative or limit the scope of the duty. Finally, the plaintiff must prove that the duty exists *towards him*.

> In *Bourhill* v. *Young* (1942), a pregnant woman heard a collision while alighting from a tram, and she suffered shock when she later saw blood on the road. Her action failed, for

she was deemed to be too far away from the accident for a duty to be owed to her. In nervous shock cases, it would seem that a duty of care is owed only where it is reasonably foreseeable that shock is likely to result.

In *McLoughlin* v. *O'Brian* (1982) one of Mrs McLoughlin's children was killed by a lorry. Her husband and two of her other children were badly injured. Mrs McLoughlin was at home two miles away at the time, but the shock of her child's death and sight of the injuries to the others made her ill. She recovered damages for her illness because ensuing shock to a *wife and mother* was a reasonably foreseeable result of the lorry driver's negligence.

2. Breach of duty

In deciding whether or not the duty of care has been broken, the standard against which the defendant's conduct will be measured is that of the so-called reasonable man. Negligence will be deemed present if the defendant did not act in a reasonable manner in the circumstances of the situation. What is reasonable will depend upon factors such as the magnitude of the risk involved, for the greater the risk, the greater the care required.

In *Bolton* v. *Stone* (1951), a batsman hit a ball out of the ground during a cricket match. It struck and injured Miss Stone, who was in the street. The top of the fence surrounding the ground was 17 feet higher than the pitch at the point where the ball crossed, and Miss Stone was about 100 yards from the batsman. It was only proved that a cricket ball had been hit out of the ground on six occasions in 30 years, and there was evidence that the shot was exceptional. It was held that, in the circumstances, the cricket club had taken reasonable care, and were not liable. It would have been otherwise if balls had landed in the road frequently.

Greater care will be required if the person exposed to the risk possesses known characteristics which either increase the likelihood of injury or, if an injury occurs, make the consequences more serious. Thus, greater care is generally expected towards children and blind persons.

In *Paris* v. *Stepney Borough Council* (1951), a fitter with only one good eye was employed on work which involved some danger to the eyes from fragments of metal. No goggles were provided. It was held that the employer acted unreasonably, and hence negligently, in not taking extra precautions.

It is also reasonable to take greater risks when acting in the public interest or in an emergency, such as driving an urgent case to hospital.

In *Watt* v. *Hertfordshire County Council* (1954), a fireman failed to recover damages when he had been injured by the movement of a heavy lifting jack which was not properly secured on a lorry. The vehicle was not properly equipped to carry the jack, but it was the only lorry available to carry the jack to free a trapped woman in danger of losing her life. The defendants had taken a reasonable risk in the circumstances.

A major problem connected with breach of duty is the *onus of proof*. Normally it is for the plaintiff to show that the defendant did not act in a reasonable manner, and in the absence of reliable evidence his action will fail. This can sometimes occur when the plaintiff is unable to say what happened, and there is no other evidence.

In *Wakelin* v. *London and South Western Railway Co.* (1886), the body of a man was found on the railway, near a level crossing, at night. He had been hit by a train, and it seemed quite possible that the railway company had been careless. On the other hand, it was equally possible that the accident was entirely the man's own fault. In the absence of evidence either way, the action failed.

There are, however, some situations where an accident happens of which the only or most likely cause must be negligence. Unattended cars do not normally run away, train doors do not normally fly open, nor do cakes contain stones. The court may then apply the maxim *res ipsa loquitur* (the thing speaks for itself) and, upon proof of the accident by the plaintiff, infer negligence from this fact, unless the *defendant* offers a reasonable explanation. The onus of proof, at this point, is reversed, and the defendant is left to prove that he was *not* negligent.

This rule of procedure can be of considerable assistance to the plaintiff in obviously negligent situations, which are normally those where the plaintiff knows little of why the accident occurred, but the defendant is or should be able to explain what has happened.

In *Richley* v. *Faull* (1965), the defendant's car skidded violently, turned round, and collided with the plaintiff's car on the wrong side of the road. It was held that this, of itself, was sufficient evidence of negligent driving. Since the defendant was unable to give a satisfactory explanation of his skid, he was held liable.

3. Resulting damage

The plaintiff must, finally, prove that he suffered loss as a result of the defendant's breach of duty of care. Loss can include damage to property, personal injuries and, in some circumstances, financial loss. Policy considerations may also apply here in determining whether the loss may be recovered.

At one time it was not clear whether personal injuries could include nervous shock, because of the problems of linking cause and effect. Medical and psychological advances have overcome this difficulty, and it is now established that nervous shock may be compensated if it gives rise to physical or mental illness, and it is just as much a form of injury as a broken leg.

Since the *Hedley Byrne* decision, financial or economic loss may be recovered if it follows from a careless statement. If such loss flows from a careless act it may only be recovered if physical damage is also caused.

In *Spartan Steel & Alloys Ltd* v. *Martin & Co. (Contractors) Ltd* (1972), careless excavation during road work damaged an electricity cable and cut off the power supply to the plaintiff's factory for 14 hours. Metal being melted in a furnace had to be removed to prevent it solidifying. Damages were recovered for the physical damage to the metal, which was now worthless, and for the (financial) loss of profit on the operation. The Court of Appeal refused to award damages for loss of profits which could have been earned on other operations while the power was off since this was economic loss independent of physical damage. Lord Denning said that, as a matter of policy, to allow claims for economic loss alone in these circumstances could lead to a very large number of claims, and it would be almost impossible to check whether these were genuine.

Finally, the resulting damage must not be too remote. Since the *Wagon Mound* case in 1961 (Unit 12) this means that the type of damage should reasonably have been foreseen by the defendant at the time when he acted carelessly.

> In *Doughty* v. *Turner Manufacturing Co. Ltd* (1964), the plaintiff was injured by an explosion caused by an asbestos cement lid being carelessly knocked into a cauldron of molten metal. His action failed for an explosion was not to be expected, according to the state of knowledge at the time, and his injuries were not therefore reasonably foreseeable. The decision could well have been different if his injuries had been caused by a foreseeable splash of metal.

B. Dangerous goods

A person who hands over dangerous goods owes a duty to the immediate recipient and, in some cases, to other persons into whose hands the goods may come.

> In *Donoghue* v. *Stevenson* (1932), a woman drank some ginger beer which had been bought for her by a friend. The beer was in an opaque bottle and, when the last of it was poured out, it was found to contain what was thought to be the decomposed remains of a snail. The woman suffered shock and became ill. The House of Lords decided that a manufacturer owes a duty of care to the consumer of his products when they are marketed in the form in which the consumer will receive them. The snail was in an opaque bottle, and there was no reasonable possibility of its being discovered between leaving the manufacturer and reaching the customer. The manufacturer was therefore liable.

This rule, which has become more important in recent years with the increasing number of prepackaged goods, is now treated as part of the general principles of negligence. Its scope has been extended by subsequent decisions and the duty is now imposed upon any person who does some work upon the goods in question. It protects any person who is likely to be injured by carelessness in that work.

> In *Stennett* v. *Hancock* (1939), Mrs Stennett, a pedestrian who had been injured by part of a lorry wheel which had broken away, successfully claimed damages from the defendants who had not carried out repairs to the lorry in a proper manner.

It must be emphasized that injury to a person caused by a dangerous defect in goods is not enough. Proof is required that the defect arose through negligence, by failure to exercise reasonable care, and that the defect was unlikely to be discovered by any reasonably foreseeable subsequent examination. The customer is often in no position to know whether the manufacturer has been careless and the courts have sometimes, therefore, applied the maxim *res ipsa loquitur* and reversed the onus of proof.

> In *Steer* v. *Durable Rubber Co. Ltd* (1958), a girl aged six was scalded when a hot water bottle split soon after being bought. The Court of Appeal held that it was for the manufacturers to prove that they had *not* been negligent, which they were unable to do.

C. Employers' liability

This is another aspect of the general principles of negligence, which deserves special mention in view of the large number of actions which arise out of injuries suffered at work. An employer owes a duty to his employees to take reasonable care to provide a safe system of work. This includes an obligation to provide reasonably competent staff, to provide reasonably safe equipment, and to provide a reasonably safe method of working. As will be seen later, this duty of care has been reinforced by a number of statutory duties imposed in the interests of safety.

The test of whether there has been a breach of duty is whether the employer has taken reasonable care in all the circumstances. Greater care will be expected towards disabled workers and young persons, as has been seen in *Paris* v. *Stepney Borough Council*. The resulting damage completing the tort is the injury suffered by the worker.

A complication arises from the fact that an injured worker will normally also receive industrial injuries or sickness benefits from the state under the national insurance schemes. The worker could, therefore, receive double compensation. Accordingly, the Law Reform (Personal Injuries) Act 1948 provides that one-half of the state insurance benefits received during the five years after the accident shall be deducted from the damages payable by the employer. The other half is not taken into account, since this is deemed to be received in respect of the worker's own insurance contributions.

D. Dangerous premises

Lawful visitors

The duty owed by an occupier of premises towards people coming on to his premises was formerly based upon complex rules which had evolved from the general principles of the tort of negligence. This duty was simplified and restated by the Occupiers' Liability Act 1957 which now largely governs the position.

The Act imposes a duty of care upon those in physical occupation and control of premises who may not necessarily be the owners. Even temporary control can be enough, as where a builder occupies part of a site during construction work. It is possible for the duty to be owed by two (or more) people in respect of the same premises, for example the occupier of a house and a builder working there, if both have some degree of control over the work being done.

The duty is owed to all lawful visitors who enter with the express or implied permission of the occupier. It covers also those who enter in exercise of a right at law, for example a police officer executing a search warrant. The Act does not apply to trespassers whose position is still governed by common law rules.

The duty concerns the state of the premises and things done or omitted to be done on them. The occupier's obligation, described as the 'common duty of care', is 'to take such care as in all the circumstances of the case is reasonable to see that the visitor will be reasonably safe in using the premises for the purposes for which he is invited or permitted by the occupier to be there'. The occupier can protect himself by warning the visitor of specific dangers but this warning must, in the circumstances, be enough to enable the visitor to be reasonably safe.

As under the previous law, the occupier must be prepared for children to be less careful than adults. What constitutes adequate warning or protection for an adult may not be deemed so for a child. In addition, some dangerous things may attract a child and these traps or allurements must be guarded against.

> In *Glasgow Corporation* v. *Taylor* (1922), a boy of seven died after eating attractive looking poisonous berries in a park. The berries were within easy reach and it was held that the warning notice was insufficient so far as young children were concerned.

Conversely, the occupier may expect that experts, for example electricians entering to repair an electrical fault, will appreciate the special risks likely to arise from their work.

> In *Roles* v. *Nathan* (1963), two sweeps were killed by carbon monoxide fumes while cleaning the flues of a coke boiler. It was held that this was a risk of which they should have been aware, and that the occupier had discharged his duty under the Act by passing on a warning he had been given by an expert.

The duty imposed by the 1957 Act may not now be excluded or modified by contract in so far as death or personal injury is concerned (Unfair Contract Terms Act 1977). The occupier may contract out of liability for other loss or damage, for example to property, provided he can show that it is reasonable to do so.

Trespassers

Trespassers must, in general, take the premises as they find them and cannot complain if they are injured. On the other hand, the occupier must act in a reasonable and civilized manner towards trespassers and the courts are now giving greater protection to trespassers, particularly children, on humanitarian grounds.

In the first place, an occupier must not inflict intentional harm upon a trespasser. Thus, while he may erect a fence of barbed wire as a reasonable means of deterring a trespasser and will not be liable for any injury thereby caused, he may not set deliberate traps intended to cause injury to trespassers who have obtained entry.

Second, if the occupier knows that trespassers are on his land or that it is likely that they are there, he cannot disregard their presence. He must not act recklessly with regard to their safety, for example, shoot in a place where they may well be. Furthermore, there may be some circumstances where he will be obliged on humanitarian grounds, to take positive steps to ensure their safety. This applies particularly to children. The Law Commission have recommended that the Occupiers' Liability Act should be extended to bring trespassers within the common duty of care but the big problem is distinguishing between the different forms of trespass, the hiker who has lost his way and the burglar.

> In *British Railways Board* v. *Herrington* (1972), children regularly played in a field next to an electrified railway. The fence guarding the line was broken down in one place, and people were known to use the gap for a short cut across the line. The Board was held liable to a boy aged six, who wandered from the field on to the line, and was badly injured by a live rail.

Finally, acquiescence in a trespass may result in the trespasser being regarded as a lawful visitor. Again, this frequently applies to children.

> In *Lowery* v. *Walker* (1911), passengers had crossed a farmer's field regularly for the last 30 years on their way to the station. It was held that, although the farmer had never expressly given permission, he had acquiesced for so long that the people were no longer regarded as trespassers. The farmer could have built a large fence, or otherwise made it clear that he no longer acquiesced, but he did not do so. Instead he put a savage horse in the field, and was held liable to someone who was attacked.

E. Breach of statutory duty

Many statutes impose duties which may give a right of action to persons injured as a result of the duty being broken. Many of these duties are simply statutory obligations to take reasonable care, but some provisions do impose strict liability.

It has long been established in English law that, in certain instances, a civil action may be brought for breach of statutory duty. This tort has become much more important in the last 100 years because of the great increase in the number of statutes.

We have seen in Unit 1 that, after the industrial revolution and growth of population in the last century, Government took an active role in many matters which had previously not concerned it. It did this largely by legislation, which often imposed new duties on public authorities, individuals, and firms. Some duties were imposed expressly, such as the duty of a factory occupier to fence dangerous machinery. Other statutes did not expressly impose a duty but, by declaring certain conduct to be unlawful, were assumed impliedly to have imposed a duty, as where the Road Traffic Act provides that it is unlawful to use a motor vehicle on a road unless there is a valid third-party insurance policy. Where the duty is owed by an individual or firm, breach will usually be a criminal offence. Difficult questions arose as to whether *all* breaches of statutory duty can give rise to a civil action. Too frequently, the statute sets out the duty in great detail, but is silent as to whether damages can be recovered by a victim in the event of breach. There are exceptions, such as the Consumer Safety Act 1978 and the Control of Pollution Act 1974, but these are rare.

At an early date, the courts decided that not all statutory duties can be made the basis of civil proceedings. A civil remedy is only available where Parliament must (in the opinion of the court) have *intended* the person harmed to be entitled to compensation. The whole question, therefore, turns on interpretation by the courts of the words used in the statute. In this task of interpretation, the courts will apply certain presumptions or guides.

1. Where the Act was designed to protect certain people, particularly from personal injury, the courts are likely to assume that a civil remedy was intended. The person injured must, of course, have been one of those to whom the duty was owed, and whom the Act was intended to protect.

    > In *Groves* v. *Lord Wimborne* (1898), a boy working in an iron works was badly injured when his arm was trapped in unfenced cog-wheels. Under legislation then in force, the

factory occupier owed a statutory duty to fence all dangerous machinery. The boy recovered damages for breach of this duty, which was clearly intended to protect people such as himself.

2. Conversely, where the statute is passed for the benefit of the public in general there is a presumption against conferring a right of action upon an individual member of the public.

> In *Cutler* v. *Wandsworth Stadium* (1949), the statute in question had provided that, where occupiers of dog-racing tracks operated a totalisator for betting, space for bookmakers should also be provided. Cutler, a bookmaker, claimed damages on the grounds that the defendants had not provided him with space. It was held that the object of the statute was to benefit the public generally—or at least a particular section of the public—by giving them some freedom of choice in their betting. It was not an Act for the protection of bookmakers and the action accordingly failed.

3. Where the statute provides its own sanctions, such as where breach is a criminal offence, the courts may assume that Parliament intended this to be the only sanction, and refuse a civil remedy. On the other hand, this is only a guideline. It is frequently held today that the Act intended to impose both civil and criminal liability, and possibly other methods of enforcement as well. In *Groves* v. *Lord Wimborne*, the occupier could also have been prosecuted, and most sections of the Factories Act 1961 can give rise both to criminal prosecution, and civil action for breach of duty.

4. Conversely, if no criminal sanction or other method of enforcing the duty is provided, the courts will be very ready to assume that civil liability was intended, otherwise the section might be just a pious hope.

> In *Reffell* v. *Surrey County Council* (1964), damages were awarded to a 12-year-old girl who put her hand through a thin pane of glass in a swing door at school. The glass was dangerous, and the local authority was held to have broken certain statutory regulations designed to ensure the safety of pupils from this type of injury. The regulations imposed a duty, and provided no criminal penalty or other means of enforcement.

5. The court will also enquire into what the Act was designed to protect against, and ask themselves whether the harm which has occurred was the 'mischief' at which the provision was aimed.

> In *Close* v. *Steel Co. of Wales Ltd* (1961), the plaintiff was injured when the bit of his electric drill shattered, and a piece entered his eye. He sued the company for breach of its statutory duty to fence dangerous parts of machinery, but his action failed. Some of the judges in the House of Lords took the view that the fencing provisions were only intended to prevent the workman coming into contact with the machine, not to fence so as to prevent parts flying out. The plaintiff's injury, therefore, was outside the 'mischief' which the section aimed to prevent.

6. Other considerations may influence the courts, such as the relation between the statutory duty and other branches of civil law.

> In *Square* v. *Model Farm Dairies Ltd* (1939), Major Square and his family contracted typhoid fever from infected milk. The court refused to allow an action by him and his

family for breach of statutory duty under the Food and Drugs Acts, because this would add a considerable complication to the existing remedies available under the Sale of Goods Act and for the tort of negligence. The court felt that Parliament could not have intended to do this in an Act dealing with food and drugs. Major Square, who had bought the milk, recovered damages for breach of contract for his own injuries and loss.

Assuming that the breach of statutory duty is actionable as a tort, it is again a question of interpretation whether the legislature intended the duty to be strict. If so, the plaintiff will recover on proof simply that the duty has been broken. If, on the other hand, it is decided that the duty is discharged if the defendant has taken reasonable care, the standard of care required will, again, depend on the wording of the Act, and the plaintiff must normally show that the defendant has failed to exercise such care.

Finally, the plaintiff must show that he has suffered harm or loss as a result of the breach. Most, but not all, of the successful actions for breach of statutory duty have involved personal injuries.

If the statutory duty is not strict, the defendant may plead the defences that may be raised in an action for negligence such as *volenti non fit injuria*, or that he had delegated the performance of the duty to an apparently competent person, or that he had generally exercised the amount of care required. If the duty is a strict one, none of these defences is available, but the defendant may reduce the damages by pleading contributory negligence.

For further consideration

1. Mary is an office cleaner. On one occasion she disconnects a piece of office machinery in order to use the electric plug for her vacuum cleaner. In so doing she receives an electric shock because of a faulty plug.

    If there are statutory regulations designed to protect office workers from dangerous electrical appliances, advise Mary on her right to claim compensation from her employer. The regulations provide for a criminal prosecution in the event of a breach but make no mention of a civil action.

2. Advise Philip whether an action for negligence is likely to succeed against each of the parties in the following circumstances.
    (a) Arthur, an accountant, upon whose advice Philip made an investment which proved to be worthless.
    (b) Bill, a barrister, who represented Philip in a recent case and conducted the case badly.
    (c) Conrad, a climber, who fell from a cliff; Philip, who was passing at the time, saw the fall and suffered a nervous shock.
    (d) Derek, a driver, whose car skidded on to the opposite side of the road where it collided with a car driven by Philip.
3. Explain whether or not a garage would be liable for injuries suffered in the following circumstances.

(a) A car mechanic from another garage calls to collect a car and slips on the oily floor.

(b) A child, playing around on an old car dumped on waste ground belonging to the garage, falls from the top of the car.

4. The Animal Diseases Research Institute carelessly allows a dangerous virus to escape. Farmer George claims compensation for the death of 20 cows, including the profit he would have gained from their sale at a later date. Auctioneer Albert claims loss of commission on a sale of cattle that is cancelled by a Government order following the escape of the virus.

Advise the Institute.

Unit 14. Torts Against Land and Goods

A. Trespass to land

The tort of trespass is committed by *direct interference with the person or property of another without lawful justification.* It can take several forms: trespass to the person—by assault, battery or false imprisonment; trespass to the goods of another; and trespass to the land of another. Trespass to land will be dealt with here.

Trespass has origins going back almost to the beginning of English legal history, and is the parent of much of our modern law of tort. At one time trespass was also a crime but, as a general rule, trespassers can no longer be prosecuted today, although there are some statutory exceptions to this rule. Thus, trespasses upon certain types of property, such as railway premises or military property, are statutory offences. Trespass for certain purposes can also be an offence, for example, in pursuit of game. A trespass with intent to commit theft or an act of violence constitutes burglary, under section 9 of the Theft Act 1968, even though the intended act is not carried out. Trespass which deliberately causes damage to property can be an offence under the Criminal Damage Act 1971. Depositing waste on the land of another can be both the tort of trespass and an offence under statutes such as the Public Health Acts and the Control of Pollution Act.

The following are the main features of the tort:

1. *Direct interference.* The interference must be direct and forcible if it is to constitute the tort of trespass. Apart from its simplest form of entry upon land, it may take many other forms, for example, throwing or placing things on land, knocking a nail into a fence or sitting on a wall. It may be committed by remaining on land when permission to be there has ended, or by using the land for an unauthorized purpose.

In *Hickman* v. *Maisey* (1900), it was held to be trespass where a private road was used by persons to watch race horses in training, and record the times, instead of for the exercise of the right of way.

Trespass may be committed by means of animals or motor vehicles. In all of these instances, however, it must be a direct interference. Thus it would be a trespass to put rubbish on another's land, but not merely to neglect your garden so that the weeds spread next door, or simply to allow the smoke from your factory to drift over other people's houses. These last two examples, being indirect interference, might amount to the tort of nuisance (see later).

2. *With the land of another.* The action will be brought by a person entitled to possession of the land. This entitlement includes not only the surface of the land, but also the air space above, and the ground (including minerals) beneath. At common law, it was technically trespass to fly an aircraft over another's land without permission, but this rule has been modified by statute. The Civil Aviation Act 1949 provides that there shall be no action for trespass (or nuisance) by reason only of a flight of a civil aircraft at a reasonable height. Conversely, there is strict liability for damage caused by aircraft or anything falling from an aircraft. A kite, or an overhead cable, could also constitute a trespass.

It is normally only the person in immediate possession who may sue. If the owner has granted a lease, the tenant normally has the right of action. The landlord could sue if permanent damage has been done, which will affect his interest at the end of the lease.

3. *Trespass is actionable per se,* in that the act alone is sufficient, without the need to prove that damage followed from the act.

Remedies for trespass

The main remedies available through the courts are as follows:

1. Damages will always be awarded but, although trespass is actionable *per se*, the damages will only compensate for loss suffered. If no loss results from the trespass, damages will be nominal unless there are aggravating circumstances.
2. An injunction may be awarded, at the discretion of the court, to order the defendant to stop his trespass, or not to commit an impending trespass.
3. If trespass to land is carried further and the wrongdoer takes possession of the land and withholds it from the rightful owner, the latter may sue for *dispossession*. If successful, he is entitled not only to judgment for possession, but also for any rents or other benefits, known as *mesne profits*, which were lost while out of possession.

In addition to his remedies in the courts, the person in possession of the land has certain other rights:

1. He has the right to ask a trespasser to leave and, if he refuses, to use such force as is reasonably necessary to remove him, but no more.

2. His right to detain trespassing animals, under the Animals Act 1971, will be discussed in Unit 15. A similar right, known as *distress damage feasant*, can be applied to other things causing damage, such as a football which breaks a window or a vehicle which crashes into a front garden.

Defences to an action for trespass

The 'general' defences to an action in tort will normally apply (Unit 12). Thus, someone expressly invited on to the land would have the defence of consent, although he must leave when asked to do so. People generally have the implied consent of the occupier to open the gate and knock on the front door, unless this consent is expressly revoked. Statutory authority can also be an important defence to this tort.

Many public authorities, for example, have statutory powers to purchase land compulsorily, although if they exceed their powers, or exercise them wrongfully, they will be liable in trespass.

In *Cooper* v. *Wandsworth Board of Works* (1863), the Board exercised its statutory powers wrongfully in demolishing the plaintiff's house, and were held liable for trespass.

Many officials, including public health inspectors, officials of electricity and gas boards, and factory inspectors have statutory powers to enter certain premises. Police officers also have various powers of entry, in some cases only with a warrant issued by a magistrate under statutory powers, in other cases without a warrant.

B. Nuisance

Private nuisance

Private nuisance arises when there is *unreasonable interference with a person's use or enjoyment of his land*. It differs from trespass to land in that the injury is indirect (see previously). The torts of negligence and nuisance sometimes overlap, and both may arise out of the same set of facts. The distinction is that, in nuisance, the plaintiff must prove that he has an interest in land which has been disturbed, whereas for negligence a breach of a legal duty of care must be established. If a tile falls off your roof and injures your neighbour who is standing in his garden, his action will be for private nuisance. If he is a visitor in your garden when this happens, he will sue for negligence, or more precisely, for breach of the Occupiers' Liability Act. If he is passing in the street at the time, he could sue for negligence or for public nuisance (see below). There can also be an overlap with the rule in *Rylands* v. *Fletcher*, except that this rule is concerned largely with isolated occurrences, whereas nuisance usually requires some continuing interference.

The main elements of private nuisance will be examined in turn.

1. *Interference*

Private nuisance may take two forms, the first comprising interference with rights in respect of land, for example, blocking a right of way, taking away a right to light, or interfering with fishing rights. The second form is concerned with interference with the enjoyment of land generally, and can cover noise, vibrations, smells, smoke, weeds, animals, and many other forms of indirect interference.

2. *Unreasonable*

People living in a community must expect to put up with a reasonable amount of inconvenience, for example, it is reasonable to keep a dog, and dogs can be expected to bark occasionally. The law expects some 'give and take' between neighbours, and an action will only lie if the interference is unreasonable. It is different if your neighbour keeps 30 dogs which bark continuously throughout the night. In deciding whether the inconvenience is sufficiently substantial to constitute a nuisance, the court will consider all of the circumstances. For example, an isolated incident is less likely to be a nuisance than a continuous interference.

> In *Bolton* v. *Stone* (1951), the cricket ball which hit Miss Stone was an exceptional occurrence. She pleaded the tort of nuisance as well as negligence, but her action failed on this ground too.
>
> In *Castle* v. *St Augustine's Links* (1922), golf balls were *often* hit on to the road, and this was held to be nuisance.

The plaintiff is only entitled to normal protection. Abnormally sensitive activities are disregarded.

> In *Bridlington Relay Ltd* v. *Yorkshire Electricity Board* (1965), the Board's power line interfered with the relaying of television broadcasts by the plaintiff. The power line would not normally have interfered with other types of activity, and it was held that the plaintiff company could not, simply because it engaged in very delicate activities, claim special protection.

The character of the neighbourhood can also be relevant, and it seems that a higher standard of amenity can be demanded in a select residential area than in an industrial one. In *Sturges* v. *Bridgman* (1879), Thesiger, LJ said, 'What would be a nuisance in Belgrave Square would not necessarily be so in Bermondsey', and similar comments have been made in other cases. If, however, the nuisance causes material damage as opposed to personal discomfort, an action may be brought whatever the locality.

The motive of the person who interferes may also be relevant. Thus malice, in the sense of deliberate intention to annoy, may affect the issue of reasonableness.

> In *Christie* v. *Davey* (1893), it was decided that, while it may be reasonable to practice a musical instrument at reasonable times of day, it is a nuisance if the neighbour deliberately retaliates by banging tin trays.

Similarly, if the defendant is negligent, and therefore creates more noise and disturbance than he need have done, this may turn a reasonable activity into an actionable nuisance.

3. *Use or enjoyment of land.*

An action for private nuisance is available to any person who has an interest in land and whose enjoyment of that land has been detrimentally affected. It is a tort which protects the *occupier* of land, but only the person who is occupier in the legal sense. Thus the tenant of a house may sue, but not members of his family, lodgers or guests, who do not have an interest in the property.

> In *Malone* v. *Laskey* (1907), the vibration from machinery next door had loosened the brackets supporting the water cistern in the lavatory of Mr Malone's house. It was held that his wife could not recover damages for private nuisance when the bracket fell on her. The tenancy was not in her name, and she was not the occupier.

The owner of land who is not in possession, for example, a landlord, may sue if the nuisance causes permanent damage which affects his interest.

4. *Harm resulting*

Most private nuisances are not actionable *per se*, and it will be apparent from the cases already mentioned that some loss of amenity or enjoyment of the land is an essential requirement. Only interferences with rights over land such as rights of way are actionable without proof of loss.

The person liable

Liability rests primarily on the person who creates or authorizes the nuisance. This liability will remain even after his occupation of the premises from which the nuisance emanates has ceased, and he no longer has the power to put an end to it.

The occupier of premises where the nuisance exists may also be liable, but only if he knowingly or carelessly permits the state of affairs which gives rise to the nuisance.

> In *Sedleigh-Denfield* v. *O'Callaghan* (1940), the occupier was held liable for the flooding of a neighbour's garden caused by a blocked pipe. The pipe had been laid on the defendant's land by a trespasser, but the defendant's servant had cleared out the ditch where the pipe was laid, and its existence was therefore either known, or should have been known.

Remedies for private nuisance

The main remedies available through the courts are damages and an injunction. The latter remedy is frequently sought, because what the occupier often wants is primarily an end to the interference rather than merely compensation. The matter is not always so simple, however. Nuisance is often committed by industrial firms discharging waste into the atmosphere or into a river, and the court might be unwilling to grant an injunction which would close the plant and throw the employees out of work. In granting the injunction, therefore, the court may suspend its operation for a time to give the firm a chance to make the alterations necessary to stop the discharge.

> In *Pride of Derby Angling Association* v. *British Celanese Ltd* (1953), an action was brought by an angling association and a landowner against various bodies which were polluting a river. An injunction was granted against one of the defendants, Derby Corporation, which was discharging sewage, but the operation of the injunction was suspended for two years to give time to build a new sewage works.

This time lag, combined with the time needed to bring proceedings and collect evidence, may often deter potential plaintiffs (Unit 8).

Apart from the remedies granted by a court, a person offended by a nuisance may take steps to remove it himself. Thus an obstruction may be removed or an overhanging tree cut back. For obvious reasons, the law does not look kindly upon such 'self-help', and if the abatement goes further than is necessary or causes unnecessary injury, the abater himself will be liable. With these restrictions, abatement is not used frequently and, when it is, requires great care.

Defences to private nuisance

The normal defences to an action in tort will be available. Consent, however, has only a limited application, since it is no defence that the plaintiff came to the nuisance. Indeed, there is no actionable nuisance until the plaintiff is affected.

> In *Sturges* v. *Bridgman* (1879), the noise and vibrations from a confectioner's premises were restrained by injunction when a doctor built a new consulting room at the bottom of his garden against the wall of the confectioner's kitchen, even though the confectioner's machinery was there before the new consulting room.

Statutory authority is an important defence to this tort as with trespass to land, but a statutory power must be exercised with all reasonable care, and so as to cause the minimum of interference with the rights of others; see *Metropolitan Asylum District* v. *Hill* (Unit 12).

Public nuisance

Public nuisance is *unlawful annoyance or harm which affects the public generally*. It is essentially a tort against persons exercising their rights as members of the public, and is not directly a tort against land. It is included here for convenience because of its close relation with private nuisance.

Because of its effect upon the public, public nuisance is primarily a crime, and the person responsible may be prosecuted. A plaintiff can only sue if he can show that he has suffered special damage, over and above that suffered by the public as a whole. Obstructing a highway will affect anyone who wishes to pass along it and, therefore, will not entitle anyone to sue. If the plaintiff is particularly affected, perhaps because the entrance to his house is blocked, he will be able to bring a civil action.

Annoyance or harm will be unlawful if it is unreasonable according to tests similar to those for private nuisance. Two of the cases already cited as illustrations, *Bolton* v. *Stone*, and *Castle* v. *St Augustine's Links*, are in fact cases on public nuisance. The forms of interference are also very similar to those for private nuisance.

> In *Halsey* v. *Esso Petroleum Co. Ltd* (1961), acid smuts from the defendant's oil depot injured the plaintiff, both by soiling clothing which was drying in his garden and by damaging the paintwork of his car which was standing in the road outside his house. It was held that damage to the clothing affected the enjoyment of his land and was a private nuisance, while damage to the car affected him as a member of the public generally, and was therefore a public nuisance (Unit 8).

C. The rule in *Rylands* v. *Fletcher*

The doctrine of *Rylands* v. *Fletcher* is perhaps the most important illustration of strict liability in tort, as contrasted with liability based on the moral fault of the defendant, for example, failure to take reasonable care in the tort of negligence. The action takes its name from the case in which the rule was formulated, but its roots go back much further in time.

> In *Rylands* v. *Fletcher* (1868), a mill-owner employed an independent contractor to construct a reservoir to provide water power. Water consequently entered some disused mineshafts, whose existence was not suspected, and flooded a neighbour's mines. In holding the mill-owner liable, the court said that, if a person brings on to his land and keeps there something likely to do damage if it escapes, he keeps it there at his peril, and will be liable for any damage which follows from an escape, even if there has been no negligence.

In order to establish that the tort has been committed, the plaintiff must show several things.

1. The occupier of land must have been actively responsible for keeping some dangerous thing on his land. He would not be responsible, for example, if water collected there in the ordinary course of nature. The thing, moreover, must have been dangerous, that is, likely to do damage if it escaped. This is a question of fact, but water, electricity, colliery waste, and even a flagpole have been held to come under this category. Some types of industrial waste, such as fumes discharged into the atmosphere or effluent into streams, could also be included.
2. The dangerous thing must constitute a non-natural use of the land, another question of fact which gives considerable discretion to the court. In recent times, it has been suggested that some industrial processes are natural uses of land, and so not within the rule.
3. There must be an escape from the land of the defendant.

    > In *Read* v. *J. Lyons & Co. Ltd* (1946), a woman munitions inspector was injured by an explosion while working in a munitions factory. It was held that the rule did not apply, since she was injured inside the plant, and not by material which had escaped. It was doubted whether a munitions factory in wartime was a non-natural use of land, but the court did not have to decide this.

4. Finally, damage to the plaintiff must have followed as a natural consequence of the escape. This is almost invariably a claim for damage to property but there seems no reason why a claim for personal injuries should not be included.

Although liability is strict, in that the plaintiff need not prove that the defendant acted carelessly, the defendant may be able to prove some defences. Inevitable accident is not a defence but, in theory, Act of God may be pleaded (see Unit 12). Protection may be given by statute, as with gas, electricity, and water undertakings. There is also no liability if the plaintiff agreed to the collection, or if the escape was caused by the default of the plaintiff or even of a third party ('act of a stranger') over whom the defendant had no control. In view of the requirements necessary to establish the application of the rule, and the defences which may be raised, its practical importance today is somewhat limited.

D. Wrongful interference with goods

Trespass to goods

This consists of *direct and unauthorized interference with goods in the possession of another*, and usually arises when the goods are taken away or damaged. The slightest interference will suffice, although this is unlikely to result in a substantial award of damages unless done in aggravating circumstances, for example, the removal of the clothes of a swimmer.

> In *Kirk* v. *Gregory* (1876), the defendant was held liable for trespass when, during a drunken party, she moved some jewellery in good faith to a place of safety and the jewellery later disappeared.

As with trespass to land this tort is designed to protect possession, but the owner out of possession has an action for permanent damage which affects his interest. A person who has been wrongly deprived of an article may retake possession of it, provided that he uses no more force than is necessary.

A trespass to goods could constitute the crime of theft, but only if there was an intention permanently to deprive the owner thereof. It might also constitute an offence under the Criminal Damage Act 1971 if there was an intention to destroy or damage the goods or recklessness as to whether the goods would be destroyed or damaged.

Conversion

If a wrongdoer *deals in the goods of another in such a way that the other's title to the goods is called in question*, an action will lie for conversion. This may take several forms such as wrongfully delivering, wrongfully taking, wrongfully withholding or wrongfully destroying the goods, but perhaps its most common form is when the goods of another are wrongfully sold. Even if this is done by mistake, or in ignorance of the true ownership, there will be no defence.

> In *Hollins* v. *Fowler* (1875), a rogue obtained some bales of cotton from the plaintiff by fraud, and re-sold them to the defendant, who then re-sold in turn to his clients. The defendant had obtained no title to the goods, and had no right to re-sell them, but was quite unaware of this. It was held that the defendant was liable to the plaintiff for conversion, and that his innocence and good faith were no defence.

It must be stressed that the wrongful dealing must be done in such a way as to challenge the plaintiff's title. A suggested test is whether the act changes the property in the goods instead of merely their position. Merely using the goods of another, for example, driving his car without permission, will not of itself amount to conversion.

In *Fouldes* v. *Willoughby* (1841), the removal of two horses from a ferry boat following an argument with the owner was held not to be conversion because there was no intention to deny the owner's title.

The usual remedy for conversion is damages, and the measure of damages is the loss to the plaintiff. This will normally, but not necessarily, be the value of the goods at the time of the conversion.

In *Wickham Holdings Ltd* v. *Brook House Motors Ltd* (1967), a person who held a car on hire purchase wrongly re-sold it to the defendants, having paid only three-quarters of the hire purchase price. The plaintiff finance company claimed damages for detinue and conversion. It was held that the damages were only the unpaid balance of the hire purchase price, not the full value of the vehicle.

Abolition of detinue

A third tort which might arise from interference with another's goods was *detinue* which consisted of the wrongful detention of the goods. It was normally used when the plaintiff sought the return of the goods themselves. The Law Revision Committee felt that detinue added an unnecessary complication to the law and it was accordingly abolished by the Torts (Interference with Goods) Act 1977. In an attempt to simplify the law, the Act also provided that, in any action for the interference with goods, whether this be for conversion, trespass or negligence, the court may order the delivery of the specific goods and/or award damages according to what is deemed appropriate relief in the circumstances.

Rights of finders

The finder of a lost article does not commit a tort by taking it into his possession if he acts reasonably in an endeavour to find the true owner and does not intend to misappropriate it. Because of the special protection given by the law to possession, the finder has a good title to the lost article against everyone but the true owner.

In *Armory* v. *Delamirie* (1722), a boy chimney sweep who had found a jewel was held to be entitled to recover it from a jeweller to whom he had taken it for valuation.

The rights of the finder may be subject to a further qualification, namely the rights of the occupier of the land where the finding occurred. If the article is attached to or under the land, it is clear that the occupier has a better claim.

In *South Staffordshire Water Co.* v. *Sharman* (1896), a workman cleaning out a pond on the plaintiff's land found two gold rings embedded in the mud. It was held that the occupier, not the workman, was entitled to them.

If the article is found on the surface of the land the position is not free from doubt. It would seem that the finder has a better title in a public place and the occupier a better title in a private place, the difficulty lying in making the distinction between these two types of place.

In *Bridges* v. *Hawksworth* (1851), the finder of a bundle of bank notes in a shop was held entitled as against the shopkeeper on the grounds that they were found in the *public* part of the shop.

For further consideration

1. A strong wind blows a number of tiles off the roof of Smith's house. Smith covers the hole in the roof with a tarpaulin but fails to fasten this down securely. Another gust of wind blows the tarpaulin into the road where Jones, a passing motorist, tries to avoid it but, in so doing, crashes his car and injures himself. At the same time further tiles are dislodged. One tile falls into a bedroom of a neighbouring house and injures Robinson, a guest who is staying there. Another falls into the garden of the same house and breaks a pane of glass in a greenhouse.

   Advise Smith of his possible liability.

2. To what extent, if at all, is it correct to say that
   (a) trespassers will be prosecuted, and
   (b) findings are keepings?

3. Leonard owns two fields which he leases to Taylor and Turner respectively. One night Seeker enters Taylor's field and digs for valuables which he believes to be hidden there. He deposits the soil which he removes on Turner's field. The following day, Seeker flies over the fields in his helicopter to see what damage he has done. Part of the helicopter falls off and damages Turner's greenhouse.

   What torts have been committed by Seeker and against whom?

4. Tom enters Fred's garage without permission one night to recover his bicycle which Fred has borrowed and not returned. In the dark he takes the wrong bicycle and in so doing damages a pipe leading from an oil tank which supplies Fred's central heating. Oil escapes and flows on to the garden of Fred's neighbour.

   Discuss.

Unit 15. Other Specific Torts

A. Trespass to the person

Any *direct interference with the person or liberty of another without lawful justification* is actionable as a trespass to the person. The following are the main features of the tort:

1. It appears that the defendant's act must be intentional. An unintentional act, even if careless, will not be sufficient.

    In *Letang* v. *Cooper* (1965), the defendant drove his car over the plaintiff's legs while she was sunbathing. The Court of Appeal held that, since the injury was inflicted unintentionally, the action lay in negligence.

2. The defendant must have had no lawful justification. An action for trespass to the person will fail if the act in question was carried out under legal authority, as when a lawful arrest has been made. Similarly, a parent or anyone acting *in loco parentis*, such as a guardian or school teacher, may inflict reasonable chastisement upon a child. It is also justifiable to use force against another in self-defence, provided that no more force is used than is necessary to ward off the attack.

Trespass to the person may take the following forms:

(a) *Assault*. This arises when a person is *threatened* in such circumstances that he reasonably believes that violence is about to be used on him. The victim must reasonably believe that the threat is about to be carried out, the actual intention of the wrongdoer being irrelevant. Thus pointing an unloaded gun could be an assault if the other believes it to be loaded. There must be some act or gesture. Words alone are not sufficient, and may even prevent what would otherwise be an assault, for example, where a threatening gesture is accompanied by a statement that only the presence of a police officer prevents the assailant carrying out his threat.

(b) *Battery*. This is the intentional *application* of force to another. In practice the term assault is often used, loosely, to include battery, but in law the two are different. Physical striking is an obvious example, but other forms include pulling away a chair, kissing a girl against her will, or setting a dog on a person. Throwing a stone at a person could be assault if the stone missed, and could also be battery if it hit. The unfortunate prisoner who, in 1631, 'ject un Brickbat' at the judge, 'que narrowly mist' was guilty only of assault; the distinction did not avail him much, since he was promptly hanged. (The report is in the Law-French used at the time.) The slightest contact will suffice, but in accordance with common sense there would be no action for touching a person in a friendly manner to attract his attention, or for reasonably jostling another in a crowd. The law would here imply consent, just as it would for the normal knocks which players can expect in a football match. In some cases, the consent will be more obvious, as where someone goes to the dentist, or a boxer enters the ring.

The amount of harm caused will affect the amount of damages, but higher damages may be awarded if the battery is committed in aggravating circumstances. It might cost a girl more to slap a boy's face (unjustifiably) in public than in private. Assault and battery are also crimes, but if the wrongdoer is prosecuted in the Magistrates' Court then, whatever the outcome, there can be no civil action based on the same facts.

(c) *False imprisonment*. This is the imposition of unlawful restraint upon another by force, by the threat of force or by a show of authority. The period of restraint is immaterial and it may last for only a few seconds, but it must be a total restraint. Partial restraint may be actionable, perhaps as a nuisance, but it is not false imprisonment.

> In *Bird* v. *Jones* (1845), a person was prevented from using one of the footpaths over a bridge, because it was enclosed for spectators watching a regatta. He could still cross on the other side of the road. His action for false imprisonment failed.

It is not essential that the plaintiff be aware of the restraint upon his liberty, as he could be asleep or drunk at the time. On the other hand, if a person fails to investigate likely and reasonable means of escape, such as trying a door to see if it is locked, there will be no false imprisonment. Similarly, a person cannot complain if he refuses to perform a reasonable condition to which he agreed upon entering the premises, for example, paying a small amount of money to leave. A defendant will also not be liable for refusing to release a person when he is under no obligation to do so.

> In *Herd* v. *Weardale Steel, Coal & Coke Co. Ltd* (1915), several miners went on strike and demanded to be brought to the surface. It was held that the colliery manager was entitled to refuse to do this until the end of the shift.

In addition to the usual remedies, an application may be made to a High Court judge for a writ of habeas corpus to secure the release of the person believed to be wrongly imprisoned.

B. Intentional physical harm

This tort consists of *a wilful act which is likely to, and actually does, cause physical harm to another*. This will not amount to trespass if there is no direct interference with the person of that other. In such a case an action may lie under this heading.

> In *Wilkinson* v. *Downton* (1897), a practical joker told a woman, falsely, that her husband had been badly injured. He was held liable to pay damages when the wife suffered nervous shock and had a serious illness in consequence.

This action has only been accepted by the courts comparatively recently, there have been few precedents and its full extent has not yet been determined. It is suggested that actions might lie under this heading for the intentional infliction of disease without the application of force, or the administration of a drug to an unwitting victim, or even frightening a person by dressing up as a ghost or by staging a mock raid as part of a student rag.

C. Malicious prosecution

This tort may be defined as the *instigation of unsuccessful criminal proceedings, maliciously and without reasonable and probable cause*. It attempts to compensate a person for the serious injury that he may suffer if he is wrongly subjected to criminal proceedings, even if these end in his favour. Although it is not a form of trespass, it sometimes accompanies false imprisonment when the restraint takes the form of an arrest followed by criminal prosecution. The plaintiff must prove the following matters:

1. that the prosecution was instigated by the defendant;
2. that the defendant did this for an improper, malicious motive;
3. without any reasonable cause for so doing; and
4. that the plaintiff has thereby suffered damage, either monetary or through loss of reputation, or by being placed in danger of loss of liberty.

The requirements for success in the action are such that it is unlikely to succeed against a person who honestly, though mistakenly, gives information to the police regarding an alleged offence. Leaving aside the questions of malice and reasonable cause, the person giving the information might not be the direct instigator of the prosecution, since the decision to prosecute would rest with the police.

D. Defamation

Defamation is *the publication of a (false) statement which tends to injure the reputation of another*. The tort exists to protect a person against infringements of his good name or reputation. It differs from other torts in that the County Court has no jurisdiction, so that an action for defamation may only be brought in the High Court. It provides the most important remaining example of trial by a civil jury. Since most people are sensitive about derogatory remarks, and may be too ready to challenge them in court, it is an action for which legal aid is not granted.

Success in an action for defamation depends upon proof of the following matters.

1. *The statement must have been defamatory*

The test is whether, in consequence, right-thinking members of society shun or avoid that person, or regard him with feelings of ridicule, hatred or contempt. It is most commonly misconduct or dishonesty which is implied, but this need not necessarily be so. Allegations of insanity, rape or insolvency—even where no blame attaches to the plaintiff—may have the effect of lowering reputation in the estimation of a third party.

> In *Youssoupoff* v. *Metro-Goldwyn-Mayer Pictures* (1934), Princess Youssoupoff recovered damages for a film which suggested that she had been raped or seduced by the Russian monk, Rasputin.

Some statements are obviously defamatory by the use of the words in their ordinary sense, for example 'X is a thief'. In other cases the words, apparently innocent, may have a secondary or hidden meaning to those who know of the special circumstances making them so. This is known as an *innuendo*, and will support an action if the plaintiff can plead, and prove, the supporting facts which show that people are likely to draw this special inference.

> In *Cassidy* v. *Daily Mirror Newspapers* (1929), a newspaper photograph of an allegedly engaged couple seemed to be innocent to most people, except those who knew that the man concerned was already married. His wife recovered damages on the grounds that those who knew them were likely to assume that she was not really his wife, but his mistress.

2. *The statement must have referred to the plaintiff*

This matter normally arises when the plaintiff either is not named, or is given a different name, and he attempts to show that other facts led reasonable people to believe that he was the person to whom the defendant was referring. Even coincidental references may be actionable.

> In *Hulton & Co.* v. *Jones* (1910), a series of newspaper articles was based upon the rather dissolute life of a fictitious person called 'Artemus Jones', who was described as being on holiday in Dieppe, with a woman who was not his wife, frequenting the Casino, and so on. Unknown to the author or the publishers, there was a real Artemus Jones, a barrister, whose friends gave evidence that they thought the articles referred to him. His action succeeded.

Liability may also arise where the statement is intended to refer to one person, and another person bearing the same name proves that people thought the statement referred to him and was defamatory of him.

The Defamation Act 1952 now affords a means whereby those committing unintentional defamation in situations such as this may be able to escape liability (see later).

If a class or group of people is defamed, no action can normally be brought, because defamation is a tort against an *individual's* reputation. On the other hand, if the group is so small that individual reputations are adversely affected, then an individual member might succeed in an action. For example, an allegation that all solicitors are dishonest would not normally give any solicitor a right of action, but an allegation that all solicitors in the town of X are dishonest might be defamatory if only two or three solicitors are in practice there.

3. *The statement must have been published*
Since a person's reputation depends upon the opinion of others, his reputation will only suffer if the defamation is communicated to a third party. Publication to the defamed person himself is not enough; you can call a man what you will to his face, so long as no one else hears. Communication to the husband or wife of the person making the statement is also insufficient; a man may say whatever he wishes to say about others to his *own* wife, so long as she does not communicate it to outsiders (in which event *she* would be liable). On the other hand, communication to the husband or wife of the defamed person would certainly be publication.

Where the defamatory statement appears in written correspondence, difficult questions can arise. It is presumed that publication takes place when 'open' communications such as postcards and telegrams are sent, even to the person defamed, because others such as post office staff will see what has been written. No publication is presumed when a letter is sent to the person defamed in an envelope, sealed or unsealed, but it could be otherwise if someone other than the addressee, such as his secretary or his wife, is likely to open and read the letter. The sender might be able to protect himself by sealing the envelope and marking it 'private and confidential'. Dictation of a defamatory letter to a secretary could also be publication.

Every 'passing on' of a defamatory statement is a separate publication and, therefore, anyone distributing defamatory matter is, in theory, liable. This could be unjust to people such as newsvendors, booksellers, and librarians, who only play an incidental part in the distribution. If such people are sued (which is unlikely in practice), they may successfully plead *innocent dissemination* provided that they did not know, and could not be expected to know, that the matter was defamatory, and that they were not negligent in any way.

4. *Resulting loss*
As will be seen below, defamation can take two forms, libel and slander. For libel it is not necessary for the plaintiff to prove any financial loss. The tort is actionable *per se*, in the sense that only harm to reputation need be shown. On the other hand, slander is not actionable unless the plaintiff can show financial loss, other than in some exceptional circumstances. Where there is monetary loss, so that the slander is actionable, the damages awarded are not limited to that loss, but can take into account general loss of reputation.

Libel and slander

For reasons which are mainly historical, there are two forms of defamation. Libel is defamation in a permanent form, usually writing, but including also sculpture, painting, the soundtrack of a film and, since 1952 when the Defamation Act clarified the position, radio and television broadcasts transmitted for general reception. The Theatres Act 1968 (which abolished censorship of plays) provided also that defamation arising from the public performance of a play should constitute libel, not merely slander. Slander is defamation in a temporary or transient form, usually speech, but including also derogatory gestures and mimes.

The main importance of the distinction is that libel is actionable without proof of resulting monetary loss, whereas for slander the plaintiff must prove loss. Exceptionally, loss need not be proved in actions for slander in four instances where the defamation is likely to be particularly damaging. These are imputations:

1. that a person is suffering from a contagious disease which is likely to lead others to shun or avoid him—venereal disease would have this effect, but not measles;
2. that a woman is unchaste (Slander of Women Act 1891);
3. that a person has committed a serious criminal offence, i.e., one punishable by death or imprisonment;
4. that a person in any office, trade or profession is unfit to hold that office or to continue to practise his trade or profession.

A further distinction, of less practical importance today, is that libel is a crime, but slander as such is not.

Defences to defamation

The possible defences which are peculiar to this tort are as follows:

1. *Offer of amends*. If the defamation is unintentional, as in the Artemus Jones type of case, there is a defence under section 4 of the Defamation Act 1952. It is available to the defendant who can show that no defamation was intended, that he was unaware of any circumstances making the statement defamatory, and that he acted with reasonable care. As soon as is reasonably practicable, the defendant must apologize with a suitable correction, for example, withdrawing copies of the book or inserting an appropriate notice in the newspaper. He must also pay costs and other expenses reasonably incurred by the plaintiff.
2. *Justification*. It is always a defence to show that the allegations are true, for no one can fairly claim that a reputation which he does not deserve has been damaged. It is sufficient to prove that the statement was substantially true.

   In *Alexander* v. *North-Eastern Rail Co.* (1865), the defendants correctly stated that the plaintiff had been convicted of an offence, but they made a slight mistake as to the sentence imposed. The plaintiff's claim failed.

   This defence can be a dangerous one for the defendant, because the onus is on him to prove that his statements were substantially true, and if he fails the damages awarded may be heavier because the defamation has now been repeated in court.

3. *Fair comment.* In the interests of free speech and criticism, opinions passed on matters which are of public concern may be defended on the grounds that they are *fair comment made in good faith on a matter of public interest.* This applies to anything which may fairly be said to invite comment or challenge public attention, such as the conduct of people in the public eye, the administration of public affairs and institutions, and the publication of plays, books, and films. The defence can be very important in connection with political comment. The views expressed by the defendant must be honestly held, even though they may be prejudiced or exaggerated. The comment ceases to be fair if it is malicious or stems from an improper motive, as when it takes the form of a personal attack on the character of the plaintiff in circumstances where his personal character is not of public concern.
4. *Privilege.* In some circumstances the public interest is thought to be more important than private reputations, and statements made in these situations are protected.

    If the privilege is *absolute*, the statement is given complete protection, irrespective of the motive or good faith of the person who made it. This applies to state communications, for example, by Ministers or senior civil servants, Parliamentary proceedings, reports issued by order of Parliament, and statements made in judicial proceedings (Unit 12). Newspaper or broadcast reports of judicial proceedings are privileged provided they are fair, accurate, and contemporaneous.

    In other situations the privilege is *qualified*, and only protects in the absence of malice, in the sense of spite or ill-will. In other words, there is protection for statements honestly, if mistakenly, made. This defence applies when there is a common or reciprocal interest between the publisher and the recipient, the former having a duty to make the statement and the latter having an interest in receiving it.

    > In *Watt* v. *Longsdon* (1930), a company letter alleging misconduct and immorality on the part of the plaintiff, an employee, was shown both to the chairman of the company and to the plaintiff's wife. It was held that the first publication was privileged in the absence of malice, for the person who had the letter had a duty to warn the chairman, who in turn had an interest in receiving it. Showing the letter to the wife, however, was not privileged, because there was no duty to communicate it to her.

    Qualified privilege can protect derogatory statements in testimonials and references, and can also apply to fair and accurate reports of Parliamentary, judicial, and other public proceedings.
5. Two other matters, although not complete defences, may be put forward in mitigation in order to reduce the amount of damages awarded:

    (a) an *apology* made in an appropriate manner as soon as there was an opportunity to do so;

    (b) *evidence of the plaintiff's bad reputation* in respect of the same sort of thing as the defamatory comments have alleged, so that although this particular statement may be untrue, the defendant's reputation was of little value anyway.

E. Deceit

The tort of deceit (fraud) is committed when one person fraudulently makes a false statement of fact intending another to act on it, the other does so act, and thereby suffers loss. We have seen earlier in the book how, in limited situations, liability can arise for *negligent* mis-statements; the tort of deceit is concerned with *intentional* or *reckless* falsehood.

A false statement of fact which induces a contract between the maker of the statement and the recipient will amount to a misrepresentation, and give a right of action for damages under section 2(1) of the Misrepresentation Act 1967 (Unit 18). In these circumstances there can be an overlap between misrepresentation and the tort of deceit. The tort can also apply in many other situations, however. It has five main elements.

1. There must be a false statement of *fact*, not merely an expression of opinion.
2. It must be made fraudulently, that is knowingly, or without belief in its truth, or recklessly, not caring whether it be true or false.

    In *Derry* v. *Peek* (1889), the directors of a tramway company carelessly made a false statement that the company had Board of Trade consent to run steam trams. In reliance on this, Peek bought shares in the company, and suffered loss when it was wound up. It was held that the directors were not liable for deceit; they had been careless, but not dishonest.

3. The plaintiff must be intended to act on the statement.
4. He must actually act in reliance on it.
5. He must thereby suffer loss, generally monetary loss.

F. Liability for animals

It is possible to commit a tort by means of an animal and, in appropriate cases, an action may lie for negligence, nuisance or trespass to the person. Other forms of liability, peculiar to the owners of animals, are now contained in the Animals Act 1971, which imposes strict liability in several important situations. The Act largely follows the recommendations of the Law Commission. It re-enacted much of the existing law, and codified certain common law rules, with amendments designed to make the rules more coherent and appropriate to modern conditions.

Strict liability

Strict liability for damage done by an animal is imposed in three instances.

1. *Dangerous animals*

Where any damage is caused by an animal which belongs to a dangerous species, its keeper is strictly liable. Such animals include those belonging to a species not commonly domesticated in the British Isles which are likely to cause severe damage, for example, tigers or bears. Strict liability is also owed for animals of a harmless species, if the particular animal has dangerous characteristics known to the keeper, for example, a vicious dog. The keeper is the person who has ownership or possession of the animal, but if this person is under the age of 16 the head of the household is responsible. Damage covers both damage to property and personal injuries and may include disease and nervous shock.

Liability is strict in the sense that it does not depend upon proof of negligence, but the Act does provide three defences to the keeper of dangerous animals. In the first place, there is no liability if the damage was wholly the plaintiff's own fault, for example, by teasing the animal. Second, there would be no liability to a person who voluntarily accepted the risk of harm, for instance by entering a lion's cage, or intervening needlessly in a dog fight; this is, in effect, the defence of *volenti non fit injuria*. Third, the keeper would not be liable to a trespasser for injuries inflicted by an animal kept on the premises, so long as the animal was not kept specially as a guard. If the animal was a guard, for example a guard dog in a factory, the keeper will only escape liability to a trespasser if he can show that keeping it there was reasonable. What is reasonable is a question of fact; it might be unreasonable to put a savage bull to guard a field where children are known to play, but a guard dog in a factory at night might be reasonable if there were warning notices, and the factory was also securely fenced.

2. Injury done by dogs to livestock

The keeper of a dog is strictly liable when it kills or injures livestock. There are two exceptions to this rule. First, the keeper is not liable if the damage was wholly the plaintiff's own fault. Second, where livestock has strayed on to land, there is no liability for injuries inflicted by a dog owned by the occupier or authorized by him to be there. The dog-owner might commit some other tort, however, such as negligence or trespass to goods, if he encourages or allows his dog to attack.

A farmer may be entitled to shoot a dog which is attacking his livestock, but only in two situations: if the dog is worrying, or about to worry, the animals and there is no other means of stopping it; or the dog has been worrying the animals, is still in the vicinity, is not in its owner's control, and there is no means of discovering the owner. In either case, the farmer must give notice to the police within 48 hours of having had to kill or injure the dog.

3. Damage caused by trespassing livestock

The owner of livestock will be strictly liable for damage done by his livestock to land or other property if it strays on to another person's land. There are two exceptions to this: where the damage was wholly the fault of the plaintiff, and where the animals were lawfully being taken along a highway and strayed from there. Where livestock has strayed on to another's land, the occupier may, in some circumstances, detain it until he is paid for damage caused, plus the expense of keeping the animals. He must give notice to the police and to the owner of the animals, if known, within 48 hours. If the owner of the animals does not pay for the damage, the occupier may sell them after 14 days to re-imburse himself.

Animals straying on to the highway

It is appropriate to mention here that, at common law, there was no obligation to fence against harmless animals straying on to the highway from adjoining land and no liability for any damage that might result, for example, from an ensuing road accident.

This exception to the general principles of negligence was deemed to be insupportable in view of the modern growth of motor traffic, and was abolished by the Animals Act. By section 8, an ordinary duty of care is owed to prevent damage from animals straying on to the highway. The duty is to take reasonable care, and all circumstances must be considered. The Act provides that account is to be taken of whether the animals had been placed by right on common land, or land situated in an area where fencing is not customary, such as moorland sheep farms.

For further consideration

1. Brenda is leaving Cutprice Supermarket when Sharp, the manager, takes hold of her arm and says in a loud voice, 'You are a regular shoplifter. Come with me to the police station.' Brenda, who is innocent, escapes from his grip by striking him with her handbag. A police officer who is passing hears Sharp's accusation, arrests Brenda and charges her with theft.
   Comment upon the legal position.
2. Copper leaves a dangerous dog to guard his scrapyard and puts up appropriate warning notices. Tommy, aged six, who cannot read, climbs over the fence and is attacked by the dog. John, who is passing, hears the child's screams and goes to his rescue. He is also badly bitten by the dog.
   Advise Copper.
3. Smith says that Peggy is expecting a baby. Margaret, who is unmarried and who is sometimes known as Peggy, wishes to take action against him for defamation. Advise Margaret of what she must prove and what defences Smith may put forward.
4. In what circumstances, if any, may a lecturer
   (a) wake up a student who has fallen asleep;
   (b) threaten to hit a student who has not prepared work for the class; and
   (c) lock the door of the lecture room without incurring liability for trespass to the person?

Unit 16. The Nature of a Contract in English Law

A. Essential requirements

There are still misconceptions about this branch of law. For many people the word contract suggests a visit to a solicitor's office and the signing of a formal document containing incomprehensible language. This is far from the truth. Most people make contracts every day of their lives, usually without realizing it. Every time they buy an article or pay for a service such as a haircut they are entering into a contract, while matters connected with their work such as holidays, and hours, are governed by the contract which they have made with their employer.

Another popular belief is that a contract must be in writing. Apart from a few exceptional instances (see later), this is not so. Most contracts are made by word of mouth. It may be desirable to have a written agreement where a lot is at stake, or where the contract has to last for a long time, but this is only for practical purposes of proof, and is usually not legally necessary.

A contract is simply *an agreement which the law will recognize*. It is of vital importance in business life, and forms the basis of most commercial transactions, such as the sale of goods and land, the giving of credit, insurance, carriage of goods, formation and sale of business organizations and, to some extent, employment.

What agreements will the law recognize?

The law will not recognize all agreements. The law of contract is concerned mainly with providing a framework within which business can operate; if agreements could be broken with impunity, the unscrupulous could create havoc. English law will intervene, therefore, and make the person who breaks an agreement pay compensation (damages) to the other party, but only if the agreement has the following essential features.

1. *Intention to create legal relations.* Unless the courts are satisfied that the parties intended the agreement to be legally binding, the courts will take no notice of it (see later).
2. *Agreement.* The courts must be satisfied that the parties had reached a firm agreement, and that they were not still negotiating. Agreement will usually be shown by the unconditional acceptance of an offer (Unit 17).
3. *Consideration.* English law will only recognize a *bargain*, not a mere promise. A contract, therefore, must be a two-sided affair, each side providing or promising to provide some consideration in exchange for what the other is to provide (see later).
4. *Form.* Certain *exceptional* types of agreement are only valid if made in a particular form, for example, in writing.
5. *Definite terms.* It must be possible for the courts to ascertain what the parties have agreed upon. If the terms are so vague as to be meaningless, the law will not recognize the agreement (Unit 17).
6. *Legality.* Certain types of agreement are so plainly 'contrary to public policy' that the law will have nothing to do with them. For example, the courts would not allow a hired murderer to recover damages if his principal refused to pay the agreed price (Unit 22).

Defective contracts

Discussion of essential requirements must also include situations where, although English law will recognize the agreement, the contract will only be given limited or no effect.

Some defects will render a contract *unenforceable*, so that although the contract does exist, neither party can *sue* the other; certain contracts, for example, need not be *in* writing, but are unenforceable unless there is written evidence of the essential terms (see later). Goods or money which pass under such a contract are validly transferred and cannot be reclaimed, but the contract cannot be sued upon if one of the parties refuses to abide by its terms.

Other defects can render a contract *voidable*. Although English law will recognize the agreement, it will allow one of the parties to withdraw from it if he so wishes. Voidable contracts include most agreements made by minors or by persons incapacitated by drunkenness or insanity, and contracts induced by misrepresentation, duress or undue influence.

Finally, there are defects which can render a contract *void*, that is, destitute of all legal effect. The expression 'void contract' is really a contradiction in terms; if the contract is void it cannot be a contract. The expression is useful, however, to describe a situation where the parties have attempted to contract but the law will give no effect to their agreement at all. Thus a contract may be void if there is a common mistake on some fundamental issue, as where the parties agree to sell a cargo which, unknown to both, has already been completely destroyed. Mistake as to the identity of the other party may also render a contract void (Unit 18).

The distinction between void and voidable contracts is important where the rights of third parties are concerned. If a contract of sale is void, ownership of the property sold will not pass to the buyer, and he cannot normally sell it to anyone else. The original seller will be able to recover the property from whoever has it. If the contract is merely voidable, it remains valid unless and until the innocent party chooses to terminate it; therefore, if the buyer re-sells *before* the contract is avoided, the sub-buyer becomes the owner, and can retain the property provided that he took it in good faith.

B. Intention to create legal relations

Many agreements are plainly never intended by the parties to be *legally* binding; there is no intention to take any dispute to a court of law.

In the case of agreements of a friendly, social or domestic nature there is a strong presumption that the parties did not intend to create a legal relationship. If friends agree to come to tea and they fail to turn up, or if a husband agrees to meet his wife and forgets, there can be no action for breach of contract, even though the complaining party may have incurred certain expenses.

> In *Balfour* v. *Balfour* (1919), a husband promised his wife an allowance before he left to take up a post abroad. When he stopped the payments, an action by the wife failed on the ground that this was not a binding contract but merely a domestic agreement with no legal obligations attached to it.

> Conversely, in *Simpkins* v. *Pays* (1955), three people sharing a house, the owner, her granddaughter, and a paying lodger, regularly entered a competition in a Sunday newspaper. The entries were sent in the name of the grandmother, but all three contributed. When an entry won, the grandmother refused to share the prize of £750. It was held that the others *were* entitled to share, because their agreement to this effect was, in the view of the court, intended to be legally binding.

On the other hand, there is a strong presumption that business agreements are intended to create legal relations. This presumption can be rebutted, but only by very strong evidence. One way in which this can be done is by a clear statement in a written contract.

> In *Rose and Frank* v. *Crompton Bros. Ltd* (1925), an English company agreed to sell carbon paper in America through a New York firm. This marketing arrangement was for a renewable period of three years and provided that 'This arrangement is not entered into . . . as a formal or legal agreement, and shall not be subject to legal jurisdiction in the Law Courts . . . '. Therefore, when the English company withdrew, it was not liable for breach of contract, although it was held liable to honour orders placed before withdrawal.

> Similarly, in *Appleson* v. *Littlewood Ltd* (1939), the plaintiff sued to recover money which he claimed to have won on a football pool. His action failed, because the printed entry form contained a statement that the transaction was 'binding in honour only'.

Most collective agreements between employers and trade unions as to wages and other terms of employment will not be legally binding. The parties are assumed to have intended the agreement to be a broad working arrangement, not a binding contract to be subject to detailed scrutiny in the courts.

C. Consideration

As stated above, the English law of contract is concerned with *bargains*, not mere promises. Thus if A promises to *give* something to B, the law will not allow any remedy if A breaks his promise. On the other hand, if B promises to do (or does) something in return, so that A's promise is dependent upon B's, this reciprocal element, the *exchange* of promises, turns the arrangement into a contract. To use legal terminology, A's promise (or action) is the 'consideration' for B's, and vice versa. Thus the promise of the seller to deliver the car is consideration for the buyer's promise to pay the agreed price.

Consideration may, therefore, be described broadly as something given, promised or done in exchange. The act, forbearance or promise of each party is the price for which the promise of the other is bought.

Consideration can be *executory* or *executed*. Executory consideration is a promise yet to be fulfilled, and most contracts start in this way, with the consideration executory on both sides. Executed consideration is the completed performance of one side of the bargain.

The existence of consideration

Consideration must exist and have some value; otherwise there is no contract. The following have no value and cannot therefore constitute consideration so as to render a promise actionable.

1. *Past consideration.* Something already done and completed by B at the time when A makes a promise to him cannot operate as consideration. A already has the benefit of what B has done, and therefore receives nothing in exchange. Thus if, unasked, I paint my neighbour's house while he is away and, upon his return, he promises me £100 for doing so, I have no remedy if he later refuses to pay me.

   In *Eastwood* v. *Kenyon* (1840), the plaintiff had been the guardian of a Miss Sutcliffe, and had spent money on her upkeep and education. When she came of age, the girl promised to repay her guardian, and her husband, Kenyon, repeated this promise when she married. It was held, however, that the guardian could not recover damages when these promises were broken, because the consideration for them was past. Any moral obligation to repay was irrelevant.

   Similarly, in *Roscorla* v. *Thomas* (1842), *after* Roscorla had bought a horse, the seller promised that it was sound and free from vice. It was held that Roscorla could not sue for breach of this undertaking, for which no new consideration had been given. (This rule would apply equally to undertakings given by a car salesman after the sale has been agreed.)

   A contrast must be drawn with those situations where, although the actual promise to pay a specific sum is made after the work has been carried out, there was an implied promise to pay (a reasonable sum) before the work was begun. If my neighbour *asks* me to paint his house, he may be impliedly promising to pay for my work.

In *Stewart* v. *Casey* (1892), Stewart, who was joint owner of some patents, asked Casey to promote them. *After* Casey had done so successfully, Stewart promised him a share in them. It was held that this promise was binding, and that the consideration was not past. The original request carried with it an implied promise to pay a reasonable amount for Casey's services. The subsequent promise to share in the profits merely put a figure to the original promise, which was given before Casey carried out his side of the bargain.

2. *A promise to perform an existing obligation to the promisee.* This will not be consideration, because the promisor is not giving anything over and above what he was already bound to give.

Therefore, if a creditor agrees to take a smaller sum in full satisfaction of a larger debt, he will be able to go back on this agreement and sue for the rest. All that the debtor has done is to pay part of what he already owed, which is no consideration for the promise to excuse him from paying the rest. If A is owed £10 by B and agrees to take £9 in full satisfaction, he can still go back later and demand the remaining £1.

In *D & C Builders Ltd* v. *Rees* (1966), the defendant owed £482 to the building company for work carried out, and refused to pay. Eventually, the builders agreed to take a cheque of £300 in full satisfaction of the debt. It was held that they were still entitled to demand the remaining £182, because there was no consideration for the earlier promise to settle for less.

On the other hand, if the debtor gives some *new* consideration for the creditor's promise to release part of the debt, the promise will bind the creditor. If, in exchange for the creditor's promise, the debtor pays off the debt earlier than he was bound to do, or at a place other than where he was bound to do, the creditor's release will be binding.

These rules apply equally to obligations other than debts, and extend to public duties as well as obligations owed directly to the promisee. Thus a promise by a public official to do something which he is already under a public duty to do will not be valuable consideration; a promise to do more than his duty *can* be enough.

In *Glasbrook Bros* v. *Glamorgan County Council* (1925), the police were offered £2200 to provide a special guard for a coal mine during a strike. It was held that they could recover this amount when the owners later refused to pay, because the special guard went beyond the ordinary police duty to protect property. (Similarly, police authorities receive payment from football clubs for providing officers inside the ground, and could sue for this sum if it were not paid.)

3. *A promise made by a third party.* In general, only a person who has given consideration may enforce a contract. For example, A may promise to pay £1 to B, if B will give a book to C. If B refuses to deliver the book, A may sue, but not C; C has given no consideration and is not a party to the contract (Unit 21, Privity of contract).

4. *Vague promises*, which are incapable of monetary value, will not be consideration. A promise to show natural love and affection or to behave as a good son should behave will be of no effect in the law of contract.

The adequacy of consideration

Provided that the consideration has some value in the monetary sense, the court will not concern itself with whether or not the value is adequate, for the value of a particular article or service is largely a matter of opinion and for the parties to decide. The court will not make a man's bargain for him. The price paid may be relevant in determining whether goods are 'merchantable' at that price (Unit 23), but this does not directly affect the existence of the contract. The fact that goods are sold for a very high or low price may also be evidence, but no more than evidence, of fraud.

Promises made by deed

There is one major exception to the rules relating to consideration. Where a person embodies his promise in a formal document called a *deed*, it can be enforced against him whether or not the promisee has given any consideration. A deed is a document signed by the person making the promise, and 'sealed' and 'delivered' by him. Promises made by deed are sometimes called *specialty* contracts, as opposed to *simple* contracts.

Equitable estoppel

Although a promise made without consideration cannot be sued upon, and will not amount to a contract, it may have limited effect as a *defence*. If A promises not to enforce his rights against B, and the promise is intended to be binding, intended to be acted upon, and is in fact acted upon by B, then A may be estopped from later bringing any action inconsistent with his promise. This defence has been called equitable or promissory estoppel.

> In *Central London Property Trust* v. *High Trees House* (1947), the lease of a block of flats proved unprofitable to the tenant because of the war, and the landlord made a written promise to reduce the rent while the war lasted. After the war, the landlord withdrew this promise and started to charge the full rent again. It was held that he was free to do this for the future, because no consideration had been given for the wartime promise. On the other hand, the court said, *obiter*, that the landlord could not have recovered the full rent for the period between making his promise and the end of the war since the tenant had relied on the landlord's promise.

D. Form

In general, the form in which a contract is made does not matter and will have no effect upon the validity of the contract. There are certain exceptions, however.

Some contracts must be by deed. Promises for no consideration, and some bills of sale (mortgages of goods), are void unless in this form. Conveyances of land and leases for over three years must be completed by deed.

Contracts which must be in writing, but not necessarily by deed, include bills of exchange, cheques and promissory notes, contracts of marine insurance, the transfer of shares in a company, and legal assignment of debts. Absence of writing will render such contracts void.

Agreements to dispose of certain consumer durable goods on credit with payment by instalments may have to comply with any Hire Purchase and Credit Sale Agreements (Control) Order currently in force, and the Order will usually render such agreements void unless made in writing and in compliance with other specified requirements. Some agreements for hiring consumer durables come under similar credit controls. Moreover, hire purchase and other regulated agreements which come within the Consumer Credit Act 1974 may be unenforceable against the borrower unless made in writing and unless they include the information required under the Act.

There is another group of contracts which, although not required to be in writing, will be unenforceable in the courts unless there is written evidence of the essential terms. This requirement derives historically from the Statute of Frauds 1677, and only affects two main types of contract today: contracts of guarantee and contracts for the sale or other disposition of land or any interest in land. This second category is now covered by section 40 of the Law of Property Act 1925, which substantially re-enacted part of the Statute of Frauds.

The written 'note or memorandum' which must be produced as evidence can come from correspondence or any other papers, whether made at or after the time of the contract. The writing must contain the names of the parties, or otherwise identify them, identify the subject-matter and, in relation to land, state the price or other consideration. It must also have been signed by the party against whom the evidence is to be used, or by his authorized agent.

The absence of written evidence does not affect the validity of the contract, but simply makes it unenforceable in the courts. A party can obtain rights under an unenforceable agreement so long as he does not have to *sue*: thus a vendor can keep the deposit paid by a prospective purchaser of a house should the latter default, whether or not there is any written evidence.

In relation to land, there is one important way of escaping this requirement of written evidence, namely through the equitable doctrine of part performance, now preserved by section 40 of the Law of Property Act 1925. The old Court of Chancery could not overrule a statute, but it would not allow it to be used as an instrument of fraud and could intervene if one party tried to take unfair advantage of the lack of written evidence. Where certain conditions are satisfied, the court may give the remedy of specific performance (Unit 20) compelling the promisor to carry out his promise, notwithstanding that there is no written note or memorandum. The conditions are as follows:

1. There must have been some act of part performance by the plaintiff, so as to carry out part of his side of the bargain.
2. The probable explanation of that act must be a contract such as is alleged to exist. The most obvious explanation for what the plaintiff has done is that he has made the contract which he claims to have made.

UNIT 16. THE NATURE OF A CONTRACT IN ENGLISH LAW

3. It must, in effect, be fraudulent of the defendant to try to rely on the absence of written evidence to escape liability.
4. Specific performance must be possible.
5. There must be sufficient oral evidence.

> In *Rawlinson* v. *Ames* (1925), Rawlinson orally agreed to lease his flat to the defendant and, at her request, carried out alterations. There was evidence that she gave continuing instructions as to what should be done. It was held that the only reasonable explanation for this was the existence of a contract such as Rawlinson alleged, and he, therefore, obtained an order for specific performance of the agreement even though there was no written evidence.

It must be remembered that the only remedy which can be given in these circumstances is specific performance (Unit 20). In the absence of written evidence, damages will not be awarded in the case of contracts to which section 40 applies.

For further consideration

1. What contracts did you make (a) today, (b) yesterday, and (c) last Saturday?
2. Explain whether or not Henry has a remedy in respect of each of the following agreements.
   (a) His daughter has a knitting machine upon which she makes jerseys in her spare time. Henry promises to sell these garments in his shop and advertises them accordingly. His daughter then gives up knitting and fails to deliver any jerseys.
   (b) He agrees to buy a consignment of socks from a wholesaler. The contract contains a clause excluding the jurisdiction of the courts. The wholesaler fails to deliver the goods.
   (c) He enters into an agreement with a trade union regarding a productivity scheme for his shop assistants. The union fails to honour the agreement.
3. (a) 'The rules of consideration ensure that English law only recognizes agreements which have a business element in them.' To what extent is this true?
   (b) Simple asks his friend, Sharp, a car dealer, if he will sell his (Simple's) car. After Sharp has sold the car Simple promises to pay him £20 for doing so. Simple later refuses to pay. Advise Sharp.
4. (a) Which type of contracts are at present required to be in a particular form? Explain in each case why you think that the requirement was imposed, and describe the consequences of non-compliance.
   (b) 'The requirement that certain contracts must be evidenced in writing can cause as many frauds as it prevents.' Do you agree? Explain your views.

Unit 17. Agreement

Unit 16 was concerned with some of the essential features which must be present in an agreement before English law will recognize it as a contract. This unit is concerned with how and when agreement is reached.

There is a difference between the situation where negotiations are in progress and the situation where a binding agreement has been reached. During negotiations, each side is free to withdraw without any sanction; after agreement has been concluded, withdrawal can amount to breach of contract. Agreement is usually shown in English law by the unconditional acceptance of an offer, and these elements will be examined in turn.

A. Offer

This is a statement of the terms on which the offeror is willing to be bound. If the offer is accepted as it stands, agreement is made.

An offer may be made to a specific person and only open to him to accept, as where A offers to sell his car to B for a stated price. An offer may be made to a class of persons, any one of whom may accept, as where the offer is only open to employees of a company or members of a particular club. An offer may, sometimes, be made to the whole world, as where the owner offers a reward to anyone who returns his lost canary.

The following are *not* offers in this legal sense.

1. *A mere invitation to treat.* This is an indication that a person is willing to enter into negotiations, but *not* that he is yet willing to be bound by the terms mentioned. Catalogues or circulars advertising goods for sale constitute such invitations. The

same applies when a large undertaking invites tenders for the supply of goods or services. A company prospectus which invites investors to buy its shares is also an invitation to treat and not an offer, because the company can still refuse to allot the shares to those who apply for them.

In many cases where a person indicates that he is willing to deal with anyone in the world, as in the examples just given, this will be treated as a mere invitation to treat; otherwise there would be an impossible situation if, for example, an advertisement to sell a car were held to be a firm offer, and 20 acceptances were received. Only in cases where the advertiser very clearly intended to be bound will an advertisement be treated as a firm offer.

Perhaps the best examples of invitations to treat are goods in a shop window, even with price tickets attached. The shopkeeper does not undertake to sell the goods. They are on display merely to invite customers to come in and offer to buy at the price shown. The shopkeeper can always refuse, although obviously he rarely does so. The same rule applies to the display of goods in a self-service store.

> In *Fisher* v. *Bell* (1961), a criminal case, the shopkeeper displayed a flick-knife in the shop window. He was charged with *offering* an offensive weapon for sale, and acquitted, because the display was only an invitation to treat. (The Restriction of Offensive Weapons Act 1961 was enacted immediately after this case to cover the display of weapons with a view to sale.)

> In *Pharmaceutical Society of Great Britain* v. *Boots Cash Chemists* (1953), another criminal case, customers selected pharmaceutical goods from self-service counters, and paid later at the cash desk, where a pharmacist was in attendance with the cashier. It was held that the display on the shelves was a mere invitation to treat. The customer made the offer when he took the goods to the cashier, who could always refuse to sell. Therefore, the pharmacist was present where the sale took place.

2. A '*mere puff*' or *boast*, which no one would take too seriously, such as a claim on the packet that 'Brand X washes whitest', will not be treated as a firm offer. There can, however, be a narrow borderline between mere boasts, and promises which a reasonable man would take seriously.

> In *Carlill* v. *Carbolic Smoke Ball Co.* (1893), the defendants advertised that they would pay £100 to anyone who caught influenza after using their smoke balls and that, as evidence of their sincerity, they had deposited £1000 with a named bank. Mrs Carlill followed their instructions, but still caught influenza, and consequently claimed £100. One of the many defences put forward was that the advertisement was not an offer. It was held that, in the circumstances, it was an offer. A reasonable person would take the promise seriously, and assume that the advertiser intended to be bound on the terms stated.

3. *A declaration of intention* is, similarly, not intended to form the basis of a contract, and is not an offer.

> In *Harris* v. *Nickerson* (1873), an auction sale was advertised and later cancelled, and the plaintiff, who had travelled to the place of sale, claimed his travelling expenses as damages. His action failed, for the advertisement was not an offer which he could accept by making the journey.

4. *Merely giving information* is not an offer.

> In *Harvey* v. *Facey* (1893), the plaintiff telegraphed 'will you sell us Bumper Hall Pen? Telegraph lowest price', and the reply was 'lowest price for Bumper Hall Pen £900'. This was held to be merely an answer to a request for information, and not an offer which could be accepted.

An offer must be communicated to the other party

Unless the offeree is aware of the offer he is unable to accept it. If X finds a wallet and returns it to the owner, he cannot claim any reward that may have been offered if he had no previous knowledge of this.

> In *Taylor* v. *Laird* (1856), the captain of a ship resigned his command in a foreign port, but later helped to work the ship home. The owners were entitled to refuse payment for these services for, by the failure to communicate the offer to them, the owners had no option of either accepting or refusing.

Duration of the offer

An offer does not continue indefinitely. While the offeree may be content *at the moment* to deal on the terms of the offer, circumstances may change. Once an offer has come to an end, it can no longer be accepted. It can end in the following ways.

1. It is possible for the offeror to *revoke* or withdraw his offer at any time up to acceptance. He is entitled to do this even if he has promised to keep the offer open for a specified time, unless the offeree had paid a sum of money or given some other consideration in return for such a promise (sometimes known as 'buying an option'). Even then, the offer can be withdrawn before the agreed time, but withdrawal will be a breach of this subsidiary contract to keep open the negotiations.

> In *Routledge* v. *Grant* (1828), Grant offered to buy Routledge's house, and gave him six weeks to decide whether to accept his offer. Before six weeks had elapsed, Grant withdrew his offer. He was held entitled to do so at any time before acceptance.

Revocation is only effective if it is communicated to the offeree, either by express words or by conduct which shows a clear intention to revoke. Selling the goods elsewhere would be an example of such conduct, but this will only revoke the offer when the first prospective buyer learns of the sale. Communication can be by the seller himself, or by another reliable source.

> In *Dickinson* v. *Dodds* (1876), the defendant had offered to sell a house to the plaintiff. Before the plaintiff accepted, the defendant sold the house to someone else. The plaintiff learned of this from a friend, Berry. It was held that, since the plaintiff had heard of the revocation from a reliable source, the original offer to him was revoked, and he could not now accept it. (On the other hand, a mere rumour would be much less likely to amount to reliable communication of revocation.)

2. An offer will *lapse* if the offeror imposes a time limit for acceptance, and the other party does not accept within that time. If no express time limit is imposed, the offer will lapse after a *reasonable* time. What is reasonable will depend on all the circumstances.

> In *Ramsgate Victoria Hotel Co.* v. *Montefiore* (1866), an investor offered in June to buy shares in the plaintiff company. He heard nothing until November, by which time he no longer wanted the shares. It was held that it was now too late for the company to accept his offer.

3. The *death* of either party before acceptance will normally terminate the offer, certainly from the moment when the other party learns of the death and, when the identity of the other party is vital, from the time of death.

4. Once the offeree has *rejected* an offer he cannot later go back and purport to accept it. A counter-offer will operate as a rejection.

> In *Hyde* v. *Wrench* (1840), an offer was made to sell a farm for £1000. A counter-offer of £950 was made and refused, whereupon the buyer tried to accept the original offer of £1000. It was held that the seller could refuse this, because the original offer had been rejected.

Acceptance subject to conditions will also be a rejection, because the offeree is trying to introduce new terms into the bargain.

> In *Neale* v. *Merrett* (1930), the defendant offered to sell land to the plaintiff for £280. The plaintiff 'accepted' this offer, sent a cheque for £80, and promised to pay the rest by instalments of £50. It was held that there was no contract; the purported acceptance introduced credit terms which the seller did not want.

Rejection, like offer and revocation, must be communicated, and is only effective from the moment when the offeree learns of it. If, therefore, the offeree sends a letter of rejection, but then changes his mind and telephones acceptance before the rejection arrives, there will be a valid contract.

5. An offer may be *conditional* upon other circumstances. If the conditions are not fulfilled, the offer will lapse. The conditions may be express or implied.

> In *Financings Ltd* v. *Stimson* (1962), a customer offered to take a car on hire purchase from Financings Ltd. Before the offer was accepted, the car was stolen from the dealer's garage where it was being kept, and badly damaged. Unaware of this, Financings Ltd purported to accept the offer. It was held that it could no longer do so. The customer's offer was subject to the implied condition that the car remain in substantially the same state between offer and acceptance.

6. *Acceptance*, by completing the contract, will bring the offer to an end. If an offer, capable of acceptance by only one person, is made to a group of people and one accepts, the offer then ceases to exist so far as the rest of the group is concerned.

B. Acceptance

This must take place while the offer is still open. It must be an absolute and unqualified acceptance of the offer, as it stands, with any terms that may be attached. As we have seen, anything else will amount to rejection.

On occasions, an acceptance may be made subject to a written or formal agreement. It is then a question of construction whether the parties intend to be bound by the initial agreement, and the writing is only for the purpose of recording this, or whether there is no intention to be bound until the more formal agreement is made. This arises frequently in contracts for the sale of land, where it is now well established that certain phrases, particularly 'subject to contract', denote the second of these alternatives. Since an agreement 'subject to contract' does not bind either party, its value may be questioned; it does, however, show that the parties are sufficiently interested to pursue the matter further.

Acceptance completes the contract, and the place where acceptance is made is, therefore, the place of the contract. This rule may be important in determining in which County Court an action for breach should be brought. If negotiations take place between parties in different countries, the rule may help to determine which system of law applies.

The manner of acceptance

Acceptance may take the form of words, spoken or written, or it may be implied by conduct, as where the offeree performs some specific act required by the offeror. Mere mental assent is insufficient, nor is it possible in English law to dispense with acceptance altogether. There must be some positive act of acceptance, and mere silence will never be enough.

> In *Felthouse* v. *Bindley* (1863), negotiations were taking place regarding the price of a horse. The plaintiff eventually wrote, 'If I hear no more about him, I consider the horse mine at £30 15s.' The defendant did not reply. It was held that, although he had intended to accept and sell at this price, his silence could not constitute acceptance, and there was therefore no sale.

Thus, where unsolicited goods arrive through the post with a note saying that unless they are returned within a specified time the recipient will be bound to pay the price, this note can be safely ignored. So long as the recipient does not treat the goods as his, by using or deliberately destroying them, his silence will not amount to acceptance. Indeed, under the Unsolicited Goods and Services Act 1971, the recipient will become owner of the goods as against the sender, unless the sender collects them within six months; the recipient can, by notice to the sender, reduce this period to 30 days. (Where the seller is a dealer, it can also be a criminal offence for him to demand payment.)

Communication of acceptance

As a general rule, acceptance must be communicated to the offeror. There is no contract until the offeror knows that his offer has been accepted. The acceptance must, moreover, be communicated by the offeree himself or his authorized agent. Unlike revocation, acceptance cannot be communicated by an unauthorized third party, however reliable.

> In *Powell* v. *Lee* (1908), the plaintiff had applied for a post as headmaster. The school managers decided to appoint him, and one of the managers, without authority, told him this unofficially. Later the managers changed their minds. It was held that they were free to do so; there was no contract with Powell, because acceptance had not been communicated by the managers.

There are two main exceptions to the rule that acceptance is only effective on communication.

1. *The offeror may dispense with communication*, and indicate that the offeree should, if he wishes to accept, simply carry out his side of the bargain without bothering to inform the offeror. Thus if a customer wrote ordering coal and, without further communication, the coal was delivered in accordance with the order, the delivery would be acceptance of the offer to buy.

   > In *Carlill* v. *Carbolic Smoke Ball Co.* (1893), another defence raised was that Mrs Carlill had not communicated to the company that she intended to use the smoke ball and catch influenza. This defence also failed; the nature of the offer made communication of acceptance inappropriate.

2. *Where the posting rule applies*, a letter of acceptance, properly addressed and stamped, is effective from the moment of posting, even if it never arrives. Three points must be emphasized about the posting rule. In the first place, the rule only applies where it must have been in the contemplation of the parties that the post would be used as a means of communicating the acceptance. This will not always be the case; if all the negotiations have taken place by telephone, and the offeror clearly expects a reply by telephone, a letter of acceptance might not be effective until it arrived. Second, there must obviously be some evidence of posting. It is not enough to give the letter to some other person to post, or even to hand it to a postman; it must be put into the hands of the postal authorities in the normal way. Finally, the posting rule only applies to acceptance; an offer, or a letter of revocation or rejection, will only be effective on arrival.

   > In *Byrne* v. *Van Tienhoven* (1880), a firm in Cardiff offered by letter to sell tin plate to a firm in New York. Later, it sent another letter revoking this offer, but while this was in transit and before its delivery, the New York firm posted a letter of acceptance. It was held that the parties clearly intended the use of the post to communicate acceptance, and posting the letter of acceptance, therefore, brought the contract into existence, since this was done before the revocation arrived.

These rules also apply to telegrams, but not to the use of the telephone or telex. In these latter cases, the communication is virtually instantaneous and is inoperative unless and until it reaches the other party.

> In *Entores* v. *Miles Far East Corporation* (1955), an acceptance sent by telex from Amsterdam to London was held to be effective only when it arrived in London, so that the contract, being made in England, could be brought before the English courts.

C. Certainty of terms

Even where offer and acceptance are apparently complete, there may still be no agreement. There can be no contract at all if it is impossible to say *what* the parties have agreed upon because the terms are too uncertain. In particular, this will be the case where the parties have still left essential terms to be settled between them. They are still at the stage of negotiation, and an agreement to agree in future is not a contract.

> In *Scammell* v. *Ouston* (1941), Ouston agreed to take a van 'on the understanding that the balance of the purchase price can be had on hire purchase terms over a period of two years'. It was held that this contract was void for uncertainty, because no one could say *what* hire purchase terms were envisaged.
>
> In *King's Motors* (*Oxford*) *Ltd* v. *Lax* (1969), an option to renew a lease 'at such rental as may be agreed upon between the parties' was similarly held void.

On the other hand, this rule is subject to some qualifications, for example:

1. The parties will be bound if, although the agreement is not complete yet, the parties have made provision to render it complete without any further negotiations between themselves.

   > In *Foley* v. *Classique Coaches Ltd* (1934), a garage owner agreed to sell land to the bus company on condition that the company would buy all its petrol from the garage 'at a price to be agreed by the parties'. A later clause provided that any dispute as to the subject-matter or content of the agreement should be referred to arbitration. The agreement as to petrol was held binding because it was part of a larger contract which the parties clearly intended to be bound by and, in the event of disagreement, the price could be referred to arbitration.

2. If the parties have agreed criteria according to which the price can be calculated, or have had previous dealings similar to the present transaction, the courts can use these matters to ascertain the terms of the contract.

   > In *Hillas & Co. Ltd* v. *Arcos Ltd* (1932), an option to buy 100 000 standards of softwood goods in 1931, without mention of detailed terms, was held binding because it was assumed to be on terms similar to those agreed in previous dealings between the parties.
   >
   > In *Brown* v. *Gould* (1972), an option was given to renew a lease 'at a rent to be fixed having regard to the market value of the premises at the time of exercising this option taking into account ... structural improvements made by the Tenant ...'. This was held binding, because the court could, if necessary, discover the market price and the value of the improvements by evidence from valuers.

3. If only a fairly minor term is meaningless, it may simply be ignored, and the rest of the contract treated as binding.

   > In *Nicolene Ltd* v. *Simmonds* (1953), the defendant agreed to sell 3000 tons of steel bars at £45 per ton, and added that he assumed that 'the usual conditions of acceptance apply'. There were no usual conditions. The court held that he was bound; the rest of the agreement made good sense, and the meaningless phrase could therefore be ignored.

For further consideration

1. For some years a farmer has sold most of his crop of strawberries to a local greengrocer's shop. Both parties are anxious to enter into an agreement regarding this year's crop. However, bad weather has made the quantity of the crop and delivery dates uncertain, and has made it difficult to fix a price.

    To what extent is it possible for the parties to enter into a binding contract and leave some of the terms to be decided later?

2. Outline the legal position of the parties and the principles of law involved in each of the following situations:
    (a) A offers to sell a car to B and states that B has five days to decide whether he wishes to buy. Three days later B hears from X that A has sold the car to C. B thereupon writes to A accepting his offer.
    (b) E offers to sell a van to F who replies to the effect that he will accept the offer if E will pay for any repairs during the next six months. E refuses to give such an undertaking, whereupon F says that he will buy without insisting upon this condition. E now replies that he no longer wishes to sell to F.

3. (a) When may a contract be formed even though the acceptance of the offer is not communicated to the offeror.
    (b) Sharp offers to sell a quantity of water-damaged textiles to Simple for sale in Simple's shop. Simple intends to accept the offer but does not reply to this effect. However, Simple does arrange for the printing of some posters and leaflets advertising the sale and Sharp happens to see these when visiting the printer for another purpose. Sharp now receives a better offer for his textiles and wishes to sell elsewhere. Advise him whether or not he has a contract to sell to Simple.

4. Consider the reason for the following rules and whether or not you feel that they should be altered.
    (a) A shopkeeper may refuse to take goods out of his window when requested to do so by a customer.
    (b) A seller may withdraw an offer at any time even though he has promised to keep the offer open for a specified period.
    (c) A letter of acceptance may be effective and conclude a contract upon posting even though it never reaches the other party.

Unit 18. Matters Which Affect the Validity of Contracts

Some contracts which appear perfectly valid may nevertheless be wholly or partly ineffective because of some defect when they were formed. The vitiating factors discussed in this unit are mistake, misrepresentation, duress, undue influence, and lack of capacity in the formation of the contract.

A. Mistake

The general rule is that mistake does *not* affect the validity of a contract. For example, if a man is mistaken as to the nature or value of what he buys, this is simply his misfortune. The law will not help him unless he has been misled by the other party (see Misrepresentation, later).

> In *Leaf* v. *International Galleries* (1950), a drawing was sold which both seller and buyer believed to be by Constable. In fact it was not. The contract was not affected by this mistake, because each side intended to deal with the physical thing sold; they were simply mistaken as to its quality and value.

A further preliminary point is that mistake of *law* will never affect the validity of a contract. Ignorance of the law is no defence. In certain circumstances, mistake of *fact* may affect the contract and, if sufficiently serious, render the contract void.

Mistakes of fact which render a contract void

Mistakes concerning the subject-matter of the contract
These mistakes, for example as to the property sold, render the contract void *if sufficiently serious*. A mere mistake as to the nature or value of the subject-matter will not be enough (see above).

A mutual mistake as to the identity of the subject-matter will render the contract void. A mutual mistake will occur where the parties are, unknown to each other, thinking about different things. Neither is right, neither is wrong; they are simply at cross purposes, and have never really agreed.

> In *Raffles* v. *Wichelhaus* (1864), a cargo of cotton was described as being on the *SS Peerless* from Bombay. There were in fact two ships of that name sailing from Bombay with an interval of three months between them. The seller intended to put the cargo on the second ship, while the buyer expected it on the first. The contract was held void.

A fundamental common mistake about the subject-matter will also leave the contract void. A common mistake occurs where both parties are under the same misapprehension; both are wrong. The clearest instance of this is where, unknown to both parties, the subject-matter does not exist.

> In *Couturier* v. *Hastie* (1856), a contract was made for the sale of a cargo of wheat which, unknown to both seller and buyer, no longer existed. The wheat had gone bad during the voyage, and the captain, in exercise of his powers, had re-sold it.

> Similarly, in *Galloway* v. *Galloway* (1914), a separation agreement between 'husband' and 'wife', disposing of property between them, was held void when it was discovered that they had never legally been married.

Mistaken signing of written documents

This may, exceptionally, be a nullity. Three elements must be present if the contract is to be void: the signing must have been fraudulently induced; the mistake must be fundamental; and the signer must prove that he or she has not been negligent. A person attempting to avoid liability under a contract on these grounds is said to plead *non est factum* (it is not my act).

> In *Foster* v. *Mackinnon* (1869), a rogue induced Mackinnon, an old gentleman with weak sight, to sign a document which Mackinnon thought to be a guarantee. In fact he was indorsing a bill of exchange for £3000, thereby incurring personal liability for this amount. It was held that, so long as he had not been negligent, he was not liable on the bill.

> Conversely, in *Saunders* v. *Anglia Building Society* (1971), a Mrs Gallie intended to assign the lease of her house so as to enable her nephew to borrow money. The assignment was prepared fraudulently by a rogue, Lee, who had promised to arrange the loan. The document which she signed transferred the lease to Lee himself, who mortgaged it to the building society and departed with the proceeds. Mrs Gallie and her nephew received nothing. Mrs Gallie claimed that the original assignment was void for mistake; she had not read it because her glasses were broken and she had not realized its effect. Her plea failed. She had intended to assign her lease, and her mistake as to the way in which she was assigning it was not so fundamental as to avoid the contract.

A mistake by one party as to the identity of the other

This type of mistake may sometimes invalidate the contract. If A contracts with B under the impression that he is really dealing with C, the contract will be void if A can prove that his mistake was material; he intended to deal with C and would not have dealt with anyone else. It may be very difficult for A to prove this, particularly where the parties dealt with each other face to face.

In *Phillips* v. *Brooks* (1919), a rogue bought a ring in a jeweller's shop. He then persuaded the jeweller that he was Sir George Bullough, and was therefore allowed to take away the ring in return for a cheque. The cheque was dishonoured, and the ring was eventually traced to a pawnbroker. The jeweller claimed that his contract with the rogue was void for mistake, but his claim failed. The jeweller had dealt with the man facing him; the question of identity was only raised when it came to payment.

Again, in *Lewis* v. *Averay* (1972), Lewis sold and parted with his car to a rogue who pretended to be Richard Greene, the film actor. The rogue paid by cheque which was dishonoured, and then re-sold the car to Averay. The contract between Lewis and the rogue was not void; Lewis could not prove that he was willing to sell only to Richard Greene and to no one else.

Where the parties did not deal with each other face to face, it may be easier for A to prove that the mistake was material.

In *Cundy* v. *Lindsay* (1878), a rogue called Blenkarn ordered linen by post from Lindsay & Co. by pretending to be Blenkiron, a reputable dealer. Blenkarn re-sold the linen to Cundy. Lindsay & Co. were able to recover it because the contract with Blenkarn was void. They satisfied the court that they intended to deal only with Blenkiron.

In *King's Norton Metal Co. Ltd* v. *Edridge, Merrett & Co. Ltd* (1897), on the other hand, the plaintiffs sold goods to a firm called 'Hallam & Co.' which placed an order by post. Hallam & Co. turned out to be a complete fiction; the real buyer was a rogue called Wallis. The contract was not void. If the plaintiffs were willing to deal with an unknown company, without checking, then the identity of the buyer was clearly not sufficiently material.

It will be apparent that most of the cases on mistake of identity are actions between two innocent parties. A will have parted with the goods to a rogue, who will have re-sold to X and departed with the proceeds. If the contract between A and the rogue was void for mistake, A can recover the goods or their value from X by an action for the tort of conversion (Unit 14); otherwise X will normally be entitled to keep the property.

Other consequences of mistake

Where there is a mistake as to the subject-matter, but the mistake is not so fundamental as to render the contract void, the court *may* nevertheless allow one party the equitable remedy of *rescission*, that is, the right to have the contract set aside *if he so wishes*. The party claiming this remedy must show that he has not been at fault in any way, and the court may impose certain conditions on granting the remedy.

In *Cooper* v. *Phibbs* (1867), Cooper agreed to lease a fishery from Phibbs. It later turned out that, unknown to both, the fishery already belonged to Cooper. The court allowed Cooper to rescind the lease, on condition that he compensate Phibbs for improvements which the latter had made.

In *Grist* v. *Bailey* (1967), Grist contracted to buy Bailey's house for £850. Both parties believed that the house was occupied by a tenant protected under the Rent Acts. In fact, unknown to both, the tenant had died. This increased the value of the house to about £2250, and Bailey refused to carry out the contract, claiming that it was void for mistake.

The contract was held *not* to be void at common law, but the court exercised its equitable power to set the original contract aside on condition that Bailey would now sell for the true value.

Mistake by one or both parties may affect other equitable remedies. For example, specific performance of a contract may be refused if one party has made a mistake which renders it unfair to enforce the agreement against him.

Where, by mistake, the terms of a written document do not represent accurately what the parties agreed orally, the court may, at its discretion, order the rectification of the document so that it does express what was agreed.

B. Misrepresentation

The conclusion of a contract is often preceded by negotiations, in the course of which one party makes statements of fact intended to induce the other to enter into the contract. If any such statement is false, it is called a misrepresentation.

A misrepresentation, then, may be defined as a false statement of fact, made by one party to the contract to the other before the contract, with a view to inducing the other to enter into it. The statement must have been intended to be acted upon, and it must actually have induced the other party to make the agreement.

It must be a representation of fact, not law. A mere boast is not regarded as a statement of fact (otherwise advertisers might incur substantial liabilities). A distinction is also made between a statement of fact and a mere expression of opinion, although this can prove difficult. Statements about a car such as 'beautiful condition' and 'superb condition' have been held in criminal cases to be statements of fact, not mere expressions of opinion.

The statement must be by one party to the contract to the other. A statement by the manufacturer which induces a customer to buy from a retail shop will not give the customer any remedy for misrepresentation against either retailer or manufacturer.

The false statement must actually have deceived the other party and induced him to make the contract. Obviously it must be false, but even a misleading half-truth can be false.

> In *London Assurance* v. *Mansel* (1879), a person seeking life assurance was asked on the proposal form what other proposals for cover he had made. He answered, truthfully, that he had made two proposals the previous year, both accepted. He did not mention, however, that he had also had several proposals rejected. This half-truth was held to be a misrepresentation. (See also non-disclosure, later.)

Many misrepresentations also amount to promises which are actually incorporated into the contract. In this event, the party deceived will normally sue for breach of contract rather than for misrepresentation, because once breach of contract is proved, damages will automatically be awarded. Where mere misrepresentation is proved, the person liable may still have a defence to an action for damages if he can prove that he reasonably believed himself to be telling the truth. The distinction between mere representations and contractual promises can be difficult, but in contracts of sale the court will normally hold that statements by a seller who is a *dealer* are contractual promises, whereas statements by a seller who is not a dealer are mere representations.

In *Oscar Chess Ltd* v. *Williams* (1957), the defendant was a private car owner, trading in his vehicle in part-exchange for another. He falsely stated that it was a 1948 model, whereas in fact it was a 1939 car. This statement was quite innocent, because the registration book had been falsified by a previous owner. It was held that his statement was a mere representation, so that his innocence was a defence.

On the other hand, in *Dick Bentley Productions Ltd* v. *Harold Smith* (*Motors*) *Ltd* (1965), a dealer sold a car which appeared from the instruments to have travelled only 20 000 miles. In fact it had done about 100 000. This was held to be breach of contract, not a mere representation, so that the buyer automatically was entitled to damages. A dealer, who knows more about the goods than his customers, is readily assumed to *promise* that his statements are true.

Remedies for misrepresentation

1. *Damages*

Under the Misrepresentation Act 1967, section 2(1), a party to the contract can recover damages for loss arising from a misrepresentation. The other party will, however, have a defence if he can prove that, up to the time of the contract, he believed that his statements were true, and had reasonable cause so to believe. It should be noted that the onus of proving this is on the defendant.

Under section 2(2), damages may also be awarded as an alternative to rescission, and in this event even the defendant's innocence may be no defence.

If the misrepresentation was made fraudulently, the party deceived can, alternatively, sue for damages for the tort of deceit (Unit 15), but since the onus of proving fraud is on the plaintiff, this will rarely be done.

2. *Rescission*

Any misrepresentation, even innocent, will give the other party a right to *rescind* the contract, that is, to end it if he so wishes. Each party must be restored to his original position; for example, the property must be returned to the seller and the price to the buyer. The contract is said to be voidable (Unit 16).

The right to rescind will be lost as soon as it becomes impossible to return the parties to their position before the contract. For example, if the property has been re-sold by the buyer, or has been destroyed by him, it will be impossible to return it to the seller.

Since rescission is an equitable right, it must be exercised reasonably promptly. It is undesirable for a contract to remain voidable for too long, because this leads to uncertainty as to the ownership of the property. If he delays unduly, therefore, the innocent party will lose his right to rescind, and be left to sue for damages. What is a reasonable time is a question of fact, and may in some cases be only a matter of days or hours.

In *Leaf* v. *International Galleries* (1950), which was mentioned earlier, the picture was sold in 1944. The plaintiff only discovered in 1949 that it was not by Constable. Although the contract was not void for mistake, the plaintiff claimed the right to rescind for innocent misrepresentation. It was held that, after a lapse of five years, any right to rescind had been lost. (The plaintiff could have claimed damages for breach of contract, but did not in fact do so.)

Normally, rescission will only be effective from the moment when it is communicated to the party at fault. This would cause injustice, however, where the misrepresentation was fraudulent and the rogue has disappeared. In this event, therefore, the rule is relaxed.

In *Car and Universal Finance Co. Ltd* v. *Caldwell* (1965), Caldwell was persuaded by a rogue to part with his car in return for a cheque which was dishonoured. On discovering this, Caldwell immediately told the police, but could do no more to rescind the contract because the rogue could not be found. It was held that, in the circumstances, Caldwell had done everything possible to make public his intention to rescind, and the rescission was therefore effective.

Finally, the right to rescind will be lost if the innocent party 'affirms' the contract, that is, elects to go on with it knowing of the misrepresentation. He cannot blow hot and cold, and once he has decided to go on, he cannot change his mind.

Section 3 of the Misrepresentation Act makes it very difficult for a party to exclude his liability for misrepresentation (Unit 19). A term in the contract which would exclude any liability or remedy for misrepresentation will be of no effect unless the defendant can show that the clause is 'reasonable' within the meaning of the Unfair Contract Terms Act 1977.

C. Duty to disclose

There is in general no duty to *disclose* facts. Silence cannot normally constitute misrepresentation even when the silent party knows that the other is deceiving himself and does nothing about it. Each party must find out the truth as best he can, and in contracts of sale this rule is known as *caveat emptor*—let the buyer beware.

There is, however, a duty to correct statements which, although originally true, have subsequently become false before the contract was made. The facts have changed, and it would be unfair to let the original statement stand.

In *With* v. *O'Flanagan* (1936), at the start of negotiations for the sale of a doctor's practice, the seller stated, truthfully, that the annual income was £2000. The seller then fell ill, and by the time that the sale took place some months later, the profits had fallen drastically. It was held that the early statement should have been corrected, and the fall disclosed.

Silence is also not enough in contracts of the unmost good faith (*uberrimae fidei*). These are, for the most part, contracts where one party alone has full knowledge of the material facts, and therefore the law does impose on him a duty to disclose. The main examples are as follows:

1. *Contracts of insurance.* There is a duty on the insured person to disclose to the insurance firm any circumstance which might influence it in fixing the premium or deciding whether to insure the risk. Failure to do this will render the contract voidable at the option of the insurance firm.

2. *In contracts for the sale of land*, the vendor must disclose all defects in *title*, but not in the property itself.
3. *Contracts to subscribe for shares in a company*. A prospectus issued by a company, inviting the public to make an offer to buy shares in the company, must disclose various matters set out in detail in the Companies Act 1948. If it does not, the contract may be rescinded.
4. *In contracts of family arrangement*, each member of the family must disclose all material facts within his knowledge.

D. Duress and undue influence

At common law, duress arose when a party was induced to enter a contract by force or the threat of force. His consent was not freely given, and hence such contracts are voidable at his option. Economic coercion can also be duress.

> In *Universe Tankships* v. *ITF* (1982), a union stopped a ship from leaving until the owners paid money to a welfare fund. The owners recovered the money, which was only paid under duress.

Equity recognizes less direct pressures.

> In *Williams* v. *Bayley* (1866), a father was induced to give security for his son's debts by the lender's threats to prosecute the son. On proof of this, the father was held not to be bound.

In other instances, equity goes further and *presumes* that there was undue influence unless the contrary is proved. This will occur where the relationship between the parties was such that one had a dominant position over the other. The main examples include doctor and patient, solicitor and client, religious adviser and disciple, parent and child (but not husband and wife). The presumption of undue influence can only be rebutted in these cases by proof that the other party had independent advice or used his own free will.

> In *Allcard* v. *Skinner* (1887), Miss Allcard joined a religious order and, in accordance with its rule of poverty, gave about £7000 to the head of the order during the eight years that she was a member. After leaving the order she waited six years and then sued to recover the money. It was held that, while the money was obtained from her by undue religious influence, her action failed because she had waited too long before suing.

Where undue influence is deemed to exist either by proof or presumption, the contract is voidable, but the right to rescind must be exercised within a reasonable time of the influence being withdrawn.

E. Lack of capacity to contract

The general rule is that everyone is fully capable of entering into contracts, and that these contracts are enforceable both by and against him. However, there are certain classes of people whose contractual capacity is limited, although the tendency in recent years has been to reduce the number of such special cases; for example, the restrictions formerly placed upon convicted persons undergoing imprisonment and upon married women have now been removed.

Minors (infants)

A minor or infant is a person under the age of 18. As a general rule, he will be able to avoid his contracts and damages will not be awarded against him. For example, he will not be bound by trading contracts which he makes.

> In *Cowern* v. *Nield* (1912), it was held that a minor who was a hay and straw merchant was not liable to repay the price of goods which he failed to deliver.
>
> In *Mercantile Union Guarantee Corporation Ltd* v. *Ball* (1937), an infant haulage contractor who took a lorry on hire purchase was held not liable for arrears of instalments.

On the other hand, a minor *can* recover damages against an adult if the latter breaks the contract. The minor can *sue*, but cannot be *sued*.
There are two main exceptions to this rule:

1. A minor must pay a *reasonable* price for *necessary* goods sold *and delivered* to him. He need not pay the contract price if this is exorbitant, and in any event he can withdraw from the contract at any time before delivery. Furthermore, this rule only applies to 'necessaries', that is, goods suitable to the minor's condition in life and to his actual requirements at the time of sale and delivery. Two aspects must be considered, therefore, to decide whether the goods are 'necessaries' in the circumstances. The *quality* aspect requires that the article be suitable to the minor's station in life; an infant duke may have higher requirements than an infant bank clerk. The *quantity* aspect relates to the minor's existing supplies; even food might not be necessary if his house is full of food.

    > In *Nash* v. *Inman* (1908), an undergraduate ordered expensive clothes from a tailor, including 11 fancy waistcoats. The minor's father was a prosperous architect, and it was argued that the clothes were suitable to the minor's station in life. Since he was already well supplied with clothes, however, these goods were held not to be necessaries.

2. Contracts of employment, apprenticeship, and education which, *taken as a whole*, are for the minor's benefit. If as a whole the contract is beneficial, the court will enforce all of the clauses, even ones which, taken in isolation, are not beneficial.

    > In *Doyle* v. *White City Stadium* (1935), an infant boxer was held bound by a clause in his contract which provided for forfeiture of his prize money if (as happened) he was disqualified. The contract as a whole was similar to apprenticeship, and the forfeiture clause encouraged clean fighting.

The Infants' Relief Act 1874 declares certain contracts made by minors to be void, but this has been treated as meaning merely void *against* the minor. He can still acquire rights under the agreement, and sue for breach. The contracts covered are ones for goods supplied or to be supplied other than necessaries, money lent or to be lent, and accounts stated, that is, IOUs or similar admissions of money due. There are two qualifications to this rule.

First, if money is lent to a minor specifically to enable him to buy necessaries, the lender can recover such part of the loan as is actually spent on necessaries at a reasonable price. Second, where the minor has acted fraudulently, for example, by falsely pretending to be full age, he can be made to return goods which he still has in his possession. If he has parted with the goods, however, the seller cannot get them back.

Special rules apply to contracts of a continuing nature which can last after the minor reaches 18. A contract such as a lease, a partnership or the holding of shares in a company will bind the minor after 18 unless he repudiates before or within a reasonable time after attaining this age.

Finally, as regards actions against the minor, the court will not hold him liable for damages in tort if this would merely be an indirect way of awarding damages for breach of contract (Unit 12).

There are also some exceptions to the rule that a minor can sue on his contracts. For example, since the remedy of specific performance will never be awarded *against* an infant, the court will not award it *to* an infant either (Unit 20). As another example, when a minor avoids the contract, as a general rule he can recover money or goods which he has handed over; but if he has received a benefit under the contract this will not be the case.

> In *Valentini* v. *Canali* (1889), a minor leased a house and agreed to buy some furniture, paying part of the price. After several months the minor left, and avoided the contract as he was entitled to do. He could not recover the payments which he made for the furniture, however, because he had received some benefit from the contract.

Insane and drunken persons

A mental patient cannot validly enter into contracts. Contracts may be made on his behalf by the Court of Protection or receivers appointed for this purpose.

If a person makes a contract while temporarily insane, or drunk, the contract is voidable if he can prove that he was so insane or drunk at the time as to be incapable of understanding what he did, and the other party knew this. The contract will be binding unless it is avoided within a reasonable time of regaining sanity or sobriety. An insane or drunken person must pay a reasonable price for necessary goods sold and actually delivered to him.

For further consideration

1. Your friend is intending to open a shop known as 'Teenage Market' for the purpose of selling a wide range of goods and services to young people. He is intending to sell both for cash and on credit terms.

    Explain the legal problems he is likely to encounter in dealing with minors and suggest measures which he might take to overcome or mitigate these problems.
2. 'Silence cannot normally constitute misrepresentation.' To what extent is this statement correct?
3. Consider the relationship where undue influence is presumed to exist. From which, if any of these relationships, would you remove this presumption? To which other relationships, if any, would you apply the presumption?

4. Rich, the elderly owner of a number of vehicles, decides to sell two of them, an expensive saloon and a less valuable van. Rogue sees the advertisement for sale in the local newspaper and calls with the intention of buying the saloon. After some negotiation a price is agreed but, while Rogue believes he is buying the saloon, Rich thinks that he is selling the van. Furthermore, Rich, whose eyesight is poor, believes that he is dealing with the local doctor to whom Rogue bears some resemblance and, on the strength of this, allows Rogue to drive away the vehicle on a promise of payment the following week. Rogue drives away the saloon, sells it to a garage and disappears with the proceeds of the sale.

Advise Rich who has now seen his saloon for sale at the garage.

Unit 19. The Terms of the Bargain

This unit deals with the rights and obligations which arise under a contract. It will also discuss one aspect of the idea of 'freedom of contract', that is, how far the parties can agree between themselves what their relations are to be, and how far the law determines their relations for them.

A. Express terms

Express terms are those specifically mentioned and agreed by the parties at the time of contracting, whether this be done in writing or by word of mouth. In simple agreements, such as small cash sales, the express terms may be very sketchy; the buyer will simply ask for what he sees before him at the price indicated, and the seller will agree to sell. There will be no need for detailed arrangements as to delivery or payment, because goods and cash will be handed over immediately.

Where the subject-matter is very valuable, where the agreement is complicated, or where the contract will last for some time, for example, because credit is allowed, the parties are likely to be much more specific as to detailed terms. In these contracts, detailed terms will often be set out expressly, frequently in a written agreement. Thus, contracts of insurance, hire purchase, or for the sale of land will be in writing and contain detailed express terms, whether or not this is required by statute or for the purpose of evidence (Unit 16).

Contractual terms, oral or written, differ in importance, and may be classified into conditions and warranties. A *condition* is an important term which is vital to the contract, so that non-observance will affect the main purpose of the agreement. Breach of condition will give the injured party a right to rescind or repudiate the contract. Alternatively, the injured party may, if he so wishes, go on with the contract, but recover damages for his loss. A *warranty* is a less important term, non-observance of which will cause loss but not affect the basic purpose of the contract. Breach of warranty will only give the injured party the right to sue for damages, not to repudiate the contract.

> In *Bettini* v. *Gye* (1876), Bettini, an opera singer, agreed to perform in Britain, and to attend for rehearsals six days before the first performance. He did not arrive until two days before the first performance. This was held to be only a breach of warranty, which entitled the management to recover damages but not to terminate the contract.

> Conversely, in *Poussard* v. *Spiers & Pond* (1876), Madame Poussard, a singer, failed to turn up for the first few performances. This was held to be a breach of condition, which entitled the management to end her contract.

Many express terms are difficult to classify so neatly in advance, and can only be classified by reference to the nature of the breach. A minor breach of the term might only be a breach of warranty, whereas a serious breach, or a breach which has serious consequences, might be a breach of condition.

> In *Hong Kong Fir Shipping Co. Ltd* v. *Kawasaki Kisen Kaisha Ltd* (1962), the plaintiffs chartered their ship to the defendants. The contract contained a term that the ship would be 'in every way fitted for ordinary cargo service'. This was a term which could not be classified in advance as a condition or a warranty, because breach could either be a minor matter if the ship were slightly defective, or a serious matter if the ship were about to sink. In fact, the engines were old, the engine-room staff were inefficient, and as a result the ship was delayed. It was held that this was only a breach of warranty, which did not entitle the defendants to repudiate the contract.

Finally, every contract contains some fundamental obligation which is the whole basis of the agreement. Thus if a man offers to buy a tractor and the seller delivers a horse, the seller has simply failed to perform his side of the bargain at all. This concept of *fundamental breach* is important in relation to exclusion clauses (see later).

B. Implied terms

Terms implied by the courts

Where the parties have not made express provision on some point, the court will sometimes imply a term to cover the position. Since the parties have not said expressly what they intend, the court will impose such obligations as, in the view of the court, they would reasonably have agreed had they thought of the matter.

> In *The Moorcock* (1889), the owner of a wharf contracted to provide a berth for a ship. The berth was unsuitable for the vessel, which was damaged when it hit a ridge of hard ground at low tide. There was no express undertaking that the berth was suitable, but the court implied a term to this effect, and the shipowner recovered damages.

The implication of additional terms is usually justified on the grounds that it is necessary in order to give business effect to the intentions of the parties; the parties obviously intended such an obligation, and the agreement makes commercial nonsense without it. If, at the time of the contract, someone had said to the parties, 'What will happen in such a case?' they would both have said, 'Of course, so and so will happen; we did not trouble to say that'. In some instances, the courts seem to have gone beyond this, and implied terms largely because this was necessary to achieve substantial justice between the parties.

In a tenancy of a furnished house, the courts will imply a term that the premises will be reasonably fit for human habitation when the tenancy begins. Under a contract of employment, the employer owes an implied duty to take reasonable care for the safety of his employees, and the latter owe a duty to show good faith and to exercise reasonable care and skill in the performance of their duties. (A careless employer may also be liable for the tort of negligence; Unit 13). In contracts for the carriage of goods by sea, the shipowner impliedly undertakes that the ship is seaworthy, that the ship will proceed on the voyage with all reasonable dispatch, and that there shall be no unnecessary deviation. In contracts of hire, the owner has an implied obligation to supply goods which are as fit for the purpose of hiring as reasonable care and skill can make them.

> In *Reed* v. *Dean* (1949), the plaintiff hired a motor launch, which shortly afterwards caught fire. The boat's fire-fighting equipment was useless, the plaintiff was injured and he lost his personal belongings. He recovered damages, even though the contract contained no express term that the boat should be safe and suitable.

It should be remembered that implied obligations only arise in the absence of any express provision on the point. Implied terms can generally be excluded by an express term to this effect.

Terms implied by statute

In some types of contract, detailed terms are implied by Act of Parliament. In many instances this has resulted from codification of the common law rules relating to such contracts. Some provisions aim simply to standardize the obligations of the parties; other provisions go further, and operate partly to redress inequality of bargaining power.

Perhaps the best example of an Act which implies terms is the Sale of Goods Act 1979, which is examined in some detail in Unit 23. The terms implied by this Act were first developed by the courts and then codified in 1893. Subsequent statutory amendments in recent years giving greater protection to consumers led to a need to consolidate and restate the law on this topic. This was done in 1979.

Some of the obligations imposed are general rules which can be freely altered by the parties if they so wish. Thus, if nothing is agreed to the contrary, delivery of the goods and payment of the price are normally concurrent conditions, that is to say, the general rule is 'cash on delivery'. The parties may, however, agree to depart from this rule, as when the buyer is allowed credit and takes possession before payment.

Other sections of the Act impose duties irrespective of the wishes of the parties and these may only be excluded in certain specific circumstances. The following are the important examples.

1. By section 12 of the Act, there is implied in a contract of sale a condition that the seller has a right to sell the goods. If the seller had no right to sell, because the goods belong to someone else, the buyer will be able to recover the full price which he paid. This obligation can be varied in some circumstances but not excluded.
2. By section 13, where goods are sold by description, there is an implied condition that the goods shall correspond with the description.
3. By section 15, where goods are sold by sample, there are implied conditions that the bulk will correspond with the sample, that the buyer will have a reasonable opportunity to compare the bulk with the sample, and that the goods will be free from any defect, rendering them unmerchantable, which would not be apparent on a reasonable examination of the sample.
4. Section 14 of the Act only implies terms into contracts where the seller sells in the course of a business. As a general rule, there is no obligation on a seller to supply goods which are of any particular quality, or fit for any particular purpose, and the maxim *caveat emptor* applies. Where the sale is in the course of a business, however, the seller does owe duties as regards quality and suitability. By section 14(2), there is an implied condition that the goods shall be of merchantable quality and, by section 14(3), where the buyer expressly or impliedly makes known the purpose for which he requires the goods, there is an implied condition that the goods will be *reasonably* fit for that purpose.

Where the buyer deals as consumer (see later), these terms cannot be excluded by the parties, and bind them automatically, whether they wish it or not.

Under the Supply of Goods (Implied Terms) Act 1973, obligations almost identical to the above are imposed on the owner of goods who lets them on hire purchase. Other statutes which imply terms into certain types of contract include the Trading Stamps Act 1964, the Defective Premises Act 1972, the Carriage of Goods by Sea Act 1971, and the Marine Insurance Act 1906.

C. Problems of unequal bargaining power

The law of contract, as we have seen it so far, has been based on the assumption that the parties freely negotiated the terms of their bargain. This is not always the case, particularly where one party is in a stronger economic position than the other.

The most obvious inequality arises where one of the parties enjoys a monopoly position. If someone wishes to acquire the goods or service which the monopolist supplies, he cannot genuinely negotiate terms to suit himself. He must either take the terms which the monopolist offers or simply do without. Thus, a passenger cannot haggle over the price of a railway ticket or the terms under which he will be carried; he must either accept the British Rail terms or travel in some other way.

The position is very similar where there are only a few suppliers. The customer does not normally negotiate over the terms of an insurance contract, a hire purchase agreement, or a mortgage. He contracts on a standard form prepared in advance by the company, which he can either take or leave. There will be little point in going to another company if all companies insist on more or less the same terms.

There may be other circumstances in which genuine bargaining is difficult. A borrower who has no money, for example, is in a weaker position than the lender who has. Even in contracts for the sale of goods, it may be difficult to negotiate where the goods are so technically complicated that the average buyer is not competent to judge the quality or fitness of what he buys. The stronger party has sometimes used his position to impose heavy duties on the other, while attempting to limit or to exclude altogether his own possible liability. Hire purchase agreements, for example, normally impose wide duties on the hirer, but are often used to contain clauses excluding any liability of the finance company for defects in the goods. Other types of contract which contain exclusion clauses will be seen from the cases mentioned later. The attitude of the courts and the legislature to such clauses will be discussed below.

D. Exclusion clauses

While it may be acceptable for parties negotiating on an equal footing to exclude or limit their liability for breach of contract, both the courts and Parliament have been reluctant to allow exclusion clauses which a stronger party has imposed on a weaker.

The approach of the courts

1. *Is the clause part of the contract?*
The courts will require the person relying on an exclusion clause to show that the other party agreed to it at or before the time when agreement was reached. Otherwise it will not form part of the contract.

(a) Where a contract is made by signing a written document, the general rule is that the signer is bound by everything which the document contains, whether he read it or not. If the document contains an exclusion clause, the other party is taken to agree to this when he signs.

> In *L'Estrange* v. *Graucob Ltd* (1934), Miss L'Estrange signed a written contract to buy an automatic machine. The document provided that 'any express or implied condition, statement or warranty . . . is hereby excluded', and the court commented that this clause was in 'regrettably small print'. Although Miss L'Estrange had not read the document, it was held that the clause bound her, and she had no remedy when the machine proved defective.

On the other hand, if misrepresentations were made as to the effect of the document before the plaintiff signed, these might prevent reliance on the exclusion clause.

> In *Curtis* v. *Chemical Cleaning Co.* (1951), the plaintiff took a wedding dress to be cleaned. She was given a document headed 'Receipt', which she was asked to sign. Before doing so, she asked the assistant what the document provided, and was told that it excluded the cleaners' liability for damage to the sequins. In fact, there was a clause excluding liability for all damage. The dress came back badly stained, and the cleaners claimed the protection of the clause. It was held that they were not protected as regards the fabric; the assistant had misrepresented the extent of the clause, and the cleaners were precluded from relying on it further.

(b) Where terms are contained in an unsigned document, the person seeking to rely on them must show that the other party knew, or should have known, that the document was a contractual one which could be expected to contain terms. He must also show that everything reasonable had been done to bring the terms to the notice of the other party. Most of the cases concern exclusion clauses in documents such as tickets, consignment notes, order forms, and unsigned receipts.

> In *Chapleton* v. *Barry UDC* (1940), the plaintiff hired a deck chair, and was injured when it collapsed. The ticket which he had received when paying contained a clause excluding liability, but he had put the ticket into his pocket without looking at it. The court decided that he was entitled to assume that the ticket was merely a receipt without conditions, and his action succeeded.
>
> On the other hand, in *Thompson* v. *LMS Railway Co.* (1930), Mrs Thompson bought an excursion ticket which contained the customary wording on the front, referring the purchaser to the back of the ticket and from there to the company's conditions and regulations in the time tables which could be obtained from the booking office. One such condition excluded liability for injury. The court upheld the company's contention that the ticket was a document which could be expected to contain terms, and that the company had done everything reasonable to draw the conditions to the attention of normal passengers. The fact that Mrs Thompson was illiterate was disregarded, and she was, therefore, not entitled to damage for injuries which she suffered on the journey.
>
> In *Roe* v. *R. A. Naylor Ltd* (1918), a 'sold note' containing an exclusion clause was simply placed in front of the business buyer at the time of sale. This document clearly contained terms, and it was held that the businessman was bound by the exclusion clause even though he had not read it. As a prudent businessman he should have done, and the seller had done everything reasonable to bring it to his notice.

(c) Any attempt to introduce an exclusion clause *after* the contract has been made will be ineffective, because the consideration for such a clause would then be past.

> In *Olley* v. *Marlborough Court Ltd* (1949), property was stolen from the plaintiff during her stay at a hotel. There was a notice in the bedroom that the proprietors accepted no responsibility for articles stolen, but this was held to be ineffective. The plaintiff only saw it *after* the contract had been made at the reception desk.
>
> Similarly, in *Thornton* v. *Shoe Lane Parking Ltd* (1971), the plaintiff made his contract with the car park company when he inserted a coin in the automatic ticket machine. The ticket which he received referred to conditions which were displayed inside the car park, which he could, therefore, only see after entry. He was injured in an accident while collecting his car. It was held that he was not bound by the conditions, which purported to exempt the company from liability for personal injury to customers. In any event, by the time he reached the ticket machine he was already committed to go into the car park. There was no space to turn round and leave if he decided that he did not like the terms mentioned on the ticket.

2. Construing exclusion clauses

If there is any ambiguity or room for doubt as to the meaning of an exclusion clause, the courts will construe it *contra proferentem*, that is, in a manner unfavourable to the person who put it into the contract.

In *Wallis, Son & Wells* v. *Pratt & Haynes* (1911), a buyer ordered seed called 'common English sainfoin'. When it grew it proved to be giant sainfoin, and therefore less valuable. When sued, the seller pleaded a clause in the contract excluding all '*warranties*, express or implied, as to growth or description'. This was held not to protect the seller, because the term broken was a *condition*, not a warranty. If the seller had wished to exclude conditions, he should have said so expressly.

Similarly, in *White* v. *John Warrick & Co. Ltd* (1953), the plaintiff hired a tricycle. The contract provided that '*Nothing in this agreement* shall render the owners liable for any personal injuries to the riders of the machines hired'. The plaintiff was injured when the saddle tilted forward. It was held that the clause only applied to actions for breach of contract, and would not protect the owner if the hirer could prove that the owner had committed the tort of negligence (Unit 13).

3. *Fundamental breach of contract*

Where one party has fundamentally broken his contract, that is, done something fundamentally different from what he contracted to do, an exclusion clause may not protect him. A court will assume as a matter of construction that the clause was not intended to apply to fundamental breach, unless it does so in the clearest possible terms. The Unfair Contract Terms Act (below), however, reverses the former rule that an exclusion clause might be disregarded if the breach was so serious as to end the contract or result in its termination.

Legislation affecting exclusion clauses

1. By the Unfair Contract Terms Act 1977, section 2, no one acting in the course of a business can, either by contractual terms or by any notice given or displayed, exclude his liability, in contract or tort, for *death or bodily injury* arising from *negligence*. He can exclude liability for other loss due to his negligence, but only if he can prove that the exemption is reasonable.
2. By section 3 of the 1977 Act, where a business contracts on its own written standard terms, it cannot exclude or vary its liability for breach of contract unless it can show that the exemption is reasonable. The same rule applies whenever a business contracts with a *consumer*, whether or not on standard terms.

    Sections 2 and 3 apply to *all* contracts, except those relating to land, patents, etc., shares, contracts affecting formation or internal management of companies, and insurance.
3. We have seen that the Sale of Goods Act imposes terms binding sellers and that, if the buyer is a *consumer*, these obligations cannot be excluded. A buyer is a consumer when he buys, for his private use, goods normally supplied for such use, from a seller selling in the course of a business. If the buyer is not a consumer, for example, if he is a retailer buying for resale, the 1977 Act, section 6, allows the seller to exclude sections 13–15 of the Sale of Goods Act if he, the *seller*, can show that the exclusion is reasonable. Section 12 cannot be excluded and, although sections 12 and 14 themselves do allow a seller limited scope to restrict his

obligations, section 14 only applies to sales in the course of a business. The 1977 Act, Schedule 2, contains rules to help determine what is 'reasonable'. Regard shall be given, for example, to the relative bargaining strength of the parties, and whether the customer was given an inducement such as a price reduction to agree to the terms.
4. The corresponding obligations imposed by the Supply of Goods (Implied Terms) Act on the owner of goods who lets them on hire purchase are subject to identical rules regarding exclusion. The 1977 Act, section 6, again applies.
5. The 1977 Act also covers exemption clauses in separate 'guarantees' given by suppliers of goods. If the goods are of a type normally supplied (for example, sold or hired) for private use or consumption, then no term in the guarantee can exclude the supplier's liability for defects while the goods are in consumer use, if the loss results from the negligence of the manufacturer or a distributor.
6. By section 3 of the Misrepresentation Act 1967, as amended in 1977, any term excluding liability for misrepresentation is void unless the person making the false statement proves that exemption is fair and reasonable having regard to the circumstances which were, or ought reasonably to have been, known to or in the contemplation of the parties when the contract was made.
7. Under the Fair Trading Act 1973, powers are conferred to make regulations prohibiting certain undesirable consumer trade practices. Such regulations may, *inter alia*, prohibit the inclusion in specified consumer transactions of terms or conditions purporting to exclude or limit the liability of a party to the transaction. Under these powers the Minister may invalidate exclusion clauses which at present are unaffected by legislation. He has banned the continued use by some traders of void exclusion clauses, which are still used to deter consumers who do not know that such clauses are ineffective.

For further consideration

1. James agreed to hire a car for a week's holiday and called at the premises of the hire firm to collect it on the morning of his departure. Advise him as to his remedies, if any, in each of the following situations.
   (a) The car is an older model with a higher petrol consumption.
   (b) The luggage boot of the car is slightly smaller than the hire firm previously stated.
   (c) Part of the bodywork of the car is in a very dangerous condition.
2. Super Cleaners Ltd offered 'to clean two garments for the price of one'. A notice was displayed in the shop to this effect but with the addition, in smaller print, of a statement that the customer must agree in return to accept full responsibility if anything should happen to the garments. A similar statement was printed on the back of the tickets which were handed to customers when they deposited the garments.

John brought two jackets for cleaning. Because of poor eyesight he was unable to read the small print on the notice, and he put the ticket in his pocket without reading it.

Some days later when John collected the jackets he saw that one had now been badly torn. After wearing the other jacket he contracted a skin disease which was caused by a chemical which the cleaner had used.

Advise John.

3. Consider the legal effect of the following notices
   (a) The owner of an open piece of land in a city has fenced it off, and allows cars to park there for payment. On the land there is a large notice which reads, 'Cars parked at the owner's risk'.
   (b) On a one-man bus, the passenger pays his fare after he enters, and is given a cyclostyled ticket bearing the notice, 'Issued subject to the company's regulations and conditions, which are available for inspection at the company's head office'.

4. 'English law consistently imposes heavier obligations on a person who sells goods in the course of a business than it does on private sellers.'

   Explain, with examples, whether this statement is correct.

Unit 20. Performance, Breach, and Remedies

A. Performance

The number of contracts broken is very small in relation to the number performed, but it is the broken contracts which attract attention. Since most contracts are made with the intention of performance, and most are so performed, this method of discharging the bargain will be discussed first.

The basic rule is that each party must perform completely and precisely what he has bargained to do.

> In *Re Moore & Co.* and *Landauer & Co.* (1921), the buyer ordered a consignment of canned fruit, to be packed in cases of 30 tins each. The correct amount was delivered, but about half was in cases of 24 tins each. It was held that the buyer was entitled to reject the whole consignment.

This rule is not always so inflexible as it seems. Difficult questions of interpretation sometimes arise as to exactly what the parties *did* promise to do, and the court will try to give a common-sense meaning to the terms agreed.

> In *Peter Darlington Partners Ltd* v. *Gosho Ltd* (1964), the seller agreed to supply a quantity of canary seed on a 'pure' basis. The seed delivered was 98 per cent pure, and evidence was given that this was the highest standard of purity which it was normally possible to obtain in the trade. The seller was held to have performed his obligation.

The court will also ignore microscopic deviations under the rule *de minimis non curat lex* (the law does not concern itself with trivial matters).

> In *Shipton, Anderson & Co.* v. *Weil Bros. & Co.* (1912), the court ignored a deviation of 55 lbs. in a consignment of 4950 tons of wheat.

If one party *has* broken his obligations, it will normally be no defence to him that the breach was not his fault. He has promised to perform his contract, and he will be liable if he does not. Only if some outside cause makes performance physically, legally, or commercially *impossible* will he have an excuse for non-performance (Unit 21). The fact that he has taken all reasonable care will be no defence to him.

> In *Frost* v. *Aylesbury Dairy Co. Ltd* (1905), the dairy supplied milk infected with typhoid germs, and Mrs Frost died of the disease. It was held that, even if the dairy could prove that it had taken all possible precautions, it was still liable for breach of its implied duty to supply milk which was reasonably fit for drinking.

The consequences of non-performance will be discussed later. If the breach is a minor one, a breach of warranty, the contract will not be discharged. Both parties must go on with it, but the injured party can recover damages. If there has been a more serious breach, breach of condition, the injured party will have a right to discharge the contract and bring it to an end.

Special rules as to performance apply to an obligation to pay money. It is the duty of the debtor to seek out and tender to the creditor, at a reasonable time of day, payment of the correct amount of money in *legal tender*, without any necessity for the creditor to give change. Legal tender consists of those coins or notes which by law must be accepted in payment of a debt. It comprises bank notes up to any amount, 50p pieces up to £10, silver (or cupro-nickel) coins of 10p or less up to £5, and bronze coins up to 20p. A cheque is not legal tender, and the creditor need not take it in payment. If a cheque is taken, it will normally be treated as conditional payment, and the debt will not be discharged until the cheque is honoured.

If the creditor refuses to take the money when tendered, the debt is not discharged; the debtor must still pay, but the creditor must now come and seek him. If money is sent by post, the risk of loss lies upon the sender unless his creditor has authorized him to use the post. In this latter event, the risk passes to the creditor, provided that the sender takes reasonable precautions for care of the money in transit.

Where a debtor owes several debts to his creditor, and pays a sum insufficient to satisfy them all, it may be important to determine which debts the payment satisfies or reduces. The creditor will prefer to appropriate the payment to the oldest debts, because after six years they may become unenforceable. The rule, however, is that the debtor has a right to appropriate at the time of payment. Only if he does not appropriate then, can the creditor appropriate at any time thereafter. Exceptionally, in the case of current accounts, the rule is that first debts are paid first, for where money is being continually paid in and out it would be difficult to carry out specific appropriation with every payment.

B. Breach of contract

Breach of contract can occur in several ways. For example, one party may expressly repudiate his liabilities and refuse to perform his side of the bargain. This can happen either at or before the time when performance was due. If a party renounces his obligations in advance, this is known as *anticipatory* breach. A person can impliedly

UNIT 20. PERFORMANCE, BREACH, AND REMEDIES

renounce his obligations by rendering himself incapable of performing them; for example, if he had contracted to sell a specific painting, he would renounce the contract by selling the painting elsewhere. Alternatively, one party may simply fail to perform the contract. He may fail altogether to perform his bargain or he may merely fail to perform one, or some, of his many obligations under the agreement. If the obligation broken was a major part of the contract, there will be *breach of condition*, if only a minor part, there will be *breach of warranty*.

Sometimes the courts have classified a breach according to whether or not it is 'fundamental', but this classification has been used mainly in relation to exclusion clauses (Unit 19).

Effects of breach

1. Every breach of contract will give the injured party the right to recover damages (see later).
2. If the breach is sufficiently serious, it will also give the injured party a right to avoid the contract and bring it to an end. This right will arise if the contract has been repudiated, or if there has been breach of condition. It will not arise for breach of warranty.

    The consequences of breach can be so serious that the injured party has no choice. He may have to treat the contract as ended if, for example, the property is destroyed. Subject to this, however, he need not end the contract unless he wants to. Two courses of action are open to him: he can avoid the agreement, in which event, the rights and obligations of each party cease, or he can go on with it and be content with his right to damages. If he does wish to avoid the contract, he must do so reasonably promptly and, as with rescission for misrepresentation, the right is lost if he 'affirms' the agreement, for example, by indicating that he has accepted the property, or by re-selling it or using it so that it cannot be returned.

    Deciding whether a term is a condition or a mere warranty is a question of fact. If a term is so wide that it is not possible to classify it in advance, the right to avoid the contract will depend on the seriousness of the breach; see *Hong Kong Fir Shipping Co. Ltd* v. *Kawasaki Kisen Kaisha Ltd* (Unit 19). Terms implied by statute almost invariably are classified in advance; for example, the terms which are implied by sections 13 to 15 of the Sale of Goods Act 1979 (Unit 23), are all conditions and breach entitles the buyer to withdraw from the contract. On the other hand, the Sale of Goods Act also provides that breach of a term as to the time of payment does *not* entitle the creditor to avoid the contract unless the parties had specifically agreed otherwise. A term as to the time set for delivery of goods almost invariably will be a condition, and failure to deliver on time will entitle the buyer to reject the goods and avoid the contract. The buyer can, alternatively, waive failure to deliver on time, but impose a new deadline, breach of which will entitle him to set the contract aside.

    In *Charles Rickards Ltd* v. *Oppenheim* (1950), the buyer ordered a new car body, to be ready in seven months' time. It was not ready then, but the buyer agreed to wait a

187

further three months. When the work was still not completed, he indicated that he would cancel the order unless it was ready within a further four weeks. It was held that he was entitled to do so, and could refuse to take the car body when it was finally tendered some months later.

3. Where a contract is to be performed by instalments, and only one or more of these is defective, it may be important to determine whether this is a minor breach, or a major one entitling the buyer to avoid the whole contract and refuse further deliveries. The tests are the relation which the size of the breach bears to the contract as a whole and the likelihood or otherwise of the breach being repeated.

> In *Munro Ltd* v. *Meyer* (1930), a first delivery of 611 tons of defective bone meal out of a contract to supply 1500 tons did entitle the buyer to refuse further deliveries.
>
> On the other hand, in *Maple Flock Co. Ltd* v. *Universal Furniture Ltd* (1934), a defect in one instalment of rag flock, the sixteenth out of twenty deliveries, did not entitle the buyer to avoid the whole contract.

4. If one party renounces his obligations and commits an anticipatory breach, the injured party has two possible courses of action. He may treat the contract as at an end and bring an action at once, either for damages for breach, or for reasonable remuneration for the work which he has performed.

> In *Hochster* v. *De La Tour* (1853), the defendant agreed in April to employ the plaintiff as a courier on a European tour as from 1 June. In May, the defendant repudiated this agreement, and the plaintiff was held entitled to commence proceedings immediately, before waiting for 1 June.

If the plaintiff does end the contract immediately, he must try to mitigate his loss by, for example, seeking alternative employment.

Alternatively, since renunciation does not automatically discharge the contract, the injured party may waive the breach and continue to press for performance until the due date arrives. The exercise of this option means that the contract continues to exist, for the benefit of both parties, until the date for performance. If, before that date, performance becomes impossible, this will discharge the contract without the party who renounced having to pay damages.

> In *Avery* v. *Bowden* (1855), a ship arrived at Odessa for a cargo of wheat and was met by a refusal to load. This renunciation was not accepted and, before the last date for performance arrived, war broke out between England and Russia. This discharged the contract, and the shipowner was unable to recover damages.

C. Damages for breach of contract

Whenever one person has broken a contract, the other can recover damages which are assessed according to the following principles:

1. The basic rule is that the plaintiff should be *compensated*, but no more than compensated, for loss which he has suffered as a result of the breach. Loss can be financial, damage to property, personal injuries or even distress to the plaintiff, as

where a holiday firm defaults on its obligations; see *Jarvis* v. *Swans Tours Ltd* (1973). Where no loss has been suffered, as where a seller fails to deliver the goods but the buyer is able to purchase elsewhere at no extra cost, the court may award *nominal* damages, a nominal sum, perhaps of £2, to mark the breach.

Exemplary or *punitive* damages, which exceed the actual loss suffered by an amount intended to punish the offending party, are not normally awarded for breach of contract, although they have been awarded in the past against banks who have dishonoured traders' cheques when the account had sufficient funds to meet them.

2. The plaintiff, however, cannot be compensated for *all* the consequences which might logically 'result' from the defendant's breach, otherwise there might be no end to liability. Some loss, therefore, will be too remote.

> In *Hadley* v. *Baxendale* (1854), a mill owner entrusted a broken crankshaft to a carrier, for delivery to an engineer who would replace it. Delivery was delayed through the fault of the carrier, and the mill stood idle longer than was necessary. The mill owner recovered damages against the carrier, but a claim for loss of profits was disallowed, because it was not shown that the carrier knew the mill would have to stand idle.

The court suggested two tests which still form the basis of the rules covering remoteness of damage. The damage or loss treated as resulting from the breach should only include:

(a) such damage as may fairly and reasonably be considered as arising naturally, that is, according to the usual course of things, from the breach; and
(b) such other loss as may reasonably be supposed to have been in the contemplation of both parties, at the time they made the contract so that the defendant in effect accepted responsibility for it.

The working of these rules can best be illustrated by some of the cases which have arisen:

> In *Horne* v. *Midland Railway Co.* (1873), Horne had a contract to manufacture boots for the French army at a price higher than the normal market price, provided that he could deliver by a certain date. The boots were consigned to the railway company, which was informed of the importance of the delivery date but not the special price. Delivery was delayed, the boots were rejected and had to be sold elsewhere at below the normal market price. Horne only recovered the difference between his re-sale price and the *market* price. His claim for the difference between the *contract* price and the price on re-sale failed, because the carriers did not know of the original contract price.

> In *Victoria Laundry* (*Windsor*) *Ltd.* v. *Newman Industries Ltd* (1949), a laundry firm ordered a new boiler which arrived late. It was held entitled to recover damages for *normal* loss of profits, because the supplier should have anticipated this. It was not, however, entitled to recover for further losses due to losing an exceptionally profitable contract of which the suppliers did not know.

> In *The Heron II* (1969), a shipowner was late in delivering a cargo of sugar to Basrah, and by the time of delivery the market price had fallen. It was held that the loss of profits could be recovered, because this possibility must reasonably have been in the contemplation of the parties.

3. The injured party has a duty to *mitigate* or minimize his loss, that is, take all reasonable steps to reduce it. A worker who is wrongly dismissed must attempt to find other work; a seller whose goods are rejected must attempt to get the best price for them elsewhere; a buyer of goods which are not delivered must attempt to but as cheaply as possible elsewhere. Loss arising from failure to take such steps will not be recovered. On the other hand, only *reasonable* steps need be taken to mitigate; the buyer, for example, need not tour the globe looking for the cheapest alternative supplier.

4. In some cases, the parties, foreseeing the possibility of breach, make an attempt in the original contract to assess in advance the damages which will be payable on breach. Such a provision for *liquidated* damage will be perfectly valid if it is a genuine attempt to pre-estimate the likely loss. If it is not a genuine pre-estimate, however, but an attempt to impose punitive damages where none would otherwise be awarded, then the liquidated damages clause will be void as a *penalty*. The essence of a penalty is that it was inserted *in terrorem*, to frighten the potential defaulter. Such clauses often used to appear in hire purchase agreements, so that if a hirer returned the goods after paying only one instalment, he might have to bring his payments under the agreements up to half or more of the original hire purchase price. The courts held such clauses to be void and, where the Consumer Credit Act 1974 applies, such penalties are invalidated by statute.

> In *Bridge* v. *Campbell Discount Co. Ltd* (1962). Bridge agreed to take a vehicle on hire purchase for £482. He paid a deposit of £105 and one instalment of £10, but then repudiated the agreement because he could afford no more. He was sued for a further £206, under a clause in the agreement requiring him to bring his total payments up to two-thirds of the hire purchase price of £482 'by way of agreed compensation for depreciation of the vehicle'. Bridge had only had the vehicle for a few weeks, had returned it in good condition, and had already paid £115. The clause was held void as penalty.

Contracts for the sale of goods and building contracts sometimes provide that, in the event of late performance, a specified sum shall be payable for each day of delay. Minimum price agreements often contain similar provisions to apply in the event of breach.

> In *Dunlop Ltd* v. *New Garage Ltd* (1915), the defendants had agreed that damages of £5 should be payable for each tyre sold below Dunlop's listed price. This clause was held valid, because even the smallest breach of the pricing arrangements could lead to widespread undercutting and severely damage Dunlop Ltd.

> On the other hand, in *Ford Motor Co.* v. *Armstrong* (1915), a promise to pay £250 for each car sold below the listed price was held void as a penalty.

D. Other remedies for breach

1. *Claims on a quantum meruit*. In some situations, a claim for damages may not be the appropriate financial remedy. This may happen where one party repudiates the contract before the other has completed his side of the bargain, but after the other

has done a good deal of work. The injured party may have suffered no direct financial loss, but he may be entitled to claim on a *quantum meruit* (for so much as he deserves) for what he has done.

> In *Planché* v. *Colburn* (1831), the plaintiff was commissioned by a publisher to write a book for £100. After he had done the necessary research and written part of the book, the publisher repudiated the contract. It was held that the plaintiff could recover £50 on a *quantum meruit*.

A claim on this basis may also be made where work has been done under a void contract. The plaintiff cannot recover damages for breach, because no contract exists, but he may recover on a *quantum meruit*.

> In *Craven-Ellis* v. *Canons Ltd* (1936), the plaintiff recovered reasonable remuneration for work which he had done as managing director of the company, when it transpired that his appointment was void.

2. *A decree for specific performance* is an equitable remedy which is sometimes granted where damages would not be an adequate remedy. It is an order of the court directing the party in breach to carry out his promises, on pain of penalties for contempt of court. Since it is equitable, it is discretionary (Unit 1); in particular, it will not be granted in the following circumstances:

   (a) It will not be awarded where damages would be enough and, for this reason, it will rarely be granted in commercial transactions. Monetary compensation will usually enable a disappointed buyer to obtain similar commodities elsewhere. In a sale of goods, the seller will normally only be ordered to hand over the article specifically where it is unique, such as an original painting.

   > In *Cohen* v. *Roche* (1927), the court refused to order specific performance of a contract to sell some Hepplewhite chairs which were rare, but not unique. Similar chairs could be bought elsewhere, albeit with difficulty.

   On the other hand, each piece of land *is* unique, and the main use of the remedy today is in contracts for the sale of land; see *Rawlinson* v. *Ames* (Unit 16). The remedy may also be granted in contracts to sell or allot shares.

   (b) The court must be sure that it can adequately supervise enforcement. Therefore contracts of a personal nature, such as employment, which depend on good faith which the court cannot ensure, will not be specifically enforced. Similarly, building contracts will not be enforced.

   (c) Specific performance will not be awarded either to or against a minor.

   (d) The court may exercise its discretion to refuse specific performance in any other situation where it is not felt just or equitable to grant it.

   > In *Malins* v. *Freeman* (1837), the remedy was refused where a bidder foolishly bought property at an auction in the belief that he was bidding for an entirely different lot. It would have been harsh to compel him to take the property; the seller could still sue for damages if he so wished.

3. *An injunction* is an order of the court directing a person *not* to break his contract. It is only appropriate to enforce a negative provision in the agreement and, being

an equitable remedy, it is only awarded on the same principles as specific performance. It can, however, be awarded to enforce a negative stipulation in a contract for services or employment.

> In *Warner Brothers Pictures Incorporated* v. *Nelson* (1937), the actress, Bette Davis, had contracted with the film company not to work as an actress for anyone else during her present contract. It was held that she could be restrained by injunction from breaking this undertaking.

On the other hand, an injunction will not be granted in contracts of employment if it would operate as an indirect way of specifically enforcing the agreement; thus, Nelson could only be restrained from working elsewhere *as an actress*, otherwise she might be faced with the alternatives of either working for Warner Brothers or starving. An employer, however, may *temporarily* be restrained from dismissing an employee; this is not tantamount to specific performance, because the employer can usually suspend the man on full pay if the employee's presence is an embarrassment.

> In *Hill* v. *C. A. Parsons & Co. Ltd* (1972), the plaintiff was dismissed with inadequate notice as a result of trade union pressure to maintain a 'closed shop'. The court granted an injunction restraining Parsons Ltd from dismissing Hill until adequate notice had been given.

As will be seen, injunctions are sometimes granted to enforce lawful restraints on trade; see cases such as *Home Counties Dairies Ltd* v. *Skilton* (Unit 22). The remedy may be granted to enforce negative promises in contracts relating to land; for example, a purchaser may be restrained from breaking his contractual promise not to build on the land sold. In exceptional circumstances, injunctions may even issue to order the seller of goods not to withhold delivery.

> In *Sky Petroleum Ltd* v. *VIP Petroleum Ltd* (1974), the parties had a 10-year agreement in 1970 that VIP would supply all Sky Ltd's petrol requirements. In November 1973 a dispute arose between the parties, and VIP withheld supplies. In the oil crisis then existing, Sky Ltd could not get supplies from any other source (contrast *Cohen* v. *Roche*, page 192). The court granted a temporary injunction restraining VIP from withholding reasonable supplies, even though this was equivalent to a temporary order of specific performance.

For further consideration

1. (a) Is a retailer liable for defects in goods which are prepacked by the manufacturer, and which the retailer could not open to check? (An example would be a tin of baked beans which, unknown to the retailer, had gone bad in the tin.)
   (b) Would the manufacturer be liable to the customer?
2. B orders 500 gallons of a specified grade of oil from S, to be delivered in five gallon drums in one month's time. Explain the rights of B in each of the following situations:
   (a) S delivers 495 gallons;

(b) S delivers in 10 gallon drums;
(c) S delivers oil of a slightly different grade;
(d) S delivers one week late.

3. William, a wholesaler, receives an order worth £500 from Richard, a retailer, for shirts which have just become fashionable. Richard would normally have paid £450 for this consignment but promises the extra £50 for delivery within three weeks. William thereupon places an order with Martin, a shirt manufacturer, for manufacture and delivery to him of the specified shirts within two weeks at a price of £350. Martin does not in fact deliver for over three weeks and when William tenders the shirts to Richard they are rejected. William sells them elsewhere for £400.

   Advise William on the damages he may expect to recover from Martin.

4. Painter agrees to undertake extensive decoration in Manor's house for a price of £1000 to be paid when the work has been completed. After Painter has committed labour and materials to the task to a value of £700, Manor claims that the work is defective and he refuses to allow Painter to enter the house to complete the work.

   Advise Painter.

Unit 21. Discharge, Limitation, and Privity

A contract may be discharged, that is, come to an end, in four main ways. Two of these, namely performance and discharge as a result of breach, arise directly out of the terms of the original contract, and were discussed in the last unit. The present unit is concerned with methods of discharge which do not necessarily arise out of what was originally agreed, but from extraneous events. These methods of discharge are new agreement and frustration.

Two other matters which affect the right to sue on a contract will also be discussed here, namely the time limits affecting *when* actions must be brought, and the rules of privity affecting *who* can sue or be sued.

A. Discharge by agreement

There are three main ways in which a contract can be discharged by agreement.
1. The parties may have made provision for discharge in their original contract. For example, the parties may have agreed at the outset that the contract should end automatically on some determining event or on the expiration of a fixed time. Thus goods may be hired, premises may be leased, or a person employed for a fixed term. On the expiration of the term, the contract will cease.

    Alternatively, the contract may contain a provision entitling one or both parties to terminate it if they so wish. Thus a contract of employment can normally be brought to an end by either party on reasonable notice to the other (subject only to statutory minimum periods of notice laid down by the Employment Protection (Consolidation) Act 1978). Hire purchase contracts usually give the hirer a contractual right to end the agreement and return the goods at any time;

where the Consumer Credit Act 1974 applies, there is also a statutory right to do this. Discharge in these ways does arise out of the terms of the original agreement.

2. Discharge can also arise, not out of the original agreement, but by reason of a new, extraneous contract. In order that the new agreement should discharge the old one, however, the new contract must be valid; for example, there must be consideration.

Where neither side of the original contract has yet been performed, there will be no difficulty; each side still owes duties, and the consideration for one party waiving his rights is the waiver of rights by the other. Thus the buyer and seller may agree to cancel an order; the seller need no longer supply the goods, and the buyer no longer has to pay.

The position is more complicated where one party has completely performed his original obligations. The agreement for discharge will only be valid if, in return for the release, the other party does or promises something which he is *not* already bound to do, such as paying earlier than he was bound to do. In the absence of such new consideration, the agreement for release will not be binding, and the original contract will stand; see *D & C Builders Ltd* v. *Rees* (1966) (Unit 16). For this reason discharge by new agreement is sometimes called discharge by accord (agreement) and satisfaction (consideration).

3. Finally, one party can release the other unilaterally, without consideration, but only if he does so by *deed*.

B. Discharge by frustration

Until the last century, the obligation to perform a contractual duty was absolute. If it became physically impossible for a party to perform his bargain, he nevertheless had to pay damages for breach, and if extraneous events took away the whole purpose of the contract without the fault of either party, they still had to continue with the agreement.

> In *Paradine* v. *Jane* (1647), a lessee was evicted during the Civil War. It was held that he still had to pay the rent; the fact that he could not enjoy the property because of events beyond his control was of no concern to the lessor, and was no excuse.

Starting with the case of *Taylor* v. *Caldwell* in 1863 (see below), the courts have developed the doctrine of frustration as an exception to this absolute rule. If some outside event occurs, for which neither party is responsible and which makes total nonsense of the original agreement, then the contract will be discharged by frustration. A radical change in circumstances can sometimes, therefore, be pleaded by a party as a valid excuse for not performing his side of the bargain. This doctrine must be approached with caution, however, because the courts have understandably been reluctant to accept anything but the most fundamental changes as frustrating events. The following are the main examples.

1. *Subsequent physical impossibility*
This will occur where, *after* the contract was made, it becomes physically impossible

or impracticable to perform it. (If this was already impossible when the contract was *made*, the agreement would be void from the outset.)

> In *Taylor* v. *Caldwell* (1863), a music hall hired for a series of concerts was burnt down before the date for the first performance. This was held to frustrate the contract, because there was no longer any hall to hire. The hirer, therefore, no longer had to pay.
>
> In *Robinson* v. *Davison* (1877), a pianist, who was engaged to give a concert on a specified date, became ill and was incapable of appearing. It was held that this frustrated the contract.

2. *Subsequent illegality*

This will occur where, *after* the contract was made, a change in the law or in the circumstances renders it illegal to perform the agreement. Thus, many contracts to export goods to Rhodesia were discharged by frustration when sanctions were introduced.

> In *Avery* v. *Bowden* (1885), the contract to load a cargo at Odessa was eventually discharged by the outbreak of the Crimean War, which made it thenceforth an illegal contract of trading with the enemy.

3. *Basis of the contract removed*

The contract may be frustrated where both parties made it on the basis of a future event which does not take place.

> In *Chandler* v. *Webster* (1904), the contract was for the hire of a room in Pall Mall for the day of Edward VII's coronation procession. The rent was over £140, because the procession would pass directly beneath the window. Unfortunately the coronation was postponed when the King became ill. This was held to frustrate the contract.

4. *Frustration of the commercial purpose of the contract*

A change may occur which makes a total nonsense of what was originally agreed, so that what the parties would have to perform bears no relation to what was originally intended. This change must be radical; an event which merely makes it more difficult or expensive for a party to perform the contract will be no excuse. It is rare that a contract will be frustrated on this ground.

> In *Metropolitan Water Board* v. *Dick, Kerr & Co.* (1918), a firm of contractors agreed in 1914 to build a reservoir. In 1916, under wartime emergency powers, the Government ordered the contractor to stop work and sell the plant. This was held to frustrate the contract. Although it might eventually be possible to start work again after the war, the enforced hold-up for an indefinite period made nonsense of the contract.
>
> On the other hand, in *Tsakiroglou Ltd* v. *Noblee & Thorl G.m.b.H.* (1962), the sellers agreed to deliver groundnuts from Port Sudan to the buyers in Hamburg, and to ship them in November or December 1956. In November 1956, the Suez Canal was closed, and the sellers would now have had to ship the goods round the Cape of Good Hope, a much longer and more expensive journey. It was held that this did *not* frustrate the contract, but merely made it more difficult to perform.

If a seller wishes to protect himself against liability to the buyer for delays due to such matters as strikes or non-delivery of raw materials, he should make special provision for this in the contract. If one party makes a promise which he fails to perform, the court is reluctant to allow him to say, in effect, 'Oh, but it's not my fault'.

The effects of frustration

Frustration automatically brings the contract to an end and renders it void. As a general rule, all sums paid by either party in pursuance of the contract before it was discharged are recoverable, and all sums not yet paid cease to be due.

> In the *Fibrosa Case* (1943), an English company agreed in 1939 to make some machinery for a Polish buyer at a price of £4800. The buyer paid an initial sum of £1000. When war broke out, Poland was occupied by the German army, and the contract was therefore frustrated by subsequent illegality. It was held that the London agent of the Polish buyer had no further liability, and could recover the £1000 already paid.

This was rather harsh on the seller, who had already done considerable work and incurred expense in manufacturing the goods. The Law Reform (Frustrated Contracts) Act 1943, therefore, restated the general rule, but introduced two exceptions to it:

1. If one party has, before the time of discharge, incurred expenses in performing it, the court may in its discretion allow him to keep or recover all or part of sums *already paid or due* under the contract.
2. If one party has, by reason of anything done by the other, obtained a valuable benefit (other than the payment of money), then the other may recover such sum as the court considers just.

The Law Reform (Frustrated Contracts) Act applies to all contracts except (a) contracts for the carriage of goods by sea, (b) contracts of insurance, (c) contracts containing special provisions to meet the case of frustration, and (d) contracts for the sale of specific goods where the agreement is frustrated because the goods perish before risk passes to the buyer. This last category is covered by the Sale of Goods Act 1979, section 7, which provides that the agreement shall be avoided, but makes no provision for the seller to recover money if he has incurred expense, or if the buyer has received benefit.

C. Limitation of actions

Contractual obligations are not enforceable for ever. Apart from other considerations, evidence becomes less reliable with the passage of time, and therefore, after a certain period, the law bars any remedy.

The Limitation Act 1980 lays down the general periods within which an action must be brought. These are as follows:

1. Actions based on a *simple* contract will be barred after six years from the date when the cause of action accrued.
2. Where the contract is made by *deed*, actions can be brought up to 12 years from the date when the cause of action accrued.

3. Actions to recover *land* can be brought up to 12 years from the date when the cause of action accrued.

A right of action 'accrues' when breach occurs. Thus, if a loan is made for a fixed time, the right will accrue when this time expires. If no time is agreed, it will be when a written demand for payment is made.

If, when the cause of action accrues, the plaintiff is under a disability by reason of infancy or unsoundness of mind, the period will not run until the disability has ended or until his death, whichever comes first. Once the period has started to run, subsequent insanity will have no effect.

If the plaintiff is the victim of fraud or acts under a mistake or if the defendant deliberately conceals relevant facts, the limitation period will not begin until the true state of affairs is discovered or should reasonably have been discovered.

> In *Lynn* v. *Bamber* (1930), some plum trees were sold in 1921 with an undertaking by the seller that they were of a particular type. Not until they matured in 1928 was it discovered that they were of inferior quality. It was held that an action for damages could still be brought, since the fraudulent misrepresentations by the seller had postponed the operation of the period of limitation.

Provided that the limitation period has not already expired, the period may be extended where the party in breach either acknowledges his liability in writing, signed by him or his agent, or makes part payment in respect of the debt or claim. Time will then begin to run afresh from the date of acknowledgement or part payment. Property obtained by theft may be recovered at any time unless it has passed to a bona fide purchaser who is protected after six years.

Equitable remedies, such as specific performance or an injunction, are not covered by the ordinary limitation periods, but will almost invariably be barred much earlier under general equitable principles. An equitable remedy must be sought reasonably promptly, because 'equity aids the vigilant, not the indolent'. A short delay, of weeks or even days, may bar the remedy.

D. Privity of contract

As a general rule, the legal effects of a contract are confined to the contracting parties. An agreement between A and B cannot confer any legally enforceable benefit on a stranger, cannot impose any obligations on a stranger, and cannot take away the rights of a stranger. Only A can sue B for breach, and vice versa.

> In *Tweddle* v. *Atkinson* (1861), a young couple were about to marry. The husband's father and the bride's father agreed between themselves that each would make payments to the couple. It was held that the husband could not sue for breach of this contract when the bride's father failed to pay.

> In *Adler* v. *Dickson* (1955), a passenger on board ship was injured by the negligence of the master and boatswain. Her ticket from the shipping company provided that 'passengers are carried at passengers' entire risk'. Nevertheless she successfully sued the master and the boatswain; the exclusion clause was in a contract between the passenger and the company, and could not protect employees.

This rule is of great importance in English law. A customer who buys a new car from a garage cannot sue the manufacturer for breach of contract, because the customer contracted only with the garage. If the car breaks down and a passenger is injured, the passenger has no contract with either the manufacturer or the garage. The plaintiff can only sue in tort in these cases, and must, therefore, prove that the defendant has been negligent (see *Donoghue* v. *Stevenson* in Unit 13). Similarly, a shareholder cannot directly take the benefit of a contract made by the company, because the company is a separate legal person (Unit 10).

There are exceptions to this general rule. For example, where an agent contracts with a third party on behalf of a principal whose existence he does not disclose, the latter may step in and sue or be sued on the contract. If two people contract with the intention of creating a trust in favour of a third person, the latter, although unable to enforce the contract, may take action as a beneficiary for breach of trust if any of the contractual obligations are broken. A lease of land may create rights and obligations which attach to the land, and bind not only the landlord and the tenant, but also future assignees of the lease.

In other situations the parties to a contract may change by operation of law or by agreement. Thus, in the case of bankruptcy, rights of action pass to the trustee in bankruptcy. In the case of death, rights of action pass to the personal representatives (Unit 29).

> In *Beswick* v. *Beswick* (1968), Peter Beswick, a coal merchant, sold his business to his nephew, John, in return (among other matters) for an undertaking by John to pay £5 per week to Peter's widow after Peter's death. Although the widow could not sue John in her own right, because she was not a party to the contract, she was able to recover payment *on Peter's behalf*, as administratrix of his estate.

Contractual rights may be assigned, in which case someone other than the original promisee may sue or be sued. Rights are easier to transfer than obligations, for if a debt is owed it matters little, to the debtor, to whom it is paid. Who is to pay does matter considerably to the creditor, and his permission to a transfer is, therefore, required.

An important situation where a third party can take the *benefit* of a contract made between two others is in connection with liability insurance, which includes compulsory motor insurance. The contract is between the insured, that is to say the driver in motor policies, and his insurance company, which promises to indemnify the driver against possible liability to third parties whom he may injure. As a general rule, only the insured can demand payment from the insurance company on this contract, not the third party. Where the insured has become bankrupt, however, the Third Parties (Rights Against Insurers) Act 1930 allows the injured party to claim directly from the insurance company; otherwise the money would go to the insured's trustee in bankruptcy, and the third party might get nothing. Moreover, in relation to motor insurance, the Road Traffic Act 1972 provides other exceptions to the privity rule; thus, a person driving with the owner's consent may be entitled to cover even though not a party to the insurance agreement and, in respect of compulsory third party risks, the person injured can recover directly from the insurance company under section 149.

The *burden* of a contract can be imposed on a stranger where a restrictive covenant is imposed on land at the time of sale, for example, a covenant prohibiting its use as an inn or alehouse; this can bind all future occupiers of the land, even though not parties to the original contract of sale (see *Tulk* v. *Moxhay* (1848) in Unit 28). Another example is the Resale Prices Act 1976, which still allows a supplier, with the consent of the Restrictive Practices Court, to impose a minimum resale price which will bind anyone who takes the goods with a view to re-sale, and who has notice of the restriction.

For further consideration

1. 'Discharge of contractual obligations by frustration should not be possible. If a person contracts to do something he should either do it or pay damages. It is possible to insure against a situation arising which makes the promise impossible to perform.' Do you agree?
2. Advise Charles as to his right to take legal action in 1982 in each of the following circumstances.
   (a) He sold and delivered goods to David in 1974. When David was pressed for payment in 1978 he admitted the debt and promised early payment. This has not been done.
   (b) He sold and delivered goods to Daniel in 1975 to the value of £80 and in 1978 to the value of £40. In 1979, Daniel paid £40 and has since refused to make any further payment.
   (c) He bought carpeting from Derek in 1975. In 1978 he noticed excessive wear and upon close examination discovered that it was of an inferior type to that which he had ordered.
3. Industrial Expansion Ltd enters into a contract to build a factory for £250 000 payable in instalments as the work progresses. The company also agrees to import and install machinery in the factory at an additional cost of £100 000 of which £30 000 is payable upon signing the contract and the balance upon completion.

   The building is started and the first progress payment of £50 000 is made. The company then discovers that because of a serious costing error the work can only be completed at a considerable loss. At about the same time the Government bars the import of foreign machinery.

   Advise Industrial Expansion Ltd, which has committed labour and materials to the extent of £30 000 and which now wishes to abandon the project.
4. Advise Bolton in both of the following situations, explaining the relevant principles of law.
   (a) Bolton bought a factory from Preston. In the agreement he promised to pay Preston a pension for life and to continue paying this to Preston's widow after

Preston's death. Preston has now died and Bolton asks for your advice on whether he is still under a legal obligation to continue paying the widow.

(b) Bolton sold and delivered goods to Chorley at a price of £500. Chorley said that he had financial problems and offered £400 in full settlement of the debt. Bolton accepted. Bolton has now heard that Chorley's business is prospering and wonders whether he can claim the outstanding £100.

Unit 22. Contracts and Public Policy

Earlier units have dealt with those agreements which English law will recognize as contracts, and the nature, effect, and discharge of such agreements. This unit refers to another aspect of the concept of freedom of contract. From the earliest days of this branch of the law, freedom of contract has been subject to overriding considerations of public policy. Some agreements have been held completely *illegal*, and the courts will normally do nothing to help parties who rely on them. Other agreements, while not being illegal, have been held *void*, so that the courts will give no remedy for breach, but will allow money paid under the contract to be recovered. Various statutes have added to the list of contractual provisions which are void or illegal as contrary to public policy at common law.

A. Contracts which are illegal at common law

1. *An agreement to commit a criminal offence or a tort* is probably the oldest example of an illegal contract. An agreement to do something in a friendly foreign country which will be an offence in that country will also be illegal in England under this head.

    In *Allen* v. *Rescous* (1676), the plaintiff paid the defendant 20 shillings to assault X and evict him. It was held that the plaintiff was not entitled to recover his money when the defendant failed in this illegal purpose.

    In *Foster* v. *Driscoll* (1929), an English partnership, formed to smuggle whisky into the United States at a time when liquor was prohibited there, was held to be illegal in English law.

2. A *contract to defraud the revenue* will be illegal for similar reasons.

> In *Miller* v. *Karlinski* (1945), an agreement between employer and employee to disguise part of the salary as expenses, so as to evade income tax, was held to be illegal. As a result, the employee was not entitled to reclaim arrears of salary from the employer.

3. *Contracts to corrupt public life*, such as contracts to bribe officials, to sell public offices, or to procure a title or honour are similarly illegal.

> In *Parkinson* v. *College of Ambulance Ltd* (1925), the secretary of the College, which was a charity, promised that he could obtain a knighthood for the plaintiff in return for a suitable donation. Parkinson donated £3000 but did not obtain a knighthood. His action for the return of the £3000 failed.

4. *Immoral contracts*. This category is limited to contracts for a sexually immoral purpose, such as a contract between a man and a woman for future cohabitation. Any contract clearly connected with an immoral purpose will be illegal.

> In *Pearce* v. *Brooks* (1866), the owner of a coach of unusual design was unable to recover the cost of hire from a prostitute who, to his knowledge, had hired it to attract clients.

A promise to pay money for past illicit cohabitation could not be sued upon since the consideration is past.

5. *Contracts for trading with the enemy*. These include all contracts with a person or firm voluntarily residing in enemy territory in time of war. If war breaks out after the contract was made but before it is performed, the contract is frustrated by subsequent illegality; see the *Fibrosa Case* (Unit 21).

6. *Contracts to impede the course of justice*. These include agreements to prevent or hinder the prosecution of a serious criminal offence, for example, by paying the victim not to report the offence or not to cooperate in the prosecution. Contracts of maintenance, where a person with no legal interest in the proceedings gives financial assistance to another to enable him to bring or defend the proceedings, and contracts of champerty, where a litigant is assisted in return for a share in the proceeds if he wins, are also illegal under this head.

Effects of illegality

An illegal contract is void. Furthermore, contrary to the general rule applying to void contracts, any money that has passed cannot be recovered. Thus in *Parkinson* v. *College of Ambulance Ltd*, Parkinson could not recover his donation. Any contract closely connected with the illegality, so as to be tainted by it, will also be void; thus the contract of hire in *Pearce* v. *Brooks* and the partnership in *Foster* v. *Driscoll* were illegal. There are, however, some exceptions to these rules:

1. Where one party was innocent of the illegality, he will be entitled to sue on the contract, although the other party cannot. This will occur where the contract appears perfectly innocent, but one party is performing it for an illegal purpose without the other's knowledge. For example, in *Pearce* v. *Brooks*, had the owner of

the coach not known the purpose for which his customer was using it, he *would* have been entitled to recover his hire.
2. Where one party repents of the illegal purpose before carrying it out, the court may allow him a remedy. On the other hand, his repentance must be genuine; if he withdraws simply because it becomes impossible to carry out the illegal purpose, the court will not believe his repentance.
3. The original owner of goods that have passed under an illegal contract may be allowed to recover the goods or his loss if, in his claim, he does not have to rely on the illegal contract. He cannot sue for breach of the contract, but he may be allowed to sue in tort.

> In *Belvoir Finance Ltd* v. *Stapleton* (1971), the plaintiffs let some cars to X Ltd under an illegal hire purchase agreement. It was held that they could recover damages for the tort of conversion (Unit 14) from Stapleton who, as salesman for X Ltd, had wrongfully re-sold the cars before the hire purchase price was paid. All that the plaintiffs had to prove was that they owned the cars and that Stapleton had wrongfully re-sold them; there was no need to rely on the illegal contract.

B. Contracts which are illegal by statute

The nature and effect of statutory illegality vary with the terms of the Act concerned. Some statutes expressly declare the whole contract illegal, with the same consequences as illegality at common law. An example of this is the Life Assurance Act 1774, under which a contract to insure a life in which the proposer has no 'insurable interest' will be illegal. In spite of its title, the Act also applies to insurance of buildings and liability insurance. The temptations which might be raised if the proposer were free to insure the life or buildings of a stranger are obvious. A proposer will normally have an insurable interest in his own life, the life of his wife, and the lives of debtors and others whose death would financially affect him.

> In *Harse* v. *Pearl Life Assurance Co.* (1904), it was held that the plaintiff had no insurable interest in the life of his mother, whose life he had insured. The policy was illegal, and the plaintiff was not entitled to recover the premiums which he had paid.

Another example is section 1 of the Resale Prices Act 1976, which declares unlawful all agreements between the suppliers of goods to 'blacklist' retailers who sell below the minimum resale price agreed by the suppliers.

At times when credit controls are in force, any agreement for sale or hire purchase of certain consumer durable goods, where credit is allowed and the money is to be paid by instalments, will be illegal unless it complies with the provisions of the current control order. At the time of writing, the Hire Purchase and Credit Sale Agreements (Control) Orders still require that minimum cash deposits be paid for most goods, the amount depending upon the type of goods, and that the period of credit be limited in most cases. Controls also exist over many hiring agreements, which will similarly be illegal if they contravene any order in force.

Some difficulty arises from statutes which, while not expressly making a contract illegal, provide that it shall only be carried out by someone who has a licence to do so. For example, licences are required by those who sell alcoholic drinks, or carry goods by road. Someone who acts without a licence commits a criminal offence, but does this render his contracts illegal? The answer depends on the purpose of the legislation in question. If, in the view of the courts, the Act was designed to forbid contracts of this type by unlicensed dealers, so as to protect the public, then the contract will be illegal. If the purpose of licensing was only to raise revenue or to help in the administration of the trade, contracts will not be affected.

> In *Cope* v. *Rowlands* (1836), an unlicensed broker in the City of London was held not to be entitled to sue for his fees, because the purpose of the licensing requirements was to protect the public against possible shady dealers.

> On the other hand, in *Archbolds (Freightage) Ltd* v. *Spanglett Ltd* (1961) a contract by an unlicensed carrier to carry goods by road was held valid, because the legislation was only designed to help in the administration of road transport.

Similar problems arise where a statute requires that certain contracts be carried out in a particular manner, with penalties in the event of breach.

> In *Anderson Ltd* v. *Daniel* (1924), the seller of artificial fertilizers was required by statute to state in the invoice the percentages of certain fertilizers. Failure to do this was held to render the contract illegal, and the seller was unable to recover the price of goods which he had delivered.

> On the other hand, in *Shaw* v. *Groom* (1970), a landlord who let furnished premises without a proper rent book did recover arrears of rent. The court took the view that the rent book requirements were not central to the contract as a whole, and that the Act did not intend the landlord to lose more in unpaid arrears than could have been imposed by way of fine.

Finally, some statutes declare certain *terms* in a contract to be illegal, without thereby affecting the rest of the contract. An example is found in the Truck Acts 1831–1940, which apply to contracts of employment. This legislation is designed to ensure that the wages of manual workers are paid in cash and not, as sometimes happened in the last century, in goods or by vouchers which could be exchanged only for goods at the company store. The Acts also prohibit certain deductions from wages by employers. A term which infringes these provisions is void and illegal, but this does not invalidate the contract of employment as a whole. The requirements as to payment in cash are now modified by the Payment of Wages Act 1960, which allows payment by cheque or through a bank if the workman requests this in writing and the employer agrees.

C. Contracts in restraint of trade

It is a long tradition of the common law that all agreements or provisions in agreements which tend to restrain trade are contrary to public policy. Most restraints are still governed by the rules of common law, but some are now extended by statute, particularly by the Restrictive Trade Practices Act 1976 and the Resale Prices Act 1976. While such restraints are void, they are not illegal.

Restraints take many forms, but the following are the main types:

1. Contracts of employment sometimes provide that the employee, after leaving his present employment, may not compete against his present employer either by setting up in business on his own or by working for a rival firm.
2. On the sale of a business, the buyer will often require the seller to promise that, in future, he will not carry on a similar business in competition with the buyer. (Otherwise the seller might set up in business nearby and attract all his old customers away from the buyer.)
3. Suppliers of goods and services sometimes agree between themselves to fix prices, restrict output, regulate the methods of supply, or otherwise influence the market for their products.
4. Retailers sometimes make 'solus' or similar agreements with suppliers, under which the retailer promises to sell only that supplier's brand of goods. The main cases have involved agreements between garages and petrol companies.

Except under the third head above, the restraint will normally be only one clause in a much wider agreement, such as a contract of employment or a sales agreement. In these circumstances, the bulk of the agreement will not be affected; the only clause in question is the one which attempts to impose the restraint.

The rules relating to covenants in restraint are basically the same for all types. Every restraint is *presumed void* unless it can be proved otherwise. It can only be proved valid if it can be shown to be reasonable in the interests of both parties *and* in the interests of the public at large.

Reasonableness between the parties depends upon whether the person for whose benefit the covenant was made had any legitimate interest in imposing it, that is, whether he had anything to lose, such as trade secrets or contact with customers. The restraint must then be measured against this interest. The nature of the restraint, its geographical area, the time for which it is to operate, and all other features must be no more than is reasonable to protect the interest in question.

Reasonableness in the public interest affects restraints which have a wide economic effect, particularly restraints under the third and fourth heads above. This is less likely to be important in restraints on employment.

Restraints on employment

In the main, the courts have not been sympathetic to restraints of this kind, which attempt to restrict the right of a person to earn his living where and with whom he likes. Furthermore, the worker may have been 'persuaded' to agree to the restraint because the employer was in a stronger bargaining position. The following cases will illustrate the rules.

In *Home Counties Dairies Ltd* v. *Skilton* (1970), a milk roundsman had to agree in his original contract of employment that, for one year after leaving his present job, he would not sell milk to customers of his present employer. The restraint applied both to setting up a rival business himself and to working for any rival firm. The restriction was held valid, and necessary to protect his employer against potential loss of customers. Skilton was restrained by injunction from breaking his undertaking.

In *Forster & Sons Ltd* v. *Suggett* (1918), the works manager of a glass-making company had agreed not to work for any rival firm for five years after leaving his present job. This was held valid, because the manager knew of secret manufacturing processes which would be of value to a rival.

On the other hand, in *Eastham* v. *Newcastle United Football Club* (1964), the Football Association's retain and transfer rules, whereby a player could not transfer to any other club without the consent of his present one, were held invalid as being wider than necessary to protect the clubs.

In *Mason* v. *Provident Clothing Co. Ltd* (1913), the clothing company had imposed a term restraining Mason, a collector and canvasser, from working for any similar business within 25 miles of London for three years after leaving. The House of Lords held that the onus was on the company to prove that such a wide restraint was reasonable to protect it, and that it had failed to do this.

Any attempt by an employer to impose restraints by indirect means will be subject to the same tests.

In *Bull* v. *Pitney-Bowes Ltd* (1966), a rule in the pensions scheme of the defendant company provided that employees should lose their pension rights if they left to work for a competing company. Bull did leave after 26 years, and went to work for a competitor. It was held that this rule in the pension scheme was void as an attempted restraint on trade.

In *Kores Ltd* v. *Kolok Ltd* (1959), an agreement between two employers that neither would employ anyone who had worked for the other in the last five years was held invalid.

Restraints on the seller of a business

The courts have been much more ready to uphold restraints imposed in these circumstances, because the buyer plainly has an interest to protect and the seller is a free agent. The restriction must, however, be no more than is necessary to protect the business which the buyer has acquired; he cannot validly prevent the seller from competing with other businesses which the buyer already owns elsewhere. The restriction must also be reasonable as to time and area.

Agreements to fix prices or regulate supplies

The common law rules described above apply to these agreements, with the public interest playing a more important part. Most such contracts are also governed by statute today, particularly the Restrictive Trade Practices Act 1976.

This Act requires such agreements to be registered with the Director-General of Fair Trading. The agreements are then presumed void unless the parties can prove to the Restrictive Practices Court that their agreement is beneficial and in the public interest. The 1976 Act sets out various 'gateways' which the parties can use in convincing the court that their agreement is acceptable; for example, an agreement to fix prices may be valid if it can be shown to benefit the public indirectly by enabling producers to cooperate rather than engage in cut-throat competition.

Resale price fixing can take place without any contract being made. We have seen in Unit 21 that a supplier can impose a minimum resale price which will bind anyone who takes the goods with a view to resale and who has notice of the restriction. The value of this to the price fixer, however, is greatly restricted by the Resale Prices Act 1976, which declares such minimum prices void unless the supplier can satisfy the Restrictive Practices Court that the restriction is in the public interest.

Restrictive trading agreements may also now be invalid in English law if they contravene Article 85 of the Treaty of Rome. This provides that all agreements between firms which may affect trade between member states, and which operate to prevent, restrict or distort competition within the Common Market, shall be automatically void.

'Solus' and similar agreements

In *Esso Petroleum Co. Ltd* v. *Harper's Garage Ltd* (1968), the garage company agreed to sell only Esso petrol for the next four years, and to keep its garages open at all reasonable hours. In return, it received a discount on the price of the petrol. This agreement, although it restricted the garage company's freedom to sell whatever petrol it wished, was held valid as being reasonable in the interests of both parties and the public at large. An agreement affecting another of Harper's garages, however, tied the garage to sell only Esso for 21 years, in return for a loan of £7000. This was held to be too long a restraint, and, therefore, against the public interest and void.

Severance of restraints

If a restraint is void, it is totally void. The court will not cut down a 25 mile or a 21 year restraint to a more acceptable figure; if the restraint is too wide, the person restrained can ignore it and set up in business next door and tomorrow.

On the other hand, if the clause restricts several different activities, it may be possible to *sever* the void restrictions from the valid ones, and allow the latter to stand.

In the *Nordenfelt Case* (1894), an inventor and manufacturer of munitions sold his business to a company and agreed not to engage in munitions business, or in any other business liable to compete in any way with that for the time being carried out by the company, in any part of the world for the next 25 years. The House of Lords held that this was really two restrictions. The munitions restraint was valid, notwithstanding its time and extent, because of Nordenfelt's importance as an inventor and the world-wide scope of the business. The second restriction, covering competition with any other activity of the company, was too wide and therefore void.

D. Other contracts which are void

Contracts prejudicial to the institution of marriage

The courts will not recognize contracts which interfere with marriage or the proper performance of marital or parental duties. A promise never to marry is deemed to be against public policy and void, though a promise not to marry a particular person or not to marry for a short period of time may be valid. If a person who is already married promises to marry someone else, this is plainly invalid, even if the promise is conditional upon divorce or the death of his or her spouse.

So far as parental duties are concerned, a parent cannot by contract deprive himself of the custody, control, and education of his children, except by certain clearly defined legal procedures such as adoption and separation agreements.

Gaming and wagering contracts

Wagering contracts are void under the Gaming Acts, and no action may be brought to enforce payment of the bet, either directly or indirectly. On the other hand, the contract is not *illegal*; a partnership formed to carry on a wagering business will be valid, and money deposited with a stakeholder can be recovered. Wagering contracts, where neither party has an 'interest' in the event concerned other than the amount of the bet, must be distinguished from insurance contracts. If X insures his own goods against theft, this is valid, because X has an insurable interest in the goods; if X insures someone else's goods, the contract will be void, because X's only interest in the goods is the amount of his bet that they will be stolen. (Note that the Life Assurance Act 1774 does not apply to insurance of goods, and so the contract is not illegal.)

Gaming contracts involve the playing of a game of chance for winnings in money or money's worth. They can be valid if they comply with certain statutory requirements, for example, that all players must have an equal chance.

Clauses excluding certain statutory requirements

Frequently an Act will expressly prohibit and declare void any attempt to contract out of its requirements. Examples include the Employer's Liability (Defective Equipment) Act 1969 (section 2), the Consumer Credit Act 1974 (section 173), the Road Traffic Act 1972 (section 148), and the Employment Protection (Consolidation) Act 1978 (section 140).

For further consideration

1. What is the reason for the rule requiring 'insurable interest' in contracts of insurance? Should a girl have an insurable interest in her fiancé's life (or vice versa). Should a young man have an insurable interest in Miss World's life? Should you be able to insure yourself against your friend's car being stolen or against the Houses of Parliament being blown up?
2. Explain and discuss whether either of the following actions would succeed.
   (a) You engage an effluent disposal contractor for one year to dispose of toxic waste from your factory. After six months, you discover that the contractor is illegally

tipping the waste on to an unlicensed tip. You cancel the contract for the future and refuse to pay fees for work already done. The contractor sues you.
   (b) You own a house which you let in furnished flats without issuing to tenants the rent books required by statute. Some time later, you sue a tenant for arrears of rent.
3. A company is about to market a new type of bicycle. It intends to sell through existing retailers and to give financial help in opening new shops where none at present exist.
   To what extent is it possible
   (a) to ensure that retailers do not stock bicycles produced by other manufacturers, and
   (b) to fix a minimum price below which its bicycles may not be sold?
4. Jazzy Jewellers Ltd owns a chain of jewellery shops in the North of England. It decides to expand into other parts of the country and buys the only jewellery shop in Barchester, a small market town in the South. Existing employees are retained including Michael, the manager, and William, a watch repairer. Both Michael and William contract that if they leave their present employment they will not for a period of three years take part in the sale or repair of watches or other items of jewellery within 10 miles of any branch of Jazzy Jewellers Ltd in England, Wales or Scotland.
   One year later, Michael and William wish to resign and become partners in a new jewellery shop which they intend to open in Barchester.
   Advise Jazzy Jewellers Ltd.

Unit 23. Sale of Goods

The law on this subject is now governed by the Sale of Goods Act 1979 which, for convenience, will simply be called 'the Act' in this unit. The Act covers the obligations and remedies of the parties, and the transfer of ownership and risk. Other matters, however, such as offer and acceptance, and consideration, are hardly affected, and are still governed by the general law of contract (Units 16–22).

The contract need not be in writing. The vast majority of *cash* sales are made orally, as where goods are sold over the counter in a shop or pub, or in a restaurant, or where a car is sold for cash. Only where credit is allowed *may* the contract have to be in writing, e.g., under the Hire Purchase Acts and the Consumer Credit Act 1974.

The Act covers contracts 'whereby the seller transfers or agrees to transfer the property in goods to the buyer for a money consideration called the price'. This applies both to a '*sale*', where ownership passes immediately to the buyer, and to an '*agreement to sell*', where the parties agree now that ownership ('property') shall pass later.

A. Obligations of the seller and the buyer's remedies

Section 27 sets out the main obligations: 'it is the duty of the seller to deliver the goods, and of the buyer to accept and pay for them in accordance with the contract of sale'. What the seller delivers, therefore, must accord with his express or implied duties under the contract, and we have seen in Unit 19 that the Act implies important terms into contracts for the sale of goods.

Title

By section 12(1) of the Act there is 'an implied *condition* on the part of the seller that in the case of a sale, he has a right to sell the goods, and in the case of an agreement to sell, he will have such a right at the time when the property is to pass'.

If the seller has no right to sell (e.g., because he had stolen the goods, or only held them on hire purchase), then he will be liable for breach of condition. The buyer can recover the full price, even if he has had the goods for some time.

> In *Rowland* v. *Divall* (1923), the buyer of a car used it for about three months, but then found that it was stolen and had to return it to the true owner. He was held entitled to recover from the seller the full price which he had paid, even though, when he had to part with it, the car was probably worth rather less. He had paid to become owner, he had not become owner, and he was therefore entitled to his money back.

Note that, if the buyer obtains no title, he must return the goods to their true owner, or be liable to him for conversion (Unit 14).

Section 12(2) also implies two warranties into contracts of sale: that the goods are free from encumbrance (such as a mortgage) not disclosed to the buyer before the contract; and that the buyer will enjoy quiet possession of the goods.

Sections 12(3)–(5) do provide limited rights for sellers to contract out of their obligations as to title, if it is made clear in the contract that the seller's title may be defective, so that the buyer knows the risk he may be taking. In this event, there is no condition that the seller has a right to sell, only various warranties to the effect, for example, that all *known* encumbrances have been disclosed, and that the buyer's quiet possession will not be disturbed *by the seller*.

Description

Section 13(1) provides that: 'Where there is a contract for the sale of goods by description there is an implied condition that the goods shall correspond with the description'.

Goods ordered through a catalogue, or a new car ordered from the manufacturer through a dealer, will always be sold by description, because this is the only way to identify what is required. Even goods seen and specifically chosen by the buyer may be described on the packet, bottle or label.

> In *Beale* v. *Taylor* (1961), a car was sold as a 'Herald Convertible, white, 1961'. The buyer discovered later that, while the rear part was accurately described, the front half had been part of an earlier model. The seller was in breach of section 13.

The word 'description' also covers statements as to quantity, weight, ingredients, even packing: see *Re Moore & Co., and Landauer & Co.* (Unit 20).

We have also seen in Unit 20 that compliance with the description must be exact, although today the courts usually try to give a common-sense meaning to descriptive terms (*Peter Darlington Partners* v. *Gosho Ltd*) and, in any event, microscopic deviations may be ignored under the *de minimis* rule.

Quality

Generally, sellers owe no obligation for the quality or suitability of the goods sold. *Where section 14 applies*, however, there are exceptions to this general rule. Unlike sections 12, 13, and 15, which apply to all sales, section 14 *only applies where the seller sells in the course of a business.*

1. Merchantable quality

Section 14(2) provides that: 'Where the seller sells goods in the course of a business, there is an implied condition that the goods supplied under the contract are of merchantable quality'.

By section 14(6) 'merchantable' means 'as fit for the purpose or purposes for which goods of that kind are commonly bought as it is reasonable to expect having regard to any description applied to them, the price (if relevant) and all the other relevant circumstances'. Thus the buyer of cheap goods must reasonably expect lower quality; similarly if he buys second hand.

Section 14(2) does *not* apply (a) as regards defects specifically drawn to the buyer's attention before the contract is made, or (b) if the buyer examines the goods before the contract is made, as regards defects which that examination ought to reveal. The second of these exceptions is often misunderstood; the buyer has *no* obligation to examine the goods and, if he chooses not to do so, he is entitled to the full protection of section 14(2).

2. Reasonable fitness for the purpose made known

By section 14(3):

> 'Where the seller sells goods in the course of a business and the buyer, expressly or by implication, makes known ... to the seller ... any particular purpose for which the goods are being bought, there is an implied condition that the goods supplied are reasonably fit for that purpose, whether or not that is a purpose for which such goods are commonly supplied, except where the circumstances show that the buyer does not rely, or that it is unreasonable for him to rely, on the skill or judgment of the seller ...'

This subsection only applies if the buyer has expressly or impliedly made known to the seller the purposes for which he requires the goods. Where the goods have only one or two obvious uses, however, it is readily assumed that the buyer wants them for their normal purpose (e.g., food for eating).

> In *Grant* v. *Australian Knitting Mills* (1936), a customer bought underpants from a shop. They still contained a chemical which had not been removed after manufacture, and this caused dermatitis. It was held that the buyer had impliedly made known that he intended to wear the pants, which were not reasonably fit for that purpose. Furthermore, they were not of merchantable quality.

The goods supplied need only be *reasonably* fit, however, and then only for the purposes made known.

> In *Griffiths* v. *Peter Conway Ltd* (1939), a lady with abnormally sensitive skin suffered dermatitis from contact with her new coat. The coat would not have affected normal skin, and the lady's action against the seller therefore failed. The coat was reasonably fit for normal purposes, and the buyer had not made known her special problems.

Section 14(3) contains one exception, namely, where circumstances show that the buyer does not rely, or that it is unreasonable for him to rely, on the seller's skill or judgment. This may apply where the buyer himself is an expert in such goods, and gives detailed instructions as to what he wants. However, even partial reliance on the seller is enough, and it can be reasonable for one dealer or expert to rely partly on another.

Sections 14(2) and (3) apply to all goods *supplied* under the contract. Therefore, when a bottle which had to be returned burst, injuring the buyer, he recovered damages under section 14 even though he had not bought the bottle, only the contents; similarly when the buyer was injured by a stray detonator hidden in the fuel which he had bought.

3. *Terms implied by usage*

Section 14(4) provides that further implied conditions and warranties as to quality and fitness may be annexed by usage.

Sample

By section 15, if goods are sold by sample, there are implied conditions: (a) that the bulk will correspond with the sample in quality; (b) that the buyer will have a reasonable opportunity of comparing the bulk with the sample; and (c) that the goods will be free from any defect, rendering them unmerchantable, which would not be apparent on reasonable examination of the sample.

Sales by sample are quite common. Things such as fitted carpets are often bought in this way, and retailers ordering in bulk from a supplier often buy by sample.

> In *Godley* v. *Perry* (1960), a boy bought a plastic catapult from a retail shop. The toy soon broke, and the boy lost an eye. The retailer had bought his catapults by sample from a wholesaler. The retailer had tested the sample by pulling back the elastic, and no defect was apparent at that stage. It was held that (a) the boy could recover damages from the retailer for breach of sections 14(2) and (3), and (b) the retailer could recover from the wholesaler under section 15(2)(c).

This case also illustrates the important point that liability under sections 12–15 is *strict*. The retailer was liable for breach of contract even though he had taken all reasonable care; see also *Frost* v. *Aylesbury Dairy Co.* (Unit 20).

Delivery

The mechanics of delivery (as opposed to *what* is delivered) are covered later in the Act. By section 28, delivery and payment are concurrent conditions, so that the seller can retain the goods until paid. Section 29(1) provides that, unless otherwise agreed, it is for the buyer to collect the goods, not for the seller to send them. Where the seller does agree to dispatch the goods, he must do so within a reasonable time. By section 31(1), unless otherwise agreed, the buyer is entitled to all of the goods at once, and need not accept delivery by instalments.

Exclusion of the seller's obligations

We have seen in Unit 19 that any clause purporting to exclude sections 13–15 is void against a person buying as a *consumer*; it may be void even against a non-consumer unless the *seller* can show that the exclusion is reasonable under the Unfair Contract Terms Act 1977. Section 12 of the 1979 Act can never be wholly excluded. On the other hand, the parties are quite free to exclude or vary provisions such as sections 28, 29, or 31 if they so wish.

The buyer's remedies

Where a seller breaks one of his obligations under the contract, the buyer may have various remedies.

1. *Damages* can always be claimed, although if no real loss has occurred the amount may be nominal. Sections 51 and 53 contain rules for measure and remoteness very similar to those in *Hadley* v. *Baxendale* (Unit 20). The basic rule is that 'the measure of damages is the estimated loss directly and naturally resulting, in the ordinary course of events, from the seller's breach of contract'. The second rule in *Hadley* v. *Baxendale* is preserved by section 54.

   An action for damages may be commenced at any time within the normal limitation period of six years.

2. *Rights to reject the goods and repudiate the contract* arise if the term broken by the seller is a *condition*, not a mere warranty. Note that most of the terms implied by sections 12–15 *are* conditions. The courts have also held that late delivery is breach of condition.

   Since these remedies derive from equity, the limitation period can be very short. By section 11(4), where the contract of sale is non-severable, the rights to reject the goods and repudiate the contract are lost as soon as the buyer *accepts* the goods or part thereof. By section 35, he is deemed to accept (a) when he intimates to the seller that he accepts the goods, or (b) (subject to section 34) when the goods have been delivered to him and he does any act in relation to them which is inconsistent with ownership by the seller, or (c) if he retains the goods for more than a reasonable time without intimating to the seller that he has rejected them.

   The second of these rules arises when the buyer treats the goods as his, by consuming or re-selling them. This, in turn, is subject to section 34: the seller must give the buyer a reasonable opportunity to examine the goods, and the buyer is not deemed to have accepted until he has had this opportunity to examine them. Therefore, if a buyer re-sells goods which were prepacked, so that he could not examine them, and then is told by the sub-buyer that they are defective, he can still reject as against the original seller, so long as only a reasonable time has elapsed. Under the third rule, 'reasonable time' is a question of fact; it may be very brief for perishable goods.

   Section 30 covers tender of a wrong quantity, or of mixed goods.

(a) If the seller delivers too small a quantity, the buyer can either reject the whole, or he can accept the lesser amount, reducing the price rateably.
(b) If the seller delivers too much, the buyer may reject the whole, accept the contract amount and reject the rest, or accept the whole and pay rateably more.
(c) If the seller delivers the goods he contracted to sell mixed with goods of a different description, the buyer may accept the goods which do accord with the contract and reject the rest, or he may reject the whole.

Section 31(2) covers instalment contracts. Section 11(4) only applies to 'non-severable' contracts, and if delivery is to be by instalments, each to be paid for separately, the contract is treated as severable. Any defective instalment can be *rejected*, notwithstanding that earlier instalments have been accepted. The difficulty arises over whether one defective instalment entitles the buyer to *repudiate* the whole contract, and refuse future deliveries, satisfactory or not. The tests to determine this are the relation which the size of the breach bears to the contract as a whole, and the likelihood or otherwise of repetition.

In *Munro Ltd* v. *Meyer* (1930), a first delivery of 611 tons of defective bone meal out of a contract for 1500 tons did entitle the buyer to refuse future deliveries.

In *Maple Flock Co.* v. *Universal Furniture Ltd* (1934), a defect in only the sixteenth instalment of rag flock did not entitle the buyer to avoid the whole contract.

Note that these rules only affect a buyer's rights to reject goods and end the contract. Even if he has lost these rights, *he can still sue for damages* within six years.

3. *Specific performance* can be claimed under section 52, but this will only be awarded where the article sold is unique, such as an original painting. Mere rarity is not normally enough; see *Cohen* v. *Roche* (Unit 20).

B. Obligations of the buyer and the seller's remedies

Buyer's obligations

The buyer must accept the goods and pay for them in accordance with the contract.

The price is normally fixed by the contract. Alternatively, it may be determined by the course of earlier dealings between the parties, or may be left to be fixed by a valuer or referee.

The time for payment is on delivery. A later date or dates may be agreed where credit is allowed. Section 10 provides that, unless otherwise agreed, delay in payment is only breach of warranty, not condition.

Acceptance of the goods is largely self-explanatory. Having ordered goods, a buyer breaks his contract if he then refuses to take them. He can only validly reject the goods if the seller is in breach of condition.

Seller's remedies

The seller can bring an *action for the price* either when ownership of the goods has passed to the buyer, or when a specific date for payment was set and has expired.

Second, if a buyer refuses to accept or pay for the goods, the seller can claim *damages for non-acceptance*, the measure being 'the estimated loss directly and naturally resulting, in the ordinary course of events, from the buyer's breach of contract' (section 50). If the market price of such goods falls between the contract and the delivery date, the damages are, prima facie, the difference between the contract price, and the market price at the time when the goods should have been accepted.

Third, an unpaid seller has certain *rights over the goods*. A common reason for non-payment is that the buyer has no money. In these circumstances, rights to sue for the price or for damages may be worthless. Therefore the following remedies may be available.

1. An unpaid seller has a *lien* or *right to withhold delivery* until he is paid. These rights exist while the goods are still in the seller's possession, and no credit has been allowed to the buyer. The rights are lost as soon as the seller parts with possession; he has no right to re-take them from the buyer. Note also that the lien gives the seller no right to *re-sell* the goods yet, only to retain them.
2. If an unpaid seller has parted with the goods to a carrier, he still has a *right of stoppage in transit* if, during the transit, the buyer *becomes insolvent* (not otherwise). The seller can order the carrier to re-deliver to the seller or his agent, so that the buyer will not get possession.
3. If an unpaid seller still has the goods, he will have a *right to re-sell* them in three circumstances: (a) where the goods are perishable; or (b) where the unpaid seller gives notice to the buyer of his intention to re-sell, and the buyer still does not pay or tender the price within a reasonable time; or (c) where, in the contract, the seller expressly reserved a right to re-sell should the buyer default.

   Where re-sale is at a profit, so that the seller gets more than the original contract price, the seller can keep the profit. If an unpaid seller re-sells wrongfully, e.g., without giving reasonable notice, the new buyer gets a good title, but in this event the seller must account to the old buyer for any profit as compared with the original contract price.
4. In addition to these statutory rights, some sellers of valuable industrial goods have, in recent years, used *reservation of title* clauses for further protection.

   In *Aluminium Industrie Vaassen BV* v. *Romalpa Aluminium Ltd* (1976), AIV sold aluminium foil to Romalpa. The written contract provided that ownership of the foil would only pass to Romalpa when the latter had paid all that it owed to AIV. If Romalpa made a new object with the foil, or incorporated or mixed it with other goods, AIV would become owner of this other object. Romalpa could sell the new object, but only on condition that its rights against the sub-buyer were handed over to AIV. When Romalpa later became insolvent, AIV successfully claimed (a) the proceeds of re-sale of some foil by Romalpa, and (b) that the foil still held by Romalpa belonged to AIV, and should be returned.

   Such clauses, in effect, extend the seller's 'real' remedies to situations where possession has already been given to the buyer. '*Romalpa*' clauses do, however, give rise to legal difficulties, and must be very carefully drafted. The case has been distinguished twice in recent years.

C. Transfer of property between seller and buyer

The purpose of sale is to transfer ownership ('property') from seller to buyer. It is important to determine exactly when this occurs largely because, by section 20, any loss or damage prima facie falls on whoever is owner at the time.

It is important first to distinguish between specific and unascertained goods. *Specific* goods are 'goods identified and agreed on *at the time a contract of sale is made*'. This includes all self-service sales (and many over-the-counter ones), most auction sales, and contracts such as the sale of a specific second-hand car. All goods which are not specific are *unascertained*. The buyer of a new car yet to be delivered from the manufacturer cannot yet point to which specific car is to be his. Most bulk orders ('100 tons of wheat') are unascertained.

In a contract for unascertained goods, items will at some stage be 'appropriated' to the contract: 100 tons of wheat from the seller's stock will eventually be set aside for the buyer. These 100 tons are now said to be *ascertained*. The 100 tons do not become specific goods, however, because they were not identified at the time of the contract. Unascertained goods cannot become specific ones under the same contract.

Passing of property in specific goods

By section 17, property in specific goods passes when the parties intend it to pass. They can make their own provision (as in the *Romalpa* case). Unless otherwise agreed, however, section 18 sets out some prima facie rules. Rule 1 states:

> 'Where there is an unconditional contract for the sale of specific goods, in a deliverable state, the property in the goods passes to the buyer *when the contract is made*, and it is immaterial whether the time of payment or the time of delivery, or both, be postponed.'

Despite the last words of Rule 1, the courts may still hold under section 17 that, if both payment and delivery are postponed, property was not intended to pass yet.

> In *Ward Ltd* v. *Bignall* (1967), the seller sold a specific car, but retained possession pending payment. Diplock L. J. said (*obiter*) that he might, if necessary, treat the car as still belonging to the seller, despite the wording of Rule 1. It was arguable that both parties regarded the car as the seller's until the buyer paid or was allowed to take delivery. The court could assume that this was their real intention.

Rule 1 applies only to goods in a 'deliverable state'; if they are not yet, then under Rule 2:

> 'Where there is a contract for the sale of specific goods and the seller is bound to do something to the goods for the purpose of putting them into a deliverable state, the property does not pass until the thing is done, and the buyer has notice that it has been done.'

Goods are only in a deliverable state 'when they are in such a state that the buyer would under the contract be bound to take delivery of them'. Therefore, if a seller agrees in the contract to fit new tyres, the car will remain the seller's property, at his risk, until the tyres are fitted *and* the buyer has notice of this.

Rule 3 is self-explanatory:

> 'Where there is a contract for the sale of specific goods in a deliverable state, but the seller is bound to weigh, measure, test, or do some other act or thing with reference to the goods for the purpose of ascertaining the price, the property does not pass until the thing is done and the buyer has notice that it has been done.'

The fourth rule applies where a buyer has asked or agreed to take goods on approval. It does *not* apply where a would-be seller sends *unsolicited* goods (see Unit 17). By Rule 4, property passes to the buyer when: (a) he signifies his approval or acceptance or does any other act adopting the transaction (e.g., re-selling the goods); or (b) if he retains the goods, without giving notice of rejection, until after the time fixed for their return has expired or, if no time was fixed, for more than a reasonable time.

Passing of property in unascertained goods

Ownership of unascertained goods cannot pass until they are ascertained (section 16). Until then, it is impossible to point out which car or bag of wheat *is* to be the buyer's.

Property does not necessarily pass even when the goods *are* ascertained (see the *Romalpa* case again). By section 18, Rule 5:

> 'Where there is a contract for the sale of unascertained ... goods by description, and goods of that description and in a deliverable state are unconditionally appropriated to the contract either by the seller with the assent of the buyer, or by the buyer with the assent of the seller, the property in the goods then passes to the buyer; and the assent may be express or implied, and may be given either before or after the appropriation is made.'

Delivery of the correct amount to a carrier for transport to the buyer is 'appropriation' for this purpose, as is any other setting aside or labelling the goods clearly for the buyer. However, ownership still does not pass unless and until the goods are in a deliverable state.

> In *Philip Head & Sons Ltd* v. *Showfronts Ltd* (1970), the seller agreed to deliver and lay fitted carpets. A carpet was delivered, but left to be laid next day. It was held still to be the seller's, so that he bore the loss when it was stolen overnight.

Passing of risk

'Risk' covers many possible mishaps, from damage or theft to total destruction. There are three times when loss can occur.

1. *Loss occurring before the contract is made*
This category of loss obviously falls on the seller. He may not only lose the goods, but also be liable to the buyer for damages if he contracts to supply goods and then cannot do so.

He will only be protected if section 6 applies: 'Where there is a contract for the sale of specific goods, and the goods without the knowledge of the seller have perished at the time when the contract is made, the contract is void.'

This section has limited scope: it only applies to *specific* goods, which have *perished* (not merely been damaged), *without the seller's knowledge*. (A seller who tries to sell goods which he knows have perished may be guilty of fraud.) However, goods can legally 'perish' without being completely destroyed, so that a cargo of dates which had sunk in the harbour and, when raised, was 'simply a mass of pulpy matter impregnated with sewage' was held to have perished. See also *Couturier* v. *Hastie* (Unit 18).

2. *Loss occurring between the contract and the passing of property*
This loss still falls on the seller under section 20(1), unless otherwise agreed. Except where section 18 Rule 1 applies, there will normally be an interval between the contract and the passing of property. The seller will again not only lose the goods, but may also be liable for damages for non-delivery.

He may be protected at this stage, however, by section 7: 'Where there is an agreement to sell specific goods and subsequently the goods, without any fault on the part of the seller or buyer, perish before the risk passes to the buyer, the agreement is avoided.'

Like section 6, this is limited to *specific* goods, which *perish, without the seller's fault*. When section 7 does apply, the Law Reform (Frustrated Contracts) Act 1943 does not. Money payable, therefore, ceases to be due, money paid must be returned, and the seller can keep or recover nothing to compensate him for any expenditure.

3. *Loss occurring after property has passed*
This category of loss normally falls on the buyer under section 20(1), even if the goods are still in the seller's possession.

> In *Tarling* v. *Baxter* (1827), a farmer sold a haystack, which remained on his farm to be collected in the spring. Before collection, it was destroyed. It was held that (a) ownership had passed to the buyer, and (b) therefore he bore the loss.

There are, however, two provisos. First, by section 20(2), if delivery is delayed through the fault of either seller or buyer, risk falls on the party at fault as regards any loss which might not have occurred but for the delay. Second, by section 20(3), 'nothing in this section affects the duties or liabilities of either seller or buyer as bailee'; therefore, a seller who remains in possession after ownership has passed to the buyer must take reasonable care of the goods.

Finally, section 20 only applies *unless otherwise agreed.*

> In *Inglis* v. *Stock* (1885), the buyer bought an unascertained part of a cargo of sugar. The contract validly provided that risk would pass when the cargo was put aboard, although by section 16 ownership could not pass until the buyer's part was ascertained.

D. Transfer of title by a non-owner

As a general rule, only the owner of goods or his agent can validly sell them. This is often expressed in the phrase *nemo dat quod non habet* (no one can give what he does not have), and the rule is embodied in section 21: '... where goods are sold by a person who is not their owner, and who does not sell them under the authority or with the consent of the owner, the buyer acquires no better title to the goods than the seller had ...'

If the buyer obtains no title, he must return the goods on demand to their true owner, or be liable for conversion. In turn, the buyer can recover from the seller for breach of section 12, but by this time the seller may have absconded.

This can be hard on buyers, who often have no means of knowing whether the seller is the owner. The issue is often between an innocent true owner and an innocent ultimate buyer, both victims of a rogue who has departed. There are other situations where the strict *nemo dat* rule would also be harsh to buyers, and several exceptions have therefore developed. These are as follows:

1. Sale by an agent

An agent acting with actual authority can pass title to his principal's goods. Even if he exceeds his actual authority, he may still pass title if he acts within his implied or apparent authority, so that the buyer has no reason to doubt his right to sell.

The Factors Act 1889, section 2(1), puts these rules into statutory form as regards *mercantile agents*. A mercantile agent is one having, in the course of his business as an independent agent (*not* merely as an employee of the principal), authority to sell or otherwise deal with goods.

> 'Where a mercantile agent is, *with the consent of the owner*, in *possession* of goods or of the documents of title to the goods, any sale, pledge or other disposition of the goods, made by him *when acting in the ordinary course of business of a mercantile agent*, shall ... be as valid as if he were expressly authorized by the owner of the goods to make the same, *provided that the person taking under the disposition acts in good faith*, and that he has not at the time of the disposition notice that the person making the disposition has not authority to make the same.'

In *Folkes* v. *King* (1923), an agent with authority to sell his principal's car for not less than £575, wrongfully sold it for only £340. The buyer obtained good title, because the agent was clearly in possession with authority to sell, and the buyer had no reason to suspect the limitation which the principal had imposed.

2. Estoppel

Section 21 itself provides another exception, where 'the owner of the goods is by his conduct precluded from denying the seller's authority to sell'. This may occur if the owner deliberately makes someone else appear to have a right to deal with the goods.

> In *Eastern Distributors Ltd* v. *Goldring* (1957), a car owner gave a dealer documents which made the dealer appear to be the owner, as part of a scheme to enable the car owner to

borrow money without adequate security. The scheme fell through, but the dealer went ahead and sold the car to a finance company. It was held that the finance company obtained a good title because, although the dealer had no right to sell, the owner's conduct estopped him from asserting this.

3. Sale in market overt (section 22)

Where goods are sold in market overt, according to the usages of the market, the buyer acquires a goods title to the goods, provided he buys them in good faith and without notice of any defect or want of title on the part of the seller. A market overt is an open, legally constituted public market, recognized as such by statute, Royal Charter, or prescription from long use. It includes all sales in the public part of shops in the City of London, by shopkeeper to customer, of goods usually sold in the shop. Sales must be according to the custom of the market, must be of goods usually sold there, between sunrise and sunset, and the buyer must take in good faith.

In *Reid* v. *Commissioner of Metropolitan Police* (1973), antiques stolen from R were sold in New Caledonian Market, Southwark, a recognized market overt. The buyer obtained no title, but only because the sale was before sunrise.

4. Sale under voidable title (section 23)

If a buyer obtains goods under a contract which is voidable (e.g., for misrepresentation or breach of condition), he can pass a good title to someone who buys from him in good faith without notice of the defect in title, provided that re-sale takes place *before* the original contract is rescinded (see Unit 16). If, however, the original contract is *void* (e.g., for mistake), no title can pass under section 23.

5. Re-sale by seller in possession (section 24)

Where a seller remains in possession of the goods, or of documents of title to them, any re-sale by him to a buyer who takes in good faith without notice of the previous sale will give a good title to the new buyer as soon as the latter takes *physical delivery* of the goods or documents. The old buyer is left to sue the seller for damages for non-delivery. A similar rule applies if a seller in possession pledges the goods or disposes of them in any other way.

6. Re-sale by buyer in possession with the consent of the seller (section 25)

Where a person who has agreed to buy obtains possession of the goods or documents of title *with the seller's consent*, any sale and delivery by the buyer who takes in good faith, without notice of any rights of the original seller to the goods, shall have 'the same effect as if the person making the delivery . . . were a mercantile agent . . .'.

Because of the words quoted, this section has limited effect. It only applies if the first buyer re-sells in such circumstances that the ultimate buyer could assume that he was buying in the ordinary course of business from a dealer.

In *Newtons of Wembley Ltd* v. *Williams* (1965), a rogue bought the seller's car with a cheque which was dishonoured. Meanwhile, the rogue had re-sold the car, to an innocent buyer, in an established street market for second-hand cars. The innocent buyer obtained a good title, because the rogue was a buyer in possession with the owner's consent, and he had re-sold in a place where he appeared to be a dealer.

Note that, as under section 24, title only passes to the new buyer if the goods are actually delivered to him, not before.

7. Motor vehicles on hire purchase (Hire Purchase Act 1964, Part III)

If a *motor vehicle* on hire purchase is sold to a *private* purchaser, who takes in good faith without notice of the hire purchase agreement, a good title will pass. A 'private' purchaser is one who is not a 'trade' purchaser (e.g., a garage) or a 'finance' purchaser (e.g., a hire purchase company). If the hirer sells to a garage, the garage gets no title under these provisions, and may be liable for conversion. However, although the garage is not protected, the first innocent private purchaser to acquire the goods thereafter does get good title.

Once the goods have become the property of an innocent private purchaser, the title is cured, and *subsequent* trade or finance purchasers are protected. A buyer is presumed to be innocent and private unless proved otherwise.

Finally, the first private person to take the vehicle may acquire it on hire purchase, and then be told before completing his payments that he has no right to it. Nevertheless he is protected so long as he was in good faith when he first took the vehicle.

8. Sale under common law or statutory powers

A pledgee has powers to sell unredeemed goods pledged with him, and others such as innkeepers and bailees (e.g., dry-cleaners) can eventually sell customers' goods to satisfy unpaid charges.

The High Court has wide powers to order the sale of goods which are affected by litigation and, for example, likely to deteriorate if kept.

For further consideration

1. David, an accountant, purchased some steel shelving from a firm specializing in the provision of office equipment. He explained that he required the shelving for the storage of files. He was shown some shelves and was asked, 'Will these do?' He said, 'I think so'.
    The shelving was unsatisfactory in use and bent under the weight of the files. Advise David.
2. Advise Richard, a retailer, in each of the following cases:
    (a) He bought 500 kg of fruit, to be delivered in 1 kg tins. Delivery was made in 2 kg tins.

(b) He bought 200 tins of biscuits and 300 tins were delivered.
(c) He bought 200 tins of beans. Delivery was made of 150 tins of beans and 50 tins of peas.

3. A furniture dealer agreed to sell two pieces of furniture:
   (a) an antique commode which the customer had chosen in the shop and to which the dealer had agreed to fit a replacement handle before delivery;
   (b) a new bureau of standard design as soon as the dealer could obtain one from the manufacturer. The dealer agreed to fit new handles to match those on the antique commode.

   When both pieces of furniture were in the shop with handles fitted and ready for collection by the customer, the shop and the furniture were accidentally destroyed by fire. Explain whether the customer still has to pay for the furniture.

4. In April, B agreed to buy 1000 rare 'Dutch Uncle' tulip bulbs from S. B paid a deposit of 5 per cent of the price, and agreed to pay the balance in September when the bulbs were to be delivered. In July, a fungus disease destroyed all the 'Dutch Uncles' in the world.

   Advise B
   (a) whether he still has to pay for the bulbs; and
   (b) alternatively, whether he can recover his deposit.

   Would it make any difference if B had chosen the specific bulbs which he wanted from B's stock?

5. Advise a television set retailer in respect of the following transactions:
   (a) a set, delivered on approval for 10 days' free trial, has been retained by the customer for one month;
   (b) a set was sold but not removed from the store, and was then sold and delivered to another customer;
   (c) a particular set was sold and then received slight damage in the course of delivery, whereupon the customer refused to accept it.

Unit 24. Credit and Security

Money may be lent and credit may be given in many ways, and on many different terms. A specified sum may be lent for a fixed term at a stated rate of interest. The whole sum may be repayable on a fixed date, or the loan may be repayable by instalments. The creditor may allow the borrower to draw varying sums on a current account up to a stated limit, as on a bank overdraft. The borrower may have a credit card which he can use to pay bills, on an arrangement that he will repay the lender (often a company controlled by his bank) in due course. Some credit is for a specific purpose, as where the supplier of goods allows his customer to pay for them by instalments, or where a building society lends money to a house buyer in return for a mortgage on the house. In other instances there may be no arrangement between lender and borrower as to how the money is to be used, as where a company issues debentures to the public.

Frequently the lender will require some *security*. We shall see later how property such as goods and land can be used in various ways as security. Other forms of property too, such as shares, can be mortgaged or charged.

The legal problems and rules can vary according to many things. The nature of the borrower may be important: the Companies Acts apply to borrowing by companies, while the Consumer Credit Act only applies to borrowing by *non*-corporate bodies. The rules can vary according to the amount owed: the Consumer Credit Act only applies where the credit does not exceed £5000. Differences also arise according to who is the lender: an individual may lend money to a corporation (by opening a savings account at a building society, for instance), or a corporation may lend to an individual (a finance company letting a car on hire purchase). This unit deals with some of the possibilities.

For as long as loans have existed, some creditors have abused their stronger bargaining position to impose harsh and unfair burdens on debtors, and many of the rules discussed below are attempts to prevent such injustices. On the other hand, creditors too need protection against debtors who will not pay. In more recent times, an added factor has been public interest in the economy. At times, national economic circumstances have been felt to demand credit restrictions, and regulations at present impose minimum cash deposits and maximum borrowing periods for most types of consumer durable goods.

A. Consumer credit

The Consumer Credit Act 1974 applies to personal credit agreements by which the creditor provides the debtor with *credit not exceeding £5000*. Credit is 'personal' when the borrower is an individual or partnership, not a corporate body. The purpose for which the money is required is immaterial; a loan for an individual's business is still 'personal'. The 'credit' is the amount *borrowed*, not necessarily the amount to be repaid. Therefore, if someone borrows £4900 but, with interest, has to pay back £5500, the agreement is within the Act. The interest is a *'charge* for credit'. There are therefore two limits on the operation of the Act: (a) as to the amount borrowed; and (b) as to the nature of the borrower.

Some agreements are 'exempt' from most provisions of the Act. The following are the main examples:

1. Loans by building societies, local authorities, and many other corporate bodies, if the loan is secured by a mortgage of land.
2. Fixed sum loans to finance the purchase of goods, services or land, if the credit is repayable by four or fewer instalments; hire purchase and conditional sale agreements, are *not* exempt, however many instalments are payable (see later).
3. 'Running-account' credits, where the whole credit *for a period* is to be repaid by a single payment; (a running-account credit is one where no specific sum is borrowed, but credit up to a certain amount is allowed). Credit card accounts, and accounts with the local greengrocer, where the bill comes and is payable, say, monthly, are usually exempt under (2) and/or (3).

The 'extortionate bargain' provisions, however, can apply even to exempt agreements and to personal credit outside the financial limits (see later).

Controls over lenders and advertising

Any person wishing to carry on consumer credit business must first obtain a licence from the Director-General of Fair Trading, who must be satisfied that the applicant is a fit person to engage in such activities. This can apply not only to potential creditors, but also to credit brokers such as retailers who have arrangements to introduce customers requiring credit to a particular finance company. Regulations govern the ways in which a licensee must conduct his business. Loans by unlicensed creditors are a criminal offence, and are enforceable against the borrower only at the Director's discretion.

The Department of Trade has made regulations controlling advertisements by credit dealers, to ensure that a fair picture is given as to the nature of the credit offered, and the true rate of interest, etc. There are similar controls over quotations by dealers as to the terms on which they offer credit. Canvassing people other than on business premises to persuade them to borrow, sending unsolicited credit tokens (credit cards), and activities persuading minors to borrow are prohibited. Breach is usually a criminal offence.

Information

In *commercial* consumer credit agreements, where the creditor acts in the course of his business, the Act aims to ensure that a prospective debtor knows what he is letting himself in for.

Before the agreement is made, the creditor must give written details of terms such as the charge for credit.

The agreement itself must be in writing, signed by the debtor personally and by or on behalf of the creditor. Signature of a form in blank, leaving it to an agent or the creditor to fill in the blanks, is not enough. Regulations cover the type, size, and in some instances colour of the print, and the document must give details of the debtor's rights as well as his duties (see later).

Copies of the agreement must be given to the debtor. He must always receive, immediately, a copy of the form which he signs. If the form then has to be sent away for completion by the creditor, the debtor must be given a second copy, of the completed agreement, within seven days of its completion, so that he can check that no alterations have been made since his signature.

Later, while a fixed-sum credit is being repaid, a debtor is entitled to information about how much he has currently paid and still owes, and to further copies of the agreement.

Rash or hasty agreements

A prospective debtor can withdraw his offer at any time before the creditor accepts it. Therefore, if the debtor's proposal has to be sent away for acceptance by the creditor (as in many hire purchase transactions), the debtor has a short interval in which to think again. He can withdraw his offer by informing the lender or any agent. The offer may also end for other reasons, as in *Financings* v. *Stimson* (Unit 17).

Second, if a credit agreement has been induced by the creditor's misrepresentations, the debtor has a reasonable time in which to rescind the contract (see Unit 18).

Third, if a commercial consumer credit agreement, within the 1974 Act, is signed by the debtor other than on the trade premises of the creditor or any dealer with whom the debtor originally negotiated, the debtor has a statutory *right of cancellation*. This particularly protects people who are persuaded by door-step salesmen to sign credit or hire purchase agreements at home (for encyclopaedias, for example). In cancellable transactions, the debtor must receive a copy of the agreement as soon as he signs, and a second statutory copy must be sent to him *by post* within seven days of its completion. He then has until the end of the fifth day following receipt of his second statutory copy in which to cancel the agreement. Cancellation must be in writing, but posting it is sufficient. Both copies of the agreement must inform him of his right to cancel.

Terms of the agreement and enforcement by the creditor

Various provisions in the Consumer Credit Act protect the debtor during the credit period. For example, the *debtor* under a regulated agreement is entitled *at any time* to pay off what he owes, on giving notice to the creditor that he intends to do so. He may also be entitled to a rebate of interest if the creditor is getting his money earlier than originally contracted for.

Second, before the *creditor* can terminate the agreement or take other action for the debtor's breach, he must serve a 'notice of default'. This must specify the alleged breach, give at least seven days in which to remedy it or pay compensation, and explain the consequences of failure to comply. If the debtor complies with the notice, 'the breach shall be treated as if it had never occurred'. Similar seven day notices must be served if the creditor wishes to enforce any of his rights in the agreement, even if there has been no breach.

Only if the debtor fails to comply with a notice of default can the creditor ask the court for an enforcement order, and even at this stage the court can give the debtor additional time to pay or grant other relief.

Third, if at any time the court finds a personal credit bargain to be *extortionate*, it may re-open the agreement so as to do justice between the parties. This can be done either in proceedings brought by the debtor, or as a defence to an action by the creditor. A bargain is extortionate if it requires the debtor, or any relative of his, to make payments which are exorbitant or grossly contravene 'ordinary principles of fair dealing'. The court has powers to set aside the whole or part of the debtor's obligations, to require the creditor to repay all or part of what the debtor has paid, and/or to alter the terms of the credit agreement.

B. Goods as security

Conditional sale and hire purchase

When customers seek goods they often need credit, which can be given in various ways. If the seller allows payment by instalments, and makes no provision for when ownership is to pass, the contract is a *credit sale*. Ownership normally passes as soon as the buyer takes possession, and the seller has no right to re-take them if the buyer defaults. Some sellers, therefore, use the goods as security, by stipulating that ownership is not to pass to the buyer until he satisfies some condition (usually payment of the last instalment). This is a *conditional sale*. The goods remain the seller's, and he can reclaim possession until the condition is met. Again, the supplier may simply hire the goods to the customer but, on payment of a specified number of hire 'instalments', the hirer will have an option to buy the goods for a nominal sum of, say, £1. This is *hire purchase*.

Frequently, the garage or retailer supplying the goods will prefer payment immediately and will, therefore, have arrangements with a finance house. In one common 'triangular' transaction of this sort, the dealer will have a stock of the finance company's hire purchase forms. If the customer wants credit, the dealer asks him to fill in his part of such a form which constitutes an offer, addressed to the finance house, to take the goods on hire purchase *from the finance house*. The dealer forwards this form together with his own offer to sell the goods for cash to the finance house. If the latter accepts both offers, it pays the dealer the cash price, becomes owner of the goods, and lets them on hire purchase to the customer (the hire purchase price being higher than the cash price). The customer collects the goods from the dealer, and the finance house rarely sees them.

Hire purchase and conditional sale to individuals or partnerships are governed by the Consumer Credit Act (and still, in part, the Hire Purchase Act 1965) within the financial limits. Notice that, for the Consumer Credit Act, it is the amount of *credit* which matters. If someone acquires a car on hire purchase for £6000, but pays a £2000 deposit, the amount of credit is only £4000, and therefore within the Act (see also page 226 above).

Some of the protections given by the 1974 Act have already been described. The controls over lenders, information to debtors, rash 'door-step' agreements, and harsh terms apply to hire purchase and conditional sale in the same way as to other agreements under the Act. There are also additional protections.

First, a hire purchaser or buyer on conditional sale can *terminate* the agreement at any time. He must give notice to the creditor, return the goods, and pay off any arrears of instalments currently due. He is then no longer liable to complete his payments under the agreement. This right to terminate the agreement and surrender the goods is in addition to his right, discussed earlier, to pay off the whole balance early (in which case he keeps the goods).

Second, the Acts protect against harsh 'minimum payment' clauses. If the hirer terminates the contract early and returns goods which have drastically depreciated, the creditor might suffer loss. Many agreements, therefore, required the debtor to bring his payments up to, say, 75 per cent of the hire purchase price if the agreement ended early. Such clauses were often in reality more attempts to penalize the debtor than to compensate the creditor and, even at common law, could probably be struck out as in *Bridge* v. *Campbell Discount Ltd* (Unit 20), whether or not the hirer was in breach.

When the 1974 Act applies it imposes statutory limits on minimum payment clauses. If there is such a clause, the payment must not exceed the amount, if any, by which one-half of the total price exceeds the aggregate of the sums paid and due immediately before termination. If the creditor's actual loss is less than this, the court may order payment of his actual loss only. On the other hand, if the debtor has not taken reasonable care of the goods, the debtor's payment will be increased, if need be, to compensate the creditor.

Third, hire purchasers and conditional sale buyers are protected against 'snatch-back'. At common law, if the hirer or buyer was late with *any* instalment, the creditor could rescind the agreement and take back the goods. This could work injustice.

> In *Cramer* v. *Giles* (1883), the hirer took a piano at a hire purchase price of 60 guineas. After paying more than 50 guineas (probably more than the piano's cash value), the hirer was late with his last two instalments. He tendered payment shortly afterwards, but this was refused. Instead, the creditor sued for return of the piano, and was held entitled to it, leaving the hirer with nothing for the instalments which he had paid.

Many creditors did not trouble to sue, but simply took the goods back summarily at the slightest default. The contract often gave the creditor right of entry to the hirer's premises for the purpose. The process often gave the creditor a considerable profit.

If the Acts apply, they protect the hirer against this. We have seen that a creditor must give at least seven days' notice of default before taking any steps against the debtor. Moreover, a creditor must not now enter any premises to take back the goods without first obtaining a court order. Even more important, when one-third of the hire purchase or conditional sale price has been paid, the goods become 'protected goods', and must not be taken back without a court order unless the debtor himself ended the agreement. If the debtor pays the whole balance of the price before the court order, the goods become his. Even if he does not do this, the court can give him additional time to pay.

If a creditor does take back protected goods without a court order, the agreement and the debtor's liabilities end, and the latter can recover *all* that he has previously paid.

> In *Capital Finance Ltd* v. *Bray* (1964), a finance company took back, without a court order, a car which Bray had on hire purchase. The car was protected goods and, when the company realized its mistake, it returned the car immediately. Bray used it for several months, refusing all requests for payment. Eventually, the company sued for possession, and this was granted. The company could not, however, recover payment for Bray's use of the car after its return to him. Moreover, Bray recovered everything which he had paid.

A creditor can only recover protected goods without a court order if the debtor voluntarily returns them, or if the debtor has abandoned them.

Finally, finance houses and other suppliers of goods on hire purchase owe obligations as regards title to the goods, description, fitness, and quality under the Supply of Goods (Implied Terms) Act 1973. This applies to all hire purchase, irrespective of the amount borrowed or the nature of the borrower. The obligations implied are almost identical to those imposed on the seller by the Sale of Goods Act, with the same limits on exclusion. Where a triangular transaction takes place, the finance company is liable for representations or promises made by the dealer.

Other uses of goods as security

When credit is needed in order to buy goods, another more drastic means by which the seller can protect himself is by a 'retention of title' (*Romalpa*) clause (Unit 23). This is often used where the buyer is a large company.

If someone who *already owns* goods wishes to use them as security, different problems arise. First he can transfer ownership to the creditor, but retain possession. The creditor will undertake to re-transfer ownership when the loan is repaid. In practice this 'mortgage' of goods will be in writing, to provide the proof needed to prevent an unscrupulous borrower from abusing his retention of the goods. Such a document is known as a *bill of sale*. It must be in a form laid down by statute, and the bill must be registered at the Central Office of the Supreme Court.

Alternatively, the borrower can *transfer possession* of the goods to the lender while retaining ownership, the reverse of the situation with a bill of sale. This is known as *pawn* or *pledge*. The goods are redeemed by repayment and, in the event of default, the lender may sell the goods either after the lapse of an agreed time or, if no time has been agreed, by giving reasonable notice to the borrower of intention to sell. There are again statutory protections, imposed now under the Consumer Credit Act.

Goods may also be subject to a *lien* when the creditor has a right to *retain possession* until a debt has been discharged. Thus a garage may retain a car as security for the cost of repairs carried out, and a hotel or dry cleaners may hold a customer's goods until the bill is paid.

C. Land as security

Mortgages

The most common method of using land as security is the mortgage. The borrower (*mortgagor*) transfers an interest in the land to the lender (*mortgagee*), and the lender may realize his interest if the loan is not repaid. The most familiar example is a loan from a building society to buy a house. The loan is repaid by the purchaser, with interest, by periodic payments.

A legal mortgage may be created today in two ways. The first is to grant a legal estate to the mortgagee in the form of a very long lease, with a proviso that the lease shall come to an end on repayment of the loan. If the property is leasehold, then a sub-lease is granted for a slightly shorter period than the original lease. The mortgagee does not take possession of the property; this remains with the mortgagor, who retains his legal estate.

An alternative and more usual method is by the execution of a deed which declares that a legal charge has been created. This is a more simple method, applicable to both freehold and leasehold, introduced by the Law of Property Act 1925. The mortgagee has the same protection as if a lease had been created.

A more informal mortgage may arise when, in return for a loan, the landowner deposits the title deeds with the lender as security. Without the title deeds, the owner would find it extremely difficult to sell or mortgage the land to another person. Deposit of the deeds only creates an equitable mortgage, over which a subsequent legal mortgage would take preference if the legal mortgagee had no knowledge of this equitable interest. Legal mortgages normally take priority according to the date of creation. This problem of priority may arise when a mortgagor defaults after raising several loans on the security of his land to a total amount which exceeds the value of the land.

If the mortgagor defaults, the lender has various remedies. He may sue for the money due. He may take possession of the land, either personally or by appointing a receiver, and recoup himself from any income arising from management of the property. He may ask the court for a foreclosure order which transfers the land to him if the mortgagor does not repay within a specified time. The most usual action is to exercise the mortgagee's power of sale, and recoup himself from the proceeds of the sale; any surplus must ultimately be returned to the borrower.

From early times, the courts have protected mortgagors from harsh and unconscionable terms. For example, they have not permitted terms which make it impossible for the borrower to redeem his mortgage for an *unreasonable* time.

> In *Fairclough* v. *Swan Brewery Co. Ltd* (1912), a 20 year lease was mortgaged on terms which made redemption impossible until six weeks before the 20 years expired. These terms were held void, and the borrower could redeem earlier.

Similarly, the courts have sometimes held void terms which give collateral advantages to the lender, but only if the advantages are unreasonable. A loan by a brewery making the mortgaged property a 'tied' public house until redemption could well be reasonable. Too long a restraint, however, might be void as an unlawful restraint of trade today, as in *Esso Petroleum* v. *Harper's Garage* (Unit 22).

If the mortgagor is an individual or partnership, the 'extortionate bargain' provisions of the Consumer Credit Act can apply to it now, with the consequences described earlier. Apart from this, however, the Act does not apply to loans secured by mortgages of land, if the lender is a building society, local authority or other body which gives loans to buy land.

Equitable liens

Equitable liens, unlike legal ones, are not merely rights to *keep* possession of property, but can exist over property in the possession of someone else. One example is that the vendor of land has an equitable lien over the property sold, even after the buyer takes possession, as security for any unpaid part of the purchase price.

D. Borrowing by companies

We have seen in Unit 11 that companies raise their capital by issuing shares. They can also raise money by borrowing it, and this can have advantages. In particular, if the company is doing well, the existing shareholders may not want to dilute their prospects by introducing new members. Moreover, although the loan will have to be repaid (unlike share capital), at least the cost of the loan, including interest, is a deduction from profits, which can save tax.

Any document issued by a company as evidence of a loan or debt is called a *debenture*. Debenture holders are therefore merely creditors of the company, not members.

Debentures can be secured or unsecured. Obviously many are secured in order to attract lenders, and various types of security can be offered. Some are secured by a *fixed charge*, the loan being charged on a specific asset of the company. A mortgage of one of the company's buildings is a debenture of this kind. If the company is wound up, the proceeds of sale of the asset are applied in paying that creditor in full, even if this means that other creditors go short. The disadvantage of a fixed charge is that it ties up the asset charged, which cannot now be dealt with without the consent of that debenture holder. Companies can, therefore, issue *floating charges*, where the loan is charged on such property as the company has from time to time. If the company sells one asset and buys another, the charge ceases to attach to the old asset, and automatically attaches to the new. It is only when the company defaults in repayments, or starts to wind up, that the floating charge 'crystallizes' and attaches permanently to the assets at that time.

In order to protect those dealing with the company, registers of debentures must be kept, so that outsiders can see what the company's debts are. At the registered office, a company must keep a register of charges, including floating charges, on its property. Often the company secretary will also keep a register of debentures of all kinds, including unsecured, although not strictly bound to do so. Most charges on the company's property must also be registered with the Registrar of Companies. Again this includes both fixed and floating charges. Charges affecting land must also be registered with the Land Charges Registry, otherwise the charge is void. These registers are open to public inspection.

On default by the company, debenture holders can have the following rights.

1. If so permitted by the terms of issue, they may appoint a receiver, who will take over management of the company from the directors so as to ensure that holders are paid.
2. Holders may bring an action for the sale of the asset(s) charged.
3. In some circumstances, debenture holders can petition for the company to be wound up.

For further consideration

1. Rash enters into a loan agreement under which he agrees to borrow £2000, and repay the creditor by 24 monthly instalments of £130 each. Soon after making the agreement, he has second thoughts and wishes to escape from this liability. Advise him.
2. A hirer takes goods on hire purchase from Finance Ltd, paying a deposit of £500,

and agreeing to pay the balance, namely £912, by equal monthly instalments over two years. The agreement provides that, in the event of it being terminated in any way at any time during the two-year period, the hirer shall make up his total payments under the agreement to 60 per cent of the hire purchase price. Explain the possible liability of the hirer to Finance Ltd should the hirer terminate the agreement after (a) two months, or (b) 12 months.

3. A buyer takes goods on conditional sale from a dealer for £6000, paying a deposit of one-third and agreeing to pay the balance by monthly instalments over two years. After two months, the buyer defaults in paying instalments. Advise the dealer as to his rights, if any, to recover possession of the goods, including the consequences of failure to observe any legal requirements.

4. A salesman in Dealer Ltd's shop, talking to a customer, describes a washing machine in the showroom as being 'in perfect condition'. The customer agrees to take the machine, but wants credit. Dealer Ltd has an arrangement with a finance company, under which Dealer Ltd sells the machine for cash to the finance company, which then lets it on hire purchase to the customer. The machine proves seriously defective, and the customer wishes to know whether he has any remedies against either the finance company or Dealer Ltd. Advise him.

5. Explain briefly the meaning of
   (a) Bill of sale
   (b) Floating charge
   (c) 'Triangular' transaction
   (d) Equitable lien
   (e) Protected goods

Unit 25. Negotiable Instruments

A. The concept of negotiability

As we shall see in Unit 27, there are forms of personal property called *choses in action*, which have no tangible existence, but which can be very valuable (shares, patents, contractual rights such as debts). These are normally evidenced by or embodied in some document. Like other property, they can be transferred, but often the transfer is hedged with legal difficulties, partly due to the very fact that the thing is intangible.

Special rules exist for things such as shares (Unit 11) and patents. More generally, choses in action such as debts can be *legally* assigned under the Law of Property Act 1925, section 136. This, however, is limited: the assignment must be in writing, it must be absolute and not merely by way of charge or mortgage, and notice must be given to the debtor or other person liable. *Equitable* assignment is easier, but the assignor cannot then sue in his own name, but must join the assignor as a party to any action. In short, both legal and equitable assignment of choses in action can be inconvenient. Moreover, in both cases, the assignee generally obtains no better title that the assignor had; the *nemo dat quod non habet* rule normally applies, as it can in sales of goods (Unit 23).

In the Middle Ages, even these limited rights of transfer were not available, and this caused difficulties for traders. For many centuries, traders have found it convenient to use documents evidencing or embodying rights to claim money. Such documents have obvious advantages for moving money without the risks of carrying actual cash. Since English law (like many other legal systems) did not provide for the transfer of such choses in action, the merchants developed their own rules, which often applied internationally, across political boundaries. They recognized certain documents embodying the right to claim money as being 'negotiable instruments', with the features described below. In the eighteenth century, the English courts too began to recognize such documents, as the courts gradually adopted much of 'the law merchant' as part of English law. Documents recognized as 'negotiable' today include bills of exchange, cheques, promissory notes, debentures payable to bearer, and bank notes. (A £1 bank note is, in *form*, simply a *promise* by the Bank of England to pay the bearer the sum of £1. If you have a £1 note, you might like to read it. Today, however, in law as well as in reality, the £1 note is recognized as *being* money, not merely a promissory note.)

Negotiable instruments all have the following features. First, the document can be assigned simply by delivery, or by delivery with 'indorsement' (signature by the transferor on the back). The advantages to merchants of such simple transferability, without the documentation required when English law did finally allow assignment of choses in action, will be apparent. Second, no notice need be given to the person owing the money; he will pay whoever eventually comes to him with the document, so long as it seems in order. (Again contrast this with the Law of Property Act.) Third, the holder of the document can sue in his own name, without having to join in all previous holders of the document (contrast equitable assignment of other choses). Fourth, the assignee may obtain a better title than the assignor had, so that the current holder in good faith need not worry whether a holder three transfers previously had been fraudulent. It is this last feature, the possibility of transfer free from previous defects in title, which distinguishes 'negotiation' of an instrument from mere assignment.

This unit concentrates on two types of negotiable instrument: bills of exchange generally, and cheques.

B. Bills of exchange

This branch of law is now largely embodied in a codifying Act, the Bills of Exchange Act 1882. By section 3(1):

> 'A bill of exchange is an unconditional order in writing, addressed by one person to another, signed by the person giving it, requiring the person to whom it is addressed to pay on demand, or at a fixed or determinable future time, a sum certain in money to or to the order of a specified person, or to bearer.'

Examples of bills of exchange

The main uses of bills of exchange are to give credit and/or transfer money without actually carrying the cash. Two examples may illustrate this. First, an overseas buyer of goods may want credit, but the British exporter will want the money as soon as possible. Both can be accommodated through a bill of exchange. The seller (S) draws a bill ordering the buyer (B) to pay the price on a date some time in the future. S sends the bill of exchange to B, who 'accepts' it (by signing across the face of the bill, usually with the date), and returns it to S. B now has his credit; he only has to pay when the bill 'matures', that is, when the payment date arrives. S obtains his money by selling ('discounting') the bill to a financial institution, usually a merchant bank, in this country at a slight discount (that is, for slightly less than B has promised to pay). B has his credit, S has his cash, and the discount house has its profit when it recovers the full price from B when the bill matures. The discount house takes the risk of non-payment and the possible problems of suing abroad.

A second method by which B can have his (usually short-term) credit while S has immediate payment is for B to draw the bill of exchange. B will have his own account with a merchant bank. B will draw a bill ordering his bank to pay S the price on a date in, say, six months' time. The bank will accept this bill and send it to S, who can then 'discount' it immediately with his own bank. The discount house will recover the money from B's bank when the bill matures. B's bank will then debit B's account or otherwise recover the money from him.

The main uses of ordinary bills of exchange today are in importing and exporting, and/or when credit is involved. Another, very specialized, form of bill of exchange is much more widely used, namely the cheque. A cheque is a bill of exchange drawn on a bank, ordering the bank to pay a specified sum to X on *demand* (that is, as soon as X, or X's bank on his behalf, presents it for payment). Cheques will be discussed later, but it should be remembered that cheques are bills of exchange, and that most of the rules discussed below apply equally to cheques.

Elements of the definition

The definition in section 3 has many important features.

First, in order to be a bill of exchange, the document must be an *unconditional order*, commanding the drawee (the buyer or the bank in the above examples) to pay. A mere request for payment is not enough. (If you have a cheque book, read the words of the cheque forms.) Second, it must be in writing, although the Act does not specify what the writing must be on; A. P. Herbert wrote a feasible but fictitious tale of a bill of exchange validly written on a cow. The bill must also be *signed* by the drawer.

Third, the bill must be *addressed by one person to another*. The person who gives the order is called the *drawer* (S in the first example above, B in the second). The person to whom the order is addressed is the *drawee* (B in the first example, B's bank in the second). The person to whom payment is to be made (S in both examples) is called the *payee*. (In the first example, S is both drawer and payee.) The drawee is only liable on a bill if and when he 'accepts' it and, therefore, the drawer or payee of an ordinary bill will usually present it for acceptance as soon as possible. If the drawee fails to accept, the bill is said to be 'dishonoured for non-acceptance'. If the drawee later fails to *pay*, whether or not he has accepted, the bill is 'dishonoured for non-payment'. We shall see the consequences later.

Fourth, a bill may be payable either *to or to the order of a specified person* or to '*bearer*'. In both of the examples given above, the bill was an 'order' bill, payable to a specified payee, S. A bill may also be a 'bearer' bill. If it is made payable to 'bearer', it can be transferred by mere delivery and, normally, whoever has possession of it is the person entitled to payment. There must, however, either be a specified payee or payees, or the bill must expressly be a 'bearer' one. A cheque form on which the customer simply instructs his bank to pay 'cash' is not a bill of exchange at all and, therefore, not a cheque. It is, however, an authorization to the bank to pay, and a bank does usually pay the drawer if he presents it for payment.

Fifth, a bill can be payable either *on demand or at a fixed or determinable future time*. In both examples above, the bill was a 'time' bill, payable on some specified future date. A bill payable at a determinable future time, such as '30 days after date' would also be a 'time' bill. If a time bill is not presented for payment on the date when it matures, or within three 'days of grace' thereafter, it becomes 'overdue', with consequences described later. If no time for payment is set, the bill is a 'demand' bill, payable immediately. It only becomes overdue if not presented for payment within a reasonable time. Cheques must, by definition (see later), be demand bills, and banks usually treat cheques as overdue if not cashed within six months. The place of payment is normally the address of the drawee/acceptor. It is often, in practice, not the payee himself who takes the bill to the drawee or acceptor for payment, but rather the payee's bank, or a subsequent assignee if the bank has discounted the bill further.

Transfer and negotiation of bills of exchange

By the 1882 Act, section 31(1), a bill is negotiated when it is transferred from one person to another in such a manner as to constitute the transferee the *holder* of the bill.

We have seen that a 'bearer' bill can be transferred by mere delivery. In fact even a thief can be 'holder' of a bearer bill, although the thief does not thereby become owner.

An 'order' bill can only be transferred by delivery with *indorsement* (signing on the back). In the examples given, S would negotiate the bill to the discount house by signing it on the back and handing it over. The discount house thereby becomes the holder, and the person entitled to payment. Indorsements can be of various types. A 'special' indorsement indicates the name of the new holder; for example, S may write on the back, 'Pay Discount House Ltd' before his signature. This bill remains an order bill, and only Discount House Ltd, the indorsee, is entitled to payment. If the payee simply signs on the back without indicating who is to be the new holder, this is an 'indorsement in blank', which converts the bill into a bearer one. Discount House, however, can itself add the words 'Pay Discount House Ltd' before S's signature, thus converting the bill back into an 'order' one. Sometimes an indorser adds the words '*sans recours*' after his signature. This means that he accepts no personal liability on the bill, even if it is subsequently dishonoured. Another possibility is a 'restrictive' indorsement, such as 'pay X only'. This transfers the bill to X, but makes it non-transferable thereafter. An indorsement 'pay X for the account of Y' would also be restrictive; X could present the bill for payment, but must then account to Y, and meanwhile could not transfer the bill to anyone else.

The rights of a holder

The 'holder' is someone in possession of an order bill of which he is payee or indorsee, or the bearer of a bearer bill. His rights depend largely on the circumstances in which he became holder. The most fortunate is the *'holder in due course'*. He is one who has taken a bill *complete and regular on the face of it, before it is overdue, without notice of any previous dishonour, in good faith, for value, and without notice of any defect in the title of the person who negotiated it to him*. A holder in due course takes free from previous defects in title, so that the fact that the bill was previously transferred fraudulently will not affect him. As we have seen, strictly the word 'negotiable' refers to such transfer free from previous defects. A person who becomes holder after a holder in due course also takes free from defects arising before the title was cured.

Notice that the holder in due course must take the bill when it is complete and regular on the face of it, and in good faith, so that there is nothing which should make him suspect any prior irregularity.

A *'holder for value'* is one who has himself given value for the bill (bought it from the payee, for example). He may or may not also be a holder in due course; even if there are suspicious circumstances, so that he does not hold in due course, he can still be holder for value. Even someone who receives the bill as a gift can be holder for value as against persons who became parties prior to the time when value was last given. Unless he is holder in due course, the holder for value has no better title than the person who transferred the bill to him. Subject to this, however, he can still recover from previous parties if the bill is dishonoured.

A *mere holder* is one who has received as a gift a bill for which value has never been given. He receives no better title than the transferor, and cannot sue on the bill if it is dishonoured. If the drawee does in fact pay him, however, this discharges the bill.

Dishonour of bills, and rights of recourse

We have seen that a bill is dishonoured if the drawee refuses to accept and/or pay it. The holder of a dishonoured bill will want to recover, from someone, the value of the bill which has been bought.

Under the 1882 Act, he has rights of 'recourse' against all 'parties' to the bill. Anyone who has signed the bill, as drawer, acceptor or indorser, is a party, and the holder can recover the value of a dishonoured bill from any of these. Sometimes bills are negotiated several times. In this event, if the current holder sues the person or bank who indorsed and negotiated the bill to him, the indorser can in turn sue any previous party.

A drawee who does not sign as acceptor is not a party and, therefore, is not liable *on the bill* either to the payee or to any subsequent holder. Nevertheless, if the drawee fails to pay, this is dishonour, and the current holder can sue anyone who *is* a party, such as previous indorsers or the drawer. (The drawee may be liable *to the drawer* for breach of another contract; for example, if he agreed to accept the bill in payment for goods supplied by the drawer, he is liable to the drawer for breach of the sale of goods contract.)

A bearer bill can be sold and transferred by mere delivery. No indorsement is necessary, and the transferor without indorsement will not become a party. He is, therefore, not liable *on the bill*. Nevertheless, by section 58, he impliedly warrants to his immediate transferee for value that the bill is what it purports to be, that he has a right to transfer it, and at the time of transfer he is not aware of any facts which render it valueless. He can be liable to his buyer for breach of these implied promises.

Matters affecting a holder's rights

If a bill was obtained or transferred by misrepresentation, fraud, duress or undue influence, these are defects in title, which are cured as against a holder in due course and subsequent parties. Some defects, however, cannot be cured.

First, if the holder's title to the bill depends upon a contract which is *void* for mistake, then he has no title. A void contract does not transfer a defective title; it transfers none at all. However, we have seen that contracts are rarely void for mistake.

> Thus in *Foster* v. *Mackinnon* (Unit 18), where the old man had been induced to indorse a bill in the belief that he was signing a guarantee, it was held that the bill would be void for mistake if—but only if—he could prove that he had not been negligent.

Second, as a general rule, no rights to a bill can be given or passed by an *unauthorized* signature. This problem arises quite frequently. If a corporate body signs a bill, it must do so through the agency of some human signer. Where a party is a partnership, signature will usually be by one or two partners on behalf of the firm. In most businesses, certain employees have authority to sign bills and cheques on behalf of the firm. In these situations, the signer himself is not liable, so long as he names or clearly identifies the company or firm on whose behalf he is signing and adds words indicating that he is merely signing as agent. Words such as 'for and on behalf of', '*per pro*', and '*p.p.*', plus the principal's name, protect the signer. The problem remains as to whether the principal, the company or firm, is liable. In general, the principal can be liable if the agent was acting within his 'usual' or 'apparent' authority (Unit 26). However, the expressions such as '*p.p.*', which make plain that it is a 'signature by procuration', operate as notice to the payee and subsequent holders that the agent's authority is limited, and in this case the principal is only bound if the agent was within his *actual* authority.

> In *Morison* v. *Kemp* (1912), a clerk who was authorized to sign cheques for his firm used such a cheque, which he signed '*per pro*' his employer, to pay off his own bookmaker. The employer was not bound, and recovered the money from the bookmaker (who should in any event have suspected that the clerk should not pay off his own gambling debts from the employer's account).

However, the principal may be bound if his conduct estops him from denying the signature's validity; see below.

Third, as a general rule, a *forged* signature is a nullity, and no rights are given by it.

However, the person whose signature is forged (or unauthorized) may exceptionally be estopped from challenging it.

> In *Greenwood* v. *Martins Bank* (1933), G's wife forged his signature as drawer on several cheques. When he discovered this, G told no one, not wishing to cause trouble. The bank, therefore, honoured the cheques, Shortly afterwards, G's wife died, and G, at that point, claimed that the bank had wrongly debited his account. It was held that G was now estopped by his original silence from denying that 'his' signatures were valid.

Fourth, a bill can be avoided by any 'material' alteration, for example, any alteration of the date, the sum payable, or the time for payment. If the alteration is visible, the bill is avoided against all parties prior to the alteration. If the alteration is not apparent, however, a holder in due course can still enforce the bill against parties prior to the alteration.

Fifth, a holder who takes a bill which in any other way is not 'complete and regular on the face of it' cannot be a holder in due course. He can acquire good title, but only if the assignor had good title to give. Thus if there is a difference between the payee's name and the name of the 'payee's' indorsement, title will only pass if the indorsement *is in fact* the payee's. To be safe, the new holder should enquire further before taking the bill.

Similarly, no one can be holder in due course of an overdue bill. The holder can still present the bill for late payment, and sue previous parties if the drawee does not pay; but the holder obtains no better title than the transferor had to give and may, therefore, be met by defences of which he knew nothing.

Finally, the signer's capacity can be important. For example, an infant cannot be personally liable on a bill or cheque. On the other hand, his signature as indorser can pass good title. Moreover, an infant's bank can validly debit his account with cheques drawn by him. A company is not normally liable on a bill or cheque if its signature as drawer, acceptor or indorser is *ultra vires* the company. However, the outsider might be protected by the European Communities Act (Unit 11), and even an *ultra vires* indorsement can pass good title to the next holder.

Discharge of bills of exchange

1. Most bills are discharged by *payment in due course* by the drawee, that is, payment at or after maturity, to the holder, in good faith, and without notice of any defect which might exist in the holder's title (section 59). An indorser can also pay in due course, but this only discharges the indorser and those who became parties after him.
2. We have seen that a material alteration which is apparent discharges all parties prior to the alteration.
3. A bill is also discharged if:
   (a) the acceptor is also the holder at maturity; or
   (b) the holder expressly waives or renounces his rights at or after maturity; or
   (c) the holder has intentionally cancelled the bill, and the cancellation is apparent thereon.

C. Cheques

By the Bills of Exchange Act, section 73, a cheque is defined as 'a bill of exchange drawn on a banker payable on demand'. Cheques, therefore, differ in certain respects from other bills of exchange. First, the drawee must be a bank. Second, a cheque must be 'payable on demand', and a 'time' bill can never be a cheque. Similarly, a 'post-dated' cheque, where the drawer signs on 1 March but dates it, say, 1 August, may be a bill of exchange, but is certainly not a cheque.

A third difference, in practice, is that the bank on which the cheque is drawn never 'accepts' it. The normal procedure is as follows. Suppose that the drawer (D) is paying the petrol station (P) by cheque for £10 worth of petrol. D will have an account with his own bank, which will have issued him with a cheque book containing printed cheque forms. When completed, D's cheque takes the form of an order, addressed to his own bank, to pay P £10. D will date and sign the cheque, and hand it *to the payee*, that is, to P. P will then present the cheque to *its* own bank, which will in turn collect payment from D's bank. Although D's bank has never 'accepted' the cheque in the sense that the drawee of an ordinary bill 'accepts', the bank will *in fact* pay if D's bank balance or overdraft facilities permit. D's bank is often called the 'paying bank', and P's bank is the 'collecting bank'.

Alternatively, P, the payee, could indorse the cheque to X in the same way as any other bill can be indorsed. X would then collect payment himself, probably through his own bank, or indorse it further. In practice, it is very rare indeed that cheques are negotiated in this way. The vast majority are collected by or on behalf of the payee.

Finally, some special rules apply to cheques but not to other bills of exchange: for instance, there are rules as to crossings on cheques, and rules which can protect the paying and collecting banks from liability.

Crossings on cheques

Unlike other bills of exchange, cheques can be 'crossed' so as to protect the drawer. A 'general' crossing is two parallel transverse lines on the face of the cheque. Many cheque forms have crossings already printed on them (look at yours), but if they do not, the drawer or any holder can add them. A general crossing is an instruction to the drawer's bank to pay out only to another bank. If it pays otherwise, it must reimburse its customer, the drawer, if the money goes to the wrong person. The payee, therefore, will only be able to collect payment through his own, the 'collecting', bank. A 'special' crossing has the same effect except that the name of a particular bank is added to the crossing, and the drawer's bank must only pay out to *that* bank. If the words 'not negotiable' are added to the crossing, the cheque *can* still be transferred by the payee, but the transferee will obtain no better title than the transferor had. If words such as 'account payee', 'a/c payee', or 'account payee only' are added, they are an instruction to the drawer's bank only to pay into the bank account of the person named as payee on the cheque. Although in theory such a cheque could still be negotiated, in practice it could not.

Protection of bankers: the paying bank

The paying bank is liable to its own customer, the drawer, if it wrongfully fails to honour his cheques, or if it pays to someone not entitled. It can also be liable for the tort of conversion to the true owner (the payee or anyone to whom he has negotiated the cheque) if it pays to someone not entitled.

This can be harsh on the paying bank, particularly if it has paid to the wrong person because of an unauthorized or forged indorsement. The paying bank only knows its own customer's (the drawer's) signature, and cannot always check the validity of an indorsement. Therefore, there are statutory protections. We have seen that, by the Bills of Exchange Act, section 59, payment of a bill of exchange 'in due course', in good faith and without notice that the holder's title is defective, discharges the bill. By section 60, if the bill is a cheque, the paying bank is deemed to have paid it in due course even if it transpires that indorsements are unauthorized or forged. This is extended by the Cheques Act 1957, section 1: where the paying bank, in good faith and in the ordinary course of business, pays a cheque which is *not* indorsed or is *irregularly* indorsed, it does not incur liability by reason *only* of the absence or irregularity. In practice, however, a bank would neither pay nor collect if a necessary indorsement was absent or irregular.

The Bills of Exchange Act, section 80, provides further protection in relation to *crossed* cheques. Payment in good faith and without negligence in accordance with the crossing has the same effect as if payment were to the true owner.

Notice that the paying bank is not protected if the *drawer's* signature is forged or unauthorized (see page 241 above). It will normally be liable, unless perhaps the drawer is estopped from denying the validity of his signature.

Protection of bankers: the collecting bank

At common law, the collecting bank would be liable to the true owner for the tort of conversion if it collected for anyone else. It could, therefore, be liable if its own customer had no title to the cheque. It is to some extent protected against this possibility by the Cheques Act, section 4: if a bank *in good faith and without negligence* (a) receives payment of a cheque for a customer, or (b) having already credited its customer's account with the amount of the cheque, collects payment for itself, the collecting bank does not incur liability by reason *only* of having collected payment.

The collecting bank escapes liability, therefore, if it can show that it has not been negligent. This is a question of fact, but the following are some examples.

1. When opening an account for a customer, the collecting bank should make reasonable enquiries about him. It should check that he is who he claims to be, and seek reasonable references. It should enquire reasonably about the customer's business or employment, although apparently it need not constantly update this information.

    In *Hampstead Guardians* v. *Barclays Bank Ltd* (1923), a rogue called B worked for Hampstead Guardians. Under the assumed name of 'Stewart', B applied to open an account with Barclays. He gave the name and address of a Mr Woolf as referee. The bank, which had never heard of Mr Woolf, wrote to him for a reference, which B himself forged. The bank then opened the account, into which B paid two cheques, drawn by B's employers in favour of the real Mr Stewart, and which B had intercepted and stolen. Barclays collected payment from the Guardians' bank and, shortly afterwards, B withdrew the money and departed. Barclays Bank was held liable to the Guardians for the amount of the cheques, because it could not show that it had taken all reasonable care to check 'Stewart's' identity.

In *Lloyds Bank Ltd* v. *Savory & Co.* (1933), a housewife paid bearer cheques, drawn by her husband's employer, into her own private account. This would obviously have been suspicious if the bank had known who her husband's employers were. The bank was held negligent because it did not know this, and had therefore wrongfully collected payment.

In *Marfani Ltd* v. *Midland Bank Ltd* (1969), the bank opened an account for a plausible and well-dressed rogue, who falsely called himself 'Eliaszade'. The bank obtained a reference from one of its known and reputable customers, who gave a good reference because he too knew the rogue as 'Eliaszade', and believed him to be honest. In fact, the rogue worked for Marfani Ltd under his true name. At work he fraudulently acquired a cheque drawn by his employer in favour of the real Mr Eliaszade, and paid this into his new account. Shortly afterwards, he withdrew the money and departed. His bank was held *not* to be liable. It had obtained a reference from a known customer, and the fact that it had not checked on its new customer's employer did not *of itself* render the bank negligent.

2. The collecting bank will be negligent if there are obviously suspicious features on the cheque itself, and it fails to enquire further. Thus it should not normally collect a cheque marked 'account payee' for anyone other than the payee. It should not normally collect for an employee's private account a cheque drawn in favour of his employer; nor should it collect for a public official's private account a cheque made payable to him in his official capacity.

In *Marquess of Bute* v. *Barclays Bank Ltd* (1954), the bank was held liable for collecting cheques drawn in favour of 'D McGaw (for the Marquess of Bute)' for McGaw's own *private* account, particularly since McGaw was an ex-employee of the Marquess.

In *Underwood Ltd* v. *Bank of Liverpool* (1924), the bank was held liable for collecting a cheque payable to a company for the private account of the managing director.

However, in *Orbit Mining and Trading Co. Ltd* v. *Westminster Bank Ltd* (1962), there was a different outcome. Orbit had an account with the Midland Bank. Cheques had to be signed by both directors, X and Y. Before X went abroad, he signed a number of blank cheque forms. Y used this opportunity to turn the blank cheque forms into 'pay cash' instruments, which he then paid into his private account with the Westminster for collection. The Westminster, rather surprisingly, was able to prove that it had not been negligent. It did not know of Y's connection with Orbit, partly because Y also had another job. It did not identify Y's signature as drawer, because the signature was illegible. The clerk at the counter did not know Y's signature, and no indorsement was needed. (Perhaps the outcome was satisfactory, in that because the Westminster was not liable, Orbit bore the loss occasioned by X's signature of blank cheques, and Y's misconduct.)

Today, by the Banking Act 1979, if a collecting bank is held negligent and liable for conversion, the damages awarded against it can be reduced for contributory negligence by the plaintiff.

It should be remembered that the Cheques Act, section 4, only protects a bank which collects for its customer, or after having credited its customer's account. It must, therefore, collect for someone who has an account with it, although it is sufficient if he opens the account with the cheque in question.

The collecting bank can also escape liability if it gives value for the cheque to the person paying it in for collection. In these circumstances, the collecting bank can become holder in due course so long as the bill is complete and regular on the face of it, and the bank takes in good faith. A collecting bank rarely gives value for the cheque when it is presented, but might do so if, for example, it allows the cheque to reduce the customer's overdraft before the cheque is cleared, or if it has a prior arrangement under which it allows the customer to draw against the cheque before it is cleared. As holder in due course, the bank could acquire the right to claim payment even if its customer's title were defective. The bank can become holder whether or not its customer has indorsed the cheque.

Cheque as a receipt

A cheque which has been paid by the paying bank is evidence that the payee has received the money, whether or not the payee has indorsed the cheque. Some paying banks used to return paid cheques to their customers, but this is rarely done today.

The relationship between banker and customer

Detailed rights and duties, express and implied, exist between a bank and its customer. These extend to cheques but also apply more widely and, therefore, are discussed further in Unit 26.

For further consideration

1. Explain the following terms in relation to bills of exchange
    (a) Drawer   (e) Dishonour
    (b) Drawee   (f) Overdue
    (c) Payee   (g) Holder in due course
    (d) Acceptance   (h) Negotiation
2. Distinguish between:
    (a) 'Time' bills and 'demand' bills;
    (b) Order bills and bearer bills;
    (c) Special indorsements and indorsements in blank.
3. Explain the meaning and effect of the following on a cheque
    (a) A general crossing
    (b) A special crossing

(c) A crossing with the words 'not negotiable'
(d) A crossing with the words 'account payee'
4. XYZ Ltd has an account with P bank. In its business, XYZ regularly has to pay large cheques, drawn on P bank, to a broker called Smith. An employee of XYZ, a rogue called R, often prepares these cheques for signature by the managing director. R secretly opens an account with C bank, falsely using the name 'Smith', and giving false but plausible references which deceive the branch manager of C bank. R then prepares a number of XYZ's cheques, drawn on P bank, ostensibly in favour of the real Smith. The managing director of XYZ signs these without asking what they are for. R then pays the cheques into his account with C bank, which collects payment for him from P bank. R then withdraws the money from C bank and absconds.
(a) Can P bank validly debit XYZ's account with these cheques?
(b) Is C bank liable to XYZ?

Unit 26. Agency, Banking, and Insurance

This unit deals with a number of contracts which have particular importance in commercial life, and which have certain features in common. In particular, in these contracts the law demands duties of care and good faith between the parties. In all cases, one party is selling a service, not property, to the other, and the personality of the parties is important.

A. Agency

An agent is a person empowered by another (the 'principal') to bring the principal into legal relations with a third party.

Agency arises in many situations. There can be independent agents, such as estate agents engaged to find a buyer for the principal's house, or travel agents engaged to book holidays or airline tickets for the principal. An employee may be agent for his employer, as where a firm employs a salesman or buyer. We have seen that corporate bodies, having no physical existence, can *only* contract through agents such as executive directors or managers (Unit 11), and that a partner may have authority to bind his firm (Unit 10).

Generally, an agent can be appointed orally, without any formalities. Strictly, there need be no contract between principal and agent, and even a young minor (sent to buy groceries on behalf of the parents) can be an agent.

Creation of agency

There are several ways in which a person can acquire authority or power to bind another by his actions. Normally, *actual authority* is *expressly* given by the principal. An agent so appointed also has *implied authority* to do everything normally incidental to his express instructions, such as incurring reasonable postage, telephone, and travelling expenses. Furthermore, where by ordinary business practice it is *usual* for a particular type of agent to have certain powers, the principal will be taken impliedly to have conferred those powers. Thus, we have seen that it is usual for partners or executive directors to make normal contracts for the business, although exactly what is usual in any instance will depend upon the person's position and the size and nature of the business. A principal can restrict the agent's usual authority, but this does not affect a third party who deals through the agent without knowledge of the restriction.

> In *Watteau* v. *Fenwick* (1893), H, manager of a public house, ordered cigars from a supplier, Watteau, for re-sale in the bar. Although H was not the owner, his name appeared over the door as licensee, and it was found to be usual for licensees to buy and re-sell cigars. H had in fact been forbidden to order cigars by Fenwick, the owner. Nevertheless Fenwick had to pay, because H was acting normally for a licensee, and there was nothing to make Watteau suspect that the licensee's usual powers were limited.

We have also seen the effect of undisclosed restrictions on the usual authority of a mercantile agent (*Folkes* v. *King*, Unit 23), and of a company secretary in a large business (*Panorama Developments* v. *Fidelis*, Unit 11). The principal's remedy in these cases is against his own agent.

A principal may also be bound if he is *estopped* from denying someone's apparent authority. This occurs if the principal, by his conduct, has 'held out' someone as having power to act on his behalf (see *Eastern Distributors* v. *Goldring*, Unit 23), and *Freeman and Lockyer* v. *Buckhurst Park Properties Ltd*, Unit 11).

Exceptionally, agency may arise from *necessity*. Four conditions must be satisfied: (a) the 'agent' must have been put in control of the principal's property; (b) a genuine emergency must have arisen, which threatens the property; (c) it must be impossible to obtain the owner's instructions in time; and (d) the agent must be acting in good faith, and solely to protect the property.

> In *Great Northern Railway Co.* v. *Swaffield* (1874), the railway company, through no fault of its own, was unable to deliver a horse consigned by rail. Unable to contact the owner, the company paid to put the horse in livery stables, and was held entitled to recover the cost from the owner.

Finally, in some circumstances, a principal can choose to *ratify* something done *in his name*, but without his authority.

> In *Re Tiedemann and Ledermann Frères* (1899), an agent who periodically bought and sold wheat on behalf of a principal, also used the principal's name, for financial reasons, in a transaction which he made on his own behalf. It was held that the principal could ratify and adopt this transaction, and take the profits.

The principal must have existed and had contractual capacity when the agent acted and, therefore, a company cannot ratify contracts made by its promoters before incorporation. In these circumstances, the promoters are personally bound by the contracts. Moreover, illegal or void acts cannot be ratified. Forged signatures, or things done *ultra vires* a company, are nullities which cannot be cured by ratification. Finally, a principal is only bound if he was aware of all material facts when he ratified.

In *Marsh* v. *Joseph* (1897), a rogue pretended to be acting on behalf of a solicitor in transactions which turned out to be fraudulent. He then gave a partial account of what he had done to the solicitor who, believing the transactions to be legitimate, 'ratified' the rogue's actions. The 'ratification' was held inoperative.

Ratification *relates back* to the time of the agent's acts, so that the position is the same as if the agent had had authority from the outset. This may have startling results.

In *Bolton Partners* v. *Lambert* (1889), Lambert made an offer to an agent who, acting without authority, purported to accept on behalf of Boltons. Lambert then tried to revoke the offer. *After* this, Boltons ratified the agent's acceptance. Lambert was held bound by the contract, because the ratification related back to the agent's acceptance, so that Lambert's revocation was too late.

The main limit on 'relation back' is that vested rights cannot be divested, so that ratification cannot affect a third party who has acquired rights to the property before ratification.

Relations with the third party

As a general rule, the agent simply drops out when the contract or other legal relationship comes into existence between principal and third party. The contract is the principal's. The agent incurs no personal liability, nor can he sue the third party.

The only major exception arises where there is an *undisclosed principal*, that is, where the agent appears to be acting for himself and does not disclose that he is merely an agent. In these circumstances, the third party has the option of holding *either* the principal *or* the agent liable. Conversely, the undisclosed principal can sue the third party, but not if this would work injustice. Therefore, an undisclosed principal cannot step in if identity is material, and the third party would not have dealt with him. Furthermore, the undisclosed principal can be met with any defence or set-off which the third party would have had against the agent.

Exceptionally, by special custom in certain trades, agents do take personal responsibility for performance by the principal or third party; and if an agent signs a document without adding words such as 'as agent', the courts may be reluctant to admit evidence that he is merely an agent.

When it comes to performing the contract, the agent is still, for the most part, just the hand and voice of his principal. If the principal gives money to his agent to pay to the third party, the principal generally remains liable if the agent defaults. If the third party pays the agent, the principal can be treated as having received the money, so long as the agent had express or implied authority to take the payment.

In tort, an agent is liable for his own wrongs; but the principal too can be vicariously liable for torts committed by his agent in the course of his authority.

Finally, problems can arise if the principal is *not* bound. A person who acts as agent impliedly promises the third party that he does have power to bind the principal. If, therefore, the agent lacks authority and exceeds his powers, so that the principal is not liable, the *agent* is liable *to the third party* for *breach of warranty of authority*. Liability is strict, and an agent can be liable even if he honestly believed that he did have authority.

In *Yonge* v. *Toynbee* (1910), solicitors, acting for their client, defended proceedings started by Yonge, and thereby put him to considerable expense. Unknown to the solicitors, their client had become insane, thereby ending their authority. Yonge recovered his legal expenses from the solicitors personally.

Duties of agent to principal

An agent owes express and implied duties to his principal. He must obey instructions. He must not delegate his functions to anyone else without his principal's permission. He must show reasonable care in carrying out his instructions, and must show such skill as he has professed.

Most importantly, an agent must show *good faith*. Therefore, he must abide by the following principles.

1. He must not buy or sell from his own principal without full disclosure, nor must he secretly act for both sides. There must be no undisclosed 'conflict of interest'.

    In *Armstrong* v. *Jackson* (1917), a stockbroker was engaged to buy certain shares for his principal. The stockbroker held some such shares himself and, without disclosing this, transferred his own shares to his principal. It was held that the principal could rescind the contract, and recover what he had paid for the shares (even though they had since fallen in value).

    In *Fullwood* v. *Hurley* (1928), an agent, engaged by the owner to sell a hotel, found someone who wanted a hotel and, without disclosing his connection with the owner, arranged the sale and claimed commission from both sides. He was not entitled to commission from the buyer.

2. An agent owes duties of confidentiality. He must not use for his own or another's benefit confidential information obtained for or from his principal. Conversely, he must not withhold information from his principal.

    In *Keppel* v. *Wheeler* (1927), K engaged an estate agent to sell his house. The agent received an offer of £6150, which K accepted 'subject to contract' (so that he was not bound yet). Five days later, the agent received another offer of £6750, but K did not learn of this until much later, after the first contract had become binding. The agent was liable to K for £600 damages, the difference between the offers.

3. An agent must account to his principal for all moneys received as agent, and must not mix his principal's money and property with his own.

4. An agent must never take a bribe, that is, any payment or gift to induce him to act in favour of the donor; nor must he make a secret profit from an unauthorized use of his position.

    In *Mahesan* v. *Malaysia Government Officers' Housing Society* (1978), M was engaged by the Society to find building land. He found a cheap and suitable site, but accepted a bribe from a property speculator to keep silent about it. This enabled the speculator to buy the site cheaply, and then re-sell it to the Society at a huge profit. The Society was entitled to recover the bribe and the speculator's profit from M.

    In *Hippisley* v. *Knee Bros* (1905), an advertising agent obtained discounts from printers with whom he regularly dealt. It was held that the discounts had to be passed on to the principal but, since the agent had not been fraudulent, he was still entitled to his commission.

We have seen that the agent must account for profits improperly made, and must compensate his principal for any loss. In the event of serious breach, the principal may end the agency without notice or compensation. An employee-agent may validly be dismissed. If the agent was fraudulent, the principal can rescind contracts made through him, and can refuse any commission. If there is bribery, both agent and donor commit criminal offences; moreover the principal can recover damages from agent or donor.

Duties of principal to agent

When the agent has completed a task, the principal must pay any commission or other payment expressly or impliedly promised. He must also indemnify the agent for expenses properly and legally incurred in exercising the agent's duties.

Termination of agency

Agency can end in various ways: by *performance*, if an agent engaged for a specific task completes it; by *death* of either party; by *bankruptcy* of the principal, and by bankruptcy of the agent if, as is usual, this renders the agent unfit for his duties; by the *insanity* of either party, if this renders him unfitted. Agency can be *frustrated*, for example, if the illness of either party defeats the commercial purpose. Finally, the principal can generally *withdraw the agent's authority* at any time (although he might be liable to the agent if this involves breach of a contract between principal and agent).

As between principal and agent, termination does not affect the agent's rights to commission already earned. As regards third parties, it must be remembered that withdrawal of the agent's *actual* authority may only affect the third party when he learns of it. Until then, the agent may still have *power* (apparent authority) to bind the principal. However, if authority is ended by operation of law, as where the principal becomes insane, this can end the agent's authority automatically, even before the third party or even the agent learns of it; see *Yonge* v. *Toynbee* again.

B. The relationship between banker and customer

A contract exists between a bank and its customer. It is a loan contract, because if the customer's account is in credit, the bank owes him that money, and vice versa if the account is overdrawn. It is also very much more. The bank undertakes to help the customer handle and take care of the money in various ways, and the parties owe duties of care and, sometimes, good faith to each other. Some rules have already been discussed in Unit 25. The following are other examples.

Duties of the bank

1. The bank must honour its customer's cheques if the account is in credit, or if the cheque is within any expressly or impliedly agreed overdraft limit. A bank which

wrongly fails to honour a customer's cheque will be liable to the customer for breach of contract, and the damages may be substantial if the customer is a trader whose financial reliability is thereby put in doubt.

The bank's duty to honour cheques is ended by: (a) notice of the customer's death or mental disorder; (b) notice of the customer's bankruptcy, or compulsory winding up if the customer is a company; and (c) if the customer countermands payment ('stops' the cheque). Countermand is only effective when actually communicated to the manager or a senior employee of the drawer's branch of his bank. Informing another branch is not enough.

> Notice also *Curtice* v. *London, City and Midland Bank* (1908), where a telegram countermanding payment was delivered to the bank after business hours, put in a box for unopened mail and, carelessly, not opened and given to the manager the following day until after the cheque had been paid. The bank was still entitled to debit its customer's account. (The customer might succeed today if he sued his bank for negligence.)

In practice, banks will *postpone* payment if the drawer telephones that he wishes to stop the cheque, but will require a written countermand signed by the drawer as soon as possible thereafter. By agreement with their customers, some banks today will not allow cheques up to £50 to be stopped at all if (a) the customer produced a credit card when handing the cheque to the payee, and (b) he signed (e.g., indorsed) the cheque in the payee's presence, and (c) the payee wrote the credit card number on the back of the cheque. In short, some banks allow their credit cards to be used to guarantee payment of certain cheques.

2. The bank must only pay a person entitled to receive payment. If, therefore, it pays on a cheque which was validly countermanded, or is void for a material alteration, or on which the drawer's signature is forged, it cannot generally debit its customer's account. The bank may, however, be protected in some circumstances: if the customer is estopped from suing as in *Greenwood* v. *Martins Bank* (Unit 25); where the customer has contributed to his own misfortune by negligently drawing the cheque (see below); or where the bank has the benefit of the statutory protections described in Unit 25. The bank may also be protected indirectly.

> In *Liggett Ltd* v. *Barclays Bank* (1928), the bank was instructed that the company's cheques must be signed by two directors. The bank wrongly paid on a cheque signed by only one director and, therefore, was not entitled to debit the company's account. It was, however, 'subrogated' to the rights of the creditor to whom the cheque had wrongly been paid. The bank, therefore, had whatever rights the creditor would have had against the company if the cheque had not been paid. If the creditor *was* entitled to the money, the customer's account could still be debited.

3. A bank impliedly undertakes to collect cheques of which its customer is payee. As we have seen, the collecting bank will present the cheque on behalf of its customer to the drawer's bank for payment. In practice, this is done through a central clearing scheme operated by the major banks.

4. A bank must observe secrecy as regards its customer's account. There are only a few exceptions to this general rule: (a) where the customer authorizes disclosure, for

example, by asking the bank to act as his referee; (b) where the bank has to disclose in order to sue for an unpaid overdraft; (c) where disclosure is required by statute, for example, under the Companies Act 1948, the Income and Corporation Taxes Act 1970, and the Bankers' Books Evidence Act 1879 under which the court can sometimes authorize a party to proceedings to inspect and copy the bank's books; and (d) exceptionally, where public policy requires disclosure.

> In *Bankers Trust Co.* v. *Shapira* (1980), the Court of Appeal ordered a bank to disclose to the plaintiff (another bank) details of an account into which two dishonest customers had paid their ill-gotten gains. The circumstances were exceptional partly because the customers themselves were unavailable, one being in prison in Switzerland, and the other having disappeared.

5. A bank owes duties of good faith towards its customers, if only because of the bank's greater strength and expertise.

> In *Lloyds Bank Ltd* v. *Bundy* (1975), the bank put pressure on its own customer, an elderly farmer, to mortgage his farmhouse to the bank, to guarantee and provide security for loans by the bank to the farmer's son. The son had financial difficulties and owed the bank a lot of money. The farmhouse was the customer's home and only major asset. The court set aside the guarantee and mortgage. At the very least, the bank should have advised the farmer to take independent advice, because there was a possible conflict of interest.

6. Although a bank has no duty to advise its customers on financial matters generally, it sometimes does so in practice. If it does, then it must show reasonable care and skill; see *Hedley Byrne* v. *Heller and Partners* (Unit 13). A bank can even owe this duty in respect of advice given before the paintiff opened an account.

> In *Woods* v. *Martins Bank Ltd* (1958), the bank was held liable when its branch manager negligently advised Woods to invest nearly £15 000 in a company which proved to be unsound, so that Woods lost his investment. Although Woods had no account with the bank when he received the advice, he was held to be a customer. He and the bank had already had dealings, and he opened an account shortly afterwards.

Duties of customer

A customer must take reasonable care when drawing cheques. If he does not, then the bank can debit his account with amounts wrongly paid out as a result.

> In *London Joint Stock Bank* v. *Macmillan and Arthur* (1918), M signed a bearer cheque on which the space for the amount in words was left blank, and simply '£2' appeared in the space for figures. A fraudulent clerk then wrote 'One hundred and twenty pounds' in the space for words, and altered the '£2' to read '£120'. The clerk cashed the cheque, and the bank was held entitled to debit M's account with the full £120.

> In *Slingsby* v. *District Bank Ltd* (1932), the drawer left a large space between the payee's name and the words 'or order' on the cheque form. A fraudulent clerk called Cumberbirch was able to write 'per Cumberbirch and Potts' in the space, and thereby obtain payment for himself. The court held that the drawer had *not* been negligent in leaving the blank space and, therefore, the bank could *not* debit his account. (This case did, however, show the possibility of such a fraud, and it might well be negligent today to leave such a space. To be safe, the drawer should add a line between the end of the payee's name and the words 'or order'.)

We have seen in Unit 25 that a customer must also disclose any forgeries of his signature to the bank; otherwise he may be estopped from denying the validity of the signature, as in *Greenwood* v. *Martin's Bank*. This is probably part of a more general duty of care which a customer owes to his bank.

C. Insurance

Most insurance contracts ('policies') are contracts of *indemnity*. One person (the 'insurer') promises, in return for a payment ('premium') to indemnify the other (the 'insured') against loss caused by some risk. A householder may insure himself against loss of or damage to his house by fire, burglary, accident, etc. A car owner may insure himself against similar risks to his car. If the risk occurs, the insurer will *idemnify* the policy holder, that is, *pay him the cost of his loss*. Another form of indemnity insurance is cover against legal liability. The insurer undertakes to pay any damages awarded against the policy holder for certain types of legal liability. Some such insurance is compulsory: the user of a motor vehicle on a road *must* be covered by a policy to indemnify him against legal liability for death or bodily injury to a third party due to accident. Use without such cover is a criminal offence, the purpose being to ensure that even the victim of an impoverished driver will recover adequate damages.

Some insurance is *non-indemnity*, because the risk covered has no direct monetary value. The policy holder can hardly be 'indemnified' against the 'cost' of personal suffering. Therefore, the insurer agrees, in return for a premium, to *pay a specified sum*, or provide benefits such as medical expenses, in the event of, for example, illness or personal injury. Life policies are also non-indemnity and, logically, should hardly be called insurance at all. The insurer undertakes to pay an agreed sum when the policy holder dies (an event which, alas, is more than a mere risk). For this reason, life policies are often called life 'assurance' rather than 'insurance'. Subject to this, the same rules apply to life policies as to other insurance.

Finally, insurance can extend to benefits in kind as well as to monetary cover.

> In *Department of Trade and Industry* v. *St Christopher's Motorists Association Ltd* (1974), a contract to provide chauffeurs for motorists who were disqualified, or unable to drive because of accident, was held to be insurance.

Formation of policies

The parties

Most *insurers*, other than Lloyd's underwriters, are companies. Under the Insurance Companies Act 1974, many types of insurance business can *only* be carried on by companies, which in turn are subject to Department of Trade supervision.

The policy holder, the *insured*, must have an *insurable interest* in the risk insured against, that is, he must stand to lose personally if the loss occurs. In the case of life policies, the policy holder can, for example, validly insure against death of himself, his/her spouse, a debtor or surety, and sometimes even an employee ('key man' policies); not, however, against death of a parent, see *Harse* v. *Pearl Life Assurance* (Unit 22). In property insurance, the owner can insure, as can a person in possession such as a tenant of land or bailee of goods. Both mortgagor and mortgagee of property can insure.

> In *Westminster Fire Office* v. *Glasgow Provident Investment Society* (1888), the holder of a debenture *secured* by a charge on assets of the comapny did have an insurable interest in the company's property.

> In *Macaura* v. *Northern Assurance Co. Ltd* (1925), the major *shareholder* insured *himself* against loss of the company's property. The policy was held void: the company was a separate legal person and, as shareholder, he did not own its property. He was also an *unsecured* creditor, but this too gave him no interest because he had no charge on the assets.

If the insured has no interest, we have seen in Unit 22 that the policy is invalidated by statute. In all policies except for loss of or damage to goods, the policy is illegal under the Life Assurance Act 1774, in which case premiums are generally irrecoverable. For insurance of goods, the policy is void as a wager under the Gaming Act 1845, but premiums are recoverable.

Offer, acceptance, and commencement of cover
The offer is usually by the would-be policy holder on the company's pre-printed proposal form. The form normally asks questions about the proposer and the risk, to help the company decide whether to accept. On acceptance, a written policy is normally issued, usually pre-printed. Cover can commence from issue of the policy, but in practice it is often postponed until the company receives the first premium. In motor policies, temporary cover is often given by a 'cover note'. This is a separate contract giving cover until a specified date, by which time the proposal form should have been accepted. The note usually incorporates such terms of the standard policy as are appropriate to temporary cover.

Dealing through agents
Insurance companies, like other corporations, must by their nature deal through agents. Problems then arise if the proposer gives information to an agent who fails to pass it on or completes a form wrongly. The company may subsequently refuse to pay. In general, the ordinary principles of agency apply. If it is within the agent's actual, usual or apparent authority to receive such information for the company, the company is deemed to have received it whether or not the agent passes it on.

> In *Stone* v. *Reliance Mutual Insurance Co.* (1972), an insurance salesman and agent had authority to help proposers to complete their proposal forms. He incorrectly wrote down some of the information which he was given. The company was treated as having received the correct details. (In practice, however, most insurers expressly provide that agents have *no* authority to help fill in proposal forms.)

Insurance *brokers* are agents of the proposer, not the company. The proposer contacts a broker to find the best terms *for him*. Therefore, the insurance company can hold the policy holder liable for false statements made by a broker who completes a proposal form for him. The client can recover damages from his broker.

Agents and brokers must not allow any conflict of interest. Under the Insurance

Companies Act 1974, anyone introducing a proposer to an insurance company must disclose any connection between himself and the company. For example, even a garage having a stock of insurance proposal forms for car buyers must disclose to its customer whether it receives commission for introducing business to the insurance company.

Duties of insured

A proposer seeking insurance cover owes high duties of good faith to his proposed insurer.

First, false statements or answers on a proposal form are misrepresentations, which can entitle the insurance company to rescind the policy and refuse to pay any claim. The policy is voidable if the misrepresentation was 'material', false, and did deceive and influence the insurance company. A 'material' statement is one likely to influence a prudent insurer in deciding whether to undertake the risk, and what premium to charge. Whether the *proposer* believed it to be material is irrelevant. Similarly, a statement can be false even if the proposer did not know that it was false; innocent misrepresentation can make the contract voidable.

> In *Merchants and Manufacturers Insurance* v. *Hunt and Thorne* (1941) the proposal form for a motor policy asked, 'Have you or any person who to your knowledge will drive the car been convicted of driving offences?' In all honesty, the proposer wrote, 'No'. Unknown to him, his son, who was also to be covered by the policy, had four convictions. Some time later, the company validly refused a claim by the father.

We have also seen in Unit 18 that a half-truth can be a misrepresentation; see *London Assurance* v. *Mansel* (page 169).

Second, most proposal forms in practice state that the answers 'shall form the basis of the contract, and shall be deemed to be incorporated therein'. This converts the statements on the proposal form from mere representations into terms of the contract. In insurance contracts, all promises and terms are called 'warranties', and if a 'warranty' is broken the insurance company can repudiate liability, whether or not the statement was 'material'.

> In *Dawsons Ltd* v. *Bonnin* (1922), the proposal form, which contained a 'basis of the contract' clause, asked where the vehicle would usually be garaged. A wrong answer was inadvertently given, but there was evidence that the proposal would still have been accepted, and the premium would have been the same, if the correct answer had been given. Nevertheless, the insurance company could refuse to pay when, later, the vehicle was destroyed by fire, quite unconnected with where it was garaged.

The harshness of this rule has been mitigated by the courts to some extent. For example, any ambiguity in the company's pre-printed proposal form or policy will be construed in favour of the policy holder. Moreover, a clause in the contract may be treated not as a warranty, but merely as defining the risk.

> In *Farr* v. *Motor Traders Mutual Insurance Society* (1920), the proposal form to insure a taxi asked whether the cab would be 'driven in one or more shifts per 24 hours'. The proposer answered, 'Just one'. The proposal, containing a 'basis of the contract' clause, was accepted. Some time later, the taxi was used briefly for two shifts while another was repaired. Later still,

when the cab was again only being used for one shift, an accident occurred. The insurance company tried to repudiate the claim for breach of warranty. It was held that the true effect of the 'one shift' clause was merely to define the risk. The vehicle was only insured while it was being used for one shift. Cover ceased while it was used for two, but re-commenced as soon as it was used for only one again.

Third, insurance is a contract *uberrimae fidei* ('of the utmost good faith'). As well as answering the proposal form truthfully, a proposer must also disclose any other 'material' information which might influence a prudent insurer. Examples of material facts are rejection of previous proposals, even for a different type of policy if rejection was for fraud; previous illness where relevant; previous motor accidents for motor policies; and previous convictions.

In *Woolcott* v. *Sun Alliance Insurance* (1978), a house owner who had insured himself against damage to his house was unable to claim when there was a fire because, although not asked when making the policy, he had omitted to disclose his criminal record, including robbery.

Where policies have to be renewed periodically, the duty to disclose probably arises again on each renewal.

Fourth, the insured's duty of good faith lasts during the policy as well. Therefore, if he makes a *fraudulently* exaggerated claim in the event of any loss, the insurance company can avoid the policy and pay nothing.

In all cases, the insurance company's right to avoid the contract is lost if it affirms the contract, for example, if it continues to accept premiums after discovering the true facts. Again, disclosure of the truth to the company's agent is disclosure to the company.

In *Ayrey* v. *British Legal Assurance* (1918), the holder of a life policy had failed to disclose when making the contract that he was in the Royal Naval Reserve. When he was called up for wartime service, his wife did tell the branch manager, and asked what they should do. The manager told her to go on paying the premiums. The company could not avoid the policy when, later, the husband died.

Duties of insurer

The insurance company's main obligations are to indemnify the policy holder, or to pay the agreed sum in a non-indemnity policy, if and when the risk insured against occurs.

If the policy holder is injured by the tort of another, the insurance company may be *subrogated* to the insured's rights against the tortfeasor. The company can insist on the insured suing the tortfeasor, and is entitled to recoup insurance payments out of the damages recovered. In indemnity policies, this prevents the policy holder from recovering the amount of his loss twice, from the tortfeasor and from the insurance company.

There are some limits on the insurance company's duties to pay. First, it need only pay if the loss was due to the risk insured. This is not always so simple as it seems. If a man is drowned after falling into a stream in the course of a fit, was his death due to accident or to illness? If a fire is caused by defective equipment which an employee negligently leaves switched on overnight, is the fire caused by the defect or the employee's negligence? It is for the policy holder to prove that the proximate cause of the loss was the risk insured against, but in cases of doubt the courts often try to give effect to the cover.

Second, as a matter of public policy, the insured is not generally allowed to benefit from his own criminal offence.

> Similarly, in *Cleaver* v. *Mutual Reserve Fund Life Assurance* (1892), a man took out a policy on his own life, under which payment was to be made to his wife when he died. She poisoned him. She was held not entitled to the policy moneys.

For motor liability policies, this rule has been limited to deliberate and serious offences. An insurance company will in fact indemnify a driver against his civil liability even if the driver was exceeding the speed limit when the accident occurred.

In property insurance, particularly on houses, the parties normally agree a maximum figure of indemnity, the 'sum insured'. This is the maximum cover which will be given, and the higher the cover, the higher the premium. As a basic rule, the policy holder will be indemnified for his full loss up to, but not beyond, the 'sum insured'. In practice, however, most policies also contain an '*average*' clause by which, in the event of loss, the amount payable is limited to *the proportion of the sum insured which the sum insured is of the true value of the property*. Therefore, if a house worth £30 000 is insured for only £20 000, the insurance company will only pay two-thirds of any loss. If the loss is £300, the policy holder will only receive £200. Average clauses protect insurance companies against under-insurance, but can badly affect a house owner if house prices are rising. Unless he regularly raises the 'sum insured', the owner may recover only *part* of any loss which he suffers.

Insurance companies often try, by clauses in the policy, to restrict or exclude their liability.

1. Most policies expressly limit the risk insured.

   > In *Wood* v. *General Accident, Fire and Life Assurance* (1948), Wood's motor policy only covered him while he was using the car for 'social, domestic, and pleasure purposes'. The policy did not cover an accident which occurred while he was driving to a business appointment (although Wood did argue that he had been enjoying the drive).

2. Most policies also contain 'exceptions', that is, circumstances in which cover will not be given, generally because of misconduct by the policy holder. For example, many motor policies only give cover while the car is in a 'roadworthy condition'.

   > In *Brown* v. *Zurich Insurance Co.*(1954), a car with bald front tyres was held not to be in a 'roadworthy condition' and, therefore, the insured was not covered.

   > However, in *Houghton* v. *Trafalgar Insurance Co. Ltd* (1953), the insurance company was held liable. A motor policy excluded the company's liability if the vehicle was used to carry an excessive '*load*'. The insurer refused to pay when an accident occurred with two extra *passengers* in the car. It was held that 'load' was intended to apply to lorries, and could not affect extra passengers in a private car. (On the other hand, *too many* extra passengers would break a 'roadworthy condition' clause.)

The courts have treated some 'exceptions' as being analogous to exclusion clauses, and construed them *contra proferentem* (see page 181). The Unfair Contract Terms Act 1977 does not apply to insurance contracts, however.

3. Many policies specify 'conditions' which the policy holder must continue to fulfil. For example, a car owner may be required to keep it garaged at night. These clauses too may be strictly construed.

> In *Re Bradley and Essex and Suffolk Accident Society* (1912), a farmer, who employed only his son, had a policy covering his liability to his employees. The policy was so badly drafted that it was difficult to tell what it meant. Tucked away in a long clause about other matters, it required the farmer to keep a wages book. He did not, and the insurance company, therefore, refused payment when the son had an accident. The company was held liable. Failure to keep the wages book was a minor breach which did not entitle the insurers to repudiate the contract. The court also commented that, in drafting the policy, the insurance company too had duties of good faith, if only to the extent of making it comprehensible.

4. Policies often contain 'notice' clauses, requiring that the insurance company be notified within, say, 14 days of any loss. If no notice is given, there is no cover.

> In *Cassel* v. *Lancashire and Yorkshire Accident Insurance Co.* (1855), a personal injury policy required that notice be given to the insurers within 14 days of any accident. The policy holder's canoe overturned on a river, in Cornwall. He suffered no immediate harm, but became ill some months later. He gave notice as soon as he became ill, but recovered nothing, because he had not given notice within 14 days *of the accident.*

Again, however, the courts have mitigated the harshness of this rule. Clauses requiring notice 'as soon as possible', for example, mean as soon as *reasonably* possible. Similarly, if the insurers have had notice of an accident from another source, such as the police, they can no longer repudiate for lack of notice from the policy holder.

5. In liability policies, admission of liability by the insured, or any other action prejudicing the issue of liability may, under the policy, entitle the insurers to repudiate liability.

Finally, we have seen that some liability insurance is compulsory. Insurance against liability for death of or bodily injury to a third party due to accident arising from the use of a motor vehicle on a road is one instance. Similarly, an employer must insure against possible liability for death or bodily injury to his employees at work. In such policies, exceptions, conditions, and notice clauses could defeat the whole purpose of compulsory insurance, namely to ensure there are enough funds for the victims. Therefore, as against the victims, liability for *compulsory* risks cannot normally be affected merely because the policy holder has broken a term in his policy.

For further consideration

1. P is a coal merchant and A is his agent. Explain the possible effects of the following transactions.
   (a) A sells his own coal to T in Newcastle in P's name.
   (b) A sells P's coal to T in Newcastle in A's own name, without disclosing that he is merely acting for P.

2. (a) Summarize the duties of an agent to his principal.
   (b) A is employed as your firm's representative, negotiating large contracts. You have just discovered that, three months ago, he received £1000 'commission' from T for arranging a contract between your firm and T. What action can your firm take?
3. (a) What is meant by 'countermanding' or 'stopping' a cheque? Explain whether and, if so, how this can be done.
   (b) Explain whether a paying bank can ever validly debit its customer's account if it pays a cheque to a person not entitled to it.
4. (a) What are the effects of (i) 'average' clauses, and (ii) 'basis of the contract' clauses in insurance law?
   (b) Explain who can validly insure a company's property.
5. Explain the following terms, and give as many examples as you can from this unit
   (a) Subrogation
   (b) Estoppel
   (c) Duty of good faith
   (d) Conflict of interest

Unit 27. Property and Legal Estates in Land

A. The nature and classification of property

Meaning of property

The word 'property' can be used in at least two different senses. It can be used to describe things capable of ownership, whether these be tangible or intangible. The early common law, arising out of the feudal system, was preoccupied with land as the main form of property in this sense, and even today people often think of land and buildings when the word is used. Property can, however, take many other forms, including goods of various types and intangible things such as patents and company shares. It can include animals as well as inanimate objects, but not human persons, although it was formerly possible to own slaves. In addition to being capable of ownership, the property must also be capable of transfer to another person by sale, by gift, or by succession on the death of the owner.

In another sense, property may be used to describe the relationship existing between a person and a thing, and the rights that the person has over the thing. Property in this sense means ownership. Thus when the Sale of Goods Act refers to the property in goods, it means the ownership of goods. For clarity, 'property' will normally be used to describe the things themselves, and 'ownership' will be used for the rights over them.

Ownership and possession

Both ownership and possession describe the relationship which exists between a person and an item of property. Ownership is a question of law while possession is more a matter of fact.

Ownership exists when the right or rights in respect of property are recognized and protected by law. The owner has the right to use and enjoy, to destroy, or to dispose of by sale or gift. The law may have restricted these rights in the interests of other people, as when I am prevented from using my land in a way that causes a nuisance to my neighbour. The owner may have granted certain rights to others, as when I grant a right of way over my land and must respect this. Subject to these qualifications, however, ownership means that all the rights relating to the property are vested by law in the owner. Proof of ownership depends upon the nature of the property. It may be evidenced by some form of title deed, but in many cases it depends upon possession.

Possession is the older concept since it is more obvious. It requires both the power of control over a thing and the intention to maintain that control. The degree of control and the necessary intention depend upon the nature of the thing. For example, I have possession of the pen in my pocket; I have possession of my car in the street outside, the keys to which are in my pocket; and I have possession of my house and the goods inside it even though I am away from home. In all of these cases, I have no intention of allowing anyone to take the property away from me.

Possession must be distinguished from mere custody, which is physical possession but without the intention to maintain this. If I hand a book to a friend while I wash my hands, he obtains custody of the book, but possession remains with me.

Possession and ownership of property may be vested in one person. They may also be separated, either unlawfully by theft, or lawfully by a form of letting or hiring. In both instances possession is transferred but the ownership remains with the same person as before.

Possession, in spite of being a matter of fact and subsidiary to ownership, is nevertheless recognized by the law and has legal consequences. It has already been noted that in many instances it is the only evidence of ownership. It is also granted legal recognition, for example, the finder of a lost object normally has a better right to it than anyone except the owner (see Unit 14), and it receives legal protection, for example, by the action of trespass. Finally, in some instances, if possession is continued for a certain period of time, it will develop into either ownership or something which is equivalent to ownership. Thus, wrongful possession of land for 12 years will, subject to certain conditions, give a good title to the possessor.

Real and personal property

The primary distinction in English law is between real property (*realty*) which comprises freehold land, and personal property (*personalty*) which comprises all other forms of property. This is a further example of how the development of English law has been influenced by procedural considerations. Rights to freehold land were enforced by a real action, that is an action to recover the land itself, from the Latin *res* meaning thing. Rights to other forms of property were enforced by an action against the person who had infringed those rights, in order to compel him to pay compensation if he refused to return the property.

Leasehold land stood in an anomalous position. Rights in respect of this were regarded as contractual and were originally enforceable against the person. Hence, even though the action of ejectment, a form of real action, was available to leaseholders as early as the beginning of the sixteenth century, leaseholds were still regarded as a form of personal property. A distinction was, however, made between leaseholds (*chattels real*) and other forms of personal property (*chattels personal*). The word 'chattel', frequently used to describe movable forms of property or goods, comes from the same root as cattle.

This distinction between real and personal property, in particular between freehold and leasehold, was important before 1926. Among other things, the succession to property in the absence of a will depended upon it, since different rules were applied in each case. The property legislation of 1925 largely abolished the necessity for the distinction which thereby became very artificial and caused unnecessary complexity. It would be of more value today if English law were to adopt the classification adopted in most other legal systems and distinguish between immovable property, or property in land, on the one hand, and movable property, or property in chattels, on the other.

Forms of personal property

Movable items of property may take many forms but fall into two main categories:

1. Things in possession (*choses in possession*) are physical or tangible objects which may be enjoyed, transferred, and even recovered from another in their material form. Examples include cars, books, ships, furniture, and animals. It is this type of property with which the Sale of Goods Act 1979 is concerned.
2. Things in action (*choses in action*) are intangible forms of property. They have no physical existence even though ownership of them may be evidenced in some documentary form. They have value and are transferable, but the rights of the owner may only be enforced by action in a court of law.

The nature of things in possession is relatively straightforward but the concept of things in action is sometimes a little more difficult to grasp. It may be of assistance to outline the principal forms: negotiable instruments; patents, trade marks and designs; copyright; company shares; contractual debts; life assurance policies; goodwill.

B. Land

Estates and interests

Rights in respect of land may take many different forms. The collection of rights relating to a particular piece of land is known as an *estate* and these rights determine the extent to which the holder of the estate may deal with the land. The rights of the owner of a freehold estate are outlined later in this unit. (Estate is also used in another sense to describe the property left upon death; Unit 29.)

If the rights relate to the land of another, the holder is said to possess an *interest*. An example of such an interest would be a right of way (see Unit 28).

English land law

Until 1926, English land law was in a very confused state. It still bore the stamp of feudalism which was based upon a system of landholding (tenures) by which everyone was a tenant, the ultimate owner of all land being the Crown. The law was largely judge-made but with some important statutes covering certain aspects.

Many different estates and interests in land existed. Some were legal, recognized by the common law, and others were equitable, protected by the Court of Chancery. Legal rights were rights in respect of the land itself (*in rem*), which could be exercised against anyone, while equitable rights existed against a person (*in personam*). If that person had purchased land in good faith with no knowledge of an existing equitable right, the holder of the right had no remedy. The purchaser's conscience was not affected and there was no justification for equitable intervention. In general, this principle still remains.

In 1925, a number of Acts were passed with the object of simplifying the land law. These Acts, of which the most important was the Law of Property Act, came into effect at the beginning of 1926 and are frequently referred to as the Property Acts or the property legislation of 1925. In the process of simplification there was an attempt to make conveyancing easier, and to this end the number of legal estates was reduced to two—freehold and leasehold—and the number of legal interests to five. All other estates and interests were declared to be equitable and only able to exist behind a trust (Unit 28). In these cases a purchaser can deal with the trustees as legal owners and need not concern himself with the complicated equitable interests.

C. Freehold

Nature of freehold

One form of legal estate existing after 1925 consists of freehold or, to use the more accurate expression, the fee simple absolute in possession. 'Fee' means that the estate can be inherited, and 'simple' denotes that this will take place according to the ordinary rules of succession (Unit 29) and will not pass on death in any special way. 'Absolute' means that the holder has an unconditional right to the estate which will not come to an end upon the happening of some event such as re-marriage. 'In possession' means that the holder is entitled to the land now, and to its rent and profits, and not at a future time when some other estate comes to an end.

The freeholder

Although in theory the Crown is the owner of all land, the holder of a fee simple is the owner for all practical purposes. He is the owner of the land itself, the air space above it and the ground below, in theory to the centre of the earth. He is the owner of any trees or growing crops, any buildings upon the land, and any fixtures which are attached either to the land or to the buildings. He has the right to catch or kill wild animals on the land. He has the right to restrict the right of entry of others and to eject trespassers, by force if

UNIT 27. PROPERTY AND LEGAL ESTATES IN LAND

necessary. He may use, enjoy, waste or neglect the land as he pleases, sell or lease it to others during his lifetime and dispose of it upon death. If the land adjoins the sea, the owner's rights terminate at the normal high water mark and the sea-shore below belongs to the Crown or the person to whom the Crown has granted it.

While the preceding paragraph outlines the general position of a freehold owner, closer examination reveals a number of restrictions upon these apparently unfettered rights. Some of these restrictions may have arisen from an agreement entered into by the owner or a previous owner, for example, the right of another to occupy the land under a lease. Other restrictions, such as the duty not to be a nuisance to neighbours, were imposed by common law. Of greatest importance are the many statutory restrictions which have been imposed, largely during the past 50 years, in the interests of the community as a whole. Social control of land for the public good has tended to take precedence over the rights of individual landowners. These various restrictions are outlined in the next section.

Restrictions on freeholders

No action may be taken in respect of civil aircraft which cross the air space above the land at a reasonable height (Civil Aviation Act 1949). Police officers may enter upon the land itself in order to prevent a breach of the peace or the commission of a serious crime, and in other cases under the authority of a warrant signed by a magistrate. Numerous statutes also give a right of entry of thousands of public officials—sanitary inspectors, planning officers, factory inspectors, inland revenue officers, gas and electricity inspectors, etc.—upon production of written authority to the occupier.

While mineral wealth under the surface normally belongs to the owner, there are exceptions in the case of gold, silver, petroleum, and coal, which belong to the state. Any valuable thing found on the land is subject to the rule of treasure trove (Unit 6). Rights over the land granted to others such as a mortgage, a right of way or a lease must be respected and, in the case of many leases, the freeholder is restricted by statute both as to the rent he can charge and as to his power to evict the tenant. In some instances the tenant even has the right to buy the freehold.

The rights of neighbours must be respected so that their light is not obstructed and their support is not taken away. The freeholder must not commit the tort of nuisance (Unit 14) nor allow the escape of dangerous things under the doctrine of *Rylands* v. *Fletcher* (Unit 14). Free disposal of the land on death is subject to the requirement that adequate provision be made for certain relatives (Unit 29).

Where a non-tidal stream flows in a defined channel through a person's land, above or below the ground, the owner of that land has certain rights in respect of the stream and its water. These are known as riparian rights from the Latin *ripa*, a river bank. The owner of the land is deemed to own the river bed and to have exclusive rights of fishing and navigation except where these have been granted to another. If the stream divides the land of two owners, the boundary is deemed to run down the middle of the stream.

At common law, the riparian owner may abstract water for ordinary purposes connected with his landholding, such as domestic use, even though other owners further down the stream are thereby deprived of water. He may abstract water for extraordinary purposes provided that the water is returned substantially the same in quantity and quality. He may not abstract water for purposes unconnected with the landholding.

In recent years the need to conserve and ensure the proper use of water supplies has led to statutory modification of these common law rights. The Water Resources Acts 1963–68 set up the Water Resources Board which in turn had power to establish river authorities. In most cases a licence is now required from an authority if more than 1000 gallons of water are to be abstracted. Under the Water Act 1973, executive power passed to 10 regional authorities and the central body became the National Water Council with purely advisory functions.

Perhaps the most important statutory interference with an owner's rights in the interests of society generally has come with control of the development and use of land under the Town and Country Planning Acts and related legislation. Planning permission is now required whenever land is to be used for a different purpose and buildings must normally comply with health, building, and housing requirements. Local authorities may make preservation orders protecting trees in the interests of amenity, and buildings which are of special architectural or historic value. Compulsory purchase orders may be made by various public authorities where land is required for public use. Compensation is paid according to specified principles and, in the event of a failure to agree upon the amount, an appeal will lie to the Lands Tribunal, an independent and specialized court for the valuation of land (Unit 6).

D. Leashold

Nature of a lease

The second form of legal estate in land existing after 1925 is leasehold or, more strictly, the *term of years absolute*. 'Term of years' means that the estate is to exist for a definite period of time, perhaps even for less than one year, and 'absolute' denotes that the holding is unconditional and cannot be brought to an end by the landlord or lessor, provided that the terms of the lease are complied with. Unlike a freehold estate, a lease need not exist 'in possession', for it can be agreed that it shall take effect from some future date.

Two essentials are required for a lease. First, the parties must have intended to create the landlord–tenant relationship under which exclusive possession of the property is given to the tenant for the period in question. A mere right to occupy the property is not sufficient. Thus, a lodger occupies his room by licence and not by lease since he does not acquire exclusive possession.

Second, the landlord–tenant relationship must be created for a definite or ascertainable term. This may be a specified period of time in which case the lease will automatically terminate at the end of that time. The period must be fixed in advance so that a lease 'for the duration of the present Parliament' would be void for uncertainty.

Alternatively, there may be a periodic lease on a yearly, quarterly or other basis which continues indefinitely until either party puts an end to it by giving notice. The period of notice required depends upon agreement or, in the absence of agreement, normally upon the period by which the rent is calculated. An exception is that a yearly tenancy, other than for agricultural land, only requires half a year's notice.

A lease to last for more than three years must be created by deed. A lease for a shorter period to take effect immediately may be created by word of mouth, though writing may be desirable for practical reasons. An agreement for a lease, being a contract concerning land, is unenforceable without written evidence or a sufficient act of part performance (Unit 16).

If a lease for more than three years is not created by deed or if there is only an agreement for a lease, the lessee will only receive an equitable and not a legal estate. While he may obtain a decree for specific performance to change this into a legal estate, he will lose this right if, in the meantime, another legal estate is created in favour of a purchaser for value who has no knowledge of the lessee's equitable rights.

Landlord and tenant

The relationship between landlord and tenant (lessor and lessee) has a strong contractual element. The express terms of the lease will depend upon agreement, but be subject to the many statutory restrictions and controls which are imposed today.

Two covenants or terms are normally found in all leases. The covenant to *repair* may impose a duty upon landlord or tenant or upon both of them; the landlord may be responsible for outside repairs, including painting, and the tenant for inside repairs. The standard required is normally that which a reasonable person would adopt for his own property. This depends, among other things, upon the neighbourhood.

The second covenant normally included is a prohibition on *assignment* or *sub-letting* by the tenant. Assignment takes place where the tenant transfers his complete interest to another, and sub-letting where the tenant lets the premises to a sub-tenant for a term shorter than the original lease. The absence of any covenant leaves the tenant free to do either of these things, which the landlord may not want because the assignee or sub-tenant could be undesirable. An absolute prohibition prevents the tenant from doing either, but the covenant is not always so rigid. If the covenant merely prohibits assignment or sub-letting without the landlord's consent, this consent must not be withheld unreasonably. The Race Relations Act 1976 further provides that it is unreasonable to withhold consent on the grounds of colour, race or ethnic origins.

In the absence of express terms, certain implied obligations rest upon the landlord in every lease. The landlord covenants that the tenant will obtain quiet enjoyment of the property and that neither he (the landlord) nor any person claiming through him will disturb that enjoyment. He covenants that he will not allow anything to be done which will prevent the property being used for the purpose for which it was leased. In the case of furnished accommodation, he covenants that it is fit for human habitation at the commencement of the lease.

In return, the tenant covenants to pay the rent and any rates and taxes except those taxes specifically payable by the landlord. He must allow the landlord to enter the premises to ascertain the state of repairs if the landlord is under an obligation to carry out repairs. The tenant must keep the premises in a reasonable state of repair and not cause damage. For breach of covenant, the landlord may bring an action for damages or, as is invariably provided in the lease, for forfeiture of the lease. In addition, for non-payment of rent, the landlord may seize and sell any personal property of the tenant found upon the premises.

During the twentieth century, the increasing pressure upon land and building has led the state to interfere and restrain landlords from taking advantage of their stronger position. Tenants have been protected by control of rents, compensation for improvements, and security of tenure. This statutory interference has applied particularly to residential property; it was largely consolidated in the Rent Act 1977. By the Leasehold Reform Act 1967 certain tenants of houses under long leases were even given the right to buy the freehold and this right was extended to tenants of local authority houses under the Housing Act 1980.

For further consideration

1. It is sometimes said that an Englishman's home is his castle and yet there are many restrictions upon a person's right to do as he pleases with it and in it. Outline these restrictions.

    In each instance, say by whom or by what body the restriction is imposed and suggest why it is imposed.
2. List as many different items of property owned by yourself or other members of your family. Explain in each case how ownership could be proved.
3. Compare the legal position of the owner of a freehold estate with that of the tenant of a leasehold.
4. To what extent is it correct to say that 'real property' and 'personal property' are simply a different way of saying 'land' and 'goods'?
5. Explain briefly
    (a) Compulsory purchase order
    (b) Riparian rights
    (c) Chose in action
    (d) Sub-letting
    (e) Possession

Unit 28. Further Aspects of Property Law

A. Interests in land

Equitable interests

A person may wish to leave his house to his widow for life and, after her death, to his son. The widow will receive a *life* interest, terminated by death, while the son will receive a *future* interest. Neither of these interests can exist as a legal estate in freehold land since the former is not 'absolute' and the latter is not 'in possession'. They may only be created as equitable interests with the use of a trust (see below).

One useful device for creating equitable interests is the *trust for sale*. This arises when the legal estate in land is conveyed to trustees and an absolute duty of sale is imposed upon them. The land is thereby freely transferable and yet the trustees have the power to postpone sale if necessary. The beneficiaries may be given varied and complex interests in the land and the rents and profits arising from it or from the proceeds of the sale. A purchaser on the other hand is only concerned with the relatively simple legal estate vested in the trustees.

In addition to trusts for sale which are expressly created, the Law of Property Act 1925 provides for the creation of certain statutory trusts for sale. The most important arise when land is held by personal representatives following an intestacy (Unit 29) and when land is held by two or more owners.

Easements and profits

Without holding an estate in land, a person may be able to exercise a legal right in respect of that land, for example, by having a right of way across it. These rights are normally attached to the land itself and bind not only the parties at the time of creation but other parties into whose hands the land later passes. Thus the holder for the time being of one plot of land will be able to exercise his right against the holder for the time being of another plot.

An *easement* is a right either to use another's land for a particular purpose or to prevent that other from using the land in a certain way. There may be a right of way on foot, for vehicles or for driving cattle, or a right to abstract or discharge water. The holder of the land may be restrained from obstructing light or the flow of air, or from taking away a right of support to a building.

Easements are sometimes created by statute but more frequently by deed. A person may sell part of his land and expressly reserve a right of way across it. Even without express words a grant may be implied if, for example, the land retained would be inaccessible without the right of way. If the right has been used continuously for a long period of time the law will presume that there has been a grant. Specified periods of time are laid down in the Prescription Act 1832, for example, use of a path as of right for 20 years, without interruption, will normally give a right of way.

A *profit à prendre* is not only the right to use the land of another but also the right to take something from it. Examples include the right to fish, to graze cattle, to shoot, and to take wood. It may be created in the same way as an easement though the prescriptive periods are longer. Another difference is that it may be owned independently of any holding of land.

Restrictive covenants

These are contractual promises not to use land in a particular way, made by one landholder to another. An example would be a promise not to carry on certain trades in order to preserve the amenities of the neighbourhood. These covenants pass with the land and may be enforced by and against subsequent holders. A person attempting to enforce a covenant against someone other than the original promisor must show that it is in substance negative in character and that he holds land which is benefited by it.

> In *Tulk* v. *Moxhay* (1848), the owner of land, which included Leicester Square in London, sold the Square itself but retained some buildings round it. The buyer covenanted not to build on the Square, but later re-sold the land and, after it had passed through several hands, an ultimate purchaser did propose to build. It was held that the original seller could restrain the present purchaser from building, because the present purchaser had taken the land with notice of the restrictive covenant.

Restrictive covenants bear some resemblance to easements in that they impose a restriction upon the right of a landholder to use his land as he pleases. They are both important when land is developed. A restrictive covenant is now an equitable right which may be protected by registration as a land charge (below). It may be modified or removed by the Lands Tribunal if it becomes unnecessary by reason of changes in the character of the neighbourhood.

B. Sale of land

The sale of land raises problems not encountered in the case of sale of goods, some of these problems arising from the nature of the property being dealt with. Land is immovable and there cannot be delivery in the form of a physical handing over; the transaction must, therefore, be carried out with a greater reliance on documents. Land is indestructible and it is more likely that people other than the seller will have an interest in the land and will be able to prove that interest; this imposes a need for greater care and more formality. Land was an early form of wealth which is still in existence; transactions are, therefore, complicated by historical developments, often of an unsystematic nature.

If the need for greater formality, more documents, and inevitably a slower procedure, is accepted, complaints may still be made that these are carried to unnecessary extremes. A common cause of complaint is the lengthy and archaic wording used in the documents. This is said to be due partly to the former, and now unjustifiable, practice of paying conveyancers according to the length of the document, and partly to the more justifiable reason that the phrases used have been accepted by the courts and that it could lead to uncertainty to alter them. In general, it is not possible to reduce land transactions to anything like the relative simplicity of other transactions and, while reforms are possible, the task facing the reformers is an immense one.

The procedure for selling land will be illustrated by examining the various steps in the sale of a private house. This will be looked at from the standpoint of a purchaser since a person's first experience of this transaction normally comes in this capacity.

Preliminary steps in buying a house

The purchaser may deal with the vendor or seller directly, or with an estate agent acting on behalf of the vendor, or less commonly he may buy the house at an auction sale. The commission charged by an estate agent or auctioneer is payable by the vendor. Negotiations may take place between purchaser and vendor until a price is agreed for the house.

An oral agreement at this stage is not legally binding because this is a contract concerning land which is unenforceable in the absence of writing or written evidence (Unit 16). If the purchaser signs a written agreement produced by the estate agent, he should take care that this contains the words 'subject to contract' and, if he pays a small deposit, that the receipt also contains these words (Unit 17). The effect is to leave both parties free to withdraw and the purchaser may also recover his deposit. At the same time it does show that the parties are sufficiently interested to pursue the negotiations further, the vendor is less likely to negotiate with other possible purchasers, and the purchaser has time to enquire into other matters.

The principal matter is likely to be whether or not the purchaser will be able to borrow sufficient money on a mortgage to cover the difference between the price and the amount of money he has available. An approach may be made to a building society which will lend if two requirements are satisfied. First, its valuation of the house must exceed the amount of the loan by a reasonable margin. This is to ensure that if house prices fall and the purchaser defaults it will be able to seize and sell the house and recover its money. Second, the mortgage repayments must not take too large a proportion of the purchaser's income so that a default is more likely. Building societies have working rules which they apply here.

The purchaser may also wish to have the house valued to ascertain both whether the price is a fair one, particularly if he is a newcomer to the district, and whether there are structural defects of which he is not aware. (The seller has no duty to warn the buyer of defects.) The building society valuation is purely for lending purposes and is not available to the purchaser.

The contract of sale

It is at this stage that solicitors are brought in. The parties exchange names of solicitors who then conduct the remainder of the transactions when legal formalities are involved and legally binding obligations entered into. The solicitors' first job is to draw up and agree the contract of sale. The purchaser's solicitor will not, however, conclude this stage until he is satisfied the purchaser has the money to complete the transaction, by mortgage or otherwise.

The parties are free to agree upon terms and it is possible to enter into an 'open' contract which does little more than record the agreement by naming the parties and fixing the price. The law will then imply an obligation upon the vendor to prove his title or right to sell by showing how this has been derived from previous transactions affecting the house (or the land upon which it has been built) for at least the preceding 15 years. In practice, a printed form of contract will be used which incorporates standard terms and conditions of sale published by the Law Society or a local Law Society. In this case, it may be agreed that the title to the property shall begin with a specified previous transaction which is less than 15 years ago. This is not as important as it was before 1969 when the title under an open contract had to go back at least 30 years. A plan will sometimes be attached to the contract showing the boundaries of the property, the extent of obligations to repair boundary fences, the position of roads, sewers and mains services and other such matters.

The contract will be drawn up in two parts, each party signing one part and the contract is concluded by the exchange of parts (or contracts). It is also customary for the purchaser to pay 10 per cent of the price as a deposit. This will be lost if the purchaser later refuses, without justification, to go through with the transaction.

The vendor still remains the legal owner but the contract of sale gives the purchaser an equitable interest in the land. Thenceforth he is entitled to any increase in value and, since he must also bear the risk of loss, he should insure the property. The vendor has a right of lien (right of retention) over the land until he is paid the balance of the purchase money and both vendor and purchaser may protect their rights by registering them as land charges. So far as the purchaser is concerned this effectively prevents the vendor from selling to someone else. If either party now refuses to complete the transaction, the other may compel this by asking a court for a decree of specific performance.

UNIT 28. FURTHER ASPECTS OF PROPERTY LAW

Proving title

After the contract, the vendor must prove that he has a good title to the property and a right to sell it by showing how the land has been dealt with for at least the past 15 years. This is done by the vendor's solicitor providing an abstract of title, which is a summary of the various transactions which have affected it during this period. The actual title deeds are retained until the completion of the purchase. The purchaser has the right to ask written questions regarding the title (requisitions on title) to which written answers will be given.

The need to examine title with every sale of land is cumbersome and expensive. The Land Registration Act 1925 accordingly provided that the title to land could be examined by, and be registered with the State, which would then issue a certificate guaranteeing ownership. Upon sale, the certificate is handed over and the name of the new owner registered. Since this is a much more simple procedure than that outlined in the previous paragraph for unregistered land, the legal fees for the transaction will be less.

Compulsory land registration is now being extended gradually to all local authority areas and the intention is that it will eventually apply to the whole country. This will be a long process, for after registration has been made compulsory in an area, registration of each piece of land is only done when that piece of land changes hands. (Do not confuse registration of title to land with registration of charges affecting land, dealt with below.)

Even though the purchaser is satisfied that the vendor has a good title, it is still necessary to check that no other person has an interest in the property which is likely to affect the sale, for example, the vendor's spouse who is in occupation. In some cases the existence of other interests may have been discovered by the physical inspection which the purchaser will certainly have made. If vacant possession is expected, the presence of 'tenants' in the house should put a purchaser on guard. There may, perhaps, be an obvious right of way across the bottom of the garden. In other cases the abstract of title may reveal that the sale is being made by executors on behalf of the beneficiaries under a trust for sale arising from a will. The purchaser may then safely pay over the money to the executors for it is no concern of his whether the money is then distributed properly among the beneficiaries.

Land charges and other interests

There may still remain other interests for which the Land Charges Act 1925 makes provision. Under this Act, a Register of Land Charges is maintained at the Central Land Registry in London where most equitable rights and a few legal rights must be registered to protect the owners of them. These rights include restrictive covenants, certain types of easements and mortgages and, as a recent addition, the claim of a deserted spouse to the matrimonial home.

If a right is registered, the purchaser is deemed to have knowledge of it and will accordingly be bound by it. A *search* must, therefore, be made of the Registry just before the purchase is completed. This is a comparatively simple matter and is done by the dispatch of a standard form asking for details of any charges against the land specified.

Local authorities are also required to keep a register of such matters as liability to road charges. Registration of these is also equivalent to notice and the purchaser will, therefore, carry out a 'local search' before contract.

The most common form of interest likely to affect the property is a mortgage by the vendor. This may be discovered by the search but is normally revealed by the abstract of title and the fact that the mortgagee will be holding the title deeds and will not part with them until the loan is repaid. Repayment to the mortgagee, usually a building society, will take place as and when the purchase is completed.

The conveyance

When the purchaser is satisfied as to the title of the vendor and the existence of other interests, the transaction is completed. If money is being borrowed on mortgage from, say, a building society, the latter will also have to be satisfied on these matters. In return for the balance of the purchase price, the vendor will hand over the title deeds to the property and the conveyance, either to the purchaser or to the mortgagee if part of the money is borrowed. The *conveyance* is a deed, signed by the vendor, which transfers the ownership of freehold land to the purchaser and which is equivalent to the physical transfer in the case of a sale of goods. If leasehold land is being transferred, this deed is known as an *assignment*. If the land is registered, the deed is a short and simple one and the land certificate is handed over instead of title deeds.

Until 1972 the fees payable to a solicitor for carrying out the above transaction depended upon a scale; the higher the price of the house, the higher the fees. Scale fees have now been abolished and solicitors may charge a fair and reasonable fee for the work involved. If a client feels that the fee is too high he may require the solicitor to obtain a certificate from the Law Society stating that the fee is fair.

C. Trusts

Nature of a trust

A trust arises when the owner of property, real or personal, is obliged to deal with that property, not for his own purposes, but for the benefit of another or others. The person creating a trust is the settlor, the owner upon whom the obligation is imposed is the trustee, and the person to benefit is the beneficiary. It is possible for one person to occupy two, or even all, of these positions. Thus a settlor may transfer property to himself and another in trust for himself and the rest of his family.

The trust arose in the Middle Ages partly as a device to avoid the feudal dues which were payable when property passed to another on death. By vesting the legal ownership in a number of trustees who could be replaced individually when they died, continuous ownership of property was obtained. The common law did not recognize the trust and regarded the trustees as legal owners, but the Court of Chancery acted on the conscience of the trustees and compelled them to administer the property on behalf of the beneficiaries. A distinction was thereby drawn between legal ownership and beneficial or equitable ownership.

The trust is one of the notable characteristics of English law and is perhaps the most important contribution made by equity. Its principal use was originally for family settlements but its flexibility, and the possibility of its application to different situations, has led to the extension of its use to many other fields, including business. The trust is used today to confer property rights upon those who cannot hold property legally, for instance, children—even those not yet born. It is used for charitable purposes. It is a useful device where property is owned by a large number of people such as an unincorporated association. It is used for the purpose of winding up the estate of a deceased person.

In general, the trust may be used for any purpose which is not illegal or contrary to public policy. Thus, a trust created to defraud creditors will be set aside. Any form of property may form the subject-matter of a trust. The earlier trusts were largely confined to land but other forms of property such as assurance policies and shares are now frequently used.

Private trusts

Trusts may be expressly created by deed or other document in writing or, less frequently, orally. In general, no particular form is required except where land is concerned, when written evidence and the signature of the settlor are necessary. Additional requirements may be necessary in certain cases, for example, a trust created by will must comply with the essentials required for a valid will (Unit 29).

A valid trust requires three certainties—of words, of subject-matter, and of objects. *Certainty of words* means that the settlor has clearly indicated that a trust is to be created. It is not sufficient to give property to A 'in the hope that he will provide for B'; there must be a clear intention by the use of such words as 'in trust for B'. In the absence of certainty of words, A will take the property beneficially and not as a trustee. *Certainty of subject-matter* means that the property in question must be clearly defined. *Certainty of objects* means a clear description of the beneficiaries or the method by which they are to be ascertained.

Once a valid trust has been completely constituted by a transfer of the property to the trustees or by a declaration of the settlor that he will henceforth act as trustee of the property, it may not normally be revoked. Revocation is only possible if the settlor has reserved to himself the right to do this. If there has been misrepresentation, mistake or duress and the parties can be restored to their original positions, the settlor may apply to the court to have the trust set aside.

Implied trusts may arise where the law presumes the existence of a trust from the conduct of the parties and the other circumstances of the transaction. If the objects of a trust fail, a trust will be implied for the benefit of the settlor. If one person advances money to another for the purchase of property and there is no evidence to the contrary, the purchaser is deemed to be trustee of that property for the benefit of the party who provided the money. (There is no such presumption, however, where the money is advanced by husband to wife or by parent to child; a gift is presumed in these circumstances.) If a person receives property from a trustee knowing that it is trust property and without giving valuable consideration for it, it will be implied that the property is held by that person as trustee.

Public (charitable) trusts

The legal definition of a charity differs a little from the everyday meaning of the word. It has been held that a trust will only be charitable if it has one of four purposes—the relief of poverty, the advancement of education, the advancement of religion, and other purposes beneficial to the community. (It is not surprising that the last of these objects particularly has caused considerable litigation.) There must in addition be an element of public benefit, except where the relief of poverty is concerned.

A charitable trust is, therefore, a public trust with the object of conferring benefit upon the public generally or upon some section of it. It must not be a private trust for the benefit of one individual or a small group of persons. The trust must be exclusively charitable with no possibility of applying any of the property for non-charitable purposes.

Charitable trusts differ from private trusts in a number of ways. They are enforced, where necessary, not by the beneficiaries, but by the Attorney-General acting for the public. They are exempt from a complex rule of law (the rule against perpetuities) which prevents property from being subject to a trust for an indefinite period of time. Perhaps the most important reason in practice for claiming that a trust is charitable is that income applied exclusively to charitable purposes is exempt from income tax.

A charitable trust will not fail for uncertainty of objects provided that it can be shown that the settlor had a general charitable intention. If this is so and it is impossible to attain this object, for example, the named charity may have ceased to exist, the property will be applied as near as can be (*cy près*) to some other charity with similar purposes.

The law relating to charitable trusts was amended by the Charities Act 1960. A Register of Charities is now maintained and there are three Charity Commissioners with power to supervise such trusts by examining accounts, authorizing schemes for dealing with trust property, and taking or authorizing legal proceedings where necessary.

Trustees

Most of the rules governing the appointment, powers, duties, and discharge of trustees are contained in the Trustee Act 1925. The settlor will usually name the trustees or make some other provision for their appointment. Any person with full legal capacity may be a trustee. In general, there is no limit to the number but, where land is concerned, there must be at least two to give a valid receipt to a purchaser and not more than four.

The appointment of additional trustees, if not provided for in the trust instrument, may be done by the existing trustee(s) or by the personal representatives of the last one to die. In the last resort, the power of appointment rests with the court. A person may refuse the appointment but, once he has embarked upon his duties, he may only retire with the consent of the other trustees. In certain specified circumstances a trustee may be replaced.

The difficulties associated with death or retirement of trustees may be overcome by the appointment of a trust corporation, recognized as such under the Trustee Act 1925; the trustee departments of banks are examples. Considerable funds are then available to guarantee the trust property and a trust corporation may act alone when two individual trustees would otherwise be required. Fees are charged for their services which may seem high in the case of a small trust.

Duties of trustees

These duties, often detailed in the trust instrument, may vary considerably, ranging from the simple duty of transferring property to a beneficiary at one extreme to extensive duties of management of property and investment of trust funds at the other. The terms of the trust must be strictly complied with and any variations approved by all the beneficiaries or sanctioned by the court.

Unless the trust instrument provides otherwise, all property must be converted into investments authorized by statute. Proper audited accounts must be kept. Delegation of duties is not allowed except where it is usual to appoint a specialist, such as a solicitor.

The trustee must not put himself in a position where his own personal interests clash with those of the trust. Thus he can only sell to or buy from the trust in very exceptional circumstances. He must not make a profit out of the trusteeship or use trust property for his own purpose. While he may recover reasonable expenses, he is not entitled to any remuneration for his services unless this is provided for. For this reason, trust corporations and professional people who act as trustees will insist upon the insertion of a charging clause in the trust instrument.

These duties can be very onerous and any breach, however innocent, constitutes a breach of trust and makes the trustee personally liable. In cases of doubt, a trustee may apply to the court for directions. In addition, he may claim from a beneficiary, who has instigated a breach of trust, or from the other trustees who are jointly liable with him. Finally, the court has the power to relieve a trustee from personal liability where he acted honestly and reasonably in the circumstances and ought to be excused.

Beneficiaries

Any person may be a beneficiary under a trust. Thus, a minor may thereby enjoy the equitable or beneficial ownership of land when he is not entitled to legal ownership. Notwithstanding the terms of the trust instrument, the beneficiaries may put an end to the trust at any time and demand that the property be transferred to them provided that they are of full age and that no other person has an interest in the property.

The beneficiaries may apply to the court if a trustee is not complying with the terms of the trust and, if necessary, bring a personal action for breach of trust against him. Trust property which has passed into the hands of others may be recovered except where it has been purchased for value without notice of the trust. This right of recovery applies even if the property has been converted into some other form provided that it remains identifiable. An action for breach of trust must normally be brought within six years.

For further consideration

1. (a) What is a charity? Criticize the legal definition.
   (b) What problems are likely to arise when a disaster causes the death of a number of people and a public appeal is made for contribution to a fund to help dependants?
2. (a) Outline the principal stages in the transfer of a house.
   (b) The legal procedure followed in the transfer of a house is often criticized as being too slow and too complicated. In what ways, if at all, could this procedure be simplified?
3. Are there any easements, *profits a prendre* or restrictive covenants affecting the house in which you live or your neighbourhood? Can you suggest any circumstances in which these rights might be created?
4. Explain briefly
   (a) Abstract of title
   (b) Life interest
   (c) Registered land
   (d) Implied trust
   (e) Trust for sale

Unit 29: Succession on Death

A. Testate succession

Nature and effect of a will

English law allows a person in his lifetime certain freedom to state who is to succeed to his property after his death. A will is the document in which such intentions are incorporated, the maker of a will being called the testator, from the Latin *testamentum* meaning a will. In addition to disposing of property, a will may include other legally binding instructions such as the appointment of executors or of guardians for children. An instruction regarding burial or the gift of the body for research may be respected but need not necessarily be complied with.

The will takes effect only upon death and until then it may be revoked either completely or partially. The property referred to is the property existing at death, which may be more or less than that existing at the time the will was made. The possibility of revocation or of diminution in the property makes an attempt to borrow money on the strength of benefits expected under a will a doubtful proposition.

Any person may benefit under a will with two exceptions. The first, to prevent fraud, is a witness, or the husband or wife of a witness; this rule was relaxed by the Wills Act 1968 which allows a witness to benefit provided that two other independent witnesses have attested the will. The second, for obvious reasons, is a person who was responsible for causing the death of the testator by homicide, such a person also being excluded from benefit from his victim's estate even where there is no will.

Property need not be left to a person at all. It may be left to some cause, or for some purpose, but only if this is charitable. Gifts for non-charitable purposes *may* be carried out by the personal representatives, but are unenforceable if the personal representatives choose not to carry out the testator's wishes. If the testator fears that this might happen, he can leave the property to a person on condition that the property be applied for the purpose specified, with a provision that the property shall pass to another if the testator's wishes are not fulfilled.

If the person to whom property was left, the beneficiary, dies before the testator, the gift to him normally *lapses*, and the property goes instead to whoever is entitled to the residue of the estate. There is one major exception to this: there is presumed to be no lapse if the dead beneficiary was a child of the testator, and left children or grandchildren alive at the testator's death. In such a case, the property will go to whoever was entitled under the beneficiary's will or intestacy.

The *commorientes* rule provides that, if two people die together and it is not certain who died first, the younger is presumed to have survived the elder. Thus if the testator and a younger spouse should die together in an accident the property could pass immediately into the family of the spouse contrary to what the testator would probably have intended. To prevent this, wills normally provide that gifts to the spouse shall only take effect if he or she survives the testator by 28 days, after which time the likelihood of both dying from the same accident is remote.

In practice, people are often unwilling to accept the inevitability of death and postpone the task of making a will until it is too late. This can be unwise. Apart from enabling the testator to choose who shall be entitled on his death, a carefully drafted will may bring substantial savings in taxation. Even if the testator is not very rich, his estate can be augmented considerably by an award of damages if death is caused by negligence. Legal advice is desirable in drawing up a will. Home-made wills, even on the standard will forms on sale to the general public, frequently contain drafting errors which may give rise to costly litigation and endless problems.

Requirements for a valid will

The formalities required for the execution of a valid will are contained in the Wills Act 1837, as subsequently amended:

1. *Writing*. A will must be in writing. Provided that it is clear, it does not matter what the testator writes on, and instances have occurred of eccentric testators using an eggshell or the side of a Dutch cheese. It is possible to refer to another existing and identifiable document, as when property is left to X for distribution in accordance with a list of bequests notified to X separately.
2. *Signature*. The testator must sign the will or otherwise acknowledge it by some mark; if he is unable to do this, it may be signed by some other person in his presence and acting on his instructions. The signature must be 'at the foot or end thereof' and anything added below the signature is of no effect.
3. *Witnesses*. Two witnesses must be present together when the testator signs or, if he has signed earlier, when he acknowledges his signature.

   In *Re Colling* (1972), the will of a hospital patient was held invalid when one of the witnesses, a nurse, was called away to attend to another patient after the testator had begun to write her name but before she had finished doing so.

   The two witnesses must then sign the will in the testator's presence. They are usually also in each other's presence when they sign, but this is not necessary unless there is an *attestation clause* which claims that they were. An attestation clause is a special form of words normally inserted before the signatures in order to raise a presumption that the statutory requirements have been met, whereupon a court will not normally require further proof of attestation. Since the process of attestation is to authenticate the testator's signature, the witnesses do not need to know the contents of the will. The restrictions upon a witness receiving any benefit under a will were noted above.

An additional requirement is that the testator shall have testamentary capacity, the power by law to make a will. He must be over the age of 18, of sound mind, and not influenced by coercion or fraud.

The above formal requirements do not apply to members of the Forces on active military service or to mariners at sea. Provided such a person is 14, any clear indication of his wishes regarding the disposal of his property after death, even made orally, is valid. Such an informal will remains valid after return to civilian life.

Family provision

Many legal systems require a person to provide for his family and dependants and only allow free disposal of a proportion of his estate. In England, testators had complete freedom until 1938 and disappointed dependants could only contest the validity of the will itself, for example, on grounds of the insanity of the testator.

The Inheritance (Provision for Family and Dependants) Act 1975 gives certain dependants a right to maintenance from a deceased person's estate. Claims may only be made by the spouse of the deceased, children (including both adopted and illegitimate), a 'child of the family' and any other person who was wholly or partially dependent upon the deceased at the date of death. The claim is based upon lack of sufficient provision by the deceased and must be made within six months from the first grant of representation to the estate, though the court may extend this period if it would operate unfairly.

The court has a wide discretion in fixing the amount of the award, if any, in determining what would be sufficient to enable the dependant to live comfortably according to his or her station in life. It will take account of the means of the claimants, both from the estate and other sources, and also their conduct towards the deceased. A man may be justified in leaving his wife nothing if her behaviour towards him in his lifetime was intolerable. To prevent the evidence on such matters being too one-sided, it is possible for a testator to make a signed statement of his reasons for leaving his family little or nothing. This is usually sealed in an envelope and retained by his solicitor in case a claim is made under the Act. There may even be an application in the estate of a well-meaning testator if, for example, there has been a provision of a gift of shares and the shares have fallen in value after the death of the testator.

The court has wide powers to make income and capital settlements and order the transfer or purchase of property. Dispositions made to avoid this legislation may be set aside. The basis of financial provision for a spouse is the same as in the case of a divorce; the criteria for other claimants is maintenance.

Alteration or revocation of a will

A will cannot be made irrevocable and a testator has by law the right to change his mind. A small alteration, for example, the addition or deletion of one legacy, may be done by the addition of another clause to the will. This supplement or postscript, known as a *codicil*, must be signed and witnessed in the same way as the will itself.

It may be written on the will itself or on a separate sheet. The same effect is achieved if the will itself is altered, but again the change must be signed and witnessed, otherwise the alterations are ignored and the original will stands.

There are several ways in which the entire will may be revoked:

1. *Express revocation.* A will may be revoked by an express statement to this effect, properly executed and attested. Such a statement usually forms the first clause of any new will which is intended to replace the old one.
2. *Implied revocation by a new will.* Even if a new will does not contain an express revocation clause, it will impliedly revoke an earlier will in so far as the two are inconsistent. If the later will is revoked, this does not revive the earlier one.
3. *Destruction with intent to revoke.* A will is revoked if the testator himself, or someone in his presence and at his request, destroys it with intent at the time thereby to revoke it. Destruction can include 'burning, tearing or otherwise destroying'. The testator must intend to revoke the will. If the destruction is accidental, the will stands and other evidence (such as carbon copies) will be admitted as to its contents.
4. *Subsequent marriage.* If the testator marries, this automatically revokes all previous wills. The only major exception to this is a will expressly made in contemplation of the marriage; such a will survives the marriage only if the future wife or husband is referred to expressly, and the will is clearly intended to survive this marriage. A will may be revived after marriage by a properly executed and attested codicil, provided that the original will has not been destroyed. In fact, with this proviso, a codicil may be used to revive any will.

B. Intestate succession

Intestacy

The Administration of Estates Act 1925, as subsequently amended, provides for the distribution of property when a person dies intestate, that is, without making a valid will. The property passes upon trust for sale to the personal representatives, who are charged with payment of all debts and expenses before distribution according to the intestacy rules.

These rules, drawn up following an examination of a large number of wills then

UNIT 29. SUCCESSION ON DEATH

held at Somerset House, attempt to dispose of the property in the way the deceased may have been expected to do if he had made a will. Some provision for a surviving husband or wife is probable and then, to keep the property in the family, equal shares to any children. If there are no children, close blood relations might be expected to benefit. However, even though the rules are statutory, their application cannot prevent a claim under the family provisions legislation (above) by an aggrieved dependant.

The rules outlined below show how these assumptions are put into effect.

Manner of distribution

The *surviving husband or wife* is entitled to all personal goods such as clothing, jewellery, and furniture. This will not include houses, money, investments or any business effects. Thus, the wife could claim the family car but not the van used for business purposes.

If there are children, the surviving spouse will also receive £40 000 absolutely, free of estate duty and carrying interest at 4 per cent from the date of death until payment. If the estate is less, he or she will receive everything. If the estate is more, he or she will receive in addition a life interest in half the remainder.

If there are no children, the spouse is entitled to £85 000 absolutely and one-half of any residue absolutely, instead of only a life interest in it. If there are no children and no parents or brothers and sisters of the whole blood, the spouse will take the entire estate absolutely.

Where there are children, creation of a life interest in favour of the spouse prevents the estate being wound up and can cause complications, particularly with small estates. Accordingly, the spouse may, within 12 months, claim a capital sum instead of an annual income. Another right normally open to the spouse is to claim the matrimonial home as part of the share of the estate taken absolutely.

The *commorientes* rule (see above) is excluded by statute in so far as intestacies are concerned. If the testator and a younger spouse die together and it is uncertain who died first, there is a presumption that the spouse did not survive the intestate. None of the above rights of the spouse will then take effect.

Children of the deceased, including adopted and illegitimate children, will ultimately succeed to the estate in equal shares, subject to any life interest of the spouse; the capital providing this life interest will only be available for distribution to the children on the death of the spouse. The property to which they are entitled will be held on trust for them until they become 18 or marry, but in the meantime reasonable sums may be made available for their maintenance, education or such other purposes as assistance with beginning a career. If one or more of the children has received a substantial sum during the lifetime of the deceased, for instance to start a business, this must be taken into account in calculating the shares. If a child has died before the intestate, leaving children of his own, these grandchildren will represent their deceased parent and share equally the proportion to which their parent would have been entitled.

Other relatives may claim the estate if there are no children, subject of course to the rights of the surviving spouse. There is an order of priority beginning with parents; if neither is alive, then brothers and sisters of the whole blood; then brothers and sisters of the half-blood; grandparents; uncles and aunts of the whole blood; uncles and aunts of the half-blood. If any of these relatives are dead, their children will take their place before anyone in the next category. If there are no relatives at all within these categories, the estate passes to the Crown.

A *partial intestacy* can arise where the testator's will does not dispose of all of his property. A will normally makes various specific gifts, and then names someone to whom all the rest or residue of the testator's property shall go. A partial intestacy will arise where, for example, there is no residuary gift of all the property, or where the person to whom the residue is left dies before the testator so that the gift lapses. The above intestacy rules then apply to the property not effectively disposed of by the will, but account is taken of anything already received by the beneficiaries under the will.

C. Administration of estates

Personal representatives

The property of a deceased person does not pass immediately to those entitled, whether by will or intestacy. The property vests first in the personal representatives of the deceased, so-called because they represent the deceased. In brief, their duties are to collect in anything due to the estate, to pay any death duties, to pay any creditors, and to distribute any balance among the beneficiaries entitled.

There are two kinds of personal representatives, executors and administrators. *Executors* are appointed by the testator in his will and their right to act is confirmed when they prove, that is obtain *probate* of, the will. *Administrators* are appointed by the court and their authority is derived from the grant to them of *letters of administration*.

Executors

An executor is usually appointed expressly by the will or by a codicil. He may be appointed by implication, as when a person is nominated to pay debts, while anyone who meddles with the estate of a deceased person is liable to find himself burdened with the responsibilities of executorship. An executor may benefit under a will, but unless there is a clear indication to the contrary, any legacy to an executor will be payable only if he accepts the office.

A person is not compelled to accept the duties of executorship but, in order to renounce these, he should file a written statement to this effect with the Probate Registry and take an oath that he has not interfered in any way with the estate. Once he has accepted office he cannot resign. It is possible for a sole executor, who may be a trust corporation, to be appointed. The number to whom probate will be granted is limited to four and, while minors may be appointed, they cannot obtain probate until 18.

If an executor dies, the remaining executors will continue to act. If the sole surviving executor dies, he will be succeeded by his own executor who will then administer both estates. This *chain of representation* will continue until an executor dies without making a further appointment when the court must be asked to appoint an administrator. The court also has power to remove an executor, for example, for unreasonable delay in carrying out his duties.

An executor can begin his duties immediately after the testator's death without any formal act and would be advised to do so to safeguard the estate. An inventory of assets is desirable, and there is an obligation to make appropriate funeral arrangements. The old practice of formally reading the will after the funeral is now virtually obsolete. An executor cannot dispose of any property before grant of probate, a document issued under the seal of the court accepting that the will is valid and confirming his right to act.

Where no dispute is probable, an application for probate 'in common form' is largely a formality, and is made to either the Principal Probate Registry in London or to a District Probate Registry, found in most large towns. Small estates with a net value not exceeding £1500, and in some circumstances higher amounts, may be dealt with without application for probate. If the grant is likely to be opposed, an application for probate 'in solemn form' will be heard in the High Court or, if the net estate does not exceed £30 000, in the County Court.

Application for probate must be accompanied by the will, an Inland Revenue Account setting out the value of the estate for the purpose of death duties, and an Executor's Oath in the form of an affidavit containing a sworn promise to administer the estate according to law. The net value of the estate may be liable to Capital Transfer Tax and the grant of probate cannot be obtained until the amount due has been paid.

Certain fees are payable and, if all is in order, a photocopy of the will is given to the executor who can then proceed with his duties. The original will is retained at the Registry. A grant of probate may be revoked later if, for example, it was improperly obtained or irregularly issued, of if a later will is discovered.

Administrators

An administrator is appointed by the court either upon an intestacy, or if a will fails to appoint executors, or if the appointed executors are unwilling or unable to act. If an administrator dies, the court must make a new appointment.

Letters of administration are granted to those considered by the court to be the most suitable persons with an interest in the estate. The grant is normally made according to the order of priority for benefit. If several people in the same class apply, the grant will be made to the first applicant and notice of the grant given to the others. A grant may be made to a creditor if the estate is likely to be insolvent.

The procedure for obtaining a grant follows similar lines to that outlined above for probate. An administration bond guaranteeing proper distribution is no longer necessary but the court may require sureties for this purpose.

A grant of letters of administration empowers the administrator to act. If there is a will, the grant is made 'with will attached' and distribution must be made according to the will. Otherwise the intestacy rules must be followed. The other rules outlined above relating to executors—liability for interfering with an estate, capacity and numbers and the revocation of a grant—largely apply also to administrators.

Winding up an estate

The powers and liabilities of personal representatives are largely contained in the Administration of Estates Act 1925 and the Trustee Act 1925. Their position is akin to that of trustees, since they must not make a profit out of their work and may claim only expenses. Remuneration may, however, be received if there is a charging clause in the will authorizing this, if the court authorizes it, or if the beneficiaries agree. They will be personally liable if they fail to perform their duties properly, for example, if property is distributed to beneficiaries when known debts have not been met. In cases of difficulty they may apply to the court for directions and they may be relieved from liability by the court if they have acted honestly and reasonably and ought fairly to be excused.

Personal representatives are normally expected to wind up an estate in one year. This may not always be possible if, for instance, shares have to be sold over a long period to prevent the price falling. While the administration should be carried out as far as possible without interference, any interested party who is dissatisfied with what is being done may apply to the court at any time.

The first duty is to ascertain and collect in the assets. This may include the collection of debts or the enforcement of rights by legal action, for example, contractual rights not extinguished by death.

The second duty is to pay all debts and satisfy any other liabilities of the estate. Advertisement in the *London Gazette* and a local newspaper specifying a time limit for claims may be desirable as a safeguard against liabilities becoming apparent later after the estate has been distributed. If the estate is insolvent, funeral expenses and costs of administration must be paid first and other debts according to the scale of priorities laid down in the bankruptcy rules. Thus rates, taxes, and wages owed will take preference over ordinary trade debts.

Finally, the remainder of the property must be distributed according to the will or the intestacy rules. Since the property is held on trust for sale, the personal representatives have the power of sale but may postpone sale should this be desirable.

For further consideration

1. Mort dies intestate leaving a widow, a son, Simon, who is aged 17 and unmarried, and two grandchildren, Jack and Jill, who are the children of another son who had died two years earlier at the age of 25.

    The estate consists of a car (value £5000), personal effects (£2000), and other assets (£40 000).

    How will his estate be divided?

2. Write a letter to your father explaining why it is desirable for him to make a will. Outline what he should bear in mind when doing so and give him any other information which you consider to be relevant.
3. Your friend has asked you if you will be an executor of his will. What are your duties if you accept?
4. To what extent may a person dispose of his property by will to whomsoever he pleases?
5. Explain briefly
   (a) Partial intestacy
   (b) Chain of representation
   (c) Codicil
   (d) *Commorientes* rule
   (e) Attestation of a will

Unit 30. The Law in Practice

Many problems arising under English law cannot be fitted neatly into compartments and considered only as a breach of contract, or as a crime, or as a question of procedure. In many instances it is necessary to draw upon a number of branches of law in order to ascertain all the legal implications of the situation. The consequences of a simple everyday incident may be very far-reaching indeed.

This final unit will, therefore, deal with two common types of situation involving socially undesirable conduct—causing an accident and selling defective goods. It will be seen that the law first attempts to prevent such conduct by legislation and sets up machinery to enforce the statutory rules. The sanctions of the criminal law are used to punish offenders and thereby try to prevent repetition of the offences.

The civil law is the principal instrument by which the victims are compensated, although the liability to pay damages may provide an additional incentive for likely offenders to comply with the law. A system of insurance, compulsory or voluntary, is frequently used to ensure that the victims actually receive the compensation awarded by the courts. On the other hand, if the insurance enables the offender to avoid his civil liability in return for a fixed premium, the incentive to comply with the law is reduced unless misconduct affects the amount of the premium.

The right to compensation may depend upon the victim proving that the wrongdoer was at fault. Moreover, in the case of accidents, the delays involved in civil litigation may leave the plaintiff without means for months or even years until the hearing and all appeals are concluded. The state social security legislation which provides the victim with immediate financial aid from public funds in the event of industrial injury, sickness or unemployment must, therefore, also be considered.

A. Accidents—the problems

Consider the facts of two accidents:

1. Marsh is driving along a narrow winding road. Soulsby approaches from behind at

a fast speed and, impatient of the possible delay, overtakes on a bend. A vehicle coming in the opposite direction causes Soulsby to cut back sharply in front of Marsh and the two cars collide. The cars are damaged, Marsh receives personal injuries and a lamp post is knocked over.
2. Machine operators employed by Dark Satanic Mills Ltd, who are paid on a piecework basis, find that they can work faster and earn more money if guards are removed from the machines. The company issues orders to all workers forbidding this practice and specifically instructs Soulsby, its foreman, that his duty is to see that the guards are used at all times. On one occasion Marsh operates his machine without a guard and Soulsby takes no action. A piece of the metal which is being worked on the machine breaks away and is thrown out. Marsh is hit in the eye and he loses the sight of that eye.

B. Prevention and criminal sanctions

Regulation of road traffic

Most of the relevant legislation on this topic has now been consolidated in the Road Traffic Act 1972. There is, in addition, a large volume of delegated legislation covering matters of detail. Much of this emanates from the responsible Ministry and applies to the whole country, for example, the Construction and Use Regulations, designed to ensure that vehicles are safely constructed and properly maintained. Some regulations of a more limited application are made by local authorities, for example, restricting the use of certain roads for passage or parking. Further guidance to road users is contained in the Highway Code and, while a failure to observe this is not an offence, such a failure may be used by a party in criminal or civil proceedings to support his case.

Thus drivers are controlled by a system of driving tests and driving licences. The safety of vehicles is regulated by test certificates and requirements regarding parts such as tyres and brakes, Excise licences control vehicle ownership and provide a source of revenue. The free flow of traffic is ensured by traffic lights, various road signs, and restrictions on parking. The safe movement of vehicles is attempted by the imposition of speed limits and the prohibition of careless driving and driving when under the influence of drink. Finally, if an accident occurs and a person is injured, the law attempts to ensure compensation by requiring that all drivers should be insured against third party risks, that is, the risk of personal injury to any person caused by the use of the vehicle on the road. Most policies also cover damage to other vehicles but this is not compulsory by law.

The enforcement of these preventive regulations is primarily in the hands of the police. The present volume of traffic means that checks can only be carried out on a sample basis and, when a driver is stopped for one offence, the opportunity is usually taken to investigate other matters. Thus, following a speeding offence, the driving licence and insurance certificate must be produced and, following an accident at night, the parties involved may be required to take a breathalyser test. For minor offences, the police have discretion as to whether to issue a warning or to prosecute and, if it is to be the latter, the actual prosecution in a Magistrates' Court is frequently conducted by a police officer.

Criminal proceedings following a road accident

With the object of mitigating the consequences of a road accident, the law imposes a duty to stop and furnish particulars in the case of an accident causing personal injury or damage to another vehicle or to an animal. This applies in Soulsby's case, since Marsh is injured and his car is damaged, but no such duty exists in respect of the lamp post. If Soulsby drives on through panic or because he does not realize that there has been an impact, he will escape liability for this offence if he reports the accident to the police with 24 hours. Furthermore, since personal injury has been caused, Soulsby must in any case report the accident and produce his certificate of insurance to the police or he will have committed another offence.

The police will investigate the accident, examining the driving licences and insurance certificates of the parties involved and taking statements from these parties and any witnesses. The vehicles will be examined and a plan made of the scene of the accident showing road measurements. Soulsby, the likely offender, must be warned at the time that he may be prosecuted or he must be served with a summons or a notice of intended prosecution within 14 days.

Soulsby will probably be charged with driving without due care and attention and further charges may be added if his driving documents are not in order or if his vehicle is found to have dangerous or unsafe parts. The more serious charge of reckless driving, which was formerly referred to as dangerous driving, may be preferred if the circumstances of the case justify this. If Marsh's injuries are fatal, Soulsby may even be charged with causing death by reckless driving, an offence introduced in 1956 because of the reluctance of juries to convict for manslaughter. If Soulsby is found, by blood or urine test, to have an alcohol content above the prescribed limit, he may also be prosecuted for this offence.

Criminal proceedings will begin by the service of a summons upon Soulsby specifying the charge or charges which he must answer. Most prosecutions for road traffic offences, including the offence of careless driving, are dealt with in a Magistrates' Court where Soulsby may either contest the charges or plead guilty by letter or by personal appearance. The more serious offence of reckless driving may be tried either summarily or on indictment and, if the court decides that the case is suitable for summary trial, Soulsby may then agree to give up his right to trial by jury. Causing death by reckless driving, maximum sentence five years, can only be tried in the Crown Court.

Sanctions

The usual penalty for a road traffic offence such as careless driving is a fine and only in extreme circumstances, for example, a number of previous convictions, is a term of imprisonment likely to be imposed. In addition, a court has important powers designed to deter or prevent an offender from future violations of road traffic regulations.

In the case of most 'moving' traffic offences, the offender's driving licence will be endorsed with the details of the offence. The conviction is thereby recorded and, if a further offence is committed, a heavier penalty is likely, Furthermore, if three endorsements are obtained in three years, the offender will be disqualified from driving for six months unless the court exercises its discretion to mitigate this on such grounds as special hardship.

Disqualification from driving for a specified period is reserved for more serious offences. For some offences such as 'drink-driving' it is compulsory; for others such as careless driving it is discretionary. If a court has doubts about the offender's ability to drive, perhaps because of old age, it may disqualify him until he passes a driving test.

If Marsh is a witness in the proceedings against Soulsby he will, of course, receive expenses. The criminal proceedings, however, will provide him with no compensation either for his injuries or for the damage to his car. Compensation for road traffic accidents is specifically excluded from the new powers of criminal courts to award compensation by the Powers of Criminal Courts Act. Motoring offences are also excluded from the Criminal Injuries Compensation Scheme. Marsh must seek redress in a civil court.

Industrial safety

Protective legislation for factory workers is contained in a number of statutes, of which the most important are the Health and Safety at Work etc. Act 1974 and the Factories Act 1961. These lay down a general framework for ensuring the health, safety, and welfare of factory workers, and empower the Ministry responsible to provide for specific matters of detail by delegated legislation. Furthermore, codes of practice, similar in effect to the Highway Code, have been introduced under the Health and Safety at Work etc. Act.

The enforcement of occupational safety legislation is primarily a matter for inspectorates under the general control of the Health and Safety Executive. Inspectors have wide powers to enter factories and to examine records and persons to ascertain whether the Acts are being complied with. They are also authorized to conduct proceedings in Magistrates' Courts.

Any person occupying a factory must notify the inspectorate at least one month before beginning to do so. There is then the right to inspect the premises but, in view of the large number of factories, this is likely to be exercised only about once every four years. The policy of the inspectorate is education and persuasion, with a criminal prosecution as a measure of last resort. Certain accidents must be notified by the occupier and the more serious ones are likely to be investigated and perhaps followed by a prosecution.

Criminal proceedings following a factory accident

Since Marsh's injury will almost certainly prevent him from earning full wages from his present job for more than three days, the accident must be reported. If Dark Satanic Mills Ltd is prosecuted and convicted, the usual penalty imposed is a fine. There are additional preventive sanctions in the Act by which the court may order the occupier to put right the contravention within a specified time or even to close down part or all of the factory until this has been done; these powers are not used frequently and would not be appropriate in the situation under consideration.

The employer may escape liability if he can prove that he has used all due diligence to enforce the Act and that the offence occurred without his consent, connivance or wilful default. The actual offender must have been convicted after being charged either by the occupier or by the factory inspector. Soulsby's omission to act will hardly constitute an offence but Marsh's removal of the guard could well do so. Marsh may, therefore, be prosecuted and fined for wilful misuse of or interference with a safety appliance. This may relieve the employer of criminal liability if the court is satisfied that the employer is blameless.

If Dark Satanic Mills is convicted, there is no reason why the court should not use its power under the Powers of Criminal Courts Act and award compensation to Marsh. (Magistrates' Courts are limited to £1000 for each charge upon which a conviction is recorded.) In view of the serious nature of the injury, the difficulty of medical evidence, and the likelihood of subsequent civil proceedings, it is unlikely that an award would be made here.

C. Compensation

Road traffic accidents

In very few instances is it necessary for the victim of a road traffic accident to resort to a court action in order to recover compensation. In most cases the claim is settled out of court, normally by negotiation between the parties' insurance companies.

If proceedings are necessary, Marsh's action against Soulsby will be for the tort of negligence. Marsh must prove that Soulsby owed him a duty of care (a duty by one road user towards other road users is well established); that this duty was broken in that Soulsby did not exercise reasonable care in the circumstances of the case; and that loss was suffered in consequence. Given the ability to prove these matters, it would seem that Marsh will succeed on the facts of the present case. If Soulsby can prove that March contributed in some way to the accident, for example by accelerating as Soulsby was overtaking, the damages will be reduced for contributory negligence.

Evidence may now be given of the result of criminal proceedings arising from the same facts. This may induce Soulsby to plead 'not guilty' to the charge of careless driving and to contest the charge vigorously, since the criminal prosecution is frequently the prelude to the civil action when more is at stake.

UNIT 30. THE LAW IN PRACTICE

Except in a few limited instances, an action cannot be brought for breach of statutory duty. The House of Lords decided in 1923, and the decision has not been challenged, that where road traffic legislation imposes a duty it is a public duty enforceable by the imposition of a fine and not by a civil action for damages by an individual.

The claim by Marsh for personal injuries must be brought within three years; the claim for damage to the car lapses after six years. Only one action is possible under each head and it is, therefore, desirable to ascertain the full extent of the loss before suing. Compensation for the damage to the car will normally be the cost of repairs with perhaps an addition for loss of use while it is being repaired. Compensation for personal injuries is more complex and will take into account such matters as loss of earnings, pain and suffering, medical expenses, and any lasting effects of the accident which cause loss of amenities.

Motor insurance

Both Soulsby and Marsh are required to have a current policy of insurance against third party claims. Soulsby's insurers will almost certainly attempt to negotiate a settlement and, if this fails and in the subsequent court action judgment is given against Soulsby, the judgment may be enforced directly against the insurers. Third party insurance will not cover the damage to Soulsby's own car and whether or not he can recover the cost of these repairs depends upon whether he has insured against this in what is sometimes called a 'comprehensive' policy. In practice, Marsh may claim from his own insurance company and leave it to the latter to pursue the claim against Soulsby or his insurers. Many insurers have a 'knock for knock' agreement under which each pays for the repairs to its own insured vehicles. If Marsh does make such a claim he may lose his 'no claim bonus' (a deduction from the annual insurance premium) for the bonus depends upon 'no claim' and not 'no blame'.

If Soulsby is uninsured, compensation, for personal injuries only will be paid to Marsh by the Motor Insurers' Bureau which was set up in 1946 by agreement between the Ministry of Transport and the motor insurers of Great Britain. Two agreements made in 1972 now govern the payment of claims made against uninsured and untraced drivers from a fund to which the insurers contribute.

Industrial accidents

Marsh, the injured worker, will also have an action in negligence against his employer for failure to provide a safe system of work, which is also a well-established duty. He must prove that the employer failed to take reasonable care for his safety and, in this respect, the employer is vicariously liable for the negligence of Soulsby, the foreman. Evidence of previous criminal proceedings, the three-year period of limitations and the basis of compensation, mentioned above, apply also to this claim. The facts, however, suggest that there was contributory negligence on the part of Marsh which, if proved, will reduce the amount of the award.

Given that the premises in question constitute a factory within the definition given in the Factories Act, a more likely action by Marsh is for breach of statutory duty. It has been established by precedent that the Act establishes positive duties for the protection of workers and that, in addition to criminal liability, a breach is remediable by a civil action for damages on the part of a worker who is injured by it.

The action will be based upon an alleged breach of the specific sections of the Act which relate to the fencing of dangerous machinery. The court must interpret these sections and decide whether the reason for the injury, the ejection of a piece of metal from the job in the machine, is covered by the wording used in the sections. If it decides that this is so, the duty placed upon the employer is strict and he cannot plead *volenti non fit injuria* or that he had delegated the performance of the duty to the foreman. The damages may still be reduced for contributory negligence.

The employer may claim that he has been obliged to pay damages as a consequence of his foreman's negligence and reclaim the amount in question from Soulsby. This is unlikely to be done in practice; Soulsby may be unable to pay the sum in question and, even if he could, this sort of action would not contribute to good industrial relations.

Marsh may receive considerable assistance in pursuing his claim from a trade union of which he is a member. Many employers have voluntarily insured against such claims in the past and, under the Employers' Liability (Compulsory Insurance) Act 1969, it is now compulsory for them to do so. Marsh's chances of receiving the compensation awarded are thereby strengthened. Finally, the award must take into account any compensation under the Powers of Criminal Courts Act and part of any social security benefits he may receive (see later).

D. Social security

Industrial injuries

The Social Security Acts 1975–80 provide a state scheme for compensating personal injuries caused by accidents arising out of and in the course of employment. All people working under a contract of employment or apprenticeship are covered and benefits are paid from a fund supported by a proportion of the national insurance contribution made by employers and workers.

A temporary injury benefit is payable for six months or until the worker returns to work, whichever is the earlier. A medical board may then assess loss of faculty, the lasting effects of the injury, to determine whether a permanent disablement benefit is payable. The assessment is made on a percentage basis according to the seriousness of the disablement. A loss of 20 per cent or more gives a pension, below 20 per cent there will be a gratuity or lump sum; the amount of the benefit depends in each case upon the extent of the percentage loss. Various supplements may be claimed for unemployability, special hardship, and dependants.

Marsh, who lost the sight of an eye while at work, would appear to have a right to benefit under this scheme which does not in any way depend upon his ability to prove negligence. The fact that he was injured at work is enough, and the breach of safety regulations on his part will neither nullify nor reduce his right. While he is away from work he will be entitled to injury benefit and, since the normal assessment for loss of the sight of one eye is 30 per cent, he should later be granted a disablement pension irrespective of whether or not the injury affects his job or his earnings. If Marsh is dissatisfied with the decision of the insurance officer on whether or not it is an industrial injury he may appeal to a Local Appeal Tribunal. If he is dissatisfied with the assessment of loss of faculty, there is a right of appeal to a Medical Appeal Tribunal. Marsh, the driver, will not be entitled to industrial injuries benefits unless he was driving in the course of his employment, for example, as a sales representative.

National insurance

A comprehensive scheme of state insurance against unemployment, sickness, old age, and similar matters likely to cause hardship is provided by the Social Security Acts 1975–80. All persons above school-leaving age and below pensionable age are insured and must pay earnings-related contributions. Under the new scheme, the contributions are now collected through PAYE and not by affixing stamps to a card as hitherto. Entitlement to the various benefits depends upon having paid a specified number of contributions.

If Marsh, the driver, is unable to work because of the accident, if he can produce a medical certificate to this effect, and if he has satisfied the contribution conditions, he will be entitled to sickness benefit. As with injury benefit, this may be increased by additional allowances for dependants. The benefit will cease when he returns to work, and no payment will normally be made for any lasting effects of the accident. In certain circumstances he may now qualify for an invalidity benefit.

The possibility of double compensation for an accident by a civil action and by state insurance is dealt with by the Law Reform (Personal Injuries) Act 1948. When damages are being assessed for loss of earnings, there must be a deduction of half of the industrial injuries or sickness benefits payable for the five years from when the cause of action arose. The other half is not taken into account since this is approximately that part of the benefit due to the worker's own contribution; it is the part due to the employer's contribution which is deducted.

Supplementary benefit

If the victim of an accident is unable to work and yet is not entitled to any of the above benefits, he may be given supplementary benefit. This is a discretionary payment, formerly called national assistance, designed to ensure that no one is left entirely without means.

E. Defective goods—the problems

Consumer protection, like safety on the roads and at work, is governed by legislation which is aimed primarily at the prevention of cheating or loss. The legislative controls are administered largely by inspectors appointed for the purpose and criminal sanctions are provided for breach.

Compensation for the victim who has bought faulty goods is normally another matter. If the supplier will not give compensation voluntarily, the victim may have to start separate civil proceedings for breach of contract, misrepresentation, or in tort. Not all consumers are so determined, or indeed can afford the time, energy, and money to do this.

Consider these transactions:

1. Soulsby buys a box of X's chocolates from Marsh's Confectionery Shop. Some of the fillings contain impurities. Soulsby, and his guests to whom he has given chocolates, become ill after eating them.
2. Soulsby buys a second-hand car from a neighbour, Marsh, who tells him in the course of negotiations that it is a 1970 model. In fact, unknown to Marsh, the car is a 1968 model, the registration book of which has been falsified by a previous owner. The car proves to be in poor condition, and Soulsby incurs considerable expense in repairing it.
3. Soulsby buys a second-hand car from Marsh (Motor Dealers) Ltd, and is told in the course of negotiations that it is a 1970 model. The rest of the facts are as in the previous situation.

F. Prevention and criminal sanctions

There is a large body of legislation which aims to prevent cheating and to protect the public against defective goods. The following are the more important matters which are controlled.

1. *False trade descriptions.* Any person who, in the course of a trade or business (a) applies a false trade description to goods, or (b) supplies or offers to supply goods to which a false trade description is applied, shall be guilty of an offence under the Trade Descriptions Acts 1968–72. It is also an offence, in the course of any trade or business, to give false indications that the goods supplied have Royal approval, or are of a kind supplied to some celebrity. It should be noted that these rules only apply where the description was applied or the goods supplied in the course of a business. A false description applied by a non-dealer will not be an offence under these sections, and may not be an offence at all unless the victim can prove the intent necessary to constitute an offence of fraud.

Other Acts prohibit misdescription of special classes of goods. For example, under section 2 of the Food and Drugs Act 1955, if a person sells, to the prejudice of the purchaser, any food or drug which is not of the nature, substance or quality of the food or drug demanded by the buyer, the seller commits an offence. The

Fair Trading Act 1973 gives the Secretary of State for Trade and Industry power to make regulations prohibiting other misleading practices.
2. *Some false or misleading indications as to the price of goods* are offences under section 11 of the Trade Descriptions Act 1968.
3. *Weights and measures* are subject to legislative controls under the Weights and Measures Acts 1963–79. Provision is made for labelling of quantity on prepacked goods, and the inspection of weighing and measuring machines. There are criminal sanctions for giving short weight or measure.
4. *An advertisement* which contains a false trade description may be sufficient to 'apply' that description to goods bought by someone who relies on the advertisement. If this occurs, the advertiser will commit an offence. More stringent controls exist over advertisements for food and drugs.
5. *The quality of goods.* As a general rule it is no offence to supply goods which are of poor quality, so long as there has been no false or misleading description. In most cases the maxim *caveat emptor* applies. On the other hand, certain goods can be extremely dangerous to the public if the quality is poor, and in these instances statutory controls are often imposed. The following examples may be given:

(a) Under section 8 of the Food and Drugs Act 1955, any person who sells any food intended for, but unfit for, human consumption shall be guilty of an offence. Regulations made under the Act cover such matters as the labelling of prepacked foods, and the ingredients of prepared foods, such as the fruit content of jams and the meat content of sausages.
(b) Under the Road Traffic Act 1972, it is an offence to sell a motor vehicle unless its mechanical quality complies with the requirements of the Motor Vehicles (Construction and Use) Regulations made under the Act. There are also requirements as to the quality of crash helmets for motor cyclists.
(c) The Consumer Protection Act 1961 and the Consumer Safety Act 1978 give the Home Secretary wide power to make regulations to protect the public against the risk of death or personal injury from defective goods. Regulations have been made about such matters as oil heaters and lead paint on toys.

Enforcement

Most of these Acts are administered by inspectors employed by the local authorities. Thus the Trade Descriptions Acts and the Weights and Measures Acts are administered by Trading Standards Inspectors, and the Food and Drugs legislation by Public Health Inspectors. Both inspectorates have wide powers to make test purchases, to enter premises, and to inspect and seize goods and documents.

Prosecutions are brought by the inspectors, and almost invariably are tried summarily in the Magistrates' Court. Offences under the Trade Descriptions Acts can be tried on indictment in the Crown Court, but this very rarely occurs.

In most cases, criminal liability for breach is strict, and all that the prosecution need show is that a false trade description has been applied, or that the food is unfit. On the other hand, many of the Acts provide a defence if the accused can show that the offence is not his fault, for example, because it was due to the act or default of another person, and that he, the accused, took all reasonable precautions and exercised all due diligence to avoid the commission of the offence. The onus of proving this defence is on the accused.

The transactions under consideration

In the first transaction mentioned above, Marsh's Confectionery Shop appears to have committed an offence under section 8 of the Food and Drugs Act and, if so, will be liable to a fine (or even imprisonment). This would be very hard on Marsh, because the chocolates reached him prepacked in a box, and he had no means of knowing that they were unfit for human consumption. The Act, therefore, provides a defence in these circumstances if Marsh can show that the offence occurred because of the act or default of another person, in this case the manufacturer, X, and that Marsh used all due diligence to secure that the provisions in question were complied with. The manufacturer would be guilty of an offence in any event.

The prosecution of Marsh or the manufacturer under the Act will not directly benefit Soulsby or his guests, unless the magistrates exercise their discretionary power to make a compensation order under the Powers of Criminal Courts Act 1973. In this event, compensation can be awarded to any person affected by the offence, which would include both Soulsby and the guests. On the other hand, compensation under this section cannot exceed £1000, and if Soulsby and his guests have been seriously ill they may wish to claim more. Moreover, if detailed medical evidence is required to assess the injury suffered, the magistrates may prefer to leave compensation entirely to separate civil proceedings.

In the second situation, Soulsby buys a second-hand car from his neighbour, Marsh, in reliance on a false description. This will not be an offence under the Trade Descriptions Acts unless Marsh sold the car in the course of a trade or business. The Act aims to catch fraudulent *dealers*, and does not apply to private sales. If the vehicle was so defective as to be in an unroadworthy condition, an offence may have been committed under the Road Traffic Act 1972.

In the third situation, Soulsby buys the car from Marsh (Motor Dealers) Ltd. If, as it appears, this sale is in the course of the business, an offence has been committed under section 1 of the Trade Descriptions Act 1968. On the other hand, Marsh Ltd may have a defence, because the false trade description was applied in reliance on information supplied by the previous owner, and was due to the act or default of that person. Marsh Ltd must also prove, however, that it has taken all reasonable precautions and exercised all due diligence to avoid committing the offence, and the company may not be able to prove this. As a motor dealer, the company should probably have checked the age of the car before re-selling it.

In this third situation, the magistrates may well be willing to award compensation under the Powers of Criminal Courts Act, since Soulsby's loss is fairly easy to assess. Orders have frequently been made on convictions under the Trade Descriptions Acts.

G. Compensation

The possibility of compensation under the Powers of Criminal Courts Act has been mentioned. The possibility of civil claim for damages rests more heavily on the initiative of the victim, who will have to start separate civil proceedings in the County Court or the High Court.

In the case of the chocolates, Marsh's Confectionery Shop had broken its contract with Soulsby. Since the sale is in the course of a business, section 14 of the Sale of Goods Act 1979 applies, and there are implied conditions that the goods shall be of merchantable quality and reasonably fit for the purpose made known, namely eating. Soulsby can, therefore, recover damages, which will compensate him for his loss, including his illness. The fact that the impurities are not the fault of the seller is quite immaterial, as we saw in *Frost* v. *Aylesbury Dairy Co. Ltd* (1905).

On the other hand, the guests who have been ill cannot sue for breach of contract, because they are not parties to any contract and are, therefore, excluded by the rules of privity. They can only sue in tort. No action for the tort of breach of statutory duty lies under the Food and Drugs Act, and in order to succeed, therefore, they will have to prove negligence. It will not be possible to prove this against Soulsby or against Marsh's Shop, because the chocolates are packed and not open to intermediate inspection. The guests must, therefore, claim from the manufacturer, X. In this event, the court may apply the maxim *res ipsa loquitur*, reverse the onus of proof, and require X to prove that he has *not* been negligent in allowing the chocolates to become contaminated. The court did this, for example, in *Steer* v. *Durable Rubber Co. Ltd* (1958).

In the case where Soulsby bought a car from his neighbour, Marsh, he will not be able to sue Marsh for breach of section 14 of the Sale of Goods Act, because that section only applies to a sale in the course of a business. He may, however, be able to sue for breach of section 13, since the car does not comply with the description '1970 model'. In this event, liability will be strict, and it will be no defence for Marsh to show that the misdescription was not his fault. On the other hand, the court may well treat a statement in the course of negotiations as a mere representation, not a term in the contract. If this is held, Soulsby can only sue for damages under section 2(1) of the Misrepresentation Act 1967, under which liability is *not* strict. It will be open to Marsh to prove that he believed, and had reasonable cause to believe, the truth of his claim that the car was a 1970 model; see *Oscar Chess Ltd* v. *Williams* (1957).

In the case where Soulsby bought a car from Marsh (Motor Dealers) Ltd, Soulsby will certainly be entitled to damages for breach of contract. Section 14 of the Sale of Goods Act will apply, and the car appears neither to be of merchantable quality, nor reasonably fit for driving. Moreover, since the statement as to the age of the vehicle was made by a dealer in this case, the contract will almost certainly be treated as a sale by description, so that section 13 will apply; see *Dick Bentley Productions Ltd* v. *Harold Smith (Motors) Ltd* (1965).

It will be noticed that both the criminal law and the civil law place much higher obligations on a seller who sells in the course of a business than upon a person who sells privately.

If Soulsby discovers the defects in the car immediately, he may be entitled to repudiate the contract, return the vehicle, and demand his money back. The right to repudiate, however, is subject to equitable rules, and Soulsby must exercise the right promptly. The contract for the sale of chocolates cannot now be repudiated, because some of the sweets have been eaten.

Finally, Soulsby will have to consider whether or not he should sue at all. If the amount of damages claimed is considerable, the decision will not be too difficult. If, on the other hand, he is only slightly sick after eating the chocolates, so that the amounts of damages is small, he must consider whether the time, effort, and cost of suing are worth while. So far as cost is concerned, he may wish to apply for legal aid, and some local legal aid committees are reluctant to grant legal aid for very small claims. If the amount is not in excess of £500, the matter may be referred to arbitration by the County Court Registrar, and this may save time and expense. The parties can agree voluntarily to such arbitration even if the amount claimed exceeds £500 and, if the parties so agree and the dispute cannot be settled otherwise, this may be the best solution.

Index

Acceptance:
    bill of exchange, of, 236, 237, 239, 242
    goods, of, 211, 215, 216, 217
    offer, of, 151, 161–3, 211, 255
Accord and satisfaction, 195
Account stated, 173
Accounts:
    companies, of, 103
    partnership, 87, 89
Acknowledgment of service, 66
Act of God, 111, 136
Act of Parliament (*see* Statute)
Administration of estates, 36, 39, 284–6
Administrative tribunals (*see* Tribunals)
Admiralty Court, 39
Adoption of children, 36, 37, 209
Advisory Committee on Legal Education, 54
Advocates general, 74
Affidavit, 66
Affiliation order, 37
Agency:
    company secretaries, of, 102
    creation of, 247–9
    directors, of, 101–2
    duties of agents, 250–1
    duties of principal, 251
    effect of, 249–50
    frustration of, 251
    partners, of, 84–7
    termination of, 251
    undisclosed principal, 199, 249
Agent:
    authority of, 247–9
    bill of exchange signed by, 240
    capacity of, 247
    duties of, 250–1
    insurance agents, 255–6
    mercantile, 221, 222
    principal, and, 250–1
    third party, and, 249–50
    warranty of authority by, 249
Aliens, 81
All England Law Reports, 22–3
Animals, 107, 147–9
Annual Practice, 66
Annual returns of companies, 103
Appeals:
    civil cases, in, 23, 39–41, 45, 47, 48, 67
    criminal cases, in, 32–3
Appellant, 23, 41
Appropriation of payments, 186
Arbitration, 50–1
    County Court, in, 37, 50–1, 300

Arrest, power of, 69
Articled clerk, 54
Articles:
    association, of, 94, 96, 97, 98
    clerkship, of, 54
    partnership, of, 83
Artificial person, 80
Assault, 140
Assembly, European Communications, of, 73
Assignment:
    bills of exchange, of, 238
    contractual rights, of, 156, 199, 235–6
    lease, of, 199, 267
Assizes, 4, 30, 31, 38
Assurance (*see* Insurance)
Attachment of earnings order, 68
Attorney-General, 59, 60, 90, 276

Bail, 30
Bank:
    collecting, 242, 243–5, 251–2
    England, of, 236
    merchant, 237
    paying, 242, 243, 251–2
Banker:
    duties to customer, 251–4
    protection of, 243–5
Bar Council, 23, 57, 60
Battery, 107, 141
Beeching Commission, 30
Benchers, 50, 55
Beneficiaries of a trust, 277
Bill, 11
    drafting of, 14
    private, 13
    private member's, 13
    public, 12, 13
Bill of exchange, 153, 167, 236 *et seq.*,
    acceptance of, 236, 237, 239, 242
    capacity, 241
    definition, 236–8
    discharge of, 241
    dishonour of, 239–40
    holder of, 239–241
    negotiations of, 238
    types of, 237–8
    (*see also* Cheques)
Bill of Sale, 231
Brief, 56
Building Societies, 81, 225, 226, 231, 271, 274
Burden of proof, 2, 67, 121–2, 170, 299
By-Law, 10, 15, 16, 17

Canon law, 8
Capacity:
    bill of exchange, and, 241
    contract, to, 80, 82, 173–4
    corporate body, of, 82, 84, 93, 100
    partnership, for, 84
    testamentary, 281
    tort, in, 113–4
    trustee, of, 276
Care, duty of, 119–121, 123, 124–5, 128, 247
    agent, by, 250
    bank, by, 253
    directors, by, 99
    drawer of cheque, by, 253
    employee, by, 178, 293–4
    employer, by, 123–4, 178, 293–4
    insured (policy holder), by, 256–7
Case law (*see* Judicial precedent)
Case stated, 32, 39, 50
Caveat emptor, 171, 179
Certification Officer, 83
Certiorari, 48
Chambers, 55, 56
Champerty, 203
Chancellor:
    Duchy of Lancaster, of, 27
    office of, 5–6
    (*see also* Lord Chancellor)
Chancery, Court of, 5–7, 43, 156
Charging order, 68
Charitable trusts, 276
Charity Commissioners, 276
Chattels, real and personal, 263
Cheques, 237, 242–5, 251–4
Children:
    adoption of, 36, 37, 209
    court jurisdiction, 36, 37, 39
    guardianship of, 39, 279
    legitimacy of, 36, 37
    succession of death, rights of, 281, 283
    trespassers, as, 125
    visitors, as, 125
Chose on action, 156, 235–6, 263
Chose in possession, 263
Church courts, 41, 43, 49
Circuit:
    administrator, 31
    County Court, 35
    Judge, 31, 32, 35, 57, 58
Civil law, 1, 2, 288–300
Clerk to the Justices, 29
Codes:
    Highway, 24, 289, 291

301

INDEX

Codes, *cont.*
  law, of, 21–2
  practice, of, 24, 289
Codicil, 282
Codification, 14, 21–2, 178, 236
Collective agreement, 152
College of Law, 54
Committal Proceedings, 29–30, 69
Committee:
  Departmental, 60
  Law Revision, 60
  Legal Education, on, 54
  Legislation, 11
  Parliamentary, 16
  Permanent Representatives, of, 73
  Stage (of bill), 12
  Whole House, of, 12
Common law, 3–6, 10, 19
Companies:
  actual returns by, 103
  capacity of, 82, 84, 93
  capital of, 94–6
  certificate of incorporation, 94
  close, 93
  debentures, 95, 232–3
  directors of, 94, 98–100, 101–2
  dividends, 96
  formation of, 55, 81, 93–4
  jurisdiction over, 36, 39
  liquidator, 103–4
  meetings, 97
  prospectus, 95, 172
  registered office, 94
  registers, 98, 103, 233
  Registrar of, 93, 98, 103
  Secretary of, 94, 98, 102
  shares in, 94–6
  shareholders, 96–7, 99–101, 102–3
  types of, 92
  ultra vires rule, 78, 82, 93, 241, 248
  winding up, of, 103–4
Compensation in criminal cases, 70, 292, 294, 298–9
Compulsory purchase of land, 47, 132, 266
Consent (*volenti*), 111–2, 132, 135
Consideration, 151, 153–5, 195
Consumer:
  protection, 296–300
  sale, 179, 182, 215
Consumer credit agreements:
  advertising, 226
  cancellation, 227–8
  exempt agreements, 226
  extortionate, 228
  information, 227
  minimum payment clauses, 229
  termination, 164–5, 229
Contempt of court, 68
Contract:
  acceptance of offer, 151, 161–3, 211, 227, 255
  agreement, discharge by, 194–5
  agreement, necessity for, 151, 158–164
  anticipatory breach, 186, 188

assignment, 156, 199, 235–6
bargaining power, 179–80
breach, 158, 186–192
capacity, 82, 84, 93, 151, 172–4, 246
certainty of terms, 151, 164
collective agreements, 152
condition, 176–9, 187
consideration, 151, 153–5, 195
corporation, by, 82, 84, 93
credit controls, 156, 204
Crown, by, 90
damages for breach, 151, 188–190, 215, 217, 299
deed, by, 155, 195, 197
discharge of, 185–193, 194–7
disclose, duty to, 171–2, 256–7
drunkenness, 151, 174
duress, 151, 172
employment, of, 173, 178, 191–2, 194, 205, 206–7
equitable estoppel, 155
essential requirements, 151
evidenced in writing, 151, 156
exclusion clauses, 171, 180–3
express terms, 176–7
family arrangements, 172
form, 151, 155–7, 211, 227, 231, 235–6
fraud, 170, 198
freedom of, 176, 202
frustration, 186, 195–7, 220, 251
fundamental breach, 177, 182, 187
gaming and wagering, 209
guarantee, 156
hire purchase, of, 156, 173, 179–80, 183, 228–30
  (*see also* Consumer credit)
illegality, 151, 196, 202–5
implied terms, 177–9, 211–16, 230, 250–1, 251–4, 299
injunction, 191–2, 198, 207
insanity, 81, 151, 174, 198
insurance, of, 171, 176, 197, 199, 204, 254–9
intention to create legal relations, 151, 152
invitation to treat, 158–9
jurisdiction in, 35, 38
limitation of actions, 197–8
minors, 80, 151, 173–4, 247
misrepresentation, 147, 151, 169–71, 183, 222, 227, 240, 256
mistake, 151, 166–9, 198, 222, 240
non est factum, 167
offer, 151, 158–161, 211, 229, 255
part performance, 156
payment of money, 186
penalty, 190, 229
performance, 155–6
privity, 198–200, 299
public policy, 151, 202–9
quantum meruit, 190–1
rectification, 169
repudiation (renunciation), 186, 187, 188
rescission, 89, 168, 170–1, 172, 187, 227

restraint of trade, in, 205–8
restrictive trade practices, 200, 205–8
sale of goods, for, 178–9, 187, 190, 197, 200
  (*see also* Goods)
sale of land, for, 155–6, 172
  (*see slso* Land)
solus agreement, 206, 208
specialty (*see* Deed)
specific performance of, 156, 174, 191, 198, 216, 272
subject to contract, 162, 271
terms, 176–183
transfer of property by, 151–2, 168
uberrimae fidei contracts, 171, 257
undue influence, 151, 172, 240
unenforceable, 151, 156, 271
void, 82, 84, 151, 155, 166–8, 173, 182–3, 197, 202–9, 220, 232, 233, 240
voidable, 84, 89, 151, 168–174, 187–8, 215, 222, 227, 256–7
warranty, 176–7, 187, 212
writing, in, 150–1, 155, 176, 180, 211, 227, 235–7, 255
writing, evidence in, 151, 156
Contribution from joint tortfeasor, 114, 294
Contributory negligence, 112, 128, 245, 293, 294
Conversion, 107, 137–8, 168, 204, 212, 221, 223, 243, 245
Conveyance, 155, 274
Corporations, 81–2, 92
  (*see also* Companies)
Costs, 37, 63, 67, 300
Council:
  Legal Education, of, 55
  Ministers, of, 73
  Tribunals, on, 48
Court:
  Admiralty, 39
  Appeal, of, 20, 22, 23, 57, 59
  (Civil Division), 40, 45, 59
  (Criminal Division), 32–3, 49, 59
  Central Criminal, (Old Bailey), 30
  Chancery, of, 5–7, 43, 156, 264, 274
  Chancery Division, 22, 36, 39, 62, 66
  Commercial, 39, 66
  Common Pleas, of, 4, 38
  County Court, 20, 35–7, 38, 40, 50–1, 53, 58, 62, 63, 66–8, 142, 162, 299, 300
  Crown Court, 29 *et seq.*, 59, 69–70, 290, 297
  Divisional, 32, 39–40, 48, 50
  European Court of Justice, 74–5, 76–7
  Exchequer, of, 4, 38
  Family Division, 22, 38, 39, 62
  High Court, 20, 22, 38 *et seq.*, 62 *et seq.*, 141, 142
  House of Lords, 20–3, 33, 40–1, 60
  Judicial Committee of the Privy Council (*see* Privy Council)
  juvenile, 29, 32

302

INDEX

Court, *cont.*
  King's Bench, of, 5, 38
  Magistrates' (*see* Magistrates' Courts)
  martial, 49
  mercantile, 7, 43
  Protection, of, 39, 174
  Queen's Bench Division, 22, 32, 33, 38 *et seq.*, 48, 50, 59, 62, 65 *et seq.*
  Restrictive Practices, 44–5
  Supreme Court, 38 *et seq.*, 58
Covenant, restrictive, 200, 270, 273
Credit, 86, 216, 225–33, 236–7
  (*see also* Consumer Credit)
Creditor, 82, 89, 102–3, 104, 225–33
Criminal law, 1, 2, 106–7, 126–7, 130, 288 *et seq.*
Crown:
  intestacy, rights on, 284
  legal status of, 90
  liability of, 24, 90, 113
  owner of land, as, 264–5
  servants, 24, 90
Custom:
  local, 3
  source of law, as, 25
Cy-près, 276

Damages:
  agency, in, 250
  breach of contract, for, 151, 188–90, 215, 217, 299–300
  exemplary, 189
  judgment for, 67–8
  liquidated, 190
  misrepresentation, for, 170, 299
  remoteness of, 123, 188–90
  sale of goods, on, 215, 217
  tort, in, 108–12, 115–6, 145, 170, 292–4
Dangerous goods, 123, 297
Dangerous premises, 124–6
Death:
  agency, effect on, 251
  contract, effect on, 161, 198
  exclusion of liability for, 182
  succession on, 279–86
  tort, effect on action in, 114–5
Debentures, 95–6, 225, 232–3
Deceit, 167, 170
Decision (in the European Communities), 76
Deed:
  contract by, 155, 195, 197
  conveyance by, 274
  partnership, of, 83
Defamation, 36, 38–9, 58, 142–6
Defence:
  civil proceedings, to, 66–7
  criminal proceedings, to, 69
Defendant, 2, 23, 65 *et seq.*
Delegated legislation, 15–17, 35, 77
Dependants:
  deceased, of, 281–2
  social security allowances, 295
  tort, claims in, 114–5

Detinue, 138
Directive, 76
Director of Public Prosecutions, 59, 60
Director-General of Fair Trading, 183, 226, 227
Discovery of documents, 66
Dismissal, 24, 90
Dispossession, 131
Distress damage feasant, 132
Divorce, jurisdiction in, 36, 37, 39
Doctrine, 77
Drunkenness, 151, 174
Duress, 151, 172

Easement, 269–70, 273
Employee:
  capacity of, 173
  Crown, of, 90
  good faith by, 178
  injunction against, 192, 206
Employer:
  care, duty of, 178, 293
  implied obligations of, 178
  vicarious liability of, 108–10, 293
Employment:
  collective agreements, 152
  illegal contracts of, 202–3
  illegal terms of, 205
  implied terms, 178, 293
  restraint of trade in, 206–7
  specific performance of, 191
Employment Appeal Tribunal, 45–6, 47
Equity, 6–7, 36, 101, 172, 191–2, 198, 215, 274–7
Equitable:
  estoppel, 155
  interest in land, 267, 269, 270
  lien, 232
  remedies, 6–7, 116, 172, 191–2, 198, 215, 267
Escape of dangerous things, 136–7
Estate:
  deceased's, administration of, 36, 279 *et seq.*, 284–6
  land, in, 263–4, 266, 269
  claim in tort for, 115
European Communities:
  Assembly (Parliament), 73
  Commission, 72–3
  Council of Ministers, 73
  law of, 8, 71–8, 208
  Treaties, 8, 71, 77, 208
Exclusion clauses, 171, 180–3, 215, 230
Executor (of Will), 284–5

Factory legislation, 291–2
Fair comment, 146
False imprisonment, 141
Fee simple, 264–6
Fieri facias (fi. fa.), 68
Finder, rights of, 138–9
Fine, 69, 290, 292, 298
Foreign sovereigns, 81
Foreclosure of mortgage, 232
Franks Committee on Tribunals, 46, 48

Fraud:
  agent, by, 250
  companies, in, 100, 103
  contract, in, 89, 170, 198
  drawer of cheque, by, 253
  limitation of actions, 117, 198
  tort of, 147
Freehold, 262–3, 264–6
Further and better particulars, 66

Gaming and wagering, 209
Garnishee order, 68
Good faith:
  agent's duties of, 250–1
  banker and customer, by, 251–4
  buyer in, 152, 221–3
  cheques, and, 243–5, 251–4
  company directors, by, 98–9
  holder of bill of exchange, and, 239, 241
  insurance, in, 171, 256–7, 259
  partners, by, 87
  personal representatives, by, 286
  shareholders, by, 100–1
Goods:
  bailment of, 223, 231
  carriage of, 178, 205
  conditional sale of, 229
  conversion of, 137–8
  credit sale of, 228–9
  dangerous, 123, 296–7
  defective, 180, 212 *et seq.*, 296–300
  finders of, 138–9
  hire of, 178
  hire-purchase of, 229–30
  lien over, 217, 231
  reservation of title clauses, 217–8, 231
  sale of, 178–9, 211–23, 228–9, 296–300
  security, as, 228–31
  specific, 218–20
  trespass to, 137
  unascertained, 218–20
  unsolicited, 162, 219
Guarantee, 155

Habeas corpus, 141
High Court (*see* Court)
Highways, 109, 135, 149
Hire purchase, 36, 38, 155, 176, 179, 180, 190, 194–5, 212, 223, 225, 228–30
Home Secretary, 33, 60
House, buying a, 271–4
House of Commons, 11–13
House of Lords:
  Appeals Committee, 40
  court, as a, 20, 22, 23, 32, 33, 40–1, 49, 59, 60
  legislative body, 12, 17
Husband and wife, 7, 113, 172, 275, 281, 283–4

Incorporated Council of Law Reporting, 19, 22
Incorporation, 80, 81, 92 *et seq.*

303

INDEX

Indemnity:
  agent's right to, 251
  insurance as, 254, 257
  joint tortfeasor, by, 110, 114
  partners, of, 87
Independent contractors, 108–10
Industrial injury benefits, 46, 294–5
Industrial tribunal (*see* Tribunals)
Inevitable accident, 111, 136
Infants (*see* Minors)
Injunction, 7, 67–9
  contract, in, 191–2, 198, 206
  employment, in, 191–2
  tort, in, 63, 116, 131, 134
Inquest, Coroner's, 49
Inns of Court, 54–5, 57
Innuendo, 143
Insanity:
  agency, effect on, 251
  capacity generally, effect on, 81
  contract, effect on, 151, 174, 198
  wills, effect on, 281
Inspectors:
  factory, 69, 291–2
  public health, 69, 297
  trading standards, 69, 297
Institute of Legal Executives, 56
Insurance:
  agents, 255–6
  average clauses, 258
  brokers, 255–6
  compulsory, 56, 126, 254, 259, 293, 294
  disclosure, duties of, 171, 256–7
  employers' liability, 259, 294
  exclusion of liability in, 258–9
  frustration, 197
  good faith in, 171, 256–7
  indemnity, 110, 254, 257
  insurable interest, 204, 209, 254–5
  marine, 155
  motor, 204, 209, 254–5
  Motor Insurers' Bureau, 293
  national (*see* Social Security)
  notice clauses in, 259
  privity of contract and, 199–200, 259
  subrogation, 110, 257
Interlocutory proceedings, 66–7
Interrogatories, 66

Joint torts, 114
Judge Advocate General, 49
Judges:
  Circuit, 31, 35, 57–8
  High Court, 31, 32, 45, 57–9
  independence of, 57–8
  presiding, 31
Judgment, 67
  enforcement of, 67–9
  reserved, 67
Judicial Committee of the Privy Council, 20, 41–2, 49, 59
Judicial precedent, 5, 6, 7, 19 *et seq.*, 46
  European Court, in, 76

Jury:
  civil, 35, 39, 67, 142
  coroner's, 49
  criminal, 27, 29, 31, 32, 69
  origins of, 4
Justice of the Peace (*see* Magistrates)

Keeping terms, 54–5
King's Peace, 3

Land:
  charges, 270, 273–4
  contracts concerning, 155–6, 172, 271–4
  estate in, 263 *et seq.*, 269–70
  interest in, 263 *et seq.*, 269–70, 273–4
  occupier's liability, 124–6
  recovery of, 36, 38, 69, 131, 198
  registration, 273
  restraint upon use of, 200, 262, 265–6, 273–4
  sale of, 155–6, 172, 271–4
  security, as, 231–2, 271–2
  torts affecting, 130 *et seq.*
  trespass to, 107–8, 130–2
Land Registry, 273
Landlord and tenant, 199, 267–8
Lands Tribunal, 40, 47, 270
Law:
  Commission, 22, 60–1, 125, 147
  Lords, 40–1, 59
  merchant, 7
  nature of, 1–3
  officers, 59–60
  origins of, 1
  reform, 60–1
  reporting, 5, 19, 22–3
Law Society, The, 15, 16, 54, 56, 60, 64, 272, 274
Lawyers (*see* Barristers and Solicitors)
Leapfrog procedure, 41
Lease (leasehold), 155, 174, 199, 262–3, 264, 266–8
Legal:
  aid and advice, 56, 63–4
  authors, books by, 25, 77
  education, 54–5, 60
  person, 80, 81–2, 101
  tender, 186
Legislation, 8, 10 *et seq.*, (*see also* Statutes, Delegated legislation)
Lending (*see* Credit)
Letters of administration, 284–6
Libel, 107, 144–5
Lien:
  common law, 231
  equitable, 232, 272
  statutory, 217
Limitation of actions:
  contract, in, 197–8
  tort, in, 117
  trust, for breach of, 277
Limited:
  liability, 82, 92, 94, 102–3
  partnerships, 89

Liquidator, 103–4
Loans, security for, 225, 228 *et seq.*
Local authorities, 81–2
Lord Chancellor, 27, 31, 39, 40, 45, 48, 57, 59
Lord Chief Justice, 31, 32, 38, 59
Lord Justices of Appeal, 32, 40, 59
Lords of Appeal in Ordinary, 40–1, 59

Magistrates, 26 *et seq.*, 37, 69–70
Magistrates' Courts, 26 *et seq.*, 37, 40, 53, 69–70, 290–2, 297–8
  appeals from, 32–3, 40
  civil jurisdiction of, 37, 40
  Committee, 29
Malicious prosecution, 142
Managing clerks, 56
Manchester Arbitration Scheme for Small Claims, 51
Mandamus, 48
market overt, 222
Marriage:
  freedom of, 208–9
  permission for, 37
  wills and, 282
  young persons and, 37, 80
Masters, High Court, 38, 66
Master of the Rolls, 32, 40, 59
Matrimonial property, 39
Memorandum of Association, 82, 93–4
Mental patient, 81, 174, 198, 281
Mesne profits, 131
Ministerial regulations, 15, 227
Ministry of Justice, 60
Minor:
  capacity generally, 80, 247
  contracts by, 80, 173–4, 198
  jurisdiction over, 39
  landholding, 80, 174
  tort, in, 80, 113–4
  will by, 80, 281
Misrepresentation, 147, 151, 169–70, 183, 222, 227, 240, 256
Mistake, 151, 166–9, 198, 222, 240
Money bill, 12
Mortgage, 7, 36, 39, 231–3, 271–2, 273, 274

National Insurance (*see* Social Security)
Natural justice, 48
Necessaries, 173
Negligence, 107, 119 *et seq.*, 132, 292–4, 299
  breach of duty, 121–2
  dangerous goods, 123, 299
  dangerous premises, 124–6
  duty of care, 119–21, 149, 292, 293
  employers' liability for, 123–4
  neighbour principle, 120
  onus of proof, 121–2, 299
  resulting damage, 122–3
  (*see also* Care, duty of)
Negotiability, 236
Negotiable instruments, 235–45, 251–3, 263

Nemo dat quod non habet, 221–3, 235
Nervous shock, 120–1, 122
Novus actus interveniens, 117
Nuisance, 107, 132–5

Obiter dicta, 21, 218
Occupiers' liability, 124–6
Offer of amends, 145
Official Secrets Acts, 59
Old Bailey (*see* Court, Central Criminal)
Onus of proof, (*see* Burden of proof)
Opinion:
    counsel's, 53, 65
    European Communities, in, 76
Order in Council, 15, 35, 77
Ormrod Committee, 54, 60
Ownership:
    nature of, 261–2
    land, of, 264
    estates and interests in land, of, 262 *et seq.*, 269–70, 274, 277
    goods, of, 211, 218–220, 221–3, 231
    negotiable instruments, of, 235 *et seq.*

Parliament, 10 *et seq.*
Parliamentary Counsel to the Treasury, 14
Partners:
    authority to bind firm, 84–6
    duties of, 87
    rights of, 87
    vicarious liability of, 108
Partnership, 83–9
    capacity to enter, 84, 174
    dissolution of, 88–9
    formation of, 83–4
    jurisdiction over, 36, 39
    legal profession, in, 55, 56
    limited, 89
    nature of, 83
Patents, 39, 263
Pawn, 231
Payment of money, 186
Perpetuities, rule against, 276
Person:
    legal, 80, 81–2, 101
    trespass to, 140–2
Personal representatives, 269, 279, 284–6
Petty Sessions (*see* Magistrates' Courts)
Plaintiff, 2, 23, 62 *et seq.*
Pleadings, 65–6
Pledge, 231
Possession, 261–2
Practising certificate, 56
Precedent (*see* Judicial precedent)
Prerogative:
    mercy, of, 33
    orders, 40, 48
    treaty making, of, 77
President of Family Division, 39
Private nuisance, 132–5
Privilege (in defamation), 146
Privy Council, 15, 41, 81
    Judicial Committee of, 20, 41–2, 49, 59
    Orders in Council, 15, 35, 77

Probate, 39, 284–5
Probate, Divorce and Admiralty Division, 39
Profit à prendre, 270
Prohibition (order of), 236
Promissory note, 236
Property:
    meaning of, 261
    types of, 262–3
    (*see also* Goods, Land, Negotiable instruments)
Provincial Courts, 49
Public:
    health, 8, 69, 297
    nuisance, 33, 132, 135
    policy, 120, 122, 202–9
Punishment of criminal offenders, 1–2, 29, 33, 69, 290–1, 292
Pupillage, 54, 55

Qualified privilege (in defamation), 146
Quantum meruit, 190–1
Quarter Sessions, 27, 30, 31
Queen (*see* Crown)
Queen's Counsel (QC), 57

Racial discrimination, 36, 45, 267
Ratio decidendi, 20–1
Real property, 262–3
Receiver, 68, 232, 233
Recommendation (in European Communities), 76
Recorder, 31, 58
Registrar:
    County Court, 37, 51
    Companies, of, 93, 94, 98, 103, 104, 233
    High Court, 66
Registration:
    bill of sale, of, 231
    charities, of, 276
    company directors, of, 98, 103
    debentures, of, 103, 233
    land charges, of, 270, 273–4
    shareholders, of, 95, 103
    title, of, 273
Remoteness of damage, 116–7, 122, 189
Rent:
    restriction, 36, 38, 268
    Tribunal, 47
Reply, 66
Representative action, 83
Requisition on title, 273
Res ipsa loquitur, 122, 123, 299
Resale price maintenance, 44, 200, 204, 207
Rescission, 7, 89, 168, 170–1, 172, 187, 227
Rescue cases, 112
Respondent, 23
Restitution of property, 70
Restrictive:
    covenants, 200, 270, 273
    Practices Court, 44–5
    trade practices, 200, 204, 205–8

Resulting trust, 275
Riparian rights, 265–6
Road traffic, 27–9, 288–91, 292–3
Roman law, 3, 8
Royal:
    Assent, 12
    Commission on Legal Services, 61
    Charter, 81
Rules of Court, 66, 83

Sale:
    chose in action, of, 235–6
    goods, of, 211 *et seq.*
    land, of, 271–4
    negotiable instruments, of, 235 *et seq.*
    shares, of, 95
    trust for, 269, 286
Salvage claims, 36, 39
Security for credit:
    bills of sale, 231
    conditional sale, 228–30
    debentures, secured, 233
    guarantee, 155
    hire purchase, 223, 226, 228–30
    lien, 217, 231, 232
    mortgage of land, 7, 231–2, 271–2, 274
    pawn or pledge, 231
    reservation of title, 217–8, 231
    shares, mortgage of, 225
    stoppage in transit of goods, 217
Self defence, 140
Senate of the Inns of Court and the Bar, 57, 60
Sequestration, 68
Settlor of a trust, 274–6
Share capital of a company, 81
    issued, 95
    nominal, 94, 95
Share certificate, 95
Shareholders:
    infant, 174
    corporate, 93
    limited liability of, 81, 82, 92, 102–3
    majority, 97, 99–101
    register of, 95
    rights of, 96, 97, 98, 255
Shares:
    companies limited by, 81, 92 *et seq.*
    nature of, 92, 96, 255
    ordinary, 96
    preference, 96
    prospectus for, 95, 172
    qualification, 98
    redeemable, 96–7
    transfer of, 95, 155
Sheriff, 49, 68
Silk, taking, 57
Slander, 144–5
Small claims, 35, 51, 64, 300
Social security, 46, 294–5
    Commissioners, 46
Solicitors, 50, 53 *et seq.*
    audience, rights of, 29, 31, 35, 53, 67
    civil proceedings, in, 62–7
    sale of house and, 271–4

INDEX

Solicitor-General, 59
Solus agreement, 208
Sources of law, 10
Specific delivery, 77
Standard of proof, 2
Statement of claim, 65
Statute:
    amending, 13
    codifying, 14, 178, 236
    consolidating, 14, 178, 289
    interpretation of, 11, 23–4
    repeal of, 13–14
    source of law, as, 8, 11–15, 23–4, 77
Statutory:
    authority, 110–11, 132, 135
    corporation, 81, 82
    declaration, 94, 104
    duty, 107, 126–8
    instrument, 15
Stipendiary magistrate, 27
Stock Exchange, 92
Strict liability:
    contract, in, 186, 299
    tort of, 107, 109, 126, 128, 136, 137
Subpoena, 6
Summary trial, 27, 290
Summing up, 67, 69
Summons for directions, 66
Supplemental List, 27
Supplementary benefit, 295

Table A, 94, 97
Taxation of costs, 63
Term of years absolute (*see* Lease)
Testamentary capacity, 80, 281
Theft, 29, 130, 137
Title:
    goods, to, 198, 221–3
    land, to, 271–4
    reservation of, to goods, 217–8, 231
Tort:
    actionable *per se*, 107–8, 131, 134, 144–5

    crime and, 106–7, 130, 135, 137, 288 *et seq.*
    Crown, by, 90, 113
    damages in, 63, 115–6, 123, 131, 138, 292–3
    death, effect of, 114–5
    defences, general, 110–13
    joint, 114
    jurisdiction in, 35–6, 38–9, 142
    limitation of actions in, 117, 293
    minors, by, 113
    nature of, 107–8
    parties, 113–5
    strict liability in, 107, 109, 126, 128, 136, 137
    vicarious liability, 108–10
Trade mark, 263
Trade union, 45, 83, 114, 152
Travaux préparatoires, 77
Treaty:
    Accession, of, 8, 75, 77, 78
    Merger, of, 72, 75
    Paris, of, 71, 75
    Rome, of, 71, 75, 208
    self-executing, 75
Trespass, 107, 130–2, 137
    livestock, by, 148–9
    (*see also* Goods, Land, Person)
Trespassers, occupiers' liability to, 125–6
Trial:
    civil, 67
    criminal, 69
    early methods of, 3
Tribunals, 43 *et seq.*
    administrative, 40, 46–9
    control over, 48
    Council on, 48
    domestic, 49–50
    Franks Committee on, 48
    industrial, 45, 47
    Lands (*see* Lands Tribunal)
    social security, 46, 295
    types of, 46–7

Trusts, 274–7
    charitable, 276
    jurisdiction, 36, 39
    origin of, 6–7
    sale, for, 269, 286
Trustee, 83, 276–7
    duties of, 277
    personal representatives as, 286
    unincorporated associations, for, 83, 275

Uberrimae fidei, 171, 257
Ultra vires, 17, 48, 78, 81, 82, 100, 101, 241, 248
Unincorporated association, 82–9, 275
Unsound mind (*see* Insanity)

Vicarious liability, 108–10
Vice-Chancellor, 39
Volenti non fit injuria, 111–2, 128, 148, 294

Wardship, 39
Warrant:
    arrest, 69
    execution, of, 68
Warranty:
    authority, of, 249–50
    contract generally, in, 177, 187
    implied, in sales of goods, 212, 214
    insurance, in, 256–7
Weekly Law Reports, 22
White Book, 66
Will, 279–82
    executors of, 284–5
    family provision, 281–2
    minor, of, 80, 281
    probate of, 284–6
Witness:
    civil action, at, 67
    criminal trial, at, 69
    will, of, 280–1, 282
Writ, 5, 65–6, 69

Year Books, 5, 22